Capital Flows, Credit Markets and Growth in South Africa

Nombulelo Gumata • Eliphas Ndou

Capital Flows, Credit Markets and Growth in South Africa

The Role of Global Economic Growth, Policy Shifts and Uncertainties

palgrave
macmillan

Nombulelo Gumata
South African Reserve Bank
Pretoria, South Africa

Eliphas Ndou
South African Reserve Bank
Pretoria, South Africa

Wits Plus, University of the Witwatersrand
Johannesburg, South Africa

School of Economic and Business Sciences
Johannesburg, South Africa

ISBN 978-3-030-30887-2   ISBN 978-3-030-30888-9 (eBook)
https://doi.org/10.1007/978-3-030-30888-9

© The Editor(s) (if applicable) and The Author(s), under exclusive licence to Springer Nature Switzerland AG 2019
This work is subject to copyright. All rights are solely and exclusively licensed by the Publisher, whether the whole or part of the material is concerned, specifically the rights of translation, reprinting, reuse of illustrations, recitation, broadcasting, reproduction on microfilms or in any other physical way, and transmission or information storage and retrieval, electronic adaptation, computer software, or by similar or dissimilar methodology now known or hereafter developed.
The use of general descriptive names, registered names, trademarks, service marks, etc. in this publication does not imply, even in the absence of a specific statement, that such names are exempt from the relevant protective laws and regulations and therefore free for general use.
The publisher, the authors and the editors are safe to assume that the advice and information in this book are believed to be true and accurate at the date of publication. Neither the publisher nor the authors or the editors give a warranty, express or implied, with respect to the material contained herein or for any errors or omissions that may have been made. The publisher remains neutral with regard to jurisdictional claims in published maps and institutional affiliations.

This Palgrave Macmillan imprint is published by the registered company Springer Nature Switzerland AG.
The registered company address is: Gewerbestrasse 11, 6330 Cham, Switzerland

Preface

This book explores the role and interaction of global economic policy uncertainties and shifts, and capital flow episodes on the South African credit markets and real economic activity. The book is divided into six parts that address the various aspects of these economic themes, whilst filling existing academic and policy research gaps. Various statistical and econometric techniques are applied to capture the various aspects of the transmission of global and domestic shocks into the South African macro-economy. Furthermore, these statistical and econometric techniques are used to assess the robustness of the empirical findings and the policy implications derived from the results. The main focus areas are given below:

- Part I deals with global economic growth, trade growth uncertainty, economic policy uncertainty and the effects of trade dynamics.
- Part II deals with global policy rates and how they are transmitted into the South African economy.
- Part III deals with capital flow surges, sudden stops and elevated portfolio inflows volatility effects.
- Part IV deals with the transmission of sovereign debt credit ratings downgrades and upgrades into credit markets and the real economy.
- Part V deals with the output gap–inflation trade-off, external shocks, labour market conditions and inflation expectations.
- Part VI focuses on the policy ineffectiveness issues.

Part I: Global Economic Growth, Economic Policy Uncertainty and The Influence of Trade Dynamics

Part I of the book investigates various channels through which global output growth shocks, global interest rates shocks, global trade shocks and economic policy uncertainty shocks are transmitted into the South African economy. We find that BRICS (Brazil, Russia, India, China and South Africa) is a big magnifier of G7 economic growth responses to positive demand shocks, followed by Emerging Market Economies (EMEs) excluding China. The propagation effects by BRICS GDP growth exceed those from Brazil, Indonesia, India, Turkey and South Africa (BIITS) economies, and the China effect alone is small. The BRICS GDP growth amplifies the effects of adverse economic growth shocks such as the global financial crisis, global trade and economic policy uncertainty. Evidence indicates that commodity price shocks lead to positive responses of G7 GDP growth and that BRICS, EMEs (excluding China) and BIITS amplify the effects of positive commodity price shocks on G7 economies.

Part II: Global Policy Rates and The South African Economy

With respect to global interest rates, evidence shows that the starting point matters in the analysis of the repo rate and the Federal Funds Rate (repo rate-FFR) spread. During the period of the Federal Funds Rate zero lower bound, the level of the repo rate was the same as the repo rate-FFR spread. The repo rate movements explain almost 42 per cent of the variation in the repo rate-FFR spread since 2000. Furthermore, we establish that there was a higher degree of synchronisation during 2005 and 2006 when the repo rate and the FFR were tightening. There are asymmetries in the repo rate-FFR spread adjustment process. The adjustments tend to persist more when the repo rate-FFR spread is widening or increasing as the change in spread exceeds the threshold. Thus, there is higher momentum in the adjustment of the repo rate when the repo rate-FFR spread is narrowing.

A key policy implication we derive from the evidence of the adjustment to the repo rate-FFR spread is that South African domestic factors dictate how policymakers adjust the repo rate. Central to the repo rate adjustments is the performance of domestic inflation relative to the inflation target. The policy implication is that low and stable inflation has benefits for the level of the repo rate-FFR spread. Furthermore, this evidence further corroborates the findings in the book that inflation below 4.5 per cent of the 3–6 per cent target has more benefits for the pass-through of a nominal demand shocks to consumer price and nominal wage inflation. Hence, the argument for lowering the inflation target band is further strengthened by these findings.

As far as the transmission of global interest rates shocks into the domestic economy is concerned, evidence in the book shows that a positive shock to global real rates leads to a contraction in domestic GDP growth and the tightening in labour market conditions. In addition, we establish that the world real interest rate plays a role in transmitting positive exchange rate shocks to domestic GDP growth. Although positive overall, permanent and transitory exchange rate volatility shocks lower GDP growth, the contraction in domestic GDP growth is larger due to elevated world real interest rate. At the same time, the amplification by the world real interest rate is negative. This means that domestic GDP growth is likely to be subdued for a prolonged period due to elevated the exchange rate volatilities and rising global real interest rates.

Part III: Capital Flow Surges, Sudden Stops and Elevated Portfolio Inflows Volatility Effects

The book analyses the (i) interaction of capital flow surges, sudden stops and elevated portfolio inflows volatility shocks with domestic GDP growth and credit growth, and the (ii) economic costs of capital flow episodes. A large body of literature shows that confidence plays a role in transmitting stimulatory policy decisions. This is underpinned by the fact that confidence contains fundamental information about the current and future states of the economy. The channel linking confidence and subsequent macroeconomic activity changes is future productivity. Evidence in the book shows that business confidence is positively related to GDP growth. At the same time, GDP growth and confidence indicators are negatively related to changes in government debt. The negative relationship is pronounced with respect to government debt and business confidence. Furthermore, government debt is negatively associated with productivity growth. But business confidence is positively related to productivity growth. This means that the productivity channel partly explains why high government debt leads to low business confidence.

Evidence in the book shows that capital flow shock effects should not be viewed in isolation of changes to global risk. Global risk appetite and aversion matters and drives capital flow episodes and net portfolio flow volatility shocks, which can amplify economic cycles and increase the vulnerability of the financial system. Heightened global risk as measured by the volatility index (VIX) and capital flow sudden stops episodes are negatively related to credit growth, imports growth, exports growth and GDP growth. Heightened VIX and capital flow sudden stops shocks lower GDP growth, while the capital flow surges shock leads to an increase. The capital flow surges shock leads to the R/US$ exchange rate appreciation and depresses money market rates and bond yields. At the same time, exports growth and imports growth decline significantly for a long period due to heightened VIX shocks. On the other hand, capital flow surges shocks increase credit growth significantly compared to the depressed state induced by a capital flow sudden stops episode and heightened VIX shocks.

The South African trade balance is mostly driven by imported intermediate goods. The results in the book imply that risk aversion shocks may lead to a significant slowdown in economic activity. Exports growth declines due to heightened VIX shocks and a capital flow sudden stops episode. Elevated global risk aversion is a significant driver of exports growth. In contrast, the capital flow surges episodes tend to increase exports growth. However, imports growth increases significantly due to the capital flow surges shock. In addition, the contraction in credit growth may lead to a slowdown in GDP growth. Thus, a global risk aversion shocks matter more than the capital flow episodes shocks in driving economic activity in South Africa.

Equity and debt inflows matter in the attainment of the price stability mandate. Rising inflation deters equity and debt inflows, in particular, equity inflows decline more compared to debt inflows. The impact of inflation on equity inflows is three times greater than that on debt inflows. Similarly, positive inflation shocks lead to a significant reduction in (i) portfolio banking and non-banking inflows and (ii) foreign direct investment (FDI) banking and non-banking inflows. High inflation deters equity, banking and non-banking inflows. The repo rate tends to respond more aggressively to positive inflation shocks in a model with equity inflows compared to that with debt inflows. Evidence shows that the differential effects could be linked to the ability of equity inflows and debt inflows shocks to influence inflation and the R/US$ exchange rate.

We test the relevance of the Samarina and Bezemer (2016) hypothesis stating that since the 1990s foreign capital inflow shocks resulted in the sectorial allocation of credit. We establish the prevalence of sectorial credit reallocations between credit to companies and households. Evidence shows that an increase in capital inflows leads to a reduction in the share of credit to households. This is the case for portfolio and FDI bank and non-bank inflows. Elevated capital inflows of all categories do not result in a strong increase in the share of credit to households on impact. The positive impact comes at a considerable lag and, even then, it is very weak.

The results in the book underscore the important role played by (i) global economic policy shifts and uncertainty, (ii) changes in global risk perceptions and the direction of capital flows, and (iii) the prevalence of the exchange rate, trade growth and output growth channels in the repo rate response to inflationary pressures. The inflation target is binding. Policymakers respond to inflationary pressures irrespective of the sources of shocks to maintain the price stability mandate. For the financial stability mandate, regulatory and prudential policies, evidence of the prevalence of credit reallocation towards companies means that capital flows can result in excesses in some market segments. To mitigate the build-up of such imbalances and the potential negative spill-over effects requires targeted regulatory and prudential tools.

Part IV: The Transmission of Sovereign Debt Credit Ratings Downgrades and Upgrades into the Credit Markets and the Real Economy

The South African GDP growth has been very weak and volatile post-2009. This period was also characterised by heightened economic policy uncertainty, various sovereign debt credit ratings downgrades, weak consumer and business confidence. In this part of the book, we dedicate a number of chapters to assess (i) the role and transmission of sovereign debt credit ratings upgrades and downgrade shocks, (ii) the role of consumer and business confidence in transmitting sovereign debt credit ratings upgrades and downgrades, (iii) the indirect role of GDP growth in transmitting sovereign debt credit ratings shocks, and (iv) the role of the cost of government borrowing in transmitting and propagating the sovereign debt credit ratings revisions shocks. We find that business confidence is positively related to GDP growth, but consumer confidence has a bigger effect on GDP growth than business confidence. These findings underscore the role of demand shocks in driving GDP growth. This is consistent with findings in Farmer (2011) that positive shocks to consumer sentiment leads to heightened private activity. Consumer and business confidence and GDP growth are negatively related to changes in government debt. There is a strong feedback between GDP growth and the sovereign debt credit ratings upgrades and downgrades shocks. A positive GDP shock tends to raise the likelihood of sovereign debt credit ratings upgrades. At the same time, the sovereign debt credit ratings downgrades (upgrades) shocks lead to lower (increases in) output growth.

A positive GDP growth shock increases the likelihood of sovereign debt credit ratings upgrades. However, a sovereign debt credit ratings downgrade lowers GDP growth. In addition, we find that there are heterogeneous effects of sovereign debt credit ratings downgrades shocks. GDP growth declines more due to the Standard & Poor's and Fitch sovereign credit ratings downgrades. The confidence channel plays an important role in the propagation of the sovereign debt credit ratings changes on GDP growth. In turn, sovereign debt credit ratings downgrades and GDP growth influence the trajectory of the repo rate towards inflation shocks. GDP growth does influence the pace of change in the policy rate responses towards positive inflation shocks.

The counterfactual responses show that the business confidence channel amplifies the GDP growth responses to sovereign debt credit ratings upgrade shocks. In addition, the business confidence channel exerts asymmetric effects on GDP growth. Negative business confidence changes are likely to depress economic growth by a big magnitude for long periods. In addition, sovereign debt credit ratings downgrades and GDP growth influence the trajectory of the repo rate towards inflation developments such as those observed at peak around 2003 and 2008. Lower business confidence and subdued GDP growth play a role in the adjustment of the repo rate to inflationary pressures. Overall, evidence shows that lower business confidence and subdued GDP growth play a role in the pace of the adjustment of the repo rate to inflationary pressures.

Part V: The Output Gap–Inflation Trade-off, External Shocks, Labour Market Conditions and Inflation Expectations

Monetary policymakers face a policy trade-off and at all times try to balance their decision-making along the efficient policy frontier captured by the Taylor curve. Evidence in this part of the book shows that inflation expectations shocks, external shocks and economic policy uncertainty shocks do shift the domestic Taylor curve. For instance, output growth volatility tends to decline with varying magnitudes due to an unexpected positive consumer price inflation and nominal wage volatility shock. A positive FFR shock leads to a delayed effect of an increase in the repo rate, a decline in the repo rate-FFR spread and the deterioration in the current account. The Taylor curve increases more when the current account is not shut off in the model. This may be because of the amplification effects of the exchange rate depreciation shock and on inflation. Foreign economic policy uncertainty shocks also result in the increase in the domestic Taylor curve, which in turn, due to increased gross capital outflows, magnifies the Taylor curve responses to elevated foreign economic policy uncertainty shocks.

Economic policy uncertainty shocks have an impact on exchange rates, commodity prices and terms of trade. A positive commodity price shock increases the Taylor curve and results in the tightening of the repo rate. On the other hand, a negative terms-of-trade shock increases the Taylor curve and the repo rate is tightened. This is because a negative terms-of-trade shock leads to the exchange rate depreciation and increases inflation but leads to a contraction in GDP growth. The combined effects of these shocks lead to increases in the inflation and output-gap volatility trade-off.

Adverse global trade shocks also impact the trade-off between the inflation and output-gap volatilities. A negative global trade shock has a significant negative effect on the Taylor curve and shifts the Taylor curve inwards. In addition, a negative global trade shock lowers the labour market conditions index, thus implying tightening in labour market conditions. A negative global trade shock induces more fluctuations in labour market conditions than on the Taylor curve. The policy implication is that labour markets adjust more to negative global trade shocks compared to the output-gap and inflation volatility trade-off. This implies that negative trade shocks which are negative demand shocks exert a disproportionately negative effect on labour market conditions than the output-gap and inflation volatilities.

Furthermore, a disaggregated analysis of the labour market conditions index shows that employment growth (quantity) adjusts more than remuneration per worker (price) to negative global trade shocks. Negative global trade shocks are transmitted more via the output growth and employment growth channels than the inflation channel. At the same time, the exchange rate depreciation following negative global trade shocks poses risks to the inflation and output-gap volatilities and neutralises the policy rate responses to inflation shocks.

Part VI: The Policy Ineffectiveness Issues

Evidence in the book shows the existence of the output gap–inflation trade-off. Real GDP growth rises due to a positive nominal demand shock. But real output rises more in a low inflation regime than in a high inflation regime. A higher degree of the output gap–inflation trade-off movements occurs in the low inflation regime. This means that the output gap–inflation trade-off is much higher in a low inflation regime relative to a high inflation regime. The policy implication is that a positive nominal demand policy shock that affects nominal demand will have a bigger effect on real output in a low inflation regime than in a high inflation regime. Inflation thresholds impact the transmission of positive nominal demand shocks to the output gap–inflation trade-off parameter. This is because inflation fluctuates more in the high inflation regime than when it is below 4.5 per cent inflation threshold. These findings indicate that policymakers have considerable scope to engage in short-run demand management policies in the low inflation regime than in high inflation regime. This is because there is a substantial degree of policy effectiveness in the low inflation regime and prices become more rigid as consumer price inflation moves below the 4.5 per cent inflation regime. Therefore, nominal demand shocks are unlikely to generate much inflation in the low inflation regime relative to the high inflation regime. In addition, the amplification effects nominal demand shocks are pronounced when inflation is below 4.5 per cent than when it is just anywhere below the 6 per cent inflation threshold. Thus, deviations from the 4.5 per cent mid-point of the 3–6 per cent inflation target range play a meaningful role in the transmission and amplification effects of nominal demand shocks to real economic activity.

Pretoria, South Africa
Nombulelo Gumata
Eliphas Ndou

Acknowledgements

We thank our colleagues at the South African Reserve Bank in the various divisions within the Economic Research Department and Economic Statistics Department, Statistics South Africa for supplying us with data. We also thank Sandile Hlatshwayo for supplying us with data for the South African economic policy uncertainty index. We owe a great deal of gratitude to the anonymous reviewers. We also thank Thomas Doan at Estima Rats software for coding assistance and their courses.

Contents

1 Introduction   1

Part I   Global Economic Growth, Economic Policy Uncertainty and The Influence of Trade Dynamics   23

2 Is BRICS GDP Growth a Source of Shocks or an Amplifier of Global Growth Responses? What Are the Policy Implications for South Africa?   25

3 Does the Trade-Openness Channel Impact the Effects of Business Confidence Shocks on Investment Growth?   55

4 Trade-Openness, Consumer Price Inflation and Exchange Rate Depreciation Shocks   69

5 Global Growth and Economic Policy Uncertainty Shock Effects on the South African Economy: Do These Reinforce Each Other?   87

6 Heightened Foreign Economic Policy Uncertainty Shock Effects on the South African Economy: Transmission via Capital Flows, Credit Conditions and Business Confidence Channels … 97

Part II   Global Policy Rates and The South African Economy   119

7 In Which Direction Is There a Momentum Effect in the Changes in the Spread Between the Repo Rate and Federal Funds Rate? … 121

8 How Do Global Real Policy Rates Impact the South African GDP Growth and Labour Market Conditions? … 141

9 To What Extent Do Capital Inflows Impact the Response of the South African Economic Growth to Positive SA-US Interest Rate Differential Shocks? … 149

Part III   Capital Flow Surges, Sudden Stops and Elevated Portfolio Inflows Volatility Effects   161

10 Economic Costs of Capital Flow Episodes in South Africa … 163

11 Capital Flow Surges, Sudden Stops and Elevated Portfolio Inflow Volatility Shocks: What is the Nature of Their Interaction with GDP Growth and Credit? … 177

12 Bank and Non-bank Capital Flows and The Sectorial Reallocation of Credit Away from the Household Sector … 195

13	Banking and Non-banking Capital Flows and The Sectorial Reallocation of Credit Away from Companies	207
14	Equity, Debt Inflows and the Price Stability Mandate	221
15	Do Local Investors Play a Stabilising Role Relative to Foreign Investors After Economic Shocks?	235
16	Do Investors' Net Purchases and Capital Retrenchment Activities Impact the Monetary Policy Response to Positive Inflation Shocks?	255

Part IV	The Transmission of Sovereign Debt Credit Ratings Downgrades and Upgrades into the Credit Markets and the Real Economy	267
17	What Role Does Business Confidence Play in Transmitting Sovereign Debt Credit Ratings Upgrades and Downgrades Shocks into the Real Economy?	269
18	Are Sovereign Debt Credit Ratings Shocks Transmitted Via Economic Growth to Impact Credit Growth?	287
19	Does the Cost of Government Borrowing Transmit Sovereign Debt Credit Ratings Downgrades Shocks to Credit Growth?	301

Part V	The Output–Inflation Trade-off, External Shocks, Labour Market Conditions and Inflation Expectations	307
20	The Output-gap, Nominal Wage and Consumer Price Inflation Volatility Trade-off	309

21	The Output-Gap and Inflation Volatility Trade-off: Do External Shocks and Inflation Expectations Shift the Taylor Curve	319
22	Do Adverse Global Trade Shocks Impact the Trade-off Between the Inflation and Output-Gap Volatilities	331
23	Do the Labour Market Conditions Shocks Impact the Trade-off Between the Inflation and Output-Gap Volatilities?	341

Part VI	The Policy Ineffectiveness Issues	351
24	The *Output Gap–Inflation* Trade-off and the Policy Ineffectiveness	353
25	Inflation Regimes and the Transmission of Positive Nominal Demand Shocks to the Price Level	365

Index — 379

List of Figures

Fig. 1.1	Global economic policy uncertainty and the US trade policy uncertainty. (Source: http://www.policyuncertainty.com/global_monthly.html)	4
Fig. 1.2	Global, US and South African GDP growth. (Source: South African Reserve Banks, IMF database and authors' calculations)	5
Fig. 1.3	Global, United States and South African GDP growth post-2009. (Source: South African Reserve Bank, IMF database and authors' calculations)	5
Fig. 1.4	Global GDP growth, trade and South African GDP growth. (Source: IMF database and authors' calculations)	6
Fig. 1.5	The repo rate and the repo rate-FFR spread. (Note: Grey-shaded area represents the period of the zero-lower bound for the US FFR. Source: South African Reserve Bank and Fred data)	7
Fig. 1.6	Headline inflation and the repo rate-FFR spread. (Source: South African Reserve Bank, Fred data and authors' calculations)	8
Fig. 1.7	Schematic representation of the sovereign debt credit ratings shock transmission to credit growth. (Source: Authors' drawing)	9

List of Figures

Fig. 1.8	Credit growth responses to sovereign debt credit ratings downgrade shocks. (Note: The grey-shaded area denotes the 16th and 84th percentile confidence bands. Source: Authors' calculations)	10
Fig. 1.9	The role of confidence and expectations in responding to stimulatory policy shocks. (Source: Authors' drawing)	11
Fig. 1.10	Exports growth responses. (Note: The grey-shaded areas denote the 16th and 84th percentile error bands. Source: Authors' calculations)	12
Fig. 1.11	Import growth responses. (Note: The grey-shaded areas denote the 16th and 84th percentile error bands. Source: Authors' calculations)	13
Fig. 1.12	Counterfactual and actual cumulative inflation responses to rand depreciation shocks. (Source: Authors' calculations)	14
Fig. 1.13	Responses of credit to household to positive capital flow shock. (Note: The shaded area denotes the 16th and 84th percentiles. Source: Authors' calculations)	14
Fig. 2.1	RICS GDP growth. (Note: Grey-shaded area represents the South African recession. Source: IMF WEO 2016)	28
Fig. 2.2	Global growth and global trade activity. (Note: Grey-shaded areas represent the South African recessions. Source: IMF WEO 2016 and authors' calculations)	29
Fig. 2.3	BRICS GDP growth and exchange rates. (Source: IMF WEO 2016)	30
Fig. 2.4	Global trade, G7 and South African GDP growth. (Source: IMF WEO 2016 and authors' calculations)	32
Fig. 2.5	Accumulated responses due to positive demand shocks and propagation effects. (Note: Emerging markets economies (EMEs) are Brazil, Russia, South Africa, Chile, Korea, Mexico, Turkey, Argentina, India and Indonesia. Source: Authors' calculations)	34
Fig. 2.6	Comparison of amplifying effects. (Note: Emerging markets economies (EMEs) are Brazil, Russia, South Africa, Chile, Korea, Mexico, Turkey, Argentina, India and Indonesia. Source: Authors' calculations)	34
Fig. 2.7	The impact of global recession, uncertainty shocks and amplification by regional growth. (Note: Emerging markets economies (EMEs) are Brazil, Russia, South Africa, Chile,	

	Korea, Mexico, Turkey, Argentina, India and Indonesia. Source: Authors' calculations)	36
Fig. 2.8	The impact of commodity price shock pre-financial crisis and amplification by regional growth. (Note: Emerging markets economies (EMEs) are Brazil, Russia, South Africa, Chile, Korea, Mexico, Turkey, Argentina, India and Indonesia. Source: Authors' calculations)	36
Fig. 2.9	Responses to negative shocks according to different sizes of shock. (Note: SD means standard deviation. Emerging markets economies (EMEs) are Brazil, Russia, South Africa, Chile, Korea, Mexico, Turkey, Argentina, India and Indonesia. Source: Authors' calculations)	38
Fig. 2.10	Various GDP growth responses to positive and negative growth shocks. (Note: SD means standard deviation. Emerging markets economies (EMEs) are Brazil, Russia, South Africa, Chile, Korea, Mexico, Turkey, Argentina, India and Indonesia. Source: Authors' calculations)	39
Fig. 2.11	Actual and counterfactual South African GDP growth. (Source: Authors' calculations)	40
Fig. 2.12	Selected Chinese indicators and work trade. (Source: IMF and World Bank)	42
Fig. 2.13	Relationship between policy uncertainty and rand exchange rate. (Source: Authors' calculations)	43
Fig. 2.14	Responses to positive Chinese policy uncertainty shock. (Note: The grey band denotes the 16th and 84th percentile confidence bands. The shock refers to one positive standard deviation shock. Source: Authors' calculations)	44
Fig. 2.15	The role of Chinese policy uncertainty on the R/US$ exchange rate dynamics. (Source: Authors' calculations)	45
Fig. 2.16	NEER responses to Chinese growth and policy uncertainty shocks. (Source: Authors' calculations)	45
Fig. 2.17	Actual and counterfactual accumulated South African GDP growth and Chinese amplifications. (Note: Responses to a positive 1 per cent GDP growth shock. Source: Authors' calculations)	47
Fig. 2.18	Actual and counterfactual accumulated South African, euro area and UK GDP growth and the amplification of Chinese GDP growth. (Note: Responses to a positive 1 per cent GDP growth shock. Source: Authors' calculations)	47

xxiv List of Figures

Fig. 2.19	SA GDP responses and third-country transmission effects. (Source: Authors' calculations)	49
Fig. 2.20	Actual and counterfactual R/US$ changes and Chinese growth effects. (Source: Authors' calculations)	50
Fig. 2.21	The evolution of domestic inflation and Chinese growth contributions. (Source: Authors' calculations)	50
Fig. 2.22	The evolution of the repo rate and Chinese growth contributions. (Source: Authors' calculations)	51
Fig. 3.1	Business confidence index and gross fixed capital formation growth in South Africa. (Note: The grey-shaded areas denote the South African recession. BCI = Business confidence index. Source: South African Reserve Bank and authors' calculations)	56
Fig. 3.2	Investment growth responses to positive business confidence shocks. (Source: Authors' calculations)	59
Fig. 3.3	Cumulative investment growth responses to positive business confidence shocks and the role of trade-openness channel. (Note: All the responses are to a one positive standard deviation business confidence shock. Source: Authors' calculations)	60
Fig. 3.4	Cumulative investment growth responses to positive business confidence shocks and the role of the components of the trade-openness channel. (Source: Authors' calculations)	61
Fig. 3.5	Cumulative investment growth responses to positive business confidence shocks and the role of the trade-openness channel in low and high inflation regimes. (Source: Authors' calculations)	63
Fig. 3.6	Cumulative investment growth responses to positive business confidence shocks and the role of the trade-openness channel in different inflation regimes. (Source: Authors' calculations)	64
Fig. 3.7	Cumulative investment growth responses to positive business confidence shocks and the role of trade-openness channel in tight and loose monetary policy regimes. (Source: Authors' calculations)	65
Fig. 4.1	The transmission of the exchange rate depreciation shocks and role of trade-openness. (Source: Authors' calculation)	70
Fig. 4.2	Trade-openness and inflation. (Note: Trade-openness equals to sum of ratio of exports and imports to GDP. Source: Authors' calculation and South African Reserve Bank)	72

Fig. 4.3	Trade-openness and time-varying ERPT. (Source: Authors' calculations)	74
Fig. 4.4	Responses to positive trade-openness shock. (Source: Authors' calculations)	75
Fig. 4.5	ERPT responses to positive trade-openness shock scenarios. (Source: Authors' calculations)	76
Fig. 4.6	ERPT responses to positive trade-openness shocks. (Source: Authors' calculations)	77
Fig. 4.7	Cumulative ERPT responses to positive trade-openness shock and the role of the business confidence channel. (Source: Authors' calculations)	78
Fig. 4.8	Cumulative ERPT responses due to a positive trade-openness gap shock and the role of the business confidence channel. (Source: Authors' calculations)	79
Fig. 4.9	Cumulative inflation responses due to the exchange rate deprecation shocks and amplification by the trade-openness channel. (Source: Authors' calculations)	80
Fig. 4.10	Cumulative inflation responses to the exchange rate deprecation shocks and amplification by the level and gaps in the trade-openness channel. (Source: Authors' calculations)	81
Fig. 4.11	Cumulative inflation responses to exchange rate the deprecation shocks and the role of the trade-openness channel. (Source: Authors' calculations)	82
Fig. 5.1	Global policy uncertainty indices. (Source: http://www.policyuncertainty.com/global_monthly.html)	88
Fig. 5.2	Cross correlations for US, euro area and SA GDP growth uncertainties. (Source: Authors' calculations)	89
Fig. 5.3	Cross correlations between the labour market conditions index, global GDP growth and trade growth uncertainties. (Source: Authors' calculations)	89
Fig. 5.4	SA GDP growth responses to positive foreign GDP growth uncertainty shocks. (Note: The grey bands denote the 16th and 84th percentile confidence bands. Source: Authors' calculations)	90
Fig. 5.5	SA GDP growth responses to positive policy uncertainty shocks and the role of foreign GDP growth uncertainties. (Note: EPU denotes Economic policy uncertainty. Source: Authors' calculations)	91

Fig. 5.6	South African labour market conditions responses to positive global uncertainty shocks. (Note: EPU denotes Economic policy uncertainty. Source: Authors' calculations)	92
Fig. 5.7	Responses to positive South African policy uncertainty shock. (Source: Authors' calculations)	93
Fig. 5.8	Repo rate responses to positive foreign growth uncertainty shocks and the role of the foreign policy uncertainty channel. (Note: EPU denotes Economic policy uncertainty. Source: Authors' calculations)	94
Fig. 5.9	Repo rate responses to positive foreign growth uncertainty shocks and the role of the global trade growth uncertainty channel. (Note: EPU denotes Economic policy uncertainty. Source: Authors' calculations)	95
Fig. 6.1	Equity inflows and foreign economic policy uncertainty indices. (Note: EPU denotes economic policy uncertainty. Source: Authors' calculations)	99
Fig. 6.2	Credit conditions index and foreign economic policy uncertainty indices. (Note: EPU denotes economic policy uncertainty. Source: Authors' calculations)	100
Fig. 6.3	Domestic GDP growth responses to positive foreign economic policy uncertainty shocks. (Note: The grey-shaded bands denote the 16th and 84th percentile confidence bands. EPU denotes economic policy uncertainty. Source: Authors' calculations)	102
Fig. 6.4	Responses of banking flows to heightened foreign economic policy uncertainty. (Note: The grey-shaded bands denote the 16th and 84th percentile confidence bands. EPU denotes economic policy uncertainty. Source: Authors' calculations)	103
Fig. 6.5	Responses of non-banking flows to positive policy uncertainty shocks. (Note: The grey-shaded bands denote the 16th and 84th percentile confidence bands. EPU denotes economic policy uncertainty. Source: Authors' calculations)	104
Fig. 6.6	The equity inflows responses to foreign economic uncertainty shocks. (Note: The grey-shaded bands denote the 16th and 84th percentile confidence bands. EPU denotes economic policy uncertainty. Source: Authors' calculations)	105

Fig. 6.7	Responses of equity inflows to different sizes of positive economic policy uncertainty shocks. (Note: EPU denotes economic policy uncertainty. Source: Authors' calculations)	106
Fig. 6.8	Cumulative responses of debt inflows to different sizes of economic policy uncertainty shocks. (Note: EPU denotes economic policy uncertainty. Source: Authors' calculations)	106
Fig. 6.9	Responses of credit conditions and GDP growth to positive economic policy uncertainty shocks. (Note: The grey-shaded bands denote the 16th and 84th percentile confidence bands. EPU denotes economic policy uncertainty. Source: Authors' calculations)	107
Fig. 6.10	Accumulated CCI responses to economic policy uncertainty shocks and the role of equity inflows. (Note: EPU denotes economic policy uncertainty; CCI denotes Credit Conditions Index. Source: Authors' calculations)	108
Fig. 6.11	Accumulated CCI responses to economic policy uncertainty shocks and the role of debt inflows. (Note: EPU denotes economic policy uncertainty; CCI denotes Credit Conditions Index. Source: Authors' calculations)	109
Fig. 6.12	Amplification of GDP responses by the business confidence channel. (Note: The grey-shaded bands denote the 16th and 84th percentile confidence bands. Source: Authors' calculations)	110
Fig. 6.13	Responses of GDP with equity inflows included in the model. (Note: The solid impulse response represents results when equity inflows are allowed to operate in the model. The dotted line represents the impulse response when equity inflows are shut off in the model. EPU denotes economic policy uncertainty. Source: Authors' calculations)	111
Fig. 6.14	GDP responses with the credit conditions index included in the model. (Note: The solid impulse response represents results when equity inflows are allowed to operate in the model. The dotted line represents the impulse response when equity inflows are shut off in the model. EPU denotes economic policy uncertainty. Source: Authors' calculations)	111
Fig. 6.15	The exchange rate and accumulated inflation responses to positive economic policy uncertainty shocks. (Note: The grey-shaded bands denote the 16th and 84th percentile confidence bands. Source: Authors' calculations)	112

xxviii   List of Figures

Fig. 6.16	Repo rate and GDP growth responses to positive inflation shocks. (Note: The grey-shaded bands denote the 16th and 84th percentile confidence bands. RR denotes repo rate. EPU denotes economic policy uncertainty. Source: Authors' calculations)	113
Fig. 6.17	The repo rate responses to positive inflation shocks and the role of credit conditions. (Note: EPU denotes policy uncertainty. Source: Authors' calculations)	115
Fig. 7.1	The US Federal Funds Rate and repo rate. (Note: Grey-shaded area represents the period of the zero-lower bound for the US FFR. Source: South African Reserve Bank and Fred data. https://fred.stlouisfed.org/)	124
Fig. 7.2	The repo rate and the repo rate-FFR spread. (Note: Grey-shaded area represents the period of the zero-lower bound for the US FFR. Source: South African Reserve Bank and Fred data)	125
Fig. 7.3	The repo rate-FFR spread relative to the long-run estimated relationship. (Note: Grey-shaded area represents the period of the zero-lower bound for the US FFR. Source: Authors' calculations)	128
Fig. 7.4	Spread between repo rate and Federal Funds Rate. (Source: Authors' calculations)	133
Fig. 7.5	Responses depending on the starting point of the spread between repo rate and Federal Funds Rate. (Source: Authors' calculations)	133
Fig. 7.6	US real interest rates and the natural rate as estimated in Laubach and Williams (2015). (Source: Laubach and Williams 2015)	135
Fig. 7.7	Ex-post real repo rate. (Source: Authors' calculations)	136
Fig. 7.8	Headline inflation and the repo rate-FFR spread. (Source: South African Reserve Bank, Fred data and authors' calculations)	137
Fig. 7.9	Comparison of responses of repo rate-FFR spread and inflation over two policy tightening episodes. (Source: Authors' calculations)	138
Fig. 8.1	GDP growth and labour market conditions responses. (Note: The grey-shaded bands denote the 16th and 84th percentile confidence bands. Source: Authors' calculations)	143

Fig. 8.2	GDP growth and LMCI responses to positive world real interest rate and role of South African policy uncertainty changes. (Source: Authors' calculations)	144
Fig. 8.3	Manufacturing output growth responses to positive exchange rate volatility shocks and the role of monetary policy volatility. (Source: Authors' calculations)	145
Fig. 8.4	GDP growth responses to positive exchange rate volatility shocks and the role of the world real interest rate. (Source: Authors' calculations)	145
Fig. 8.5	Labour market conditions responses to positive world real interest rate shocks and the role of transitory exchange rate volatility. (Source: Authors' calculations)	146
Fig. 9.1	Responses of the domestic economy following a tight US monetary policy shock under the Mundell-Fleming model. (Source: Authors' drawings)	150
Fig. 9.2	Capital inflows and the interest rate differential. (Source: Authors' calculation)	153
Fig. 9.3	Cumulative GDP growth responses to a positive interest rate differential shock and the role of portfolio inflows shock. (Source: Authors' calculations)	155
Fig. 9.4	Cumulative GDP growth responses to a positive interest rate differential shock and the role of the capital inflows shock. (Source: Authors' calculations)	155
Fig. 9.5	Cumulative GDP growth responses to a positive interest rate differential shock and the role of the capital inflows shock. (Source: Authors' calculations)	156
Fig. 9.6	Cumulative GDP growth responses to a positive interest rate differential shock and the role of the capital inflows shock in an expanded model. (Source: Authors' calculations)	157
Fig. 9.7	Cumulative GDP growth responses to a positive interest rate differential shock and the amplification by the debt and equity inflows channels. (Source: Authors' calculations)	158
Fig. 10.1	VIX, net purchases by non-residents and the R/US$ changes. (Note: The shaded area denotes periods when VIX was equal to 31 per cent, which is equal to the size of VIX shock we use in the impulse response analysis)	164
Fig. 10.2	Selected indicators of economic activity and net purchases by non-residents. (Note: The shaded area denotes the annual	

	periods when VIX was equal to 31 per cent, which is equal to the size of VIX shock we use in the impulse response analysis. Source: South African Reserve Bank, Fred data and authors' calculations)	165
Fig. 10.3	Cross correlations. (Source: Authors' calculations)	166
Fig. 10.4	Bilateral cross correlations. (Source: Authors' calculations)	168
Fig. 10.5	Cross correlations between trade components and capital flow episodes. (Source: Authors' calculations)	169
Fig. 10.6	Comparisons of GDP responses to VIX, capital flow sudden stops and capital flow surges shocks. (Source: Authors' calculations)	170
Fig. 10.7	Comparison of the exchange rate responses. (Source: Authors' calculations)	170
Fig. 10.8	Short-term interest rates responses. (Source: Authors' calculations)	171
Fig. 10.9	Bond yield responses. (Source: Authors' calculations)	172
Fig. 10.10	Stock market responses. (Source: Authors' calculations)	172
Fig. 10.11	Exports growth responses. (Source: Authors' calculations)	173
Fig. 10.12	Import growth responses. (Source: Authors' calculations)	174
Fig. 10.13	Credit growth responses. (Source: Authors' calculations)	174
Fig. 11.1	Relationship between GDP growth, credit growth and net capital flows. (Source: Authors' calculations)	179
Fig. 11.2	South African bank assets and liabilities: 2000 to 2014. (Data for 2014 ends in December. Source: South African Reserve Bank and authors' calculations)	181
Fig. 11.3	South African bank deposits as per cent of liabilities to the public. (Source: South African Reserve Bank and authors' calculations)	181
Fig. 11.4	South African bank interbank deposits as a percentage of total deposits. (Source: South African Reserve Bank and authors' calculations)	182
Fig. 11.5	Responses of credit growth. (Note: The grey-shaded areas denote the 16th and 84th percentile error bands. Source: Authors' calculations)	184
Fig. 11.6	Contributions of different capital flow categories' shocks to credit growth over time. (Source: Authors' calculations)	185
Fig. 11.7	Fluctuations in credit growth explained by different capital flow shocks. (Source: Authors' calculations)	186

List of Figures

Fig. 11.8	The accumulated impulse responses to an unexpected positive one standard deviation VIX shock. (Note: The grey-shaded areas denote the 16th and 84th percentile error bands. Source: Authors' calculations)	187
Fig. 11.9	Comparison of GDP growth and credit growth responses to capital flow episodes shocks. (Note: The grey-shaded areas denote the 16th and 84th percentile error bands. Source: Authors' calculations)	188
Fig. 11.10	Actual and counterfactual GDP growth. (Source: Authors' calculations)	189
Fig. 11.11	Actual and counterfactual credit growth. (Source: Authors' calculations)	190
Fig. 11.12	Contributions of categories of various capital flow episodes on credit growth. (Source: Authors' calculations)	191
Fig. 11.13	Fluctuations in GDP growth and credit growth. (Source: Authors' calculations)	191
Fig. 12.1	Share of credit to households and companies. (Source: South African Reserve Bank)	196
Fig. 12.2	Relationship between credit to households, total FDI flows and total portfolio capital flows. (Source: South African Reserve Bank and authors' calculations)	198
Fig. 12.3	Bilateral relationships between credit to households and capital flows. (Source: South African Reserve Bank and authors' calculations)	199
Fig. 12.4	The sensitivity of the credit to household relationship to disaggregated capital flows. (Source: Authors' calculations)	199
Fig. 12.5	Cross correlations between credit to households, banking and non-banking flows. (Source: Authors' calculations)	200
Fig. 12.6	Responses of credit to household to positive capital flow shock. (Note: The shaded area denotes the 16th and 84th percentiles. Source: Authors' calculations)	201
Fig. 12.7	Fluctuations in credit to households due to FDI, portfolio flows, bank and non-bank flows. (Source: Authors' calculations)	202
Fig. 12.8	The contributions of aggregated bank flows. (Source: Authors' calculations)	203
Fig. 12.9	The contributions of aggregated non-bank flows. (Source: Authors' calculations)	203

Fig. 13.1	Relationship between credit to companies and bank and non-bank capital flows. (Source: South African Reserve Bank and authors' calculations)	208
Fig. 13.2	Bilateral relationships between credit to companies and capital flows. (Source: South African Reserve Bank and authors' calculations)	210
Fig. 13.3	Sensitivity of credit to companies to disaggregated capital flows. (Source: Authors' calculations. Note: Capital flows are expressed as a percentage of GDP)	211
Fig. 13.4	Responses of credit to companies to positive capital inflow shocks. (Note: The shaded area denotes the 16th and 84th percentiles. Source: Authors' calculations)	212
Fig. 13.5	Credit to companies' responses to bank and non-bank flows shocks. (Note: The shaded area denotes the 16th and 84th percentiles. Source: Authors' calculations)	213
Fig. 13.6	Fluctuations in credit to companies due to FDI, portfolio, bank and non-bank flows. (Source: Authors' calculations)	213
Fig. 13.7	Relationships between credit to companies and selected macroeconomic indicators. (Source: South African Reserve Bank and authors' calculations)	214
Fig. 13.8	Cumulative repo rate responses to positive inflation shocks and amplification by portfolio flows channel. (Source: Authors' calculations)	215
Fig. 13.9	Cumulative repo rate responses to positive inflation shocks and amplification by various capital flow categories. (Source: Authors' calculations)	216
Fig. 13.10	Actual and counterfactual credit to companies and the contributions of bank flows. (Source: Authors' calculations)	216
Fig. 13.11	Actual and counterfactual credit to companies and the contributions of bank and non-bank flows. (Source: Authors' calculations)	217
Fig. 13.12	Household and corporate credit share relationship with inflation. (Source: South African Reserve Bank and authors' calculations)	218
Fig. 13.13	Household and corporate credit growth relationship with inflation. (Source: South African Reserve Bank and authors' calculations)	219

Fig. 14.1	Comparison of descriptive statistics. (Source: Authors' calculations)	222
Fig. 14.2	Relationship between inflation, equity inflows and debt inflows. (Source: South African Reserve Bank and authors' calculations)	223
Fig. 14.3	Comparison of bilateral relationships. (Source: Authors' calculations)	224
Fig. 14.4	Repo rate, GDP growth and credit growth responses to a positive inflation shock. (Note: The grey-shaded areas denote the 16th and 84th percentile error bands. Source: Authors' calculations)	225
Fig. 14.5	Responses to the R/US$ exchange depreciation shocks. (Note: The grey-shaded areas denote the 16th and 84th percentile error bands. Source: Authors' calculations)	226
Fig. 14.6	Capital inflow responses to positive inflation shocks. (Note: The grey-shaded areas denote the 16th and 84th percentile error bands. Source: Authors' calculations)	227
Fig. 14.7	Responses to rand depreciation and positive inflation shocks. (Note: The grey-shaded areas denote the 16th and 84th percentile error bands. Source: Authors' calculations)	227
Fig. 14.8	Households and companies credit share responses to positive capital inflow shocks. (Source: Authors' calculations)	228
Fig. 14.9	Repo rate responses to positive inflation shocks and the role of equity and debt inflows. (Source: Authors' calculations)	229
Fig. 14.10	Responses to equity and debt inflow shocks. (Note: The grey-shaded areas denote the 16th and 84th percentile error bands. Source: Authors' calculations)	230
Fig. 14.11	Comparison of fluctuations induced by positive equity and debt inflow shocks. (Source: Authors' calculations)	230
Fig. 14.12	Repo rate responses to positive inflation shocks and the role of equity and debt outflows. (Source: Authors' calculations)	231
Fig. 14.13	Repo rate responses to positive inflation shocks and the role of banking and non-banking flows. (Source: Authors' calculations)	232
Fig. 15.1	Relationship between repo rate and FFR. (Source: South African Reserve Bank, Fred and authors' calculations)	237

Fig. 15.2	Relationship between the US and SA GDP growth. (Source: South African Reserve Bank, IMF and authors' calculations)	237
Fig. 15.3	Relationship between the repo rate and gross capital inflows and outflows. (Source: South African Reserve Bank and authors' calculations)	239
Fig. 15.4	Responses to positive US GDP growth and FFR shocks. (Note: The grey-shaded areas denote the 16th and 84th percentile error bands. Source: Authors' calculations)	241
Fig. 15.5	Relationship between the repo rate-FFR spread and gross capital flows. (Note: The grey-shaded areas denote the 16th and 84th percentile error bands. Source: Authors' calculations)	242
Fig. 15.6	The repo rate-FFR differential and South African gross capital outflows. (Note: The grey-shaded areas denote the 16th and 84th percentile error bands. Source: Authors' calculations)	243
Fig. 15.7	Responses of repo rate-FFR spread and domestic gross capital outflows due to positive US GDP growth shock. (Note: The grey-shaded areas denote the 16th and 84th percentile error bands. Source: Authors' calculations)	245
Fig. 15.8	The impact of pure and growth-driven US interest rate shock. (Note: The grey-shaded areas denote the 16th and 84th percentile error bands. Source: Authors' calculations)	246
Fig. 15.9	Responses of US and SA GDP growth to positive VIX shocks. (Note: The grey-shaded areas denote the 16th and 84th percentile error bands. Source: Authors' calculations)	247
Fig. 15.10	Comparison of responses to positive domestic GDP growth and repo rate shocks. (Note: The grey-shaded areas denote the 16th and 84th percentile error bands. Source: Authors' calculations)	248
Fig. 15.11	The impact of persistent and non-persistent repo rate shocks on gross capital flows. (Source: Authors' calculations)	249
Fig. 15.12	The impact of persistent and non-persistent positive GDP growth shocks on gross capital flows. (Source: Authors' calculations)	250
Fig. 15.13	Comparison of domestic gross capital flow responses. (Source: Authors' calculations)	250
Fig. 15.14	Proportion of fluctuations in gross capital outflows and inflows due to US positive GDP growth and FFR shocks. (Source: Authors' calculations)	251

Fig. 15.15	Proportion of fluctuation in gross capital outflows and inflows due to positive SA GDP growth and repo rate shocks. (Source: Authors' calculations)	252
Fig. 16.1	Responses to the rand per US dollar exchange rate depreciation shocks. (Note: The grey-shaded areas denote the 16th and 84th percentile error bands. Source: Authors' calculations)	259
Fig. 16.2	Responses to positive inflation shocks. (Note: The grey-shaded areas denote the 16th and 84th percentile error bands. Source: Authors' calculations)	260
Fig. 16.3	Counterfactual and actual cumulative GDP growth responses to positive repo rate shocks. (Source: Authors' calculations)	261
Fig. 16.4	Counterfactual and actual cumulative inflation responses to the rand per US dollar exchange rate depreciation shocks. (Source: Authors' calculations)	262
Fig. 16.5	Counterfactual and actual cumulative repo rate responses to positive inflation shocks. (Source: Authors' calculations)	263
Fig. 16.6	Comparison of the cumulative effects of total and net purchases of domestic shares by non-residents. (Source: Authors' calculations)	264
Fig. 17.1	The role of confidence and expectations in responding to stimulatory policy shocks. (Source: Authors' drawings)	271
Fig. 17.2	GDP growth, consumer and business confidence. (Source: South African Reserve Bank and Authors' calculations)	271
Fig. 17.3	Government debt growth, GDP growth, and consumer and business confidence. (Source: South African Reserve Bank and authors' calculations)	273
Fig. 17.4	Government debt growth, labour productivity and business confidence. (Source: South African Reserve Bank and authors' calculations)	274
Fig. 17.5	Responses of sovereign debt credit ratings to positive GDP growth shocks. (Note: The grey-shaded area bands denote the 16th and 84th percentile confidence bands. SP denotes Standard & Poor's. Source: Authors' calculations)	275
Fig. 17.6	GDP growth responses to sovereign debt credit ratings upgrades and downgrades shocks. (Note: The grey-shaded area bands denote the 16th and 84th percentile confidence bands. SP denote Standard & Poor's. Source: Authors' calculations)	276
Fig. 17.7	The responses to positive business confidence shocks. (Source: Authors' calculations)	277

Fig. 17.8	GDP growth responses to positive CDS and EMBI shocks. (Note: The grey-shaded area bands denote the 16th and 84th percentile confidence bands. Source: Authors' calculations)	278
Fig. 17.9	GDP growth responses to negative business confidence shocks. (Source: Authors' calculations)	278
Fig. 17.10	Business confidence responses to downgrades shocks and the role of post-2008 periods. (Source: Authors' calculations)	279
Fig. 17.11	Selected GDP growth responses to downgrades shocks. (Source: Authors' calculations)	280
Fig. 17.12	GDP growth responses to sovereign debt credit ratings upgrades shocks. (Note: SP denotes Standard & Poor's. Source: Authors' calculations)	280
Fig. 17.13	Cumulative responses of GDP growth to S&P sovereign debt credit ratings revisions shocks and the role of consumer confidence. (Source: Authors' calculations)	282
Fig. 17.14	Actual and counterfactual repo rate responses to GDP growth shocks. (Source: Authors' calculations)	283
Fig. 17.15	Actual and counterfactual repo rate responses and the role of sovereign debt credit ratings downgrades confidence shocks. (Source: Authors' calculations)	283
Fig. 18.1	Schematic representation of the transmission of the sovereign debt credit ratings downgrades and upgrades shock to credit growth. (Source: Authors' drawings)	288
Fig. 18.2	Responses of credit growth to sovereign debt credit ratings downgrades and upgrades shocks and the role of economic growth. (Source: Authors' calculations)	290
Fig. 18.3	Responses of credit growth to the ratings agency sovereign debt credit ratings downgrades and upgrades shocks and the role of economic growth. (Note: SP denotes Standard and Poor's. Source: Authors' calculations)	291
Fig. 18.4	Credit growth responses to sovereign debt credit ratings downgrades and upgrades shocks. (Note: The grey-shaded areas denote the 16th and 84th percentile confidence bands. Source: Authors' calculations)	292
Fig. 18.5	Credit growth responses to sovereign debt credit ratings downgrades and upgrades shocks in the endogenous–exogenous model. (Note: The grey-shaded areas denote the 16th and 84th percentile confidence bands. Source: Authors' calculations)	293

Fig. 18.6	Percentage of fluctuations in credit growth explained by the sovereign debt credit ratings downgrades and upgrades shocks. (Source: Authors' calculations)	294
Fig. 18.7	Credit growth responses to sovereign debt credit ratings downgrades and upgrades revisions shocks in the endogenous–exogenous model. (Note: The grey-shaded areas denote the 16th and 84th percentile confidence bands. Source: Authors' calculations)	295
Fig. 18.8	Percentage of fluctuations in credit growth explained by shocks to sovereign debt credit ratings revisions to downgrades and upgrades. (Source: Authors' calculations)	295
Fig. 18.9	Credit growth responses to sovereign debt credit ratings downgrades and upgrades shocks in a counterfactual VAR model. (Source: Authors' calculations)	296
Fig. 18.10	Credit growth responses to sovereign debt credit ratings downgrades and upgrades shocks in a counterfactual VAR model. (Note: SP denotes Standard and Poor's sovereign debt credit ratings. Source: Authors' calculations)	297
Fig. 18.11	Credit growth amplifications by GDP growth response to sovereign debt credit ratings agency downgrades and upgrades shocks. (Note: SP denotes Standard and Poor's sovereign debt credit ratings. Source: Authors' calculations)	297
Fig. 19.1	Credit growth responses to sovereign debt credit ratings downgrades shocks. (Note: The grey-shaded area denotes the 16th and 84th percentile confidence bands. Source: Authors' calculations)	303
Fig. 19.2	Credit growth, cost of government debt and gross government loan-to-GDP ratio responses to a sovereign debt credit ratings downgrades shock. (Source: Authors' calculations)	304
Fig. 19.3	Credit growth responses to rating agency-specific sovereign debt credit downgrades shocks. (Note: SP denotes Standard and Poor's. Source: Authors' calculations)	305
Fig. 20.1	Efficient policy frontier. (Source: Authors' drawings)	310
Fig. 20.2	Trade-off between output growth volatility and inflation volatility. (Note: IT means inflation targeting period. Source: Authors' calculations)	313
Fig. 20.3	Scatterplot between output growth volatility and inflation volatility. (Source: Authors' calculations)	313

xxxviii   List of Figures

Fig. 20.4	Impulse responses, cross correlation and scatterplot between output volatility and nominal wage inflation volatility. (Source: Authors' calculations)	314
Fig. 20.5	Effects of positive demand and supply shocks on conditional volatilities. (Source: Authors' calculations)	315
Fig. 21.1	Responses to a positive Federal Funds Rate shock. (Source: Authors' calculations)	321
Fig. 21.2	Cumulative responses to positive UK and US economic policy uncertainty shocks. (Source: Authors' calculations)	322
Fig. 21.3	Responses to positive commodity price shocks. (Source: Authors' calculations)	323
Fig. 21.4	Responses to a negative terms-of-trade shock. (Source: Authors' calculations)	324
Fig. 21.5	The Taylor curve responses to the Rand per US dollar exchange rate shock. (Note: S.D. denotes the standard deviation shocks. Source: Authors' calculations)	324
Fig. 21.6	The responses of the Taylor curve to positive expectations shocks. (Note: The grey-shaded bands denote the 16th and 84th percentile confidence bands. Source: Authors' calculations)	325
Fig. 21.7	The responses of the Taylor curve to positive inflation expectations shocks. (Note: The grey-shaded bands denote the 16th and 84th percentile confidence bands. Source: Authors' calculations)	326
Fig. 21.8	The responses of the Taylor curve to negative inflation expectations shocks relative to the 6 per cent inflation threshold. (Source: Authors' calculations)	327
Fig. 22.1	Labour market conditions index. (Source: Authors' calculations)	332
Fig. 22.2	Responses to a negative global trade shock and in a longer sample. (Note: The grey-shaded bands denote the 16th and 84th percentile confidence bands. Source: Authors' calculations)	333
Fig. 22.3	Tax revenue growth and selected labour market indicators responses to negative global trade shocks. (Source: Authors' calculations)	334
Fig. 22.4	The Taylor curve responses based on the endogenous–exogenous VAR approach. (Note: The grey-shaded bands denote the 16th and 84th percentile confidence bands. Source: Authors' calculations)	335

Fig. 22.5	Proportion of fluctuations induced by global trade shocks. (Source: Authors' calculations)	336
Fig. 22.6	Cumulative responses to a negative global trade shock and the role of the labour market conditions index (1995Q1 to 2014Q1). (Source: Authors' calculations)	337
Fig. 22.7	Cumulative responses to a negative global trade shock and the role of labour market conditions index (2000Q1 to 2014Q1). (Source: Authors' calculations)	337
Fig. 22.8	Cumulative responses and fluctuation due to a negative global trade shock. (Source: Authors' calculations)	338
Fig. 23.1	Labour market conditions index. (Source: Authors' calculations)	342
Fig. 23.2	Taylor curve responses to loose and tight labour market conditions shocks. (Note: LMCI denotes labour market conditions index. Source: Authors' calculations)	343
Fig. 23.3	Taylor curve responses based on the endogenous–exogenous VAR approach. (Note: LMCI denotes labour market conditions index. Source: Authors' calculations)	344
Fig. 23.4	Taylor curve responses based on the endogenous–exogenous VAR approach (1995Q1 to 2014Q4). (Note: LMCI denotes labour market conditions index. Source: Authors' calculations)	345
Fig. 23.5	Responses from a counterfactual VAR approach. (Note: LMCI denotes labour market conditions index. Source: Authors' calculations)	346
Fig. 23.6	Taylor curve responses to labour market conditions shocks and role of the 6 per cent inflation threshold. (Note: LMCI denotes labour market conditions index. Source: Authors' calculations)	346
Fig. 23.7	Output-gap and inflation volatility responses to loose and tight labour market conditions shocks. (Note: The grey-shaded bands denote 16th and 84th percentile confidence bands. LMCI denotes labour market conditions index. Source: Authors' calculations)	347
Fig. 23.8	Cumulative responses to tight labour market shocks and the role of the output-gap and inflation volatility shocks. (Source: Authors' calculations)	348
Fig. 24.1	Theoretical effects of expansionary policy shock on output and inflation. (Source: Authors' drawings)	354

Fig. 24.2	Responses to a positive nominal demand shock. (Note: The grey-shaded bands denote the 16th and 84th confidence bands. Source: Authors' calculations)	357
Fig. 24.3	Responses to a positive nominal demand shock in different VAR models. (Note: The grey-shaded bands denote the 16th and 84th confidence bands. Source: Authors' calculations)	359
Fig. 24.4	Responses to a positive nominal demand shock in high and low inflation regimes. (Note: The grey-shaded bands denote the 16th and 84th confidence bands. Source: Authors' calculations)	360
Fig. 24.5	Inflation responses and fluctuations to positive a nominal demand shock. (Source: Authors' calculations)	361
Fig. 24.6	Cumulative responses to positive a nominal demand shock and the role of inflation. (Source: Authors' calculations)	362
Fig. 24.7	GDP responses to positive a nominal demand shock in models with nominal wage inflation. (Source: Authors' calculations)	363
Fig. 24.8	Nominal wage responses to a positive nominal demand shock in high- and low inflation regimes. (Source: Authors' calculations)	364
Fig. 25.1	Theoretical depiction of the price level response to a positive nominal demand shock. (Source: Authors' drawings)	366
Fig. 25.2	Inflation responses and fluctuations due to a positive nominal demand shock in 1990Q1 to 2017Q1 period. (Note: The grey-shaded bands denote the 16th and 84th percentile error bands. Source: Authors' calculations)	371
Fig. 25.3	Inflation responses and fluctuations due to a positive nominal demand shock during the inflation targeting period. (Note: The grey-shaded bands denote the 16th and 84th percentile error bands. Source: Authors' calculations)	372
Fig. 25.4	Real GDP growth responses due to a positive nominal demand shock and the role of inflation regimes during the inflation targeting period. (Note: The grey-shaded bands denote the 16th and 84th percentile error bands. Source: Authors' calculations)	372
Fig. 25.5	Accumulated actual and counterfactual real GDP growth responses due to a positive nominal demand shock and the role of inflation regimes (2000Q1–2017Q1). (Source: Authors' calculations)	373

Fig. 25.6	Accumulated actual and counterfactual real GDP growth responses due to a positive nominal demand shock and the role of inflation regimes (1990Q1–2017Q1). (Source: Authors' calculations)	374
Fig. 25.7	Comparison of amplification of nominal demand shocks by inflation regimes. (Source: Authors' calculations)	375
Fig. 25.8	Robustness based on 1980Q1–2017Q1 sample. (Note: The grey-shaded bands denote the 16th and 84th percentile error bands. Source: Authors' calculations)	377

List of Tables

Table 2.1	Granger causality effects	32
Table 7.1	Synchronisation of the repo rate and FFR during inflation targeting	126
Table 7.2	Cointegration and asymmetry tests	130
Table 7.3	Granger causality test	132
Table 7.4	Mean nominal repo rate-FFR spread, real repo rate and inflation	137
Table 17.1	Sovereign debt credit ratings of South Africa's government long-term debt	285
Table 25.1	Unrestricted cointegration rank test (trace)	368
Table 25.2	Unrestricted cointegration rank test (maximum eigenvalue)	369
Table 25.3	Estimates of the long-run coefficients based on the inflation regimes	369
Table 25.4	The speed of price adjustment or the error-correction coefficients	370
Table 25.5	Unrestricted cointegration rank test (trace)	376
Table 25.6	Unrestricted cointegration rank test (maximum eigenvalue)	376
Table 25.7	Estimates of the long-run coefficients based on the inflation regimes	377
Table 25.8	The speed of adjustment or error-correction	377

xliii

1

Introduction

The period subsequent to the global financial crisis highlighted that global demand plays an important role in driving economic recoveries. At the time, when global policy uncertainties have become elevated and global interest rates reached low levels to mitigate the adverse effects of these uncertainties. Current global growth is characterised by diverging GDP growth rates with the United States of America (US) growing at a high pace while the Chinese growth is slowing down. The World Bank and IMF downgraded the world economic growth forecasts, following heightened trade tensions between China and the US. We apply a variety of econometric techniques to capture various aspects of the transmission of global and domestic shocks into the South African macroeconomy. We test several hypotheses to determine whether they are agreeable and relevant for the South African economy. In all instances, we use various econometric techniques to assess the robustness of the empirical findings and the policy implications derived from the results.

Recent developments which happened during the writing of this book include the following:

- Most central banks in advanced economies have not wound down their balance sheet policies, some embarked on negative interest rate policies and have extended forward guidance to assist them to meet their price, financial and macroeconomic stability mandates.
- South Africa's sovereign debt credit ratings has been downgraded further by the Standard and Poor as well as the Fitch rating agencies. However, Moody's rating agency is still maintaining South Africa's investment rating level.
- The US Federal Reserve Bank (Fed) raised the policy rate at the end of 2015 in an effort to normalise the policy rate settings. This monetary policy stance was supported by high economic growth, very low unemployment and a promising rebound of inflation towards the target. However, the Fed has since reversed course in July 2019 and started easing the monetary policy stance in order to achieve its price stability mandate and support the growth expansion. This contrasts with South Africa, which has had to deal with extremely low growth, a recessionary environment accompanied by increasing unemployment, bouts of sharp exchange rate depreciation shocks and elevated inflationary shocks. This has implications for capital flows and the financing of the current account. Changes in investor risk perceptions are evident in the changes in the direction of the purchases of domestic assets by non-residents.
- Trade tensions between the US and China continue to weigh on global trade activity. China also experienced a slowdown in economic growth in recent times. These global developments have heightened global growth and trade policy uncertainties regarding the momentum of global growth.
- The South African Bureau of Economic Research business confidence index has remained below the midpoint for most of the time post-2009, indicating the persistently low levels of confidence.
- Domestic credit growth has also remained weak even during times of elevated capital flows.

This book is divided into six parts which cover diverse themes. Part I covers the effects of global economic growth and trade uncertainty on the South African economy. Part II focuses on global interest rates and how they are transmitted into the South African economy. Part III deals with capital flow surges, sudden stops and elevated portfolio inflow volatility shock effects. Part IV focuses on the transmission of sovereign debt credit ratings downgrades into government debt costs and real economic activity. Part V deals with the output–inflation trade-off and the role of external shocks, labour market conditions and inflation expectations in shifting the Taylor curve in South Africa. Part VI focuses on the policy ineffectiveness issues.

1.1 Why Do We Author This Book?

We dedicate a number of chapters in the book to deal with the role and transmission of global economic and trade policy uncertainty, the policy normalisation process by the US Fed, global real policy rates and the role of Brazil, Russia, India, China and South African (BRICS) GDP growth as sources of shocks and/or amplifiers of global growth. The book also deals with the policy trade-offs as captured by the Taylor curve. We explore how external shocks; labour market conditions and inflation expectations shocks shift the South African Taylor curve. We also dedicated a number of chapters to explore the transmission of sovereign debt credit ratings downgrades, consumer and business confidence shocks into the South African credit markets and the real economy. This is accompanied by various chapters which deal with the role and interaction of capital flow surges, sudden stops and elevated portfolio inflow volatility shocks. We explore the nature of their interaction with output and credit growth and their economic costs, thereof.

1.1.1 There Are Policy Shifts in the Global Economy Which Include Trade Policies and the Role of Global Economic Growth Impulses

Figure 1.1 shows that global economic policy and trade uncertainty have increased. These economic uncertainty indices have featured strongly in academic and policy discussions and debates in recent years. It remains unclear as to how these global policy shifts and trade uncertainties will be

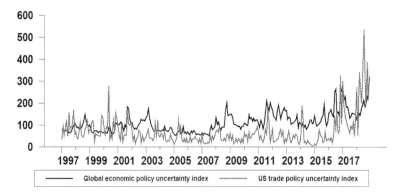

Fig. 1.1 Global economic policy uncertainty and the US trade policy uncertainty. (Source: http://www.policyuncertainty.com/global_monthly.html)

resolved and their effects on the domestic economy thereof. At the same time, the direction of capital flows and the availability of global liquidity are interlinked and transmitted through various channels to affect the domestic economy. This book fills academic and policy research gaps on the transmission of global economic policy uncertainty, capital flow episodes and sovereign debt credit ratings shock effects into the South African macroeconomy.

1.1.2 The Extent to Which BRICS Growth Could Be a Source of Shocks and an Amplifier of Global Growth Responses Is Unknown

The South African GDP growth has been very weak and volatile post-2009. However, pre-2009, South African (SA) GDP growth was more comparable to global GDP growth and well above that of the US as shown in Fig. 1.2. Furthermore, SA GDP growth has remained well below its 2000–2016 average growth since 2011. At the same time, US growth recovered and has oscillated around its 2000–2016 average growth.

Of note is the fact that post-2009, US and SA average growth converged towards 1.5 per cent, the positive association and correlation has increased and yet, the US economy has managed to lower the unem-

1 Introduction 5

ployment rate to pre-2009 levels in stark contrast to the SA experience. What might explain this divergence? In part, the divergence might be explained by the persistent divergence and decline in SA GDP growth post-2013 when global and US recovered and continued to increase as shown in Fig. 1.3. The implication of global and US GDP trends is that, had SA GDP growth remained at minimum 2010 and 2011 growth

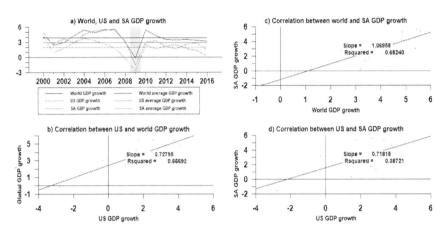

Fig. 1.2 Global, US and South African GDP growth. (Source: South African Reserve Banks, IMF database and authors' calculations)

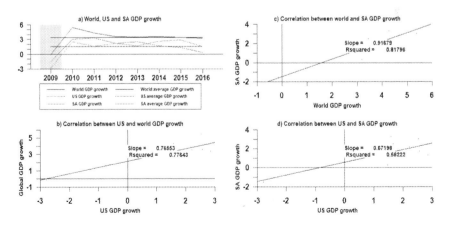

Fig. 1.3 Global, United States and South African GDP growth post-2009. (Source: South African Reserve Bank, IMF database and authors' calculations)

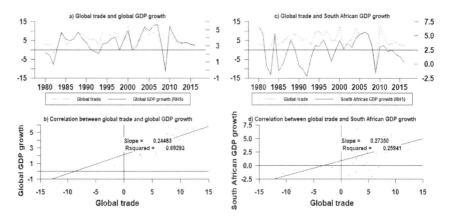

Fig. 1.4 Global GDP growth, trade and South African GDP growth. (Source: IMF database and authors' calculations)

rates and maintained these levels of growth momentum, SA GDP growth would have compared favourably with average global and US GDP growth.

At the same time, the 2009–2016 average global GDP growth of 3.4 per cent in Fig. 1.3 would have been more than enough to persistently lower the unemployment rate in South Africa as suggested by vast empirical evidence. In addition, Fig. 1.4 shows that SA growth is positively associated with global trade albeit, very weak relative to global growth. These trends indicate that SA can use the "exports-led GDP growth" strategy to benefit from global trade growth. The association of SA GDP growth with global trade growth indicates that there is room for improvement.

1.1.3 Changes in the US Fed Funds Rate, Global Real Policy Rates Matter for the South African Economy

The US Fed normalised its policy settings December 2015. We explore the implications of this by assessing the direction in which there is a momentum effect in the changes in the long run spread between the repo

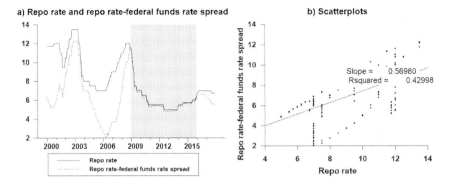

Fig. 1.5 The repo rate and the repo rate-FFR spread. (Note: Grey-shaded area represents the period of the zero-lower bound for the US FFR. Source: South African Reserve Bank and Fred data)

rate and the Federal Funds Rate (FFR). Evidence shows that the starting point matters for such an analysis as shown in Fig. 1.5. The repo rate-FFR spread hardly moved during the period of the FFR zero-lower bound. The level of the repo rate was the same as the repo rate-FFR spread. This means that the repo rate movements explain all the variation in the repo rate-FFR spread during the zero-lower bound of the FFR. However, the spread has adjusted as the US Fed started to increase the policy rate. The scatterplots in Fig. 1.5(b) indicate that the repo rate movements explain almost 42 per cent of the variation in the repo rate-FFR spread over the sample period.

Central to the repo rate adjustments is the performance of domestic inflation relative to the inflation target as shown in Fig. 1.6. The scatterplots in Fig. 1.6(b) show that inflation is positively associated with repo rate-FFR spread. In addition, inflation explains about 34 per cent of the movements in the repo rate-FFR spreads. The slope of the relationship suggests that a one per cent rise in inflation raises the repo rate-FFR spread by about 0.52 per cent. The policy implication is that low and stable inflation has benefits for the level of the repo rate-FFR spread. Furthermore, this evidence further corroborates the findings in the book indicating that inflation below 4.5 per cent within the target range reduces the pass-through of positive nominal demand shocks to inflation.

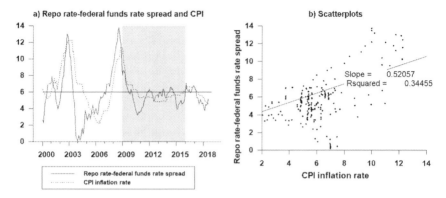

Fig. 1.6 Headline inflation and the repo rate-FFR spread. (Source: South African Reserve Bank, Fred data and authors' calculations)

1.1.4 To Show That the Policy Trade-off Between Inflation and Output Volatilities Is Impacted by Domestic and Global Factors

The book looks at the trade-off between the inflation, nominal wage and output-gap volatilities. Evidence shows that output growth volatility tends to decline with varying magnitudes due to an unexpected positive consumer price inflation and nominal wage volatility shock. This trade-off is evident in the samples for pre- and post-inflation targeting framework. Furthermore, it is a time-varying process. Output growth volatility increases due to elevated consumer price inflation and nominal wage volatility. The negative relationship between consumer inflation, nominal wage volatility and output growth volatility is strong pre- and post-inflation targeting. In addition, the results show that the effects of demand and supply shocks on consumer price inflation, nominal wage and output-gap volatilities are not persistent. Hence, departures or deviations from the Taylor curve should be short-lived if the central bank operates efficiently.

1.1.5 To Show the Asymmetry in the Reaction of the Real Economic Activity to Sovereign Debt Credit Ratings Downgrades and Upgrades Shocks

We dedicate several chapters in the book to assess the role and transmission sovereign debt credit ratings upgrades and downgrades shocks. We pay attention to (i) the role of business confidence; (ii) the indirect role of GDP growth in transmitting sovereign debt credit ratings shocks; and (iii) the cost of government borrowing. The direct and indirect transmission channels of sovereign debt credit ratings downgrades and upgrades shocks effects shown in Fig. 1.7 are explored. The *indirect channel* is transmitted via economic growth, which implies that GDP growth is the main transmitter of the sovereign debt credit ratings shocks. Thus, sovereign debt credit ratings upgrades and downgrades imply that changes in the cost at which government borrows are transmitted directly and indirectly to credit growth via GDP growth.

The book conducts detailed analysis to determine what the simultaneous occurrence of low business confidence and the heightened risk of a sovereign debt credit ratings upgrade and downgrade do to the domestic real economy. Barsky and Sims (2009) categorise the approaches to the role of confidence in macroeconomics into two views. The animal spirits view which suggests the autonomous fluctuations in beliefs that in turn have causal effects on economic activity. The news view

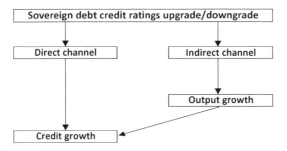

Fig. 1.7 Schematic representation of the sovereign debt credit ratings shock transmission to credit growth. (Source: Authors' drawing)

which regards the causal relationship between confidence and the subsequent macroeconomic activity. This is to be underpinned by the fact that confidence measures contain fundamental information about the current and future states of the economy. In most studies, the channel linking confidence and subsequent macroeconomic activity is changes in future productivity.

Evidence in the book shows that a sovereign debt credit ratings downgrade shock lowers credit growth and the decline is bigger when the cost of government debt and borrowing is endogenous in the model than when it is exogenous as shown as shown in Fig. 1.8. This means that allowing for the feedback of the cost of government debt and borrowing propagates the adverse shock effects of the sovereign debt credit ratings downgrade on credit growth. The cost of government debt and borrowing exert negative amplification effects on credit growth following a sovereign credit downgrade ratings shock. This is because the sovereign debt credit ratings downgrade shocks raises the cost of government debt and borrowing as well as the ratio of government gross loan debt to GDP.

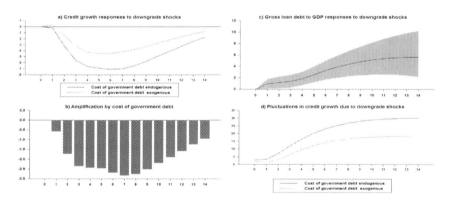

Fig. 1.8 Credit growth responses to sovereign debt credit ratings downgrade shocks. (Note: The grey-shaded area denotes the 16th and 84th percentile confidence bands. Source: Authors' calculations)

1.1.6 To Show that VIX and Elevated Portfolio Inflows Volatility Impact GDP Growth and the Interaction Between Credit Growth, Capital Flow Surges, Sudden Stops and Capital Flow Retrenchments

The book explores the (i) interaction of capital flow surges, sudden stops and elevated portfolio inflow volatility shocks with GDP growth and credit, and the (ii) economic costs of capital flow episodes.

1.1.7 To Show that Confidence Plays a Role in Transmitting Stimulatory Policy Decisions

Figure 1.9 illustrates the role of confidence and the responses of expectations to expansionary monetary policy. A decline in interest rates results in a much higher response in output (Y_0 to Y_2) when confidence is high, and agents have better expectations about the economic outlook, compared to Y_0 to Y_1, when confidence and expectations are low. Evidence in the book shows that business confidence is positively related to GDP growth. At the same time, GDP growth and confidence are negatively related to changes in government debt.

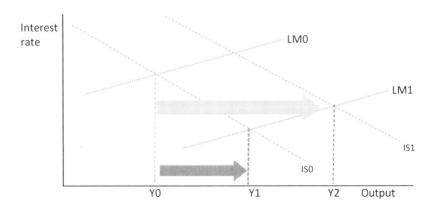

Fig. 1.9 The role of confidence and expectations in responding to stimulatory policy shocks. (Source: Authors' drawing)

1.1.8 To Show the Role of Government Debt on the Macroeconomy

Evidence in the book shows that the negative relationship between government debt and business confidence is pronounced. Furthermore, government debt is negatively associated with productivity. But business confidence is positively related to productivity growth. This means that the productivity channel partly explains why high government debt leads to low business confidence.

1.1.9 To Show That the Trade Channel Matters

We find that the South African trade balance is susceptible to risk aversion shocks and this may lead to a significant slowdown in economic activity. Figure 1.10 shows that exports growth declines significantly for a long period due to heightened VIX shocks. In contrast, the capital flows surge episodes tend to increase exports growth. However, a sudden stop shock depresses exports growth, which is later followed by a transitory improvement. Elevated global risk aversion is a significant driver of exports growth.

However, imports growth increases significantly due to the capital flow surges shock in Fig. 1.11. This contrasts with a decline due to heightened VIX and sudden stop shocks. In addition, the contraction in credit

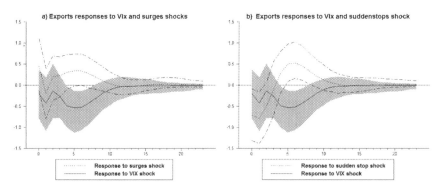

Fig. 1.10 Exports growth responses. (Note: The grey-shaded areas denote the 16th and 84th percentile error bands. Source: Authors' calculations)

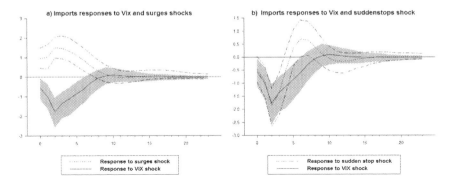

Fig. 1.11 Import growth responses. (Note: The grey-shaded areas denote the 16th and 84th percentile error bands. Source: Authors' calculations)

growth may lead to a slowdown in GDP growth. Thus, a global risk aversion shocks matter more than the capital flow episode shocks in driving economic activity in South Africa.

1.1.10 To Provide Empirical Evidence Showing That Equity and Debt Inflows Matter

Evidence in the book shows that the repo rate tends to respond more aggressively to positive inflation shock in a model with equity inflows compared to that with debt inflows. Evidence shows that the differential effects could be linked to the ability of equity inflows and debt inflows shocks to influence inflation and the R/US$ exchange rate, as shown in Fig. 1.12. The actual inflation response is lower in the presence of net purchases and domestic capital retrenchment compared to the counterfactual inflation rate. In contrast, the inflation response is higher in the presence of VIX than when it is shut off in the model. The domestic investors' capital flow retrenchment has a bigger impact in dampening inflationary pressures due to the R/US$ exchange rate depreciation than due to net purchases by non-residents.

The results in the book show that the equity inflow shocks leads to the appreciation of the R/US$ exchange rate by a higher magnitude and for a prolonged period compared to debt inflows shocks. Thus, equity inflows lower inflation, appreciate the R/US$ exchange rate and affect the rate at which the repo rate responds to inflationary shocks. Hence,

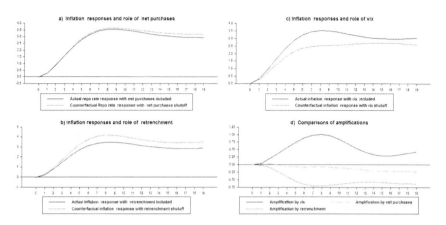

Fig. 1.12 Counterfactual and actual cumulative inflation responses to rand depreciation shocks. (Source: Authors' calculations)

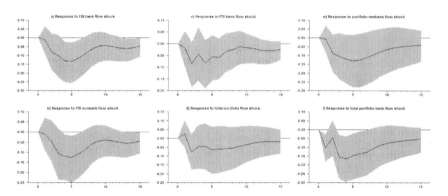

Fig. 1.13 Responses of credit to household to positive capital flow shock. (Note: The shaded area denotes the 16th and 84th percentiles. Source: Authors' calculations)

equity inflows matter more in the attainment of the price stability mandate. We test the relevance of the Samarina and Bezemer (2016) argument, that since the 1990s foreign capital inflow shocks have resulted in the sectorial allocation of credit. We establish the prevalence of sectorial credit reallocations between credit to companies and households. Evidence in the book shows that an increase in capital inflows leads to a reduction in the share of credit to household, as shown in Fig. 1.13.

This is the case for portfolio and foreign direct investment (FDI) bank and non-bank flows. Elevated capital flows of all categories do not result in a strong increase in the share of credit to households on impact. The positive impact comes at a considerable lag and even then, it is very weak.

1.2 Selected Main Findings

It is imperative for South African policymakers to deal with structural issues in the economy, to have economic growth driven by domestic factors which minimises the exposure of the domestic economy from global adverse effects. The implications of the results contained in the book is that the persistent loss of SA GDP growth momentum post-2009, although was in part influenced by global factors, is largely explained by domestic factors in particular heightened policy uncertainty in recent years and the lack of bold supply-side policy interventions. Hence, South Africa did not benefit from the rebound in global growth post-2009. In addition, SA growth is positively associated with global trade, albeit very weak relative to global growth, as shown in Fig. 1.4. But the association of SA GDP growth with global growth indicates that there is room for improvement.

The BRICS can exert adverse effects on global economic growth with wide repercussions. Evidence in the book shows that BRICS is a big magnifier of G7 economic growth responses due to positive demand shocks, followed by EMEs (excluding China). Furthermore, the propagation effects by BRICS growth exceed those from BIITS economies and the China effect alone is small. The BRICS amplify the effects of adverse economic shocks such as the global financial crisis and uncertainty. Evidence indicates that commodity price shocks lead to positive responses of G7 growth and that BRICS, EMEs (excluding China) and BIITS amplify the effects of positive commodity shock on G7 economies.

BRICS growth shocks lead to asymmetric G7 GDP growth. Large negative BRICS GDP growth shocks lead to large declines in G7 GDP growth compared to smaller negative shocks. Global business cycles impact each other in an asymmetric way, especially due to negative GDP shocks. These asymmetric responses suggest that economic growth in advanced economies is more likely to remain subdued, prompting monetary policy to be more accommodative for a longer period. Domestically, this means that interest rate differentials will be driven more by adverse factors inflation.

Elevated Chinese policy uncertainty contributed to the sharp depreciation in the R/US$ exchange rate compared to the effects emanating from US policy uncertainty. Furthermore, the South African exchange rates depreciate more due to weak Chinese GDP growth and the negative effects are propagated by China policy uncertainty. Evidence shows that Chinese GDP growth via the sharp R/US$ exchange rate deprecation poses a threat to inflationary pressures and the monetary policy stance. In addition, China growth shocks and those of advanced economies are transmitted via other countries (third countries) before impacting South Africa. We find that robust Chinese growth is important for sustaining high South African GDP growth in response to positive US, euro area, G7 and Chinese GDP growth shocks. Robust Chinese growth amplifies the response of euro area GDP growth response to positive US GDP growth shocks. This suggests that these economies will grow more when US GDP growth occurs concurrently with robust Chinese growth.

The co-movement between the repo rate and Federal Funds Rate varies and we establish that there was a higher degree of synchronisation during 2005 and 2006 when the repo rate and the FFR were tightening. The estimates of the Geweke feedback measures show that there was some degree of synchronisation, although weak when the policy stance was loosening. We establish that the long-run repo rate is at 7 per cent. The repo rate-FFR spread has been below the long-run repo rate since 2010. There are asymmetries in the repo rate-FFR spread adjustment process. The adjustments tend to persist more when the repo rate-FFR spread is widening or increasing as the change in repo rate-FFR spread exceeds the threshold. We conclude that this evidence points to higher momentum in the adjustment of the repo rate when the repo rate-FFR spread is narrowing. The repo rate-FFR spread adjusts non-linearly depending on the starting point.

South African domestic factors will dictate how policymakers adjust the repo rate. A key policy implication we derive from evidence in the book is that, irrespective of whether the future Fed interest rate adjustments are constrained by the zero lower bound and the lower neutral rate, South

African domestic factors, especially inflation will dictate how policymakers adjust the repo rate.

Unexpected tightening in global real interest rates leads to a contraction in domestic GDP growth and tightening in labour market conditions. In addition, we establish that the world real interest rate plays a role in transmitting positive exchange rate shocks to domestic GDP growth. We find that positive overall, permanent and transitory exchange rate volatility shocks lower GDP growth. But, the contraction in domestic GDP growth is larger due to elevated world real interest rates than when this variable is shut off in the model. Furthermore, the amplification by the world real interest rate is negative. This means that domestic GDP growth is likely to be subdued for a prolonged period due to elevated exchange rate volatilities and rising global real interest rates.

Inflation expectations, external and uncertainty shocks impact the trade-off between inflation volatilities and output volatility, and this shifts the Taylor curve. Evidence in the book shows that a positive FFR shock leads to a delayed effect of an increase in the repo rate, a decline in the repo rate-FFR spread and the deterioration in the current account. In addition, the Taylor curve increases more when the current account is not shut off in the model. This may be because of the amplification effects of the exchange rate depreciation on inflation. At the same time, foreign policy uncertainty shocks also result in the increase in the domestic Taylor curve, which in turn, due to increased gross capital outflows, magnify the Taylor curve responses to elevated policy uncertainty shocks.

Policy uncertainty, exchange rates, commodity prices and terms-of-trade impact the trade-off between inflation and output volatilities. A positive commodity price shock increases the Taylor curve and results in the tightening of the repo rate. On the other hand, a negative terms-of-trade shock increases the Taylor curve and the repo rate is tightened. This is because a negative terms-of-trade shock leads to the exchange rate depreciation and induces inflation but leads to a contraction in GDP growth. The combined effects of these shocks lead to increases in the inflation and output volatilities trade-offs.

Adverse global trade developments also impact the trade-off between the inflation and output volatilities. A negative global trade shock has a significant negative effect on the Taylor curve, suggesting that the Taylor curve shifts inwards. In addition, a negative global trade shock lowers the labour market conditions index implying that labour market conditions tighten. A negative global trade shock induces more fluctuations in labour market conditions than on the Taylor curve. The implication of these results is that labour markets adjust more to negative global trade shocks compared to the output and inflation volatilities trade-offs. This means that negative trade shocks which are negative demand shocks exert a disproportionately negative effect on labour market conditions than on the output and inflation volatilities.

Sovereign debt credit ratings developments have an impact on domestic credit dynamics. We examine the extent to which weaker credit growth post-recession in 2009 could be linked to various rounds of sovereign debt credit ratings downgrades and whether subdued GDP growth can exacerbate the transmission of these shocks to credit growth.

We find that business confidence is positively related to GDP growth, but consumer confidence has a bigger effect on GDP growth than business confidence. This is consistent with findings in Farmer (2011) that consumer sentiment leads private activity. Consumer and business confidence and GDP growth are negatively related to changes in government debt. There is a strong feedback between GDP growth and the sovereign credit upgrades and downgrades. A positive GDP growth shock tends to raise the likelihood of a sovereign debt credit ratings upgrade. At the same time, the sovereign debt credit ratings downgrades (upgrades) leads to a decline (increase) in output.

The confidence channel plays an important role in the propagation of the sovereign debt credit ratings changes on GDP growth. The counterfactual responses show that the business confidence channel amplifies the GDP growth responses to sovereign debt credit ratings upgrade shocks. In addition, the business confidence channel exerts asymmetric effects on GDP growth. Negative business confidence changes are likely to depress economic growth by big a magnitude for long periods. In addition, sovereign debt credit ratings downgrades and GDP growth influence the trajectory of the repo rate towards inflation developments such as those observed around 2003 and 2008. Lower business confidence and subdued GDP growth play a role in the adjustment of the repo rate to inflationary pressures.

Negative shocks to global demand via the trade channel exert pronounced adverse effects on labour market conditions than on the Taylor curve. A disaggregated analysis of the labour market conditions index shows that employment growth (quantity) adjusts more than remuneration per worker (price) to negative global trade shocks. Negative global trade shocks are transmitted more via the output and employment channels than the inflation channel. At the same time, the exchange rate depreciation shock poses risks to the inflation and output volatilities and neutralises the policy rate responses to inflation shocks. Thus, a negative global trade shock shifts the Taylor curve inwards and the labour market conditions tighten.

There is a need to raise GDP growth as it increases the likelihood of sovereign debt credit ratings upgrades. However, a sovereign debt credit ratings downgrade lowers GDP growth. In addition, we find that there are heterogeneous effects of the sovereign debt credit ratings downgrades shocks. GDP growth declines more due to the Standard & Poor's and Fitch sovereign debt credit ratings downgrades.

With respect to the indirect effects of the sovereign debt credit ratings downgrade shocks transmitted via the cost of government debt and borrowing, evidence in this book shows that the sovereign debt credit ratings downgrade shocks are transmitted via the cost of government debt and borrowing to impact credit growth. A sovereign debt credit ratings downgrade shock lowers credit growth and the decline is bigger when the cost of government debt and borrowing channel is included in the model. The cost of government debt and borrowing channel exerts negative amplification effects on credit growth following a sovereign debt credit ratings downgrade shock. This is because the sovereign debt credit ratings downgrade shocks raises the cost of government debt and borrowing as well as the ratio of government gross loan debt to GDP.

Thus, policymakers should implement policies that avert sovereign debt credit ratings downgrades, as the sovereign debt credit ratings downgrades shocks spill-over into credit growth via the cost of government debt and borrowing channel.

Global risk appetite and aversion matter and drive capital flow episodes and net portfolio flow volatility shocks which can amplify economic cycles and increase the vulnerability of the financial system. We find that that heightened global risk (as measured by VIX) and sudden stop episodes are negatively related to credit growth, imports growth, exports growth and GDP growth. Heightened VIX and sudden stops shocks lower GDP growth, while the capital flow surges shock leads to an increase in GDP growth. The capital flow surges shock leads to the R/US$ exchange rate appreciation and depresses money market rates and bond yields. At the same time, exports and imports growth decline significantly for a long period due to heightened VIX shock. Capital flow surges shock increases credit growth significantly compared to the depressed state induced by a sudden stop and heightened VIX shocks.

The South African trade balance is susceptible to risk aversion shocks, and this may lead to a significant slowdown in economic activity. Exports growth declines significantly for a long period due to heightened VIX shock. In contrast, the capital flows surge episodes tend to increase exports growth. However, a sudden stop shock depresses exports growth, which is later followed by a transitory improvement. Elevated global risk aversion is a significant driver of exports growth.

However, imports growth increases significantly due to the capital flow surges shock. This contrasts with a decline due to heightened VIX and sudden stop shocks. In addition, the contraction in credit growth may lead to a slowdown in GDP growth. Thus, a global risk aversion shock matters more than the capital flow episode shocks in driving economic activity in South Africa.

Evidence in the book also establishes that equity and debt inflows matter in the attainment of the price stability mandate. Rising inflation deters equity and debt inflows, but equity inflows decline more compared to debt inflows. The impact of inflation on equity inflows is three times larger than that on debt inflows. Similarly, positive inflation shocks lead to a significant reduction in (i) portfolio banking and non-banking flows and (ii) foreign direct investment (FDI) banking and non-banking inflows. High inflation deters equity, banking and non-banking inflows.

We test the relevance of the Samarina and Bezemer (2016) argument that, since the 1990s, foreign capital inflows shocks resulted in the sectorial allocation of credit. We establish the prevalence of sectorial credit reallocations between credit to companies and households. Evidence shows that an increase in capital inflows leads to a reduction in the share of credit to households. This is the case for portfolio and FDI bank and non-bank flows. Elevated capital flows of all categories do not result in a strong increase in the share of credit to households on impact. The positive impact comes with a considerable lag, and even then, it is very weak.

References

Barsky, B., and Sims, E.R. 2009. *Information, Animal Spirits, and the Meaning of Innovations in Consumer Confidence*. NBER Working Paper No. 15049.

Farmer, R.E.A. 2011. *Confidence, Crashes and Animal Spirits*. NBER Working Paper No. 14846.

Samarina, A., and Bezemer, D. 2016. Do Capital Flows Change Domestic Credit Allocation? *Journal of International Money and Finance*, 6(C), 98–121. Elsevier.

Part I

Global Economic Growth, Economic Policy Uncertainty and The Influence of Trade Dynamics

2

Is BRICS GDP Growth a Source of Shocks or an Amplifier of Global Growth Responses? What Are the Policy Implications for South Africa?

Learning Objectives

- Assess whether BRICS is a source or amplifier of positive G7 GDP growth and demand shocks.
- Explore whether BRICS GDP growth shocks lead to asymmetric G7 GDP growth.
- Establish whether elevated Chinese economic policy uncertainty and GDP growth pose a threat to the monetary policy conduct in South Africa.
- Find whether Chinese GDP growth shocks amplify the response of euro area and UK GDP growth to US GDP growth shocks
- Show the implications of the asymmetric responses to G7 GDP growth shocks for global monetary policy and the SA-US interest rate differentials.
- Compare the contribution of elevated Chinese policy uncertainty on the R/US$ exchange rate to those due to US policy uncertainty.
- Establish whether Chinese GDP growth shocks and those of advanced economies are transmitted via other countries (third countries) before impacting South Africa.

- Determine whether robust Chinese GDP growth amplifies the response of the euro area GDP growth response to positive US GDP growth shocks.

2.1 Introduction

In 2016, global growth was largely characterised by economies growing at lower rates than before the financial crisis. Forecasts of global growth have been persistently downgraded,[1] and this happened despite central banks in advanced economies (AEs) embarking on various unconventional monetary policy easing policies.[2] In addition, the period subsequent to the financial crisis has highlighted the role global demand plays as a key mechanism that drives economic recoveries. At the same time, expectations indicated the likelihood that the recovery in AEs will lift the global economy out of the subdued growth environment is very small. Similarly, growth in most emerging market economies (EMEs) and, in particular, BRICS,[3] was slowing down. Hence, this chapter explores whether BRICS GDP growth shocks are a source of global GDP growth shocks or an amplifier of the responses to global GDP growth shocks. Do BRICS GDP growth shocks amplify (G7) GDP growth shock effects and positive demand shocks? In addition, do BRICS GDP growth shocks lead to an asymmetric G7 GDP growth response?

This, is motivated by China being a significant contributor to the global economy and a BRICS member which has, in recent times, exerted volatility and uncertainty in the global economy. In addition, we are motivated by the availability of the Chinese economic policy uncertainty index constructed by Scott et al. (2015) to capture the effects of the Chinese economic policy uncertainty.[4] As a consequence, there is need to determine, whether the elevated Chinese economic policy uncertainty and GDP growth deviation from the mean level pose a threat to the monetary policy conduct in South Africa. This includes showing the importance of the Chinese GDP growth as

---

[1] See, for example, World Bank (2016), OECD Economic Outlook (2016) and IMF WEO (October 2015).
[2] The share of the global economy guided by central banks with negative interest rates was at 23.3 per cent in 2016. http://on.wsj.com/1RQJbo2. See also Fig. 2.1 in Chap. 2.
[3] Comprises of Brazil, Russia, India, China and South Africa.
[4] http://www.policyuncertainty.com/index.html.

we assess how it amplifies the responses amongst advanced economies. Does the Chinese GDP growth shock amplify the response of euro area and UK GDP growth to US GDP growth shocks?

We fill policy research gaps as we differ from Chap. 3 of the World Bank Global economic prospects January 2016 objectives, which looked at (i) What are the key channels of spill-overs from the major emerging markets? (ii) Do business cycles in BRICS move in tandem with those in other emerging markets and frontier markets? (iii) How large are spill-overs from major emerging markets? And (iv) What are the policy implications? The questions explored in this chapter and the findings give much needed insight on important policy questions from the South African perspective.[5] Second, we fill policy research gaps determining the ability of BRICS and EMEs to amplify G7 growth responses to positive global demand shocks. This is because the role of global demand shocks is relevant given the policy initiatives to stimulate global demand. In addition, if US GDP growth shocks are transmitted via China GDP growth to impact other economies, then third-country effects need to be explored. Third, the chapter fills research gaps by giving more insight into the relationships by breaking down the preceding questions into the following sub questions. Are the Chinese growth shocks and those of AEs transmitted via other countries (third countries) before impacting South African GDP growth? If so, how relevant are these third-country effects? What do the counterfactuals from shutting off Chinese GDP growth dynamics in the estimated models imply for the South African exchange rate, inflation and monetary policy?

To contextualise the analysis in this chapter, Fig. 2.1 shows that GDP growth among BRICS is slowing. Hence, there is a need to determine whether negative BRICS GDP growth shocks exert asymmetric effects on G7 and South African growth dynamics. We apply different techniques such as the modified versions of Pentecôte and Rondeau (2015) and the Cerra and Saxena (2008) to determine the amplification abilities and to ascertain the robustness of the evidence contained in the chapter.

---

[5] This chapter differs from the questions explored by the World Bank report for January 2016. See Chap. 3 page 180 of the World Bank Global economic prospects January 2016 (i) What are the key channels of spill-overs from the major emerging markets? (ii) Do business cycles in BRICS move in tandem with those in other emerging markets and frontier markets? (iii) How large are spill-overs from major emerging markets? What are the policy implications?

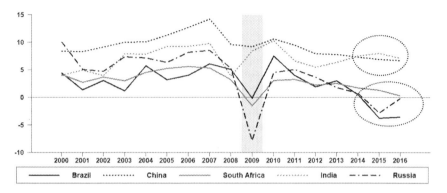

Fig. 2.1 RICS GDP growth. (Note: Grey-shaded area represents the South African recession. Source: IMF WEO 2016)

Furthermore, we use the Kilian and Vigfusson (2011) structural near-VAR model approach to establish the asymmetric effects to the size and sign of the GDP growth shock. But due to the prevailing weak GDP growth, we place more emphasis on analysing the asymmetric effects of negative GDP growth shocks rather than positive shocks. In addition, we explore the role of the Chinese policy uncertainty on the South African economy. Last, we use the Poirson and Weber (2011) counterfactual VAR approach to capture the amplification effects and the prevalence of third countries transmission effects.

2.1.1 Global Growth and Global Trade Activity

The underlying theme that has emerged after the global financial crisis is the prevalence of a serious disconnect of the key mechanisms that drive economic recoveries. The key factor underlying the disconnect is weak demand, particularly from the cyclical perspective (OECD 2016). Further to this, Bayoumi (2015) points to the fact that current circumstances demonstrate that it is difficult for governments and central banks to stimulate growth and inflation when demand is weak. The slowdown in demand is particularly evident in annual world trade activity shown in Fig. 2.2(b).

If growth in global trade is synonymous with global demand through export and import activity, then, based on Fig. 2.2(d), the current slow-

2 Is BRICS GDP Growth a Source of Shocks or an Amplifier... 29

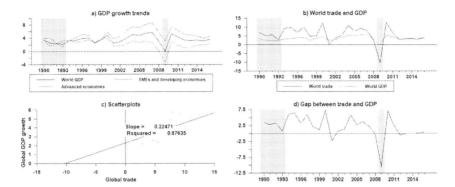

Fig. 2.2 Global growth and global trade activity. (Note: Grey-shaded areas represent the South African recessions. Source: IMF WEO 2016 and authors' calculations)

down in world trade which matches global GDP growth must imply muted global demand pressures. In this respect, Hoekman (2016) asserts that it is important for global trade to grow faster than global GDP growth. This is because global trade is a source of demand. In turn, growth in imports and exports lead to economic activity which generates employment and income. The gap between global GDP growth and trade growth has closed in Fig. 2.2(d) following a drop in global trade. The scatterplot in Fig. 2.2(c) shows that world trade is positively associated with world GDP growth and explains around 68 per cent of the variation in global GDP growth. Therefore, policies that will raise global trade activity relative to income as shown in Eq. (2.1) will have to focus on global demand via the absorption channel. This absorption channel includes consumption, investment and government (fiscal) spending channels as shown in Eq. (2.2). The difference operator Δ implies growth rates.

$$\Delta \text{Trade activity} - \Delta \text{Income} = \Delta \text{Residual} \qquad (2.1)$$

where the ΔResidual in Eq. (2.2) gives the variables that policymakers can directly or indirectly influence via different policy initiatives.

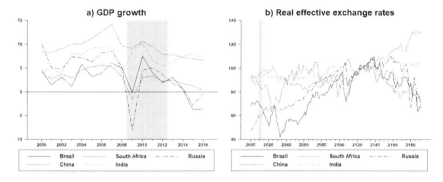

Fig. 2.3 BRICS GDP growth and exchange rates. (Source: IMF WEO 2016)

$$\Delta \text{Residual} = \Delta \text{Investment} + \Delta \text{Consumption} + \Delta \text{Government spending} \quad (2.2)$$

Based on the residual identity in Eq. (2.2), both monetary policy and fiscal policy can be used to widen the gap between trade growth and economic activity. However, it is worth noting that evidence so far shows that unconventional monetary policies in AEs have neither spurred global growth, nor has business investment responded to the extraordinary low cost of capital and liquidity injections.[6] Despite this situation, nearly half of the AEs have embarked on negative policy rates. In addition, Fig. 2.3 shows that the inverse transmission is equally evident in the other BRICS economies. The large exchange rate depreciations, contrary to theoretical predictions, have neither spurred trade activity nor economic growth.

But of immediate concern about the trends shown in Fig. 2.3 is the divergence within the BRICS economies. It is undeniable that China and India GDP growth have not experienced recessions, but their GDP growth rates have deviated from the long-term mean growth rates. Hence, in the later sections of the chapter, we argue that their standard deviation of GDP growth rate from the mean growth matters. We also use the standard deviation of the Chinese and India GDP growth rates from their mean growth in the empirical analysis to determine the effects of the

---

[6] In this respect, evidence in Gumata and Ndou (2017) showed the inverse transmission of the unconventional monetary policies into South Africa via the exchange rate and trade channels.

shocks in negative deviation of growth rates from the mean growth level of BRICS countries on G7 GDP growth.

2.1.2 South African GDP Growth, G7 Growth and Global Trade

For the empirical analysis, the study uses quarterly (Q) data from 1999Q1 to 2015Q3.[7] The economies assessed include BRICS, G7,[8] BIITS[9] and EMEs (excluding China).[10] First, we use the stylised facts to assess the nature of the relationship between global trade, SA and G7 GDP growth for the period 2000 to 2016 on an annual basis. Evidence in Fig. 2.4(b) shows that SA GDP growth tracks G7 growth, but the scatterplots indicate that G7 growth dynamics explain around 47 per cent of the variation in SA GDP growth.

In addition, Fig. 2.4(d) shows that SA GDP is positively related to world trade growth and world trade growth explains roughly 60 per cent of domestic growth. The trends in Fig. 2.4 show that there are direct and indirect ways in which SA GDP growth benefits from G7 GDP growth and global trade. It is noteworthy that, post 2009, SA GDP growth continues to diverge from global trade growth, possibly pointing to the disconnect between the exchange rate depreciations via the exports growth and GDP growth channels.

So far, we have shown the trend analysis and bilateral correlations. But what do the causality tests say about the direction of causation from BRICS, G7, China and EMEs growth? In Table 2.1, we use quarterly (Q) data from 1999Q1 to 2015Q3 to test for the direction of causality.

The results in Table 2.1 indicate the prevalence of interdependency between GDP growth in these economies with bidirectional relationship between BRICS and G7, EMEs and G7, China and EMEs (excluding China). This shows that economies are interdependent, pointing to possible spill-over effects.

---

[7] The data is obtained from the OECD and IMF and South African Reserve Bank.
[8] Comprises of the US, UK, Germany, France, Italy, Canada and Japan.
[9] Comprises of Brazil, Indonesia, India, Turkey and South Africa.
[10] Comprises of Brazil, Russia, South Africa, Chile, Korea, Mexico, Turkey, Argentina, India and Indonesia.

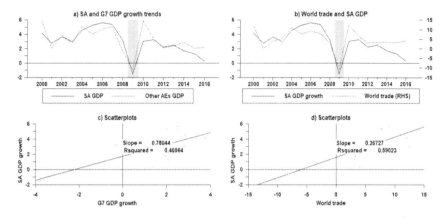

Fig. 2.4 Global trade, G7 and South African GDP growth. (Source: IMF WEO 2016 and authors' calculations)

Table 2.1 Granger causality effects

Null hypothesis	F-Statistic	p-value	Decisions
BRICS growth does not granger cause G7 growth	17.26	(0.00)	Reject
G7 growth does not granger cause BRICS growth	9.58	(0.00)	Reject
EMEs growth does not granger cause G7 growth	11.10	(0.00)	Reject
G7 growth does not granger cause EMEs growth	10.38	(0.00)	Reject
China growth does not granger cause BRICS (excl. china) growth	3.87	(0.05)	Reject
China growth does not granger cause EMEs growth	3.24	(0.08)	Reject

Source: Authors' calculations

2.2 How Important Are BRICS and Other EMEs GDP Growth in Propagating Demand Shock Effects on G7 Economies?

The empirical investigation begins by looking at the propagation abilities of regional economic growth in the transmission of demand shocks to G7 growth. Demand arises when the national income identity is decomposed into domestic and external demand in Eq. (2.3). This is not restricted to domestic demand, but can also refer, for instance, to regional demand.

$$\Delta GDP = \Delta\text{domestic demand} + \Delta\text{External sector demand} \quad (2.3)$$

To answer the question posed in this section, we modify the Pentecôte and Rondeau (2015) approach to determine the response of G7 to a positive demand shock.[11] We use the growth Eq. (2.4) with demand shocks as defined by the error term ε_t.

$$G7growth_t = constant + \sum_{i=1}^{4}\beta_i G7growth_{t-i}$$
$$+ \sum_{i=1}^{4}\beta_i Other\_GDPGrowth_{t-i} + \varepsilon_t \quad (2.4)$$

where *Other_GDPGrowth* denotes China GDP growth, BRICS, BRICS (excluding China) and BIITS. Each of these *Other_GDPGrowth* variables are added individually in the model. The counterfactual response is determined by setting the coefficients of the *Other_GDPGrowth* variables to zero in Eq. (2.4) leading to Eq. (2.5).[12]

$$G7growth_t = constant + \sum_{i=1}^{4}\beta_i G7growth_{t-i} + \varepsilon_t \quad (2.5)$$

The propagating (magnifying) or restraining (stifling) abilities of specific channels are determined by the gap between actual and counterfactual responses.

2.2.1 The Impact of Positive Demand Shocks

Figure 2.5(a), (b) and (c) show that BIITS, BRICS, BRICS (excluding China), Chinese GDP growth and EMEs (excluding China) amplify G7 GDP growth shocks to global demand shocks. This result points to the importance of inter-linkages among these economies.

---

[11] The analysis in this chapter differs from Pentecôte and Rondeau (2015) and Wong (2015).
[12] This is consistent with the Cerra and Saxena (2008) as a baseline model.

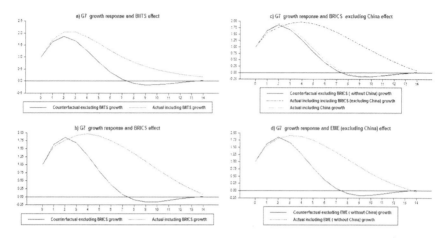

Fig. 2.5 Accumulated responses due to positive demand shocks and propagation effects. (Note: Emerging markets economies (EMEs) are Brazil, Russia, South Africa, Chile, Korea, Mexico, Turkey, Argentina, India and Indonesia. Source: Authors' calculations)

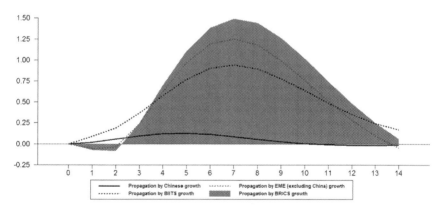

Fig. 2.6 Comparison of amplifying effects. (Note: Emerging markets economies (EMEs) are Brazil, Russia, South Africa, Chile, Korea, Mexico, Turkey, Argentina, India and Indonesia. Source: Authors' calculations)

The magnitudes of the propagations by these economic groupings are shown in Fig. 2.6. The evidence based on the peak effects shows that BRICS is a big magnifier of G7 economic growth responses to positive demand shocks, followed by EMEs (excluding China). Furthermore, Fig. 2.6 reveals that the propagation effects by BRICS GDP growth exceed those from BIITS economies, and that the China effect alone is small.

2.2.2 Impact of the Global Recession and Periods of Uncertainty Shock

This section uses the growth Eq. (2.6) with demand shocks as defined by the error term ε_t and D refers to dummy variables that capture specific economic shocks or episodes, *Other_GDPGrowth* denotes Chinese GDP growth, BRICS, BRICS (excluding China) and BIITS. Each of these *Other_GDPGrowth* variables is added individually in the model.

$$G7growth_t = constant + \sum_{i=1}^{4} \beta_i G7growth_{t-i}$$
$$+ \sum_{i=1}^{4} \beta_i Other\_GDPGrowth_{t-i} + d_i \times D + \varepsilon_t \quad (2.6)$$

The amplification ability of a particular channel is calculated as the difference between the response in the baseline model in Eq. (2.5) and the other response to the global recession shock. We use D as a dummy variable, which is defined as the global recession and subsequent global economic uncertainty. The dummy variable D is defined to equal one for the period 2008Q1 to the end of the sample and zero otherwise. Figure 2.7(a) shows that G7 growth responses decline more when GDP growth from other economic regions is included and the amplification magnitudes by the BRICS GDP growth are large compared to the other economic block groupings in Fig. 2.7(b).

This evidence shows that BRICS, EMEs (excluding China) and BIITS amplify the effects of positive global demand shocks on G7 economies. In addition, these economies amplify the effects of adverse economic shocks such as the global financial crisis and economic policy uncertainty.

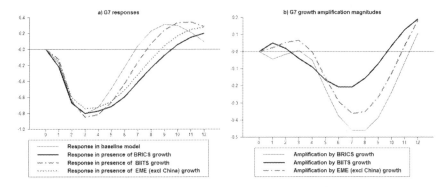

Fig. 2.7 The impact of global recession, uncertainty shocks and amplification by regional growth. (Note: Emerging markets economies (EMEs) are Brazil, Russia, South Africa, Chile, Korea, Mexico, Turkey, Argentina, India and Indonesia. Source: Authors' calculations)

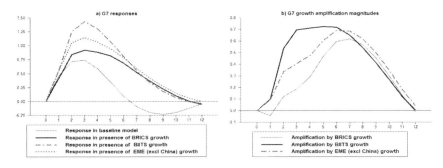

Fig. 2.8 The impact of commodity price shock pre-financial crisis and amplification by regional growth. (Note: Emerging markets economies (EMEs) are Brazil, Russia, South Africa, Chile, Korea, Mexico, Turkey, Argentina, India and Indonesia. Source: Authors' calculations)

2.2.3 The Impact of Commodity Price Shock Before the Financial Crisis

This section illustrates the positive amplification effects of positive global demand shock and the channels of transmission prior to the financial crisis. We use a dummy variable for the commodity price boom equal to one between 2003Q2 and 2007Q3 and zero otherwise. Evidence indicates that commodity price shocks lead to positive responses of G7 growth in Fig. 2.8(a). In addition, evidence in Fig. 2.8(b) shows that

BRICS, EMEs (excluding China) and BIITS amplify the effects of positive commodity shock on G7 economies.

2.3 Are There Asymmetric BRIC Growth Shock Effects on G7 and South African GDP Growth?

This section applies the second approach to determine the asymmetric effects of BRICS GDP growth shock on G7 and US GDP growth. We stated earlier that China and India GDP growth rates have not experienced recessions. But their GDP growth rates have deviated from the long-term mean growth rates. Hence, the thrust of the analysis in this section is that the standard deviation of the GDP growth rate from the mean growth matters. We, therefore, determine the effects of the negative deviation of GDP growth rates from the mean GDP growth rates of BRICS countries on G7 economies.

The estimations in this section use the Kilian and Vigfusson (2011) structural near-VAR model. The VAR model is estimated using two lags and 10,000 bootstraps draws.[13] We modify this approach to determine the effects of (i) shocks of negative deviations of BRICS GDP growth rates from their mean growth rates on G7 and US GDP growth; (ii) shocks of negative deviations of BRIC GDP growth from their mean growth on South African GDP growth; (iii) shocks of negative deviations of EMEs (excluding China) GDP growth from their mean GDP growth on G7 GDP growth; and (iv) euro area GDP growth responses to China GDP growth shocks.

2.3.1 Is There an Asymmetric GDP Growth Response to Different Sizes of GDP Growth Shocks?

First, we assess the asymmetric responses due to the size of the negative GDP growth shock followed by the sign of the shock. The asymmetric effects are assessed based on different sizes of negative GDP growth

---

[13] Kilian and Vigfusson (2011) is used in the model to determine the asymmetric effects of oil price increases and decreases shocks on GDP growth in the US.

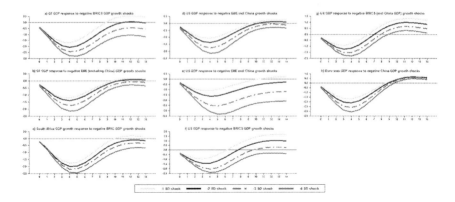

Fig. 2.9 Responses to negative shocks according to different sizes of shock. (Note: SD means standard deviation. Emerging markets economies (EMEs) are Brazil, Russia, South Africa, Chile, Korea, Mexico, Turkey, Argentina, India and Indonesia. Source: Authors' calculations)

shocks of one-, two-, three- and four-standard deviation shocks. Figure 2.9 shows the responses to the effects of negative BRICS GDP growth shock as well as negative EMEs GDP growth shock on G7 and other economies. The results in Fig. 2.9 indicate evidence of asymmetric responses due to the magnitude of the negative shock. The four-standard deviation negative shocks lead to a big decline in GDP growth compared to the one-standard deviation shocks. This means that bigger negative shocks lead to large declines in GDP growth compared to smaller negative shocks. The responses are large and show evidence of asymmetric effects.

Fact 1 *Large negative BRICS GDP growth shocks lead to large declines compared to smaller negative shocks indicating asymmetry response.*

2.3.2 Is There Asymmetric Response to the Sign of the Shock?

The preceding section identified asymmetric responses with respect to the size of the negative shocks. But the size aspect of asymmetry alone does not reveal the asymmetric response due to the sign (positive or negative) of the shock. Hence, this section compares G7, US, euro area GDP

2   Is BRICS GDP Growth a Source of Shocks or an Amplifier...

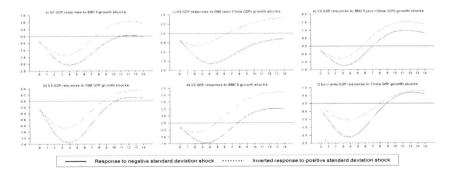

Fig. 2.10 Various GDP growth responses to positive and negative growth shocks. (Note: SD means standard deviation. Emerging markets economies (EMEs) are Brazil, Russia, South Africa, Chile, Korea, Mexico, Turkey, Argentina, India and Indonesia. Source: Authors' calculations)

growth rate responses to negative BRICS, EMEs, EMEs (excluding China) and BRICS (excluding China), Chinese GDP shock to those from a positive shock. For ease of comparison of responses to positive and negative shocks, we invert responses from a positive shock, as shown in Fig. 2.10.

The results in Fig. 2.10 reveal that negative BRICS and EMEs GDP growth shocks lead to more contraction in advanced economies' GDP growth compared to positive shocks. The asymmetry in response due to the sign of the shock implies that a slowdown in EMEs, BRICS and the Chinese economy may indeed require a gradual and, in extreme cases, further stimulus in AEs via reduced policy rates. This means that the concerns about the external conditions raised by US policymakers are founded and well placed. Global business cycles impact each other in an asymmetric way, especially due to negative GDP shocks. For the South African economy, this means that the interest rate differentials will be driven very much by how policymakers respond to domestic inflationary factors.

Fact 2 *Global business cycles impact each other in an asymmetric way, due to negative GDP shocks. Growth in advanced economies is more likely to remain very low and monetary policy more accommodative for longer periods due to the asymmetric transmission of negative GDP growth from EMEs.*

2.3.3 What Are the Implications for South African Economic Growth?

We have established that negative BRICS GDP growth shocks have an asymmetric impact on G7 GDP growth. Based on these findings, we extend the analysis to determine the implications for South African GDP growth. We estimate a three variable VAR model using G7, BRIC and South African GDP growth rates using two lags and 10,000 Monte Carlo simulations. Thereafter, we apply the historical decomposition approach to separate the South African growth into trend component, its own contributions and those contributions from both BRIC and G7 GDP growth.

What are the implications of BRIC and G7 growth dynamics for South African economic growth? Figure 2.11 shows that South African GDP growth was lower than the counterfactual, which excludes the combined effects of G7 and BRIC growth between 2007 and 2010.

This suggests that both G7 and BRIC GDP growth deviations from the mean growth have contributed to lower SA growth. In addition, post 2012 actual South African GDP growth is lower than the counterfactual, suggesting that the slowdown in G7 and BRIC GDP growth contributed

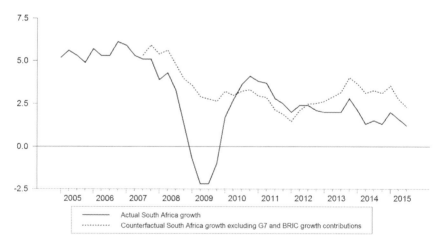

Fig. 2.11 Actual and counterfactual South African GDP growth. (Source: Authors' calculations)

to lower South African GDP growth than would be the case in their absence.

These results indirectly imply that in part lower SA actual and potential output (output-gap) is due to external GDP growth factors. The finding further shows that global demand pressures are indeed muted. This further corroborates earlier findings that muted global demand and the output-gap are not the main drivers of domestic inflationary pressures. The inverse transmission of unconventional monetary policies largely via the sharp depreciation in the exchange rate results in inflationary pressures, as opposed to exports growth.

Fact 3 *The negative output-gap can be attributed to muted external GDP growth developments rather than to domestic factors only. This is particularly the case since 2012.*

2.4 How Important Is China GDP Growth for the Transmission of External GDP Growth Shocks to South Africa?

This section explores the importance of the Chinese GDP growth shocks to South Africa (SA) via the counterfactual and third countries effects. First, we deal with the recent uncertainty surrounding policy execution by the Chinese authorities. We use the Chinese policy uncertainty index constructed by Baker et al. (2015) and assess the threats from the unexpected elevation in this index on the South African economy. We then determine how SA GDP growth impulses would be when Chinese GDP growth is shut off as the transmission channel of external GDP growth shocks. Thereafter, we determine whether the Chinese growth shocks get transmitted via other countries before affecting South Africa.

Briefly, Fig. 2.12 shows recent developments in selected economic indicators for the Chinese economy. In line with the slowdown in the global economy and world trade, the Chinese current account surplus narrowed. In addition, the Chinese authorities have been implementing policies aimed at rebalancing the economy, and this has induced shocks on the global economy.

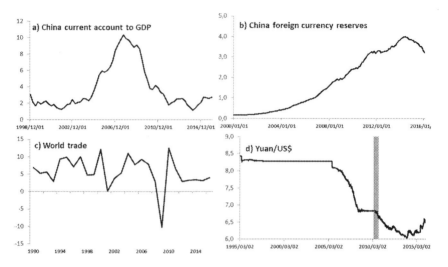

Fig. 2.12 Selected Chinese indicators and work trade. (Source: IMF and World Bank)

However, the Chinese exchange rate developments have made more headlines. The authorities have been intervening in currency markets to support the exchange rate, and Fig. 2.12 shows that the forex reserves have declined leading to further uncertainty in markets.

2.4.1 Threats from Chinese Policy Uncertainty Shock

With that background, this section determines the channels through which the Chinese policy uncertainty impacts South African monetary policy. We note that it is also true that the US policy normalisation has exerted uncertainty. Therefore, for the comparison of the impact of uncertainty, we use the US and China policy uncertainty measures in the empirical analysis. First, the cross correlations in Fig. 2.13(b) show a positive relationship between annual changes in the US and China policy uncertainty measures and annual rand per US dollar (R/US$) changes. The positive relationships suggest that the R/US$ depreciates more when preceded by elevated Chinese policy uncertainty compared to US policy uncertainty in the first four quarters. The scatterplots in Fig. 2.13(d) and

2 Is BRICS GDP Growth a Source of Shocks or an Amplifier...

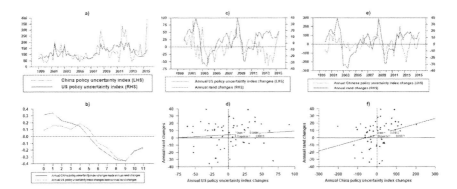

Fig. 2.13 Relationship between policy uncertainty and rand exchange rate. (Source: Authors' calculations)

(f) indicate that the Chinese policy uncertainty explains about 9.9 per cent of R/US$ movements, which is large compared to 4.8 per cent due to US policy uncertainty. We conclude that Chinese policy uncertainty contributed to the sharp depreciation in the R/US$ exchange rate compared to the effects emanating from US policy uncertainty.

Having established that Chinese policy uncertainty plays a bigger role than the US policy uncertainty in the dynamics of the R/US$ exchange rate, we apply a fourth approach to determine the exogenous effects of Chinese policy uncertainty on the GDP growth rates for China, South Africa, the South African exchange rates and consumer price inflation. We estimate a three variable model with Chinese GDP growth, South African GDP growth and other South African variables as endogenous variables. The other South African variables are included separately in the model. The Chinese policy uncertainty is included as an exogenous variable. All growth rates are at an annual rate.

The responses to the positive exogenous Chinese policy uncertainty shock shown in Fig. 2.14(a) and (b) indicate that an unexpected increase in Chinese policy uncertainty shock leads to a significant Chinese and South African GDP growth slowdown. The Chinese policy uncertainty shock leads to a significant depreciation in all the exchange rate measures, namely, the R/US$, nominal effective exchange rate (NEER) and real effective exchange rate (REER). To the extent that the REER represents competitiveness relative to the trading partners, the sharp depreciation is

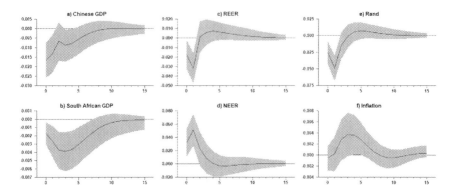

Fig. 2.14 Responses to positive Chinese policy uncertainty shock. (Note: The grey band denotes the 16th and 84th percentile confidence bands. The shock refers to one positive standard deviation shock. Source: Authors' calculations)

welcome. However, the policy uncertainty shock indirectly via the exchange rate depreciation leads to inflationary pressures in Fig. 2.14(f). As a result, policymakers act to curb inflationary pressures, and this contributes to the significant slowdown in GDP growth in Fig. 2.14(b).

The above analysis does not show the contributions of annual Chinese policy uncertainty changes to actual annual R/US$ changes. For this exercise, we estimate a model with Chinese policy uncertainty index changes, South African GDP growth and R/US$ changes.[14] Figure 2.15 shows that since mid-2014, the actual R/US$ depreciation exceeded the counterfactual, suggesting that the Chinese policy uncertainty contributed to the sharp exchange rate depreciation.

For further analysis of the impact of the Chinese policy uncertainty on SA exchange rates, we show the actual and counterfactual NEER responses to positive Chinese policy uncertainty responses in Fig. 2.16. We compare the response on the NEER when the Chinese GDP growth is included to when it is excluded in the model. This helps us to ascertain whether Chinese growth matters for the impact of Chinese policy uncertainty on the South African exchange rate.

Yes, we find that the South African NEER depreciation would be very shallow due to positive Chinese policy uncertainty shock if Chinese GDP

---

[14] For robustness issues, we estimated the model which includes China policy uncertainty index, China GDP growth, South African GDP growth and the R/US$ exchange rate.

2 Is BRICS GDP Growth a Source of Shocks or an Amplifier...

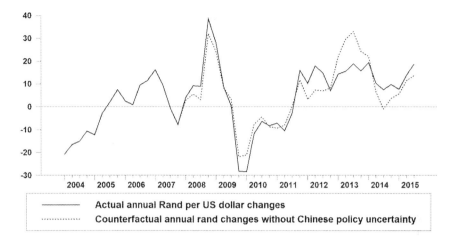

Fig. 2.15 The role of Chinese policy uncertainty on the R/US$ exchange rate dynamics. (Source: Authors' calculations)

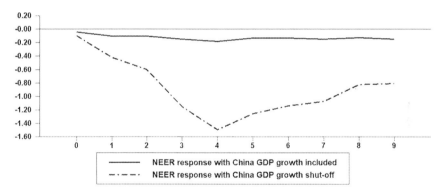

Fig. 2.16 NEER responses to Chinese growth and policy uncertainty shocks. (Source: Authors' calculations)

growth was robust in Fig. 2.16. As a result, the NEER depreciates sharply when Chinese GDP growth is shut off in the model. This shows that the Chinese policy uncertainty shock has pronounced effects on South African exchange rates in the absence of Chinese GDP growth.

Fact 4 *South African exchange rates depreciate more due to weak Chinese growth in the presence of China policy uncertainty.*

2.4.2 South African GDP Growth Impulses in the Absence of Chinese GDP Growth

This section extends the analysis of the effects of China GDP growth by exploring how South African GDP growth impulses would be in the absence of Chinese GDP growth as a transmission channel of external GDP growth shocks. We apply a fifth approach to determine role of Chinese GDP growth in the transmission of external growth shocks to South Africa. We use a modified Poirson and Weber (2011) VAR approach to determine the extent to which Chinese GDP growth amplifies or dampens the South African GDP growth response to external shocks. We estimate a four-variable VAR model which includes the GDP growth of a large economy, China GDP growth, BRIC (excluding China) GDP growth and SA GDP growth.

The three large economy's GDP growth consist of US, G7 excluding US, and euro area GDP growth. These are included separately in the model. We estimate the model using two lags and 1000 Monte Carlo draws. We distinguish between the actual and counterfactual responses. The actual responses refer to SA GDP response in the presence of all variables and the counterfactual response is when we purge the influence of China GDP growth. The gap between actual and counterfactual SA GDP growth responses due to large economies' shocks is the amount by which Chinese GDP growth amplifies or dampens the response of SA GDP growth to external GDP growth shocks.

Figure 2.17 shows that, in most cases, the actual SA GDP growth responses exceed their counterfactuals, which suggests that robust Chinese GDP growth amplifies SA GDP growth responses to external growth.

Fact 5 *Robust Chinese growth raises the response of South African and other economies to positive US GDP growth.*

Figure 2.18 shows the responses of (i) SA growth to positive euro area GDP growth shock and (ii) euro area and UK GDP growth to positive

2 Is BRICS GDP Growth a Source of Shocks or an Amplifier... 47

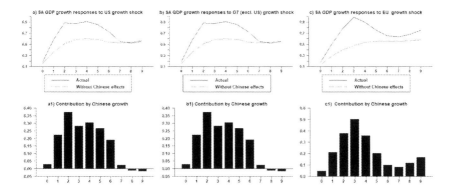

Fig. 2.17 Actual and counterfactual accumulated South African GDP growth and Chinese amplifications. (Note: Responses to a positive 1 per cent GDP growth shock. Source: Authors' calculations)

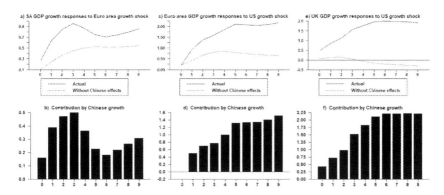

Fig. 2.18 Actual and counterfactual accumulated South African, euro area and UK GDP growth and the amplification of Chinese GDP growth. (Note: Responses to a positive 1 per cent GDP growth shock. Source: Authors' calculations)

US GDP growth shocks in the presence and absence of Chinese GDP growth. Evidence shows a widening gap between the actual and counterfactual responses, indicating that robust Chinese GDP growth is important for these economies too. This suggests that these economies will grow more when US GDP growth occurs concurrently with robust Chinese GDP growth.

2.4.3 Are There Significant Third-Country Transmission Effects?

To answer this question, the analysis on this section applies a sixth approach to determine the role of other countries in the transmission of GDP growth shocks into South Africa. We explore whether there is significant evidence that external GDP shocks are transmitted via other countries before they impact South Africa. We modify the Poirson and Weber (2011) approach to assess the relevance of third-country effects. We also show the extent to which external shocks are transmitted into South Africa via other countries before impacting South Africa. We estimate a four-variable VAR model which includes selected large economy GDP growth, China GDP growth, BRIC excluding China GDP growth and South African GDP. The large economies are included separately in the models and these are the US, G7 excluding US, and euro area GDP growth.

The model is estimated using two lags and 10,000 Monte Carlo draws. The actual responses refer to SA GDP responses in the presence of all variables. The counterfactual response is the response in the absence of third countries, which is calculated when we purge the influence of all third countries included in the model in response to specific external GDP growth shocks. The gap between the actual and counterfactual SA GDP growth responses to large economies' shocks captures the role of third countries on SA GDP growth to external GDP growth shocks.

The evidence in Fig. 2.19 shows that positive US, G7 (excluding US), Chinese and euro area GDP growth shocks are transmitted into South Africa via third countries, and this amplifies the SA GDP growth response. Thus, in the absence of these third countries, the SA GDP growth responses would be significantly different and much lower. This suggests that SA will achieve much better GDP growth rates in the presence of robust growth in other countries. Otherwise, in the absence of positive global GDP growth spill-overs, the South African economy will achieve anaemic growth rates.

Fact 6 *Robust Chinese growth is important for sustaining high South African GDP growth in response to positive US, euro area, G7 GDP and Chinese GDP growth shocks.*

2 Is BRICS GDP Growth a Source of Shocks or an Amplifier...

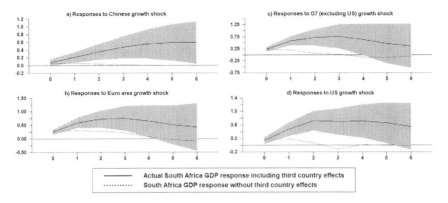

Fig. 2.19 SA GDP responses and third-country transmission effects. (Source: Authors' calculations)

2.5 What Are the Policy Implications of Chinese GDP Growth for the South African Economy and Monetary Policy?

Earlier sections and Figs. 2.13, 2.14, 2.15 and 2.16 showed that Chinese policy uncertainty and growth play a meaningful role in determining developments in SA economic variables. This section extends this analysis by estimating a counterfactual VAR model with GDP growth for China and South Africa, and South African headline CPI inflation and R/US$ exchange rate. All growth rates are at an annual rate. We adopt the counterfactual VAR approach to draw policy implications for the role the Chinese growth effects exert on SA.

2.5.1 Implications for R/US$ Exchange Rate

First, we show the effects of the Chinese growth on the evolution of the R/US$ exchange rate in Fig. 2.20. We excluded the contributions of Chinese growth on the R/US$ to calculate the counterfactual R/US$ changes. The results in Fig. 2.20 show that, since mid-2014, the actual R/US$ changes were much weaker than the counterfactual. This indicates that weak Chinese economic growth contributed to the R/US$ depreciation.

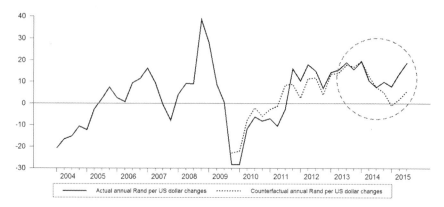

Fig. 2.20 Actual and counterfactual R/US$ changes and Chinese growth effects. (Source: Authors' calculations)

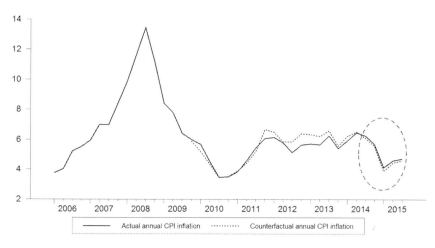

Fig. 2.21 The evolution of domestic inflation and Chinese growth contributions. (Source: Authors' calculations)

2.5.2 Implications for Domestic Inflation

We compare the actual and counterfactual inflation rates in Fig. 2.21 and find that between 2011Q3 and 2014Q2 actual inflation was lower than the counterfactual despite the R/US$ exchange rate sharp depreciation. But since mid-2014, actual inflation exceeded the counterfactual, suggesting that the sharp R/US$ exchange rate depreciation due to the slowdown in Chinese growth contributed to elevated inflation.

2.5.3 Implications for Domestic Monetary Policy

We conclude the analysis by looking at whether Chinese GDP growth dynamics impact the repo rate responses to inflation. The impact of the Chinese GDP growth shocks may not be direct, but transmitted indirectly via the depreciation of the exchange rates and GDP growth effects as suggested in the earlier analysis. Indeed, the results in Fig. 2.22 show that the actual policy rate is higher than the counterfactual. This suggests that the policy stance was appropriate given that the actual exchange rate and inflation rates were higher than the counterfactual since late 2014. In addition, between 2012 and mid-2014, the actual repo rate was much lower than the counterfactual, which coincides with periods of low exchange rate pass-through to inflation. Thus, the repo rate was more accommodative during the period of low pass-through of exchange rate to inflation.

Fact 7 *Chinese GDP growth contributed to the sharp R/US$ exchange rate deprecation which poses a threat to inflationary pressures and the monetary policy stance.*

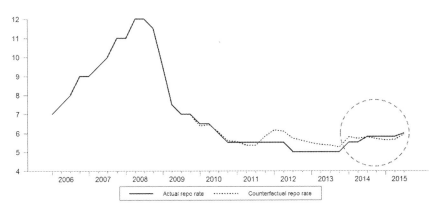

Fig. 2.22 The evolution of the repo rate and Chinese growth contributions. (Source: Authors' calculations)

2.6 Conclusion and Policy Implications

This chapter assessed whether BRICS is a source and amplifier of positive G7 GDP growth and demand shocks. Evidence shows that BRICS is a big magnifier of G7 economic growth responses to positive demand shocks, followed by EMEs (excluding China). Furthermore, the propagation effects by BRICS growth exceed those from BIITS economies and the China effect alone is small. The BRICS amplify the effects of adverse economic shocks such as the global financial crisis and uncertainty. Evidence indicates that commodity price shocks lead to positive responses of G7 growth and that BRICS, EMEs (excluding China) and BIITS amplify the effects of positive commodity shock on G7 economies.

Furthermore, BRICS growth shocks lead to asymmetric G7 GDP growth. Large negative BRICS GDP growth shocks lead to large declines in G7 GDP growth compared to smaller negative shocks. Global business cycles impact each other in an asymmetric way, especially due to negative GDP shocks. These asymmetric responses suggest that economic growth in advanced economies is more likely to remain subdued, prompting monetary policy to be more accommodative for a longer period. Domestically, this means interest rate differentials will be driven more by adverse factors inflation.

Evidence indicates that elevated Chinese economic policy uncertainty contributed to the sharp depreciation in the R/US$ exchange rate compared to the effects emanating from US economic policy uncertainty. Furthermore, the South African exchange rates depreciate more due to weak Chinese GDP growth, and the negative effects are propagated by China economic policy uncertainty. Evidence shows that Chinese GDP growth via the sharp R/US$ exchange rate deprecation poses a threat to inflationary pressures and the monetary policy stance. Hence, we conclude that the China policy uncertainty poses a threat to SA, to the extent that induces and contributes to sharp currency depreciation, which are in turn passed through to inflationary pressures.

In addition, China growth shocks, and those of advanced economies transmitted are via other countries (third countries) before impacting South Africa. We find that robust Chinese growth is important for sustaining high South African GDP growth in response to positive US, euro area, G7 and Chinese GDP growth shocks. Robust Chinese growth amplifies the response of euro area GDP growth response to positive US GDP growth shocks. This suggests these economies will grow more when US GDP growth occurs concurrently with robust Chinese growth.

References

Baker, R.S., Bloom, N., and Davis, S.J. 2015. *Measuring Economic Policy Uncertainty*. NBER Working Paper No. 21633.

Bayoumi, T. 2015. *The Dog That Didn't Bark: The Strange Case of Domestic Policy Cooperation in the "New Normal"*. IMF Working Paper WP/15/156.

Cerra, V., and Saxena, S.W. 2008. Growth Dynamics: The Myth of Economic Recovery. *American Economic Review*, 98(1), 439–57.

Gumata, N., and Ndou, E. 2017. *Bank Credit Extension and Real Economic Activity in South Africa: The Impact of Capital Flow Dynamics, Bank Regulation and Selected Macro-prudential Tools*. Palgrave Macmillan. ISBN 978-3-319-43551-0.

Hoekman, B. 2016. *The Global Trade Slowdown: A New Normal?* A VoxEU.org ebook. https://voxeu.org/sites/default/files/file/Global%20Trade%20Slowdown_nocover.pdf.

IMF WEO. October 2015. Adjusting to Lower Commodity Prices.

IMF World Economic Outlook. 2016. Too Slow for Too Long. https://www.elibrary.imf.org/view/IMF081.

Kilian, L., and Vigfusson, R.J. 2011. Are the Responses of the U.S. Economy Asymmetric in Energy Price Increases and Decreases? *Quantitative Economics*, 2(3), 419–53.

OECD Economic Outlook. 2016. Escaping the Low Growth Trap? Effective Fiscal Initiatives, Avoiding Trade Pitfalls. http://www.oecd.org/eco/outlook/economic-outlook-november-2016.htm

Pentecôte, J.S., and Rondeau, F. 2015. Trade Spill Overs on Output Growth During the 2008 Financial Crisis. *Journal of International Economics*, 143, 36–47.

Poirson, H., and Weber, S. 2011. *Growth Spill-over Dynamics from Crisis to Recovery*. International Monetary Fund WP/11/218.

Scott, R.B., Bloom, N., and Davis, S.J. 2015. *Measuring Economic Policy Uncertainty*. NBER Working Paper 21633.

Wong, B. 2015. Do Inflation Expectations Propagate the Inflationary Impact of Real Oil Price Shocks? Evidence from the Michigan Survey. *Journal of Money, Credit and Banking*, 47(8), 1673–89.

World Bank. 2016. Global Economic Prospects: Divergences and Risks. June 2016. World Bank Group http://pubdocs.worldbank.org/en/842861463605615468/Global-Economic-Prospects-June-2016-Divergences-and-risks.pdf

3

Does the Trade-Openness Channel Impact the Effects of Business Confidence Shocks on Investment Growth?

Learning Objectives

- Examine the extent to which the trade-openness channel impacts the relationship between business confidence and gross fixed capital formation (investment growth).
- Determine if the exposure to international trade increases the sensitivity of investment growth to positive business confidence shocks
- Examine whether the role of trade-openness is influenced by price stability and monetary policy changes

3.1 Introduction

In 2018, the United States of America (the US) imposed tariffs on goods imported from China, South Africa and other economies.[1] In an ideal situation, the imposition of tariffs on goods imported to the US should make these imports expensive in the US. This may reduce volume of

---

[1] The US imposed tariff on steel and aluminium imports from South Africa. The Minister of trade and industry has indicated recently that this reduces the benefits from Africa Growth and Opportunity Act.

imports demanded in the US. The decline may depend on the ease of their substitutability and the prevalence of import-substituting goods, *ceteris paribus*. The imposition of the US trade tariffs makes SA exports expensive thereby reducing their demand in the US. The decline may impact the size of SA trade-openness measured as the sum of exports and imports. The decline in South African exports may happen via two ways. First, it may be due to the direct imposition of US tariffs on SA goods. Second, this may happen indirectly via reduction in the demand of intermediate goods from SA by other countries that export goods to the US. This is referred to as *"third country transmission effects"*. This chapter argues that the size of trade-openness may impact the transmission of positive shocks to business confidence to gross fixed capital formation growth (investment growth) in South Africa.

As a precursor to the empirical analysis, Fig. 3.1 shows that business confidence has been weak and gross fixed capital formation growth (investment growth) has been mostly negative since 2014. So, to what extent does the trade-openness channel impact the relationship between business confidence and gross fixed capital formation? Alternatively, does great exposure to international trade increase the sensitivity of investment growth to positive business confidence shocks? Is the role of trade-openness influenced by price stability and monetary policy changes?

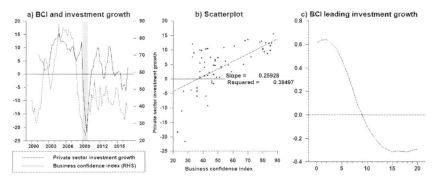

Fig. 3.1 Business confidence index and gross fixed capital formation growth in South Africa. (Note: The grey-shaded areas denote the South African recession. BCI = Business confidence index. Source: South African Reserve Bank and authors' calculations)

Why does the inclusion of the trade-openness channel matter in this analysis? First, the role of the trade-openness channel has been assessed in transmitting monetary policy shocks to output. Certain studies find that trade-openness impacts the transmission of monetary policy shocks to output (Povoledo 2018; Peersman and Smets 2005). Second, this is because firms may find an opportunity to increase their investment spending when exports are increasing, especially when firms are doing well. Third, the increase in intermediate imports may lead to increased capital formation, and this may be bigger when the currency appreciates by large magnitude. Fourth, the investment saving (IS) schedule suggests a negative relationship between interest rates and the trade balance. This suggests that the trade balance deficits should rise as interest rates increase. Therefore, it would be incomplete to have this discussion without determining the effects of price stability based on the influence of the 4.5 per cent and 6 per cent inflation thresholds. The 6 per cent threshold is currently the upper part of the inflation target band. The analysis further examines whether expansionary and contractionary monetary policy changes affect how trade-openness impacts the transmission of positive business confidence shocks to investment growth.

Evidence reveals that investment growth rises irrespective of whether the trade-openness channel is included or not. In addition, the actual investment growth increases more when the trade-openness channel is included in the model relative to that suggested by the counterfactual. Moreover, the exports channel is the biggest amplifier of the positive business confidence shocks on investment growth. Therefore, policymakers should implement policies that boost business confidence to stimulate investment growth and the effects could be amplified by increasing exports competitiveness. Evidence reveals that the trade-openness channel has bigger amplifying effects on investment growth (1) in the low inflation regime than in the high regime and (2) when monetary policy is expansionary than when it is contractionary. This evidence suggests that the attainment of the low inflation objective matters for the effects of positive business confidence to stimulate investment growth.

Policymakers should note that the slowdown in investment growth, may be accentuated via the third-country transmission channel, following the impositions of trade tariffs by the US on South African trade partners. This happens when South African exports to China are used as intermediate inputs in the production of the Chinese goods, which are then exported to the US. Hence, the imposition of the US trade tariffs on Chinese goods may indirectly reduce the demand of their intermediate imports from South Africa. Therefore, policymakers should quantify the costs of US tariffs, linked to third-country transmissions of South African exports to China, to know the magnitudes of additional threats to economic growth recovery.

3.2 The Response of Investment Growth to Positive Business Confidence Shocks

The preliminary analysis begins by determining the reaction of investment growth to positive business confidence shocks. The analysis uses quarterly (Q) data spanning 1990Q1 to 2018Q1. The model uses trade-openness, the BER confidence indicator and gross fixed capital formation in South Africa. Trade-openness is measured as the sum of exports and imports as a percentage of GDP. The variables are expressed as quarter-on-quarter growth rates. The growth in gross fixed capital formation (Inv_growth) captures growth in investment. Eqs. (3.1) and (3.2) include a dummy for the recession in 2009Q1–2009Q3. The dummy equals one during this period and zero otherwise. Both Eqs. (3.1) and (3.2) are estimated using 10,000 bootstrap draws.

$$Inv\_growth_t = constant + \sum_{i=0}^{4} Inv\_growth_{t-i}$$
$$+ \sum_{i=0}^{2} Business\_confidence\_growth_{t-i}$$
$$+ \sum_{i=0}^{1} Trade\_openness\_growth_{t-i}$$
$$+ Recession\_dummy + \varepsilon_t \quad (3.1)$$

3 Does the Trade-Openness Channel Impact the Effects...

$$Inv\_growth_t = constant + \sum_{i=0}^{4} Inv\_growth_{t-i}$$
$$+ \sum_{i=0}^{2} Business\_confidence\_growth_{t-i}$$
$$+ \sum_{i=0}^{1} Trade\_openness\_growth_{t-i}$$
$$+ \sum_{i=0}^{2} Repo\_rate\_changes_{t-i}$$
$$+ Recession\_dummy + \varepsilon_t \qquad (3.2)$$

Figure 3.2 shows the responses of investment growth to positive business confidence shocks. In Fig. 3.2 the positive business confidence shocks raise investment growth for nearly a year. The increase in investment growth happens irrespective of whether the change in the policy rate is included (in Fig. 3.2(b)) or excluded (in Fig. 3.2(a)). Therefore, the increase in investment growth, due to a positive business confidence shock is robust to the inclusion of the policy rate.

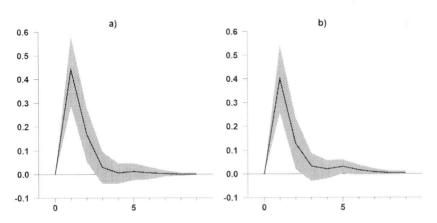

Fig. 3.2 Investment growth responses to positive business confidence shocks. (Source: Authors' calculations)

3.3 Does the Trade-Openness Channel Matter for the Effects of Business Confidence on Investment Growth?

This section examines the role of the trade-openness channel in the transmission of positive business confidence shocks to investment growth. This is assessed via the counterfactual VAR analysis as discussed in Ndou et al. (2018). The estimated baseline counterfactual VAR model includes growth in business confidence, growth in investment and growth in trade-openness. The counterfactual VAR model is estimated using two lags and 10,000 Monte Carlo draws. The exogenous variables include the dummy that captures the recession in 2009. The counterfactual investment growth response is determined by shutting off the trade-openness channel in transmitting positive business confidence shocks to investment growth. The gap between the actual and counterfactual responses measures the role of the trade-openness channel.

In Fig. 3.3(a), investment growth rises irrespective of whether the trade-openness channel is included or not. However, actual investment growth increases more when the trade-openness channel is included in the model in comparison to that suggested by the counterfactual.

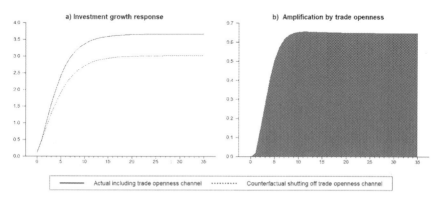

Fig. 3.3 Cumulative investment growth responses to positive business confidence shocks and the role of trade-openness channel. (Note: All the responses are to a one positive standard deviation business confidence shock. Source: Authors' calculations)

3 Does the Trade-Openness Channel Impact the Effects... 61

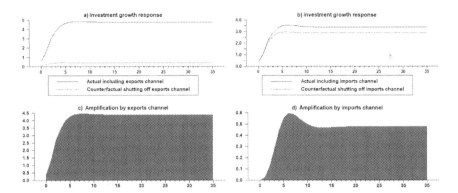

Fig. 3.4 Cumulative investment growth responses to positive business confidence shocks and the role of the components of the trade-openness channel. (Source: Authors' calculations)

How robust is the importance of the trade-openness channel when decomposed into the export and import components? The robustness analysis separates the role of the trade-openness channel into the exports and imports channels. This will determine the channel which has a bigger amplifying effect on the investment growth reaction to positive business confidence shocks. These components replace the trade-openness measure in the preceding model.

In Fig. 3.4(a) and (b), actual investment growth rises more than the counterfactual responses. This suggests that the export and import channels amplify the investment growth increases to positive business confidence shocks. In addition, the export channel is the biggest amplifier of the positive business confidence shocks on investment growth. This suggests that increased exports from South Africa to the rest of the world may be the needed amplifier to spur the economic recovery at the time when investment growth is pulling down or is a drag on economic growth. It is more likely that the increase in exports growth will raise South African firms' profits. There is a possibility that some portion of retained earnings may be invested in capital formation. Therefore, the imposition of trade tariffs on the South African exports to the US may lead to depressed investment growth despite increased business confidence. This slowdown in the investment growth may be accentuated via a third-country transmission channel. This happens when SA exports to China are used as intermediate inputs in the production of the Chinese goods, which are then exported to the US. Hence, the imposition of US trade tariffs on Chinese goods may indirectly reduce the demand of intermediate imports from South Africa. It should also be noted that the import growth channel seems to play a smaller role than the export growth channel.

3.3.1 Does the Price Stability Channel Matter?

As indicated in the introduction, this analysis examines the extent to which the consumer price inflation channel affects how the trade-openness channel impacts the transmission of positive business confidence shocks to investment growth. This section further examines the role of the inflation threshold based on the 4.5 per cent, in impacting how trade-openness transmits positive business confidence shocks to investment growth.

The analysis separates the influence of inflation on the trade-openness channel by showing whether this depends on (i) inflation above the 4.5 per cent inflation threshold, (ii) inflation below the 4.5 per cent inflation threshold. The determination of the influence of the inflation threshold effects is achieved by creating two trade-openness dummy variables. The first trade-openness dummy equals to the value of growth in trade-openness when inflation is below or equal to 4.5 per cent, and zero otherwise. The second trade-openness dummy equals to the value of growth in trade-openness when inflation is above the 4.5 per cent threshold and zero otherwise. These trade-openness dummy variables are included in the baseline counterfactual VAR model separately.

In Fig. 3.5(a), investment growth rises due to positive business confidence shocks. The actual investment growth rises more than the counterfactual suggests. This suggests that the trade-openness channel in the low inflation regime amplifies the increase in investment growth following a positive business confidence shock. In Fig. 3.5(b) actual investment growth rises less than the counterfactual suggests. This implies that the trade-openness channel in the high inflation regime dampens the investment growth response due to a positive business confidence shock.

The findings reveal that the trade-openness channel has a bigger influence in the low inflation regime than in the high regime. This evidence

3 Does the Trade-Openness Channel Impact the Effects... 63

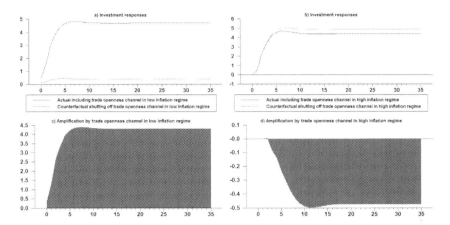

Fig. 3.5 Cumulative investment growth responses to positive business confidence shocks and the role of the trade-openness channel in low and high inflation regimes. (Source: Authors' calculations)

shows that the role of inflation regimes matters for the efficacy of the trade-openness channel in transmitting positive business confidence shocks to investment growth. This suggests that the attainment of low inflation objective matters for the effects of positive business confidence to stimulate investment growth.

To what extent would the role of trade-openness based on the inflation threshold value of 4.5 per cent differ from that of using the 6 per cent limit? We further examine if the influence of the consumer price inflation on the trade balance channel depends on whether the inflation threshold is below 4.5 or 6 per cent. This determines if these thresholds exert different influences on the role of trade-openness as a conduit in transmitting positive business confidence shocks to investment growth.

Consequently, we separate the role of the trade-openness channel based on the consumer price inflation of the 6 per cent threshold. The 4.5 per cent threshold in the preceding model is replaced with 6 per cent. In Fig. 3.6(a), the investment growth rises higher than the counterfactual suggests when inflation is below 6 per cent. This suggests that the low inflation regime (inflation below 6 per cent) enables the trade-openness channel to amplify the rise in investment growth. By contrast, a high inflation regime (inflation above 6 per cent) makes the trade-openness

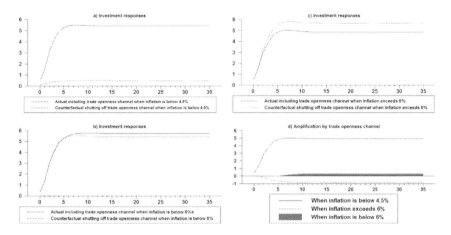

Fig. 3.6 Cumulative investment growth responses to positive business confidence shocks and the role of the trade-openness channel in different inflation regimes. (Source: Authors' calculations)

channel dampen the rise in investment growth to positive business confidence shocks.

Do the inflation thresholds matter? To answer this question, we compare the sizes of the amplifications based on inflation below the 4.5 per cent and 6 per cent thresholds, respectively. In Fig. 3.6(d), the trade-openness channel has bigger amplifying effects on investment growth when inflation is below the 4.5 per cent threshold than when inflation is below 6 per cent. This indicates that an inflation threshold of 4.5 per cent may enable business confidence to have bigger effects. This shows that the inflation threshold matters, and the 4.5 per cent is very important. This evidence reveals that price stability matters. This suggests that policymakers should enforce a low inflation environment to enable the amplifying effects of the trade-openness channel in the transmission of the effects of positive business confidence shocks to stimulate investment growth.

3.3.2 Do Monetary Policy Changes Matter?

This chapter concludes the analysis by looking at the extent to which the expansionary and contractionary monetary policy stances influence the

3 Does the Trade-Openness Channel Impact the Effects... 65

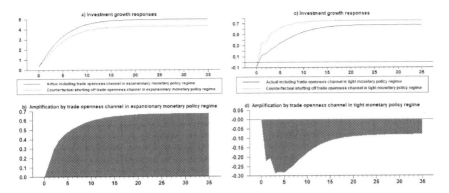

Fig. 3.7 Cumulative investment growth responses to positive business confidence shocks and the role of trade-openness channel in tight and loose monetary policy regimes. (Source: Authors' calculations)

trade-openness channels in transmitting positive business confidence shocks to investment growth. This is achieved by creating two trade-openness dummy variables. The first trade-openness dummy equals to the value of growth in trade-openness when the repo rate changes are positive (contractionary monetary policy changes) and zero otherwise. The second trade-openness dummy equals to the value of growth in trade-openness when repo rate changes are negative (expansionary monetary policy) and zero otherwise. These trade-openness dummy variables are included separately in the counterfactual VAR model. The VAR model includes growth in business confidence, investment growth and the trade-openness dummy. The model is estimated using two lags and 10,000 Monte Carlo draws.

In Fig. 3.7(a), actual investment growth rises more than the counterfactual suggests. This reveals that the trade-openness channel amplifies investment growth response to the positive business confidence shock when monetary policy is expansionary. In contrast, in Fig. 3.7(b) counterfactual investment growth exceeds the actual reaction when monetary policy is contractionary. This evidence reveals that monetary policy changes do impact the role of trade-openness in transmitting positive business confidence shocks to investment growth.

3.4 Conclusion and Policy Implications

This chapter examines the extent to which the trade-openness channel impacts the relationship between business confidence and gross fixed capital formation. Does great exposure to international trade increase the sensitive of investment growth to positive business confidence shocks? Is the role of trade-openness influenced by price stability and monetary policy changes? Evidence reveals that investment growth rises irrespective of whether the trade-openness channel is included or not. In addition, the actual investment growth increases more when the trade-openness channel is included in the model relative to that suggested by the counterfactual. Moreover, the exports channel is the biggest amplifier of the positive business confidence shocks on investment growth. Therefore, policymakers should implement policies that boost business confidence to stimulate investment growth and the effects could be amplified by increased exports competitiveness. Evidence reveals that the trade-openness channel has bigger amplifying effects on investment growth (i) in the low inflation regime than in the high regime and (ii) when monetary policy is expansionary than when contractionary. This evidence suggests that the attainment of low inflation objective matters for the effects of positive business confidence to stimulate investment growth.

Policymakers should note that the slowdown in investment growth may be accentuated via third-country transmission channels following the impositions of trade tariffs by the US. This happens when South African exports to China are used as intermediate inputs in the production of the Chinese goods, which are then exported to the US. Hence, the imposition of the US trade tariffs on Chinese goods may indirectly reduce the demand of their intermediate imports from South Africa. Therefore, policymakers should quantify the extent of costs of US tariffs linked to third-country transmissions of the South African exports to China to know the magnitudes of additional threats to the economic growth recovery.

References

Ndou, E., Gumata, N., and Ncube, M. 2018. *Global Economic Uncertainties and Exchange Rate Shocks: Transmission Channels to the South African Economy.* Palgrave Macmillan.

Peersman, G., and Smets, F. 2005. The Industry Effects of Monetary Policy in the Euro Area. *Economic Journal*, 115(503), 319–42.

Povoledo, L. 2018. Pricing Behavior and the Role of Trade Openness in the Transmission of Monetary Shocks. *Journal of Macroeconomics*, 57, 231–47.

4

Trade-Openness, Consumer Price Inflation and Exchange Rate Depreciation Shocks

Learning Objectives

- Show the extent to which the trade-openness channel impacts the reaction of inflation to exchange rate depreciation shocks
- Assess the relationship between the ERPT and trade-openness in South Africa

4.1 Introduction

The rising trade tensions between China and the United States of America (US) may impact the size of the South African trade-openness, measured by the sum of exports and imports as a per cent of GDP. The sum of imports and exports captures the size of the external sector in the national income identity. At the same time, theoretical predictions suggest that elevated trade tensions will slow down global and regional economic growth prospects. However, nothing has been said regarding the possible influence of the trade tensions on the size of the exchange rate pass-through (ERPT). This includes central bankers whose primary mandates include price stability. Regarding the

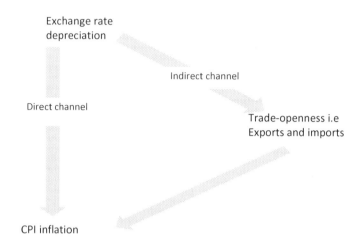

Fig. 4.1 The transmission of the exchange rate depreciation shocks and role of trade-openness. (Source: Authors' calculation)

price stability mandate, empirical studies indicate that trade-openness may impact the size of the ERPT, but the direction of influence is ambiguous.

Hence, Fig. 4.1 depicts the theoretical framework to be used in this study. The depiction shows that the exchange rate depreciation can impact the consumer price inflation (*hereafter referred to as inflation*) directly and indirectly. The direct relationship is based on the law of one price. However, the weakness of this law is the non-consideration of the role of the trade-openness channel. Hence, this channel is included in Fig. 4.1 as an indirect channel. The indirect channel arises when the exchange rate changes are transmitted via the trade-openness channel to impact inflation. The second part of the indirect channel has serious implications for the ERPT dynamics amidst the current trade tensions. Romer (1993) found that trade-openness is inversely related to inflation. Therefore, the overall sign of the correlation between the ERPT and trade-openness can be either positive or negative.[1]

---

[1] A high degree of the exchange rate pass-through for developing economies has been cited as the rationale for the developing countries' well documented fear of floating. Whether the ERPT is high or not matters for the determination of the trade balance.

These possibilities point to the need for an empirical investigation to identify the sign of the relationship based on the data to enable the prescription of appropriate policy recommendations. So, to what extent does the trade-openness channel impact the reaction of inflation to the exchange rate depreciation shocks? What is the relationship between the ERPT and trade-openness in South Africa? There are no studies that have applied a counterfactual approach to show the importance of the trade-openness channel in the reaction of inflation to the exchange rate depreciation shocks. Answers to these questions have implications on whether monetary policy and trade policy can be used as tools to induce expenditure-switching effects needed to spur economic activity to adjust given the current trade tensions.

What is the motivation for looking at the role of trade-openness in relation to the ERPT? The first motivation is because of the policy implications derived from the link between high trade-openness and the low ERPT. The low exchange rate pass-through has implications for monetary policy. According to Goldfajn and Werlang (2000) the smaller exchange rate pass-through to inflation implies that the difference between inflation expectations and inflation targets is much smaller. This implies that a small pass-through should generate minor inflation forecast errors. This could improve the transparency of the inflation path following minor volatilities in the price variation in the economy. These are important in raising social welfare and monetary policy efficiency. In addition, Devereux et al. (2006) suggest that when pass-through is very low, the exchange rate no longer acts as an expenditure-switching device that alters the relative prices of home and foreign goods. Hence, the exchange rate remains important in stabilising demand through cushioning the effective real interest rate faced by consumers and firms.

The second motivation is due to the negative relationship between trade-openness and inflation depicted by a scatterplot in Fig. 4.2. The negative relationship supports the empirical evidence in Romer (1993). This negative relationship may arise due to the globalisation of economic activity, which increases competition and contestability of markets, thereby reducing the pricing power of the dominant firms in the tradeable sector (Mihaljek and Klau 2008). Rogoff (2006) argues that increased

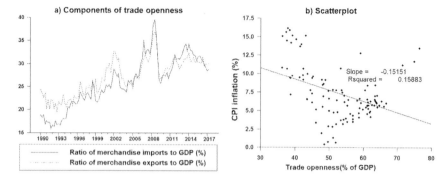

Fig. 4.2 Trade-openness and inflation. (Note: Trade-openness equals to sum of ratio of exports and imports to GDP. Source: Authors' calculation and South African Reserve Bank)

competition drives prices down and makes prices and wages more flexible. In addition, output and employment tends to be higher with greater competition. Under these conditions Rogoff suggests the real effects of unanticipated monetary policy became smaller and transitory. Furthermore, Mihaljek and Klau (2008) state that the reduction in the pricing power may spur firms to absorb some temporary costs which arise from increased exchange rate depreciations, thereby lowering the size of the exchange rate pass-through coefficient.

It should be noted that literature offers different explanations as to why trade-openness may lower the ERPT.[2] First, Lopez-Villavicencio and Mignon (2017) suggest that a negative relationship happens when trade-openness influences the degree of competition, which impacts the pricing strategies and the degree to which domestic firms sell their products in the internal market. Second, Gust et al. (2010) suggest that the decline in the exchange rate pass-through to import prices is due to high trade integra-

---

[2] Literature findings and theory do not only point to a negative relationship between trade-openness and the ERPT, but to an ambiguous association. For instance, Ozkan and Erden (2015) suggest that the impact of trade-openness on the ERPT is rather ambiguous from a theoretical perspective. High trade-openness may enable the exchange rate changes to be easily transmitted, and this gives rise to a high ERPT. Moreover, Benigno and Faia (2010) argue that globalisation (or trade-openness) reflected by greater competition implies a higher ERPT. This arises when greater competition due to the increase in the share of foreign products in a specific industry raises the degree of the exchange rate pass-through.

tion and increased complementarity in price setting. The greater the trade integration, the lower the ERPT becomes due to the prevailing strategies that involve complementarity in price setting. Hence, the firms' pricing strategies depend on the marginal cost and prices set by competitors. Third, Lopez-Villavicencio and Mignon (2017) argue that high trade-openness may lead to higher international competition for the multinational firms, which may lead to pricing to market practices. The implementation of the pricing to market strategies should reduce the ERPT. Fourth, Goldfajn and Werlang (2000) found a negative relationship between trade-openness and ERPT. They suggest that the negative relationship may happen when firms want to maintain profit margins through outsourcing productions to lower cost countries, which includes the economies to which these firms are exporting too, and this further lowers the size of the exchange rate pass-through.

This analysis fills policy and academic research gaps in various ways. First, given the two possible outcomes in the relationship between trade-openness and the ERPT, there is a need for an empirical analysis to disentangle the role of the trade-openness channel in influencing the ERPT dynamics in South Africa. Hence, the analysis examines the potency of the trade-openness channel in impacting the reaction of inflation to exchange rate depreciation shocks using a counterfactual approach. This will reveal whether the trade-openness channel indirectly mitigates or amplifies the rise in inflation due to exchange rate depreciation shocks. Second, the analysis fills policy and academic research gaps by determining whether increased trade-openness directly impacts the size of the ERPT coefficient.

Evidence reveals that increased trade-openness lowers the ERPT and mitigates the increase in inflation following the exchange rate depreciation shocks. This finding implies that, as long as rising trade tensions between China and the US do not lead to a reduction in the size of the South Africa trade-openness, the size of the ERPT coefficient will remain smaller compared to when trade-openness declines. This probably reflects the influence of increased competition on lowering prices. It is also important to heed the advice of Sbordorne (2008) that globalisation managed to lower the level of inflation, which may indicate that there is less incentive to revise price often since the cost of price misalignment may have been lowered.

4.2 Empirical Results

The analysis begins by examining the direct effects of a positive trade-openness shock on the evolution of the time-varying exchange rate pass-through to inflation. The time-varying ERPT is estimated in Ndou et al. (2019).[3] The time varying exchange rate pass-through is estimated using time-varying techniques and not the rolling regression approach whose results are based on an arbitrarily chosen moving window. The time-varying approach estimates the pass-through at each period. In this section the analysis uses quarterly (Q) data spanning 1990Q1 to 2018Q2. Trade-openness is equal to the sum of exports and imports as a ratio of GDP and is expressed as percentage. The scatterplot in Fig. 4.3 shows a negative relationship between the time varying ERPT and trade-openness. This preliminary evidence indicates that high trade-openness reduces the size of the ERPT.

The empirical analysis begins by estimating two VAR models to determine the dynamic responses of the ERPT over time. The first model (Model 1) includes trade-openness, time-varying ERPT and the policy rate. The exogenous variables in the model include a constant and a dummy for the recession in 2009Q1 to 2009Q3 and zero otherwise. The model uses quarterly (Q) data from 1990Q1 to 2018Q2. The impulse responses are shown in

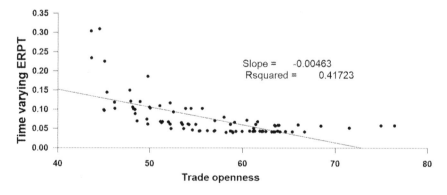

Fig. 4.3 Trade-openness and time-varying ERPT. (Source: Authors' calculations)

---

[3] The book is titled "Exchange rate passthrough, second round effects and inflation process: Evidence from South Africa".

4 Trade-Openness, Consumer Price Inflation and Exchange... 75

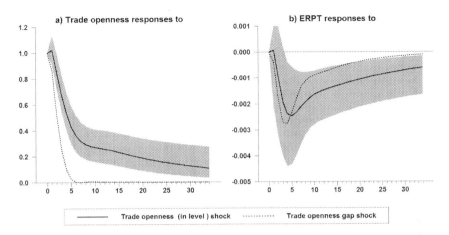

Fig. 4.4 Responses to positive trade-openness shock. (Source: Authors' calculations)

Fig. 4.4. The rise in trade-openness tends to be persistent in Fig. 4.4(a). In addition, the ERPT declines significantly over all horizons. This suggests that an unexpected increase in trade-openness significantly lowers the size of the ERPT coefficients. The second model (Model 2) is estimated to test the robustness of these results. Both models are estimated using two lags and 10,000 Monte Carlo draws. In Model 2, the trade-openness is replaced with quarter-on-quarter changes in trade-openness. Similarly, the results show that a positive trade-openness shock significantly lowers the ERPT.

An (2006) finds that the more persistent the exchange rate changes become, the higher the size of the exchange rate pass-through coefficient.[4] Hence, the analysis examines whether the persistence of a positive trade-openness shock matters in the ERPT dynamics and distinguishes between the persistent and non-persistent shocks. In Fig. 4.5, the ERPT declines more due to a persistent positive trade-openness shock compared to that due to a non-persistent shock. This evidence shows that the persistence of positive trade-openness shocks matters. The results are robust to different model specifications. This evidence corroborates earlier results showing that positive trade-openness has a direct impact on the size of the ERPT and lowers it.

---

[4] This could be explained by foreign exporters' willingness to maintain market shares in large markets.

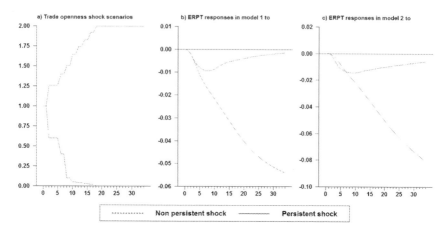

Fig. 4.5 ERPT responses to positive trade-openness shock scenarios. (Source: Authors' calculations)

4.2.1 How Robust Are the Results to Different Model Specifications?

The analysis examines the robustness of the finding that an unexpected increase in trade-openness lowers the ERPT using different models. Two models are estimated using Eqs. (4.1) and (4.2) based on 10,000 bootstrap draws.

$$ERPT_t = constant + \sum_{i=0}^{2} ERPT_{t-i} + \sum_{i=0}^{2} Trade\_openness_{t-i}$$
$$+ \sum_{i=0}^{2} Business\_confidence\_neg_{t-i}$$
$$+ \sum_{i=0}^{2} Repo\_rate_{t-i} + Recession\_dummy + \varepsilon_t \quad (4.1)$$

$$ERPT_t = constant + \sum_{i=0}^{2} ERPT_{t-i} + \sum_{i=0}^{2} Trade\_openness_{t-i}$$
$$+ \sum_{i=0}^{2} Repo\_rate_{t-i} + Recession\_dummy + \varepsilon_t \quad (4.2)$$

where *Business_confidence_neg* denotes a dummy, which is equal to the negative values of the business confidence index deviations from 50 index points and zero otherwise. Both equations include the dummy which equals one for the recession in 2009Q1–2009Q3 and zero otherwise. Figure 4.6 shows the ERPT responses to a once-off 1 per cent unexpected increase in trade-openness. In both instances, the ERPT declines significantly for nearly four quarters. We therefore conclude that the reduction in ERPT due to a positive trade-openness shock is robust to the different model specifications.

In addition, the analysis examines whether the business confidence channel influences the effects of a positive trade-openness shock on the ERPT dynamics. The business confidence index has been below or close to the 50 index points for a long time post-2009. And this has implications for the macroeconomic dynamics, and possibly how businesses decide on pricing strategies. Consequently, the analysis examines the role of the negative deviations of the business confidence from the midpoint of 50 index points in transmitting the positive trade-openness shocks to the ERPT. The estimated model includes the trade-openness, the ERPT and the dummy which equals the values of the negative deviations of the business confidence index from the midpoint and zero otherwise. Ndou et al. (2018) found that depressed business confidence developments explained the reduced ERPT post-2008. The counterfactual VAR model is estimated with two lags and includes other exogenous variables as explained above. The counter-

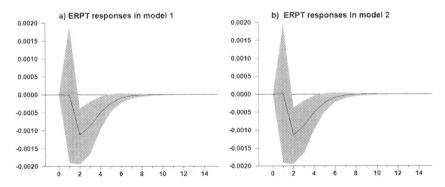

Fig. 4.6 ERPT responses to positive trade-openness shocks. (Source: Authors' calculations)

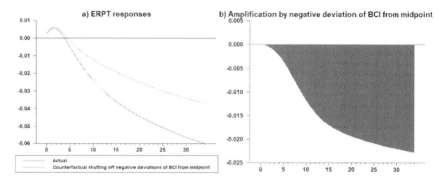

Fig. 4.7 Cumulative ERPT responses to positive trade-openness shock and the role of the business confidence channel. (Source: Authors' calculations)

factual models shut off the business confidence channel in transmitting positive trade-openness shocks to the ERPT. The cumulative responses of the ERPT to a one positive standard deviation increase in trade-openness are shown in Fig. 4.7. The actual ERPT declines much more than the counterfactual. This finding suggests that the depressed business confidence environment amplifies the reduction in the ERPT following a positive trade-openness shock. This happens when weak confidence translates into subdued demand in the economy.

How robust are the results to using the gap of trade-openness? The trade-openness gap is measured as deviations of Hodrick-Prescott filtered trend of trade-openness from the actual trade-openness. The preceding model is used to determine the robustness of the role of the trade-openness gap in impacting the ERPT. In addition, this will show how the preceding evidence is impacted by the inclusion of the negative deviations of the business confidence index from the midpoint and GDP growth developments post-2008Q1. Two dummy variables are created, and these are included separately in the model. The business confidence dummy is defined as in the preceding analysis. The GDP dummy equals to the value of the GDP growth post-2008Q1 and zero otherwise.

Figure 4.8 shows that a positive trade-openness gap shock lowers the size of the ERPT coefficients. The decline in the ERPT is amplified by the negative deviations of the business confidence index (BCI) from the midpoint and volatile economic growth developments post-2008Q1. The

4 Trade-Openness, Consumer Price Inflation and Exchange... 79

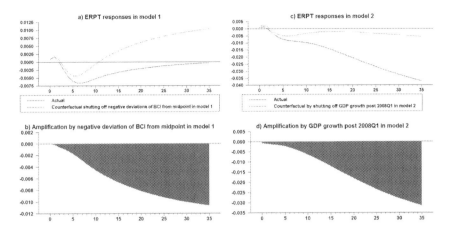

Fig. 4.8 Cumulative ERPT responses due to a positive trade-openness gap shock and the role of the business confidence channel. (Source: Authors' calculations)

ERPT decline due to a positive trade-openness shock is robust to the influence of different economic conditions.

4.2.2 Does the Trade-Openness Channel Impact the Reaction of Inflation to Exchange Rate Depreciation Shocks?

The preceding evidence indicates the importance of the direct effects of a positive trade-openness shocks on the time-varying ERPT. In addition, evidence lends credence to the findings in Romer (1993), that increased trade-openness lowers inflation. Furthermore, a positive trade-openness shock lowers the ERPT, and the decline in the ERPT is accentuated by the negative deviations of the business confidence index from the midpoint. Consequently, the next section assesses the relevance of the indirect role of the trade-openness channel in transmitting exchange rate depreciation shocks to inflation. This encompasses estimating various counterfactual VAR models to determine the role of the trade-openness channel. The counterfactual VAR models shut off the trade-openness channel in determining the reaction of inflation to the exchange rate depreciation shocks. The exchange rate depreciation equals the positive growth rates in the nominal effective exchange rate and zero otherwise.

4.3 Evidence from the Three Variables Counterfactual VAR Models

The determination of the indirect role of the trade-openness channel begins by estimating counterfactual VAR models. Two models are estimated using three endogenous variables. The models include the exchange rate depreciation, inflation and trade-openness as endogenous variables. The exogenous variables include the GDP gap and the repo rate. The gap is measured as percentage deviations of the Hodrick-Prescott filter log GDP trend from the actual log GDP. The models are estimated with two lags. The GDP gap and annual GDP growth are included separately in the models. The exchange rate depreciation equals the positive growth rates of the nominal effective exchange rate and zero otherwise. In Fig. 4.9, the actual and counterfactuals indicate that inflation increases due to exchange rate depreciation shocks. However, the actual inflation rate rises less than the counterfactual suggests. This shows that the trade-openness channel dampens the increase in inflation due to the exchange rate depreciation shocks.

Evidence indicates that, irrespective of the model specifications, actual inflation rises less than the counterfactual suggests. The negative amplifications shown in Fig. 4.9 indicates that the trade-openness channel

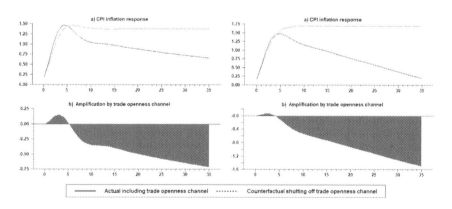

Fig. 4.9 Cumulative inflation responses due to the exchange rate deprecation shocks and amplification by the trade-openness channel. (Source: Authors' calculations)

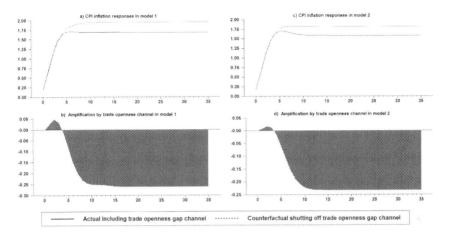

Fig. 4.10 Cumulative inflation responses to the exchange rate deprecation shocks and amplification by the level and gaps in the trade-openness channel. (Source: Authors' calculations)

dampens the increase in inflation due to the exchange rate depreciation shocks. Thus, high trade-openness dampens the increase in inflation due to the exchange rate depreciation shocks.

So, how robust is the evidence to using the trade-openness gap in the counterfactual VAR model. The analysis shows the robustness of the results using the trade-openness gap as a transmission channel. Thus, the trade-openness level is replaced with the trade-openness gap as defined above. The results show that the increase in actual inflation is lower than the counterfactual response. This indicates that the positive trade-openness gap dampens the increase in inflation due to the exchange rate depreciation shocks. Thus, both the level and the trade-openness gap dampen the increase in inflation due to exchange rate depreciation shocks in Fig. 4.10.

4.3.1 Evidence from the Counterfactual VAR Models with Additional Variables

How robust is the evidence to including additional variables in the preceding model? The analysis concludes by determining the robustness of the evidence of the indirect role of the trade-openness channel in impacting the

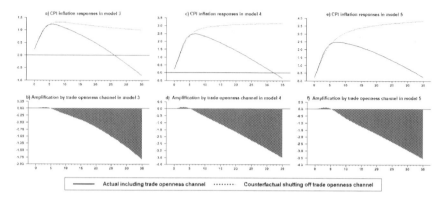

Fig. 4.11 Cumulative inflation responses to exchange rate the deprecation shocks and the role of the trade-openness channel. (Source: Authors' calculations)

response of inflation to the exchange rate depreciation shocks. Three counterfactual VAR models are estimated. Model 3 includes the exchange rate depreciation dummy, inflation, repo rate and the trade-openness channel. Model 4 includes the exchange rate depreciation dummy, repo rate, inflation, the consumer confidence index and the trade-openness channel. The trade-openness channel is shut off to determine its role in transmitting shocks. Model 5 includes the exchange rate depreciation dummy, repo rate, inflation, growth in the business confidence index and the trade-openness channel. The exchange rate depreciation dummy equals to the positive growth rates of the nominal effective exchange rate and zero otherwise. In all models, the impulse responses in Fig. 4.11 indicate that inflation rises less than the counterfactual responses. This indicates that the trade-openness channel dampens the actual increase in inflation from what would be the case if this channel was shut off.

4.4 Conclusion and Policy Implications

This chapter examines whether the unexpected increase in trade-openness has any direct effect on the exchange rate pass-through (ERPT) and if it also impacts the reaction of inflation to the exchange rate depreciation shocks. Evidence indicates that an unexpected increase in trade-openness significantly lowers the size of exchange rate pass-through to inflation. In addition, the trade-openness channel mitigates the rise in inflation due to the exchange rate depreciation shocks. Inflation rises less in the presence of the trade-openness channel than what would be the case when the trade-openness channel is not considered. This evidence implies that if the rising trade tensions between China and the United States of America do not reduce the size of the South African trade-openness, the size of the ERPT will be smaller than when trade-openness starts shrinking significantly. This implies that the size of the interest rate adjustments based on the projected interest rate path probably exhibits an upward bias, if they do not consider that increased trade-openness reduces the size of the ERPT. Therefore, monetary policymaking may benefit from considering the influence of increased trade-openness on the size of the ERPT. This will lend credence to heightened concerns about the US imposing trade protectionist policies as this affects the exchange rate pass-through, which in turn impacts price stability.

References

Akofio-Sowah, N.A. 2009. Is There a Link between Exchange Rate Pass-Through and the Monetary Regime: Evidence from Sub Saharan Africa and Latin America. *International Advanced Economic Research*, 15, 296–309.

An, L. 2006. Three Essays on Exchange Rate and Monetary Policy. University of Kentucky Doctoral Dissertations, 491. https://uknowledge.uky.edu/gradschool_diss/491.

Baharumshah, A.Z., Sirag, A., and Nor, N.H. 2017. Asymmetric Exchange Rate Pass-Through in Sudan: Does Inflation React Differently During Periods of Currency Depreciation. *African Development Review*, 29(3), 446–57.

Benigno, P., and Faia, E. 2010. *Globalization, Pass-Through and Inflation Dynamics*. NBER Working Paper No. 15842.

Betts, C., and Devereux, M.B. 2000. Exchange Rate Dynamics in a Model of Pricing to Market. *Journal of International Economics*, 50(1), 215–44.

Campa, J.M., and Goldberg, L.S. 2005. Exchange Rate Pass-through into Import Prices. *The Review of Economics and Statistics*, 87(4), 679–90.

Choudhri, E.U., and Hakura, D.S. 2006. Exchange Rate Passthrough to Domestic Prices: Does Domestics Inflation Environment Matter? *Journal of International Money and Finance*, 25(4), 614–39.

Daniels, J.P., and Vanhoose, D.D. 2010. Exchange Rate Pass-Through, Openness and the Sacrifice Ratio. *Journal of International Money and Finance*, 36(C), 131–50.

De Souza, R.M., Maciel, L.F.P., and Pizzinga, A. 2013. State Space Models For The Exchange Rate Passthrough: Determinants and Null Full Passthrough Hypotheses. *Applied Economics*, 45(36), 5062–75.

Devereux, M.B., and Engel, C. 2002. Exchange Rate Passthrough, Exchange Rate Volatility and Exchange Disconnect. *Journal of Monetary Economics*, 49, 913–40.

Devereux, M.B., and Yetman, J. 2002. *Price Setting and Exchange Rate Pass-Through: Theory and Evidence*. HKIMR Working Paper No. 22/2002.

Devereux, M.B., Engel, C., and Storgaard, P.E. 2003. Endogenous Exchange Rate Passthrough When Nominal Prices are Set in Advance. *Journal of International Economics*, 63, 263–91.

Devereux, M.B., Lane, P.R., and Xu, J. 2006. Exchange Rate and Monetary Policy in Emerging Market Economies. *The Economic Journal*, 116, 478–506.

Frankel, J., Parsley, D., and Wei, S. 2005. *Slow Pass Through Around the World: A New Import for Developing Countries?* Working Chapter Number 11199, NBER.

Froot, K., and Klemperer, P. 1989. Exchange Rate Pass-Through When Markets Shares Matters. *American Economic Review*, 79(4), 637–54.

Gagnon, J.E., and Ihrig, J. 2004. Monetary Policy and Exchange Rate Pass-Through. *International Journal of Finance and Economics*, 9, 315–38.

Ghosh, A., and Rjan, R.S. 2009. What is the Extent of the Exchange Rate Passthrough in Singapore? Has it Changed Over Time? *Journal of the Asia Pacific Economy*, 14(1), 61–72.

Goldfajn, Iand, and Werlang, S. 2000. *The Pass-through from Depreciation to Inflation: A Panel Study*. Working Chapter No. 423, Department of Economics, PUC-Rio.

Gust, C., Leduc, S., and Vigfusson, R. 2010. Trade Integration, Competition and the Decline in Exchange Rate Pass Through. *Journal of Monetary Economics*, 57(3), 309–24.

Ho, C., and MaCauley, R. 2003. *Living with Flexible Exchange Rates: Issues and Recent Experiences in Inflation Targeting Emerging Market Economies*. Working Chapter 130, BIS.

Jasova, M., Moessner, R., and Takats, E. 2016. *Exchange Rate Passthrough: What Has Changed Since the Crisis?* BIS Working Chapters, Number 583.

Krugman, P. 1989. *The Delinking of Exchange Rate from Reality, Chapter 2 in Exchange Rate Instability*. MIT Press.

Lopez-Villavicencio, A., and Mignon, V. 2017. *On the Seemingly Incompleteness of Exchange Rate Pass-Through to Import Prices: Do Globalization and or Regional Trade Matter*. CEPII Working Chapter.

Mihaljek, D., and Klau, M. 2008. Exchange Rate Pass-Through in Emerging Market Economies: What Has Changed and Why?, BIS Chapters. In: Bank for International Settlements (ed.), *Transmission Mechanisms for Monetary Policy in Emerging Market Economies*, vol. 35, 103–30. Bank for International Settlements.

Monacelli, T. 2005. Monetary Policy in Low Passthrough Environment. *Journal of Money, Credit and Banking*, 37(6), 1047–66.

Ndou, E., Gumata, N., and Ncube, M. 2018. *Global Economic Uncertainties and Exchange Rate Shocks: Transmission Channels to the South African Economy*. Palgrave Macmillan.

Ndou, E., Gumata, N., and Tshuma, M.M. 2019. *Exchange Rate Pass Through, Second Round Effects and Inflation Process, Evidence from South Africa*. Palgrave Macmillan. ISBN 978-3-030-13931-5.

Ozkan, I., and Erden, L. 2015. Time-Varying Nature and Macroeconomic Determinants of Exchange Rate Pass-Through. *International Review of Economics and Finance*, 38, 56–66.

Rincon-Castro, H. and Rodriguez-Nin, N. 2018. *Nonlinear State and Shock Dependence of Exchange Rate Pass-through on Prices*. BIS Working Chapters Number 690.

Rogoff, K. 2006. Globalisation and Global Disinflation. *Jackson Hole Symposium*, August 28–30.

Romer, D. 1993. Openness and Inflation: Theory and Evidence. *Quarterly Journal of Economics*, 108(4), 869–903. November 1993.

Sbordorne, A.M. 2008. *Globalisation and Inflation Dynamics: The Impact of Increased Competition*. Federal Reserve Bank of New York Staff Chapters Number 324.

Soon, S., Baharumshah, A.Z., and Wohar, M.E. 2018. Exchange Rate Passthrough in the Asian Countries: Does Inflation Volatility Matter. *Applied Economics Letters*, 25(5), 309–12.

Steel, D., and King, A. 2004. Exchange Rate Passthrough: The Role of Regimes Changes. *International Review of Applied Economics*, 18(3), 301–22.

Zorzi, M.C., and Hahn, E. 2007. *Exchange Rate Pass-through in Emerging Markets*. European Central Bank Working Chapter Series Number 739.

5

Global Growth and Economic Policy Uncertainty Shock Effects on the South African Economy: Do These Reinforce Each Other?

Learning Objectives

- Explore what happens to domestic economic growth and labour market conditions amid heightened foreign economic growth uncertainty.
- Determine whether foreign economic growth and policy uncertainties affect the evolution of the repo rate.
- Show what the counterfactual approach suggests the repo rate would have been if the effects of global trade growth uncertainty and global policy uncertainty are shut off.
- Show the counterfactual GDP growth and the labour market conditions index responses to the SA policy uncertainty shock and the role of global trade growth uncertainties.

5.1 Introduction

This chapter explores the impact of global policy uncertainty shown in Fig. 5.1. It is evident that the global policy uncertainty index by Baker et al. (2016) has remained elevated since 2015 with bouts of increases due to selected recent events as shown in Fig. 5.1.

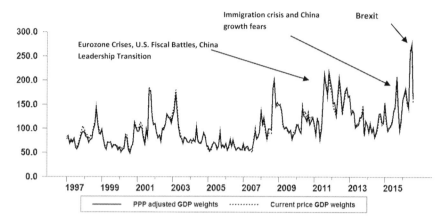

Fig. 5.1 Global policy uncertainty indices. (Source: http://www.policyuncertainty.com/global_monthly.html)

This chapter explores what happens to domestic economic growth and labour market conditions amid heightened foreign economic growth uncertainty. Do foreign economic growth and policy uncertainties affect the evolution of the repo rate? If so, what does the counterfactual approach suggest the repo rate would have been if the effects of global trade growth uncertainty and global policy uncertainties are shut off in the modelling? Given recent developments regarding the sources of economic growth uncertainties, the focus of the analysis is on the global, United States (US) of America, United Kingdom (UK) and the euro area economic growth and policy uncertainties.

5.2 Selected Stylised Relationships

This section starts the analysis by looking at the cross correlations between the US, euro area and South African (SA) GDP growth uncertainties. The GDP (economic) growth uncertainties are measured as standard deviations from their means. The analysis uses quarterly (Q) data from 1998Q1 to 2016Q2. All growth rates are at annual rate. The data is sourced from the South African Reserve Bank, International Monetary Fund and Organization for Economic Co-operation and Development databases. Figure 5.2 shows that higher GDP growth uncertainty in the

5 Global Growth and Economic Policy Uncertainty Shock Effects... 89

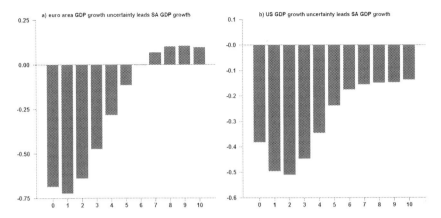

Fig. 5.2 Cross correlations for US, euro area and SA GDP growth uncertainties. (Source: Authors' calculations)

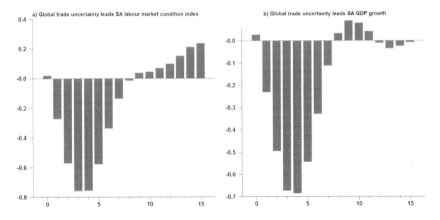

Fig. 5.3 Cross correlations between the labour market conditions index, global GDP growth and trade growth uncertainties. (Source: Authors' calculations)

US and the euro area are followed by a decline in SA GDP growth. In addition, South African GDP growth declines more when preceded by the euro area GDP growth uncertainty.

On the other hand, Fig. 5.3(a) shows a negative relationship when SA GDP growth and the labour market conditions index (LMCI)[1] are preceded by elevated global trade growth uncertainty. This indicates that

---
[1] The labour market conditions index (LMCI) is sourced from Gumata and Ndou (2017).

labour market conditions tighten following elevated global trade growth uncertainty. In addition, the negative relationship in Fig. 5.3(b) shows that SA GDP growth declines when preceded by increased global trade growth uncertainty.

5.3 Empirical Evidence

Figure 5.4 shows the responses of SA GDP growth and the LMCI to positive foreign GDP growth and trade growth uncertainty shocks. Evidence indicates that elevated foreign GDP growth and trade growth uncertainty shocks lead to a significant decline in SA GDP growth for at least five quarters depending on the foreign GDP growth uncertainty shock. In addition, the LMCI declines, which implies that labour market conditions tighten following elevated foreign GDP growth uncertainties shock.

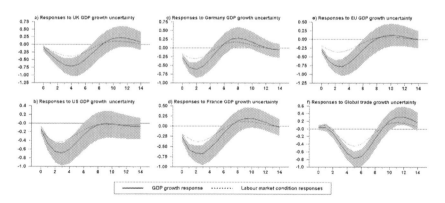

Fig. 5.4 SA GDP growth responses to positive foreign GDP growth uncertainty shocks. (Note: The grey bands denote the 16th and 84th percentile confidence bands. Source: Authors' calculations)

5.4 Counterfactual GDP Growth Responses to Policy Uncertainties and the Role of Foreign GDP Growth Uncertainties

This section compares the actual and counterfactual GDP growth responses derived from the counterfactual VAR model. The counterfactual responses refer to the GDP growth response which arises when the foreign economic growth uncertainties are shut off in the model. The gap between the actual and counterfactual responses indicates the size of the SA GDP growth accentuated by foreign policy uncertainties.

Figure 5.5 shows that a positive policy uncertainty shock lowers SA GDP growth. This happens irrespective of whether foreign GDP growth uncertainties are included or not in the model. Thus, we conclude that positive foreign policy uncertainty shocks have adverse effects on SA GDP growth and the effects are accentuated by elevated foreign GDP growth uncertainties. The US and euro area GDP growth uncertainties worsen the SA GDP growth contraction by about 0.2 percentage points, respectively.

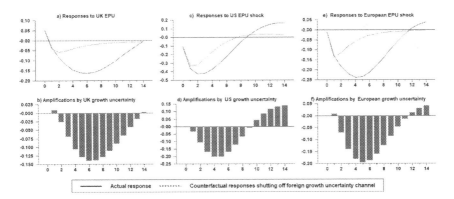

Fig. 5.5 SA GDP growth responses to positive policy uncertainty shocks and the role of foreign GDP growth uncertainties. (Note: EPU denotes Economic policy uncertainty. Source: Authors' calculations)

5.5 Counterfactual Labour Market Conditions Index Responses to Policy Uncertainties and The Role of Global Trade Growth Uncertainties

We show the role of global trade growth uncertainty in the transmission of positive foreign policy uncertainties shock to LMCI in Fig. 5.6.

The results show that the worsening of the LMCI is more severe when global trade uncertainty is included than when it is shut off in the model. This suggests that elevated global trade uncertainty amplifies the tightening in the labour market conditions following increased foreign policy uncertainty shocks.

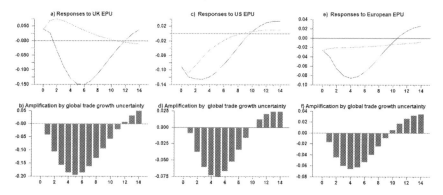

Fig. 5.6 South African labour market conditions responses to positive global uncertainty shocks. (Note: EPU denotes Economic policy uncertainty. Source: Authors' calculations)

5.6 Counterfactual GDP Growth and LMCI Responses to Positive SA Policy Uncertainty Shocks and the Role of Global Trade Growth Uncertainties

This section extends the analysis by exploring the propagation effects of SA policy uncertainty. Figure 5.7(a) shows that SA GDP growth declines more due to a positive SA policy uncertainty shock in the presence of foreign GDP growth uncertainties than when these are shut off in the model. On the other hand, Fig. 5.7(b) shows that GDP growth contraction is amplified by elevated global trade growth uncertainty. In addition, Fig. 5.7(c) shows that the LMCI tightens more when global trade growth uncertainty is included than when it is shut off in the model. The size of the amplification effects is shown in the second row of Fig. 5.7. The negative amplification indicates that elevated foreign GDP growth and global trade growth uncertainties during SA policy uncertainty shocks worsen the SA GDP growth contraction and labour market conditions tighten.

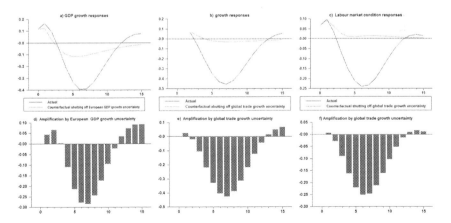

Fig. 5.7 Responses to positive South African policy uncertainty shock. (Source: Authors' calculations)

5.7 What Are the Implications for The Repo Rate Adjustments from Elevated Foreign Policy and Global Trade Growth Uncertainty?

We conclude the analysis in this chapter by looking at the actual and counterfactual repo rate responses to a positive foreign GDP growth uncertainty shock and the role of the foreign policy uncertainty channel. Similar to earlier sections, we estimate a counterfactual VAR model to determine the actual and counterfactual impulse responses. The counterfactual response refers to the repo rate when the foreign policy uncertainty channel is shut off in the model. The gap between the actual and counterfactual repo rate responses measures the size of the amplification effects induced by the foreign policy uncertainty channel. Figure 5.8 shows that the repo rate declines, and this is magnified by elevated foreign policy uncertainties.

Figure 5.9 shows that the policy rate is loosened more following elevated UK and euro area GDP growth uncertainty shocks when the global trade growth uncertainty channel is allowed to operate in the model than when it is shut off. However, the global trade growth uncertainty channel has less amplifying impact in the decline of the repo rate following

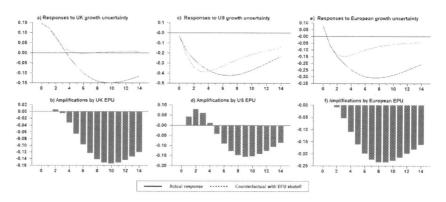

Fig. 5.8 Repo rate responses to positive foreign growth uncertainty shocks and the role of the foreign policy uncertainty channel. (Note: EPU denotes Economic policy uncertainty. Source: Authors' calculations)

5 Global Growth and Economic Policy Uncertainty Shock Effects... 95

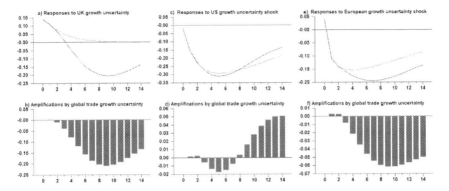

Fig. 5.9 Repo rate responses to positive foreign growth uncertainty shocks and the role of the global trade growth uncertainty channel. (Note: EPU denotes Economic policy uncertainty. Source: Authors' calculations)

elevated US GDP growth shocks. This suggests that the global trade growth uncertainty channel amplifies the loosening in repo rate.

5.8 Conclusion and Policy Implications

This chapter explored what happens to domestic economic growth and labour market conditions amid heightened foreign and SA economic growth uncertainty and global trade growth uncertainty. Evidence shows that higher GDP growth uncertainty in the US and the euro area are followed by a decline in SA GDP growth. The South African GDP growth declines more when preceded by the euro area GDP growth uncertainty. Furthermore, there is a negative relationship between SA GDP growth, the LMCI and elevated global trade growth uncertainty. The results indicate that SA GDP growth declines and the labour market conditions tighten for at least five quarters following elevated global trade growth uncertainty. Similarly, foreign and SA policy uncertainty shocks lower domestic GDP growth and tighten the LMCI. Foreign GDP growth and trade growth uncertainties accentuate the effects of elevated foreign policy uncertainties. Furthermore, evidence shows that the repo rate declines due to positive foreign GDP growth uncertainty shocks, and the global trade growth uncertainty channel amplifies the loosening in repo rate.

References

Baker, S.R., Bloom, N., and Davis, S.J. 2016. Measuring Economic Policy Uncertainty. *Quarterly Journal of Economics*, 131(4), 1593–636. November.

Cerra, V., and Saxena, S.W. 2008. Growth Dynamics: The Myth of Economic Recovery. *American Economic Review*, 98(1), 439–57.

Gumata, N., and Ndou, E. 2017. *Bank Credit Extension and Real Economic Activity in South Africa: The Impact of Capital Flow Dynamics, Bank Regulation and Selected Macro-prudential Tools*. Palgrave Macmillan. ISBN 978-3-319-43551-0.

IMF World Economic Outlook. 2016. Too Slow for Too Long. https://www.elibrary.imf.org/view/IMF081

Kilian, L., and Vigfusson, R.J. 2011. Are the Responses of the U.S. Economy Asymmetric in Energy Price Increases and Decreases? *Quantitative Economics*, 2(3), 419–53.

OECD Economic Outlook. 2016. Escaping the Low Growth Trap? Effective Fiscal Initiatives, Avoiding Trade Pitfalls. http://www.oecd.org/eco/outlook/economic-outlook-november-2016.htm.

Pentecôte J.S., and Rondeau, F. 2015. Trade Spill Overs on Output Growth During the 2008 Financial Crisis. *Journal of International Economics*, 143, 36–47.

Poirson, H., and Weber, S. 2011. *Growth Spill-over Dynamics from Crisis to Recovery*. International Monetary Fund WP/11/218.

Scott, R.B., Bloom, N., and Davis, S.J. 2015. *Measuring Economic Policy Uncertainty*. NBER Working Paper 21633.

6

Heightened Foreign Economic Policy Uncertainty Shock Effects on the South African Economy: Transmission via Capital Flows, Credit Conditions and Business Confidence Channels

Learning Objectives

- Determine whether foreign economic policy uncertainty shocks are transmitted via capital flows, credit conditions and the business confidence channels to impact SA GDP growth.
- Establish how heightened foreign economic policy uncertainty impacts the direction of capital flows into the South African economy.
- Show that heightened economic policy uncertainty shocks and tight credit conditions shocks impact the monetary policy responses to positive inflation shocks.
- Establish the impact of low business cycles indicators, consumer and business confidence levels on the South African economic activity.
- Determine if there is evidence of asymmetric effects induced by the size of global economic policy uncertainty shocks and their implications for South African policymakers in response to external shocks.

6.1 Introduction

The spill-over effects of the United Kingdom's (UK) decision to leave the European Union (EU) to the rest of Europe and the global economy are yet to fully manifest. However, the initial responses of financial markets have shown that uncertainty and financial shocks can dampen confidence and destabilise economic prospects if not addressed.[1] Indeed, the transmission of uncertainty, risk and financial shocks to global financial markets differs as evidenced by the 2007–2008 financial crises and the 2010–2011 sovereign debt crises.[2] Nonetheless, Caldara et al. (2014) show that positive uncertainty shocks have a significant macroeconomic impact in situations where they elicit a tightening of credit and financial conditions. In addition, Farmer (2011) shows that not only do market participant's expectations or beliefs exert an independent influence on economic activity, they also tend to select an equilibrium.

As a result, this chapter extends the analysis of the global economic uncertainty shock effects on the South African economy by examining selected financial transmission channels into the domestic economy. The key question we examine is whether global economic uncertainty shocks are transmitted via capital flows, credit conditions and business confidence[3] channels to impact GDP growth. Do foreign policy uncertainty and credit conditions impact the monetary policy responses to positive inflation shocks? Furthermore, given low consumer and business confidence levels; and the slowdown in the coincident and leading business cycle indicators, what do policy uncertainty shocks mean for the domestic economy? Is there evidence of asymmetric effects induced by the size of global uncertainty shocks and what are the implications for South

---

[1] Hence, the Bank of England, ECB and other central banks stated that the priority is to reduce uncertainty and to foster confidence. This is underpinned by the understanding that uncertainty tends to risk spill-overs including contagion effects between interconnected markets.

[2] For instance, Chudik and Fratzscher (2012) show evidence of the evolving nature of the transmission of shocks during the 2007–2008 financial crises and the 2010–2011. They find that the flight-to-safety phenomenon due to the rise in risk and risk aversion characterised the pattern of capital flows in 2007–2008. The pattern of flows in 2010–2011 was different and investor decisions seemed to be informed by (i) a country's sovereign rating (ii) quality of institutions and (iii) financial exposure.

[3] For example, see Barsky and Sims (2008) for models in which confidence is an independent driver of economic activity.

African policymakers in response to external shocks? Furthermore, a large body of literature shows evidence of the role of the financial sector as an amplifier of other types of shocks. For instance, Kiyotaki (1999) shows that relatively small and temporary shocks through collateral constraints and financial frictions can be propagated differently, generating large and persistent fluctuations in output and asset prices.[4]

6.2 What Is the Nature of the Relationship Between Economic Policy Uncertainty, Equity Inflows and Credit Conditions?

We start the analysis by showing the bilateral relationships between country-specific measures of economic policy uncertainty as measured by Baker et al. (2013), equity inflows as a percentage of GDP and the credit conditions index (CCI). We use quarterly (Q) data spanning 2000Q1 to 2015Q4. The economic policy uncertainty indices shown in Fig. 6.1 are for the United States of America (US), United Kingdom (UK), China,

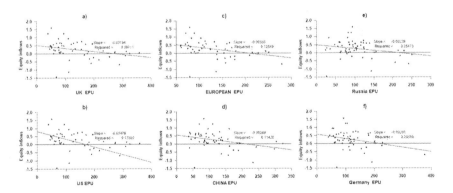

Fig. 6.1 Equity inflows and foreign economic policy uncertainty indices. (Note: EPU denotes economic policy uncertainty. Source: Authors' calculations)

---

[4] Similar to Bernanke et al. (1996) of amplification of shocks via the financial accelerator mechanism.

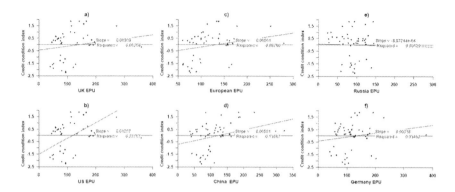

Fig. 6.2 Credit conditions index and foreign economic policy uncertainty indices. (Note: EPU denotes economic policy uncertainty. Source: Authors' calculations)

Russia, Germany, France and Europe. The credit conditions index (CCI) is used to proxy the credit conditions channel. The CCI captures diverse variables and potential channels of transmission from debt markets and the banking sector.[5]

The slopes of the relationships in Fig. 6.1 indicate that foreign economic policy uncertainties are negatively related with equity inflows. This means that elevated economic policy uncertainty deters equity flows into the domestic economy.

In addition, Fig. 6.2 shows a positive relationship between foreign policy uncertainty and the domestic CCI. The slopes of the scatter plots indicate are positive, meaning that domestic credit conditions tighten in response to elevated foreign policy uncertainties.

6.3 The Empirical Analysis

This section conducts the empirical analysis of the transmission channels of the foreign uncertainties into the domestic economy. We use a VAR model and quarterly (Q) data spanning the period 2000Q1 to 2015Q4. The data is sourced from the South African Reserve Bank database. All growth rates are at annual rate. The analysis estimates several VAR models

---

[5] The credit conditions index (CCI) is sourced from Gumata and Ndou (2017).

to establish the nature of the transmission channels of heightened foreign policy uncertainty into the South African economy. The analysis in this section uses variables which include the foreign economic policy uncertainty indices, GDP growth, consumer price level or repo rate, the exchange rates, and bank capital flows as a percentage of GDP. The foreign economic policy uncertainty indices are sourced from Baker et al. (2013) and are included separately in the VAR models. The exchange rates include the Rand per foreign currency, that is, US dollar (US$), Euro (€), Chinese Yuan (CNY) and British Pound (£). Data for banking and non-banking flows refers to combined foreign direct investment and portfolio banking and non-banking flows. The flows are expressed as per cent of GDP.

The economic policy uncertainty indices and exchange rates are included separately in the models. All the variables were log transformed and multiplied by 100 so that they are interpreted as per cent deviation from the trend, except for the repo rate which is in per cent, and bank capital flows as a percentage of GDP. In the estimations, for proper identification of economic policy uncertainty shocks, foreign economic policy uncertainty measures are placed first and then followed by domestic variables. The models use two lags as chosen by AIC and 10,000 Monte Carlo draws. The shocks refer to a one positive standard deviation shock which implies increased or heighten economic policy uncertainty.

6.3.1 How Does Domestic GDP Growth Respond to Heightened External Economic Policy Uncertainty?

Bloom (2014) suggests that high uncertainty about future productivity and demand conditions generates fluctuations in investment, hiring and productivity. The higher uncertainty generates a slowdown as firms postpone activity and wait for uncertainty to subside. Another channel of transmission pointed out by Dixit (1989) suggests that an uncertain environment affects firm entry and exit decisions. So how does domestic GDP growth respond to various foreign economic and policy uncertainty indices? Figure 6.3 shows evidence that heightened foreign economic policy

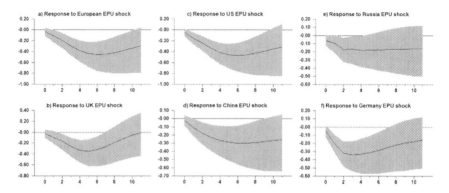

Fig. 6.3 Domestic GDP growth responses to positive foreign economic policy uncertainty shocks. (Note: The grey-shaded bands denote the 16th and 84th percentile confidence bands. EPU denotes economic policy uncertainty. Source: Authors' calculations)

uncertainty shocks lower domestic GDP growth. The adverse foreign economic policy uncertainty shocks lower domestic GDP growth significantly for long periods except for the Russian economic policy uncertainty shock. In most cases, domestic GDP growth tends to deviate from its trend by nearly 0.5 per cent. This is consistent with evidence in Fornari and Straccay (2011) who find that financial shocks can separately exert a significant influence GDP growth and investment growth.

What are the channels that could explain the decline in domestic GDP growth? We examine these in more detail in the next sections focusing on the role of capital flows and credit conditions in transmitting these foreign economic policy uncertainty shocks. For example, Baker et al. (2013) found that economic policy uncertainty indices adversely impact investment and hiring and reduced GDP growth and employment growth. The negative effects of heightened economic policy uncertainty in these economies can spill-over into the domestic economy via several channels such as confidence, low global demand and firm survival as posited by Byrne et al. (2015).[6]

---

[6] Byrne et al. (2015) posit that during crisis and periods of heightened uncertainty, bank-dependent economies are the most affected.

6.4 The Transmission of Economic Policy Uncertainty Shocks via the Capital Flows Channel

Vast empirical studies establish evidence that positive capital inflow shocks lead to credit booms. For instance, Igan and Tan (2015) show evidence that capital inflows create liquidity thus enabling banks to extend credit. So how does foreign economic policy uncertainty impact the direction of capital flows into South Africa? Is the composition of capital flows affected? To assess for the changes in the composition of capital inflows, we separate the effects between banking and non-banking flows.

6.4.1 The Role of Banking and Non-banking Flows

Figure 6.4 shows that positive foreign economic policy uncertainty shocks lead to a significant reduction in banking flows. The decline lasts longer, following the European and US economic policy uncertainty shocks at about 7 and 9 quarters, respectively. The decline in banking flows due to UK economic policy uncertainty lasts for about six quarters. On the

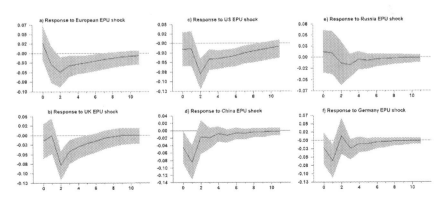

Fig. 6.4 Responses of banking flows to heightened foreign economic policy uncertainty. (Note: The grey-shaded bands denote the 16th and 84th percentile confidence bands. EPU denotes economic policy uncertainty. Source: Authors' calculations)

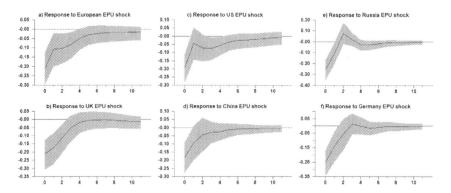

Fig. 6.5 Responses of non-banking flows to positive policy uncertainty shocks. (Note: The grey-shaded bands denote the 16th and 84th percentile confidence bands. EPU denotes economic policy uncertainty. Source: Authors' calculations)

other hand, the Russian economic policy uncertainty shock has no significant effect on banking flows.

In Fig. 6.5, non-banking flows decline significantly on impact. The decline lasts between one and four quarters. Thus, evidence suggests that both banking and non-banking flows decline in response to heightened foreign policy uncertainty shocks.

6.4.2 What About Equity Inflows?

Figure 6.6 shows that equity inflows decline on impact to positive foreign economic policy uncertainty shocks. However, the decline is significant and lasts four quarters to positive European and US economic policy uncertainty shocks. The decline lasts two quarters to Germany economic policy uncertainty shocks. In contrast, the declines are not significant due to positive Chinese and Russian economic policy uncertainty shocks.

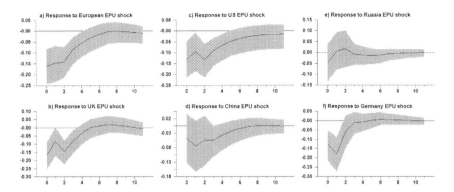

Fig. 6.6 The equity inflows responses to foreign economic uncertainty shocks. (Note: The grey-shaded bands denote the 16th and 84th percentile confidence bands. EPU denotes economic policy uncertainty. Source: Authors' calculations)

6.5 Are There Asymmetries Related to the Size of Positive Economic Policy Uncertainty Shocks?

This section examines the presence of asymmetric response of equity and debt inflows to selected positive foreign economic policy uncertainty shocks. We apply the bivariate Kilian and Vigfussion (2011) asymmetric approach to determine the asymmetric responses of equity and debt inflows to positive economic foreign economic policy shocks. In the analysis, we focus on Europe, China, UK and US economic policy uncertainty shock effects. Figures 6.7 and 6.8 show that large-sized shocks tend to depress equity inflows more than smaller economic policy uncertainty shocks.

Thus, positive economic policy uncertainty shocks have asymmetric effects on equity inflows based on the size of the shocks. This evidence suggests that elevated foreign economic policy uncertainty deters equity and debt inflows into South Africa. This has implications for domestic price and financial stability and requires mechanisms that mitigate these adverse effects.

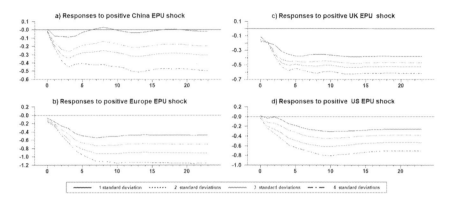

Fig. 6.7 Responses of equity inflows to different sizes of positive economic policy uncertainty shocks. (Note: EPU denotes economic policy uncertainty. Source: Authors' calculations)

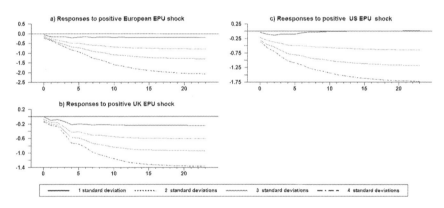

Fig. 6.8 Cumulative responses of debt inflows to different sizes of economic policy uncertainty shocks. (Note: EPU denotes economic policy uncertainty. Source: Authors' calculations)

6.6 Transmission via the Credit Conditions Channel

This section examines the role of the credit conditions channel in transmitting foreign economic policy uncertainty shocks. In the initial VAR estimations, we replace the capital inflow variables with the credit

6 Heightened Foreign Economic Policy Uncertainty Shock... 107

conditions index. The intention is to assess the presence of endogenous credit cycles or the financial accelerator in propagating the initial economic policy uncertainty shock. This can be for example, because of the effects of heightened economic policy uncertainty that is translated into an increase in sovereign bond yields thus tightening financial and credit conditions.

Figure 6.9 shows that credit conditions increase (tighten) due to heightened economic policy uncertainty shocks. The responses indicate prolonged periods of credit conditions tightening due to positive European, US and China economic policy uncertainty shocks. The tightening in credit and financial conditions can result in higher agency costs and external premiums for raising capital in financial markets.

However, the results in Fig. 6.9 indicate that elevated UK, Russia and Germany economic policy uncertainty shocks lead to short periods of tightening in credit conditions. In addition, the tighter credit conditions are often accompanied by GDP growth contractions, albeit at differing magnitudes.

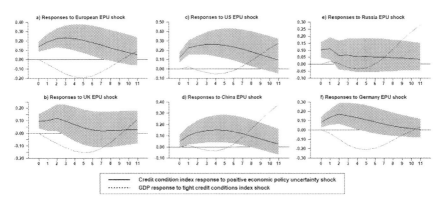

Fig. 6.9 Responses of credit conditions and GDP growth to positive economic policy uncertainty shocks. (Note: The grey-shaded bands denote the 16th and 84th percentile confidence bands. EPU denotes economic policy uncertainty. Source: Authors' calculations)

6.6.1 Do Equity and Debt Inflows Amplify the Response of the Credit Conditions Index?

Earlier results showed that equity and debt inflows respond negatively to positive foreign economic policy uncertainty shocks. However, do equity and debt inflows lead to differential amplification effects on credit conditions? We use the counterfactual scenarios approach to assess responses in the presence and absence of equity and debt inflows in the model. Figure 6.10 shows that the credit conditions index tightens irrespective of whether the equity and debt inflows are included or shut off in the model. The counterfactual scenarios indicate that credit conditions tighten due to positive foreign economic policy uncertainty shocks. In addition, the excess responses of actual over counterfactual responses imply that the decline in equity inflows amplifies the tightening of credit conditions compared to that due to debt inflows. The implication is that firms with poorer indicators of creditworthiness will be more constrained than those which are creditworthy, and this can negatively affect investment and growth. Glichrist et al. (2013) find evidence that positive uncertainty shocks influence investment largely through the widening of spreads as they are associated with a decline in output.

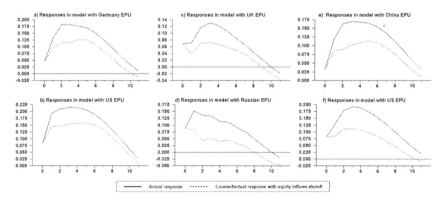

Fig. 6.10 Accumulated CCI responses to economic policy uncertainty shocks and the role of equity inflows. (Note: EPU denotes economic policy uncertainty; CCI denotes Credit Conditions Index. Source: Authors' calculations)

6 Heightened Foreign Economic Policy Uncertainty Shock... 109

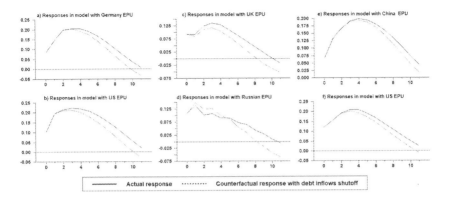

Fig. 6.11 Accumulated CCI responses to economic policy uncertainty shocks and the role of debt inflows. (Note: EPU denotes economic policy uncertainty; CCI denotes Credit Conditions Index. Source: Authors' calculations)

What about the role of debt inflows? Similar to the preceding findings of the impact of equity inflows, the results show that the actual credit conditions index (CCI) exceeds the counterfactual scenario responses in Fig. 6.11. This suggests that the decline in debt inflows amplify the tightening in credit markets and conditions. Earlier, evidence showed that foreign economic policy uncertainty shocks have adverse effects on equity and debt inflows. Evidence in this section shows that the responses of equity and debt inflows propagate the adverse effects of heightened economic policy uncertainty via tight credit conditions.

6.6.2 The Role of the Business Confidence Channel in Propagating GDP Responses to Positive Foreign Economic Policy Uncertainty Shocks

This section applies the endogenous–exogenous VAR approach to capture the influence of the business confidence index in transmitting positive foreign economic policy uncertainty shocks. The business confidence is included as an endogenous variable in one model and is an exogenous variable in the other model. Thereafter, the gap between the impulse responses gives an indication of the size of the influence of the business confidence channel. The VAR models include foreign economic policy

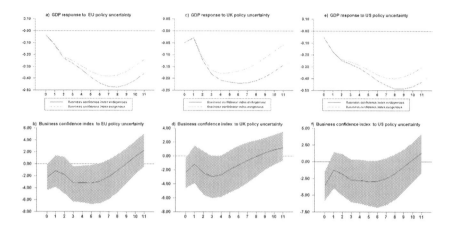

Fig. 6.12 Amplification of GDP responses by the business confidence channel. (Note: The grey-shaded bands denote the 16th and 84th percentile confidence bands. Source: Authors' calculations)

uncertainty, GDP, consumer price level, repo rate and business confidence index. The models are estimated using two lags and 10,000 Monte Carlo draws.

Figure 6.12 shows that GDP declines more when the business confidence index is endogenous in the model than when it is exogenous in the model. This shows that the deterioration in the business confidence as shown in the second row of Fig. 6.12 leads to further deterioration in GDP due to foreign economic policy uncertainty shocks.

6.6.3 Does the Effect of Monetary Policy Tightening on GDP Depend on Equity Inflows and Credit Conditions?

The preceding section found that credit conditions tighten, and equity and debt inflows decline for some time due to positive economic policy uncertainty shocks. So, to what extent are the responses of GDP to the monetary policy tightening shocks influenced by the equity inflows and credit conditions channels? We use a counterfactual scenario approach to assess for the differential responses. Figure 6.13 shows that equity inflows worsen the decline in GDP due to monetary policy tightening shocks.

6 Heightened Foreign Economic Policy Uncertainty Shock... 111

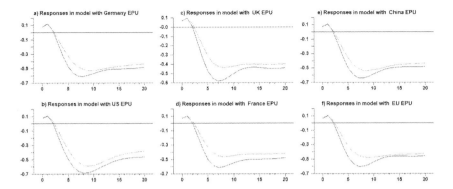

Fig. 6.13 Responses of GDP with equity inflows included in the model. (Note: The solid impulse response represents results when equity inflows are allowed to operate in the model. The dotted line represents the impulse response when equity inflows are shut off in the model. EPU denotes economic policy uncertainty. Source: Authors' calculations)

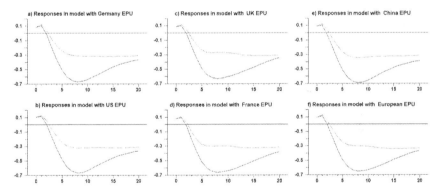

Fig. 6.14 GDP responses with the credit conditions index included in the model. (Note: The solid impulse response represents results when equity inflows are allowed to operate in the model. The dotted line represents the impulse response when equity inflows are shut off in the model. EPU denotes economic policy uncertainty. Source: Authors' calculations)

On the other hand, Fig. 6.14 shows that GDP declines much more when credit conditions are not shut off than when they are shut off in the model. This suggests that tighter credit conditions lead to a bigger decline in GDP following a monetary policy tightening shock.

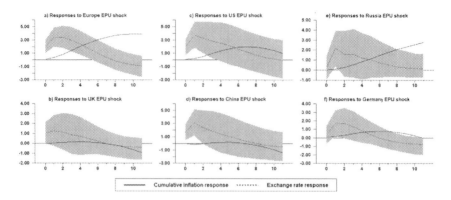

Fig. 6.15 The exchange rate and accumulated inflation responses to positive economic policy uncertainty shocks. (Note: The grey-shaded bands denote the 16th and 84th percentile confidence bands. Source: Authors' calculations)

If credit conditions propagate the impact of monetary policy tightening on GDP, do foreign economic policy uncertainty and credit conditions impact the adjustment of monetary policy in response to inflationary pressures? To answer this, we start by looking at the effects of foreign economic policy uncertainty shocks on the exchange rate of the Rand to the US dollar (US$), Euro (€), Chinese Yuan (CNY) and British Pound (£) as risks to inflation and the accompanying inflation developments.

Evidence in Fig. 6.15 suggests that positive economic policy uncertainty shocks lead to the Rand depreciation against the US dollar (US$), Euro (€), Chinese Yuan (CNY) and British Pound (£). However, the inflationary pressures based on the cumulative inflation responses show a delayed build-up in inflation. This has implications for policy adjustments to curb inflation and mitigate inflation via forward looking policy conduct.

6.6.4 The Role of Foreign Economic Policy Uncertainty: Inferences from the Endogenous–Exogenous VAR Model

Bloom (2014) posits that when uncertainty is high, monetary and fiscal policy tools become less effective because firms and consumers are more likely to respond cautiously to stimulus via interest rates and tax cuts. So,

6 Heightened Foreign Economic Policy Uncertainty Shock... 113

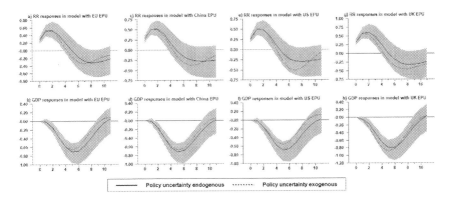

Fig. 6.16 Repo rate and GDP growth responses to positive inflation shocks. (Note: The grey-shaded bands denote the 16th and 84th percentile confidence bands. RR denotes repo rate. EPU denotes economic policy uncertainty. Source: Authors' calculations)

to what extent does economic policy uncertainty matter for the responses of the repo rate and GDP to positive inflation shocks?

We apply an endogenous–exogenous VAR approach to capture the influence of economic policy uncertainty. The economic policy uncertainty is included as an endogenous variable in one model and an exogenous variable in another model. Thereafter, the gap between the impulse responses gives an indication of the size of the influence of the economic policy uncertainty. The models include changes in foreign economic policy uncertainty, GDP growth, inflation and repo rate and equity inflows as a percentage of GDP. The models are estimated using two lags and 10,000 Monte Carlo draws.

Figure 6.16 (first row) compares the repo rate responses to positive inflation shocks when foreign economic policy uncertainty is endogenous in one model and is exogenous in the other model. This is to determine the robustness of the amplification effects from foreign economic policy uncertainty. Indeed, the repo rate rises to curb positive inflationary pressures irrespective of whether foreign economic policy uncertainty shocks are endogenous or are introduced exogenously in the model. However, there is no statistically significant difference in the repo rate responses to curb inflation as both responses are within the same error bands.[7] This means that

---

[7] The finding is robust to different counterfactual techniques using the shutting off approach.

monetary policy enforces price stability irrespective of whether foreign economic policy uncertainty is endogenous or exogenous in the model, albeit in small magnitudes, as indicated by the duration and the transitory natures of the responses. Thus, we conclude that domestic economic conditions matter over and above the foreign economic policy uncertainty shocks.

In addition, the second row of Fig. 6.16 shows the role of foreign economic policy uncertainty on GDP growth responses due to the repo rate tightening shocks based on the endogenous–exogenous VAR approach. Evidence indicates that GDP growth declines more when economic policy uncertainty is endogenous in the model than when it is exogenous. The gaps at the peak effect indicate that economic policy uncertainty accentuates the GDP growth decline due to monetary policy tightening shocks.[8]

6.6.5 Do Credit Conditions Impact the Monetary Policy Response to Positive Inflation Shocks?

This section replaces equity inflows as a percentage of GDP in the model estimated in the previous section with the credit conditions index. However, to make comparisons of the impact of credit conditions in this section, we do not use the endogenous–exogenous approach but shut off the effects of credit conditions in the interest rate equation in the VAR model.

Figure 6.17 shows that the counterfactual repo rate exceeds the actual repo rate. This implies that tighter credit conditions due to elevated foreign economic policy uncertainty induce a slow pace of tightening in the repo rate due to positive inflation shocks. This means that credit conditions matter for both the magnitude and speed of the policy rate adjustment.

6.7 Conclusion and Policy Implications

Do economic policy uncertainty and credit conditions impact the monetary policy responses to positive inflation shocks? First, we establish that foreign economic policy uncertainties are negatively related with equity inflows. This means that elevated policy uncertainty deters equity

---

[8] But the error bands indicate the effects are not statistically different.

6 Heightened Foreign Economic Policy Uncertainty Shock... 115

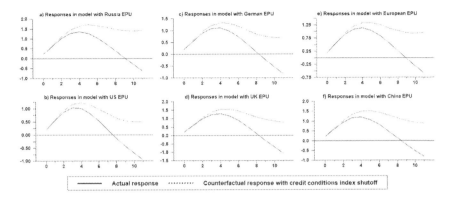

Fig. 6.17 The repo rate responses to positive inflation shocks and the role of credit conditions. (Note: EPU denotes policy uncertainty. Source: Authors' calculations)

flows into the domestic economy. On the other hand, heightened foreign economic policy uncertainty tightens credit conditions. Heightened foreign economic policy uncertainty shocks lower domestic GDP growth. At peak, decline domestic GDP can deviate from long-term trend by nearly 0.5 per cent.

Second, positive foreign economic policy uncertainty shocks lead to a significant reduction in capital inflows. However, the decline lasts longer following elevated European and US economic policy uncertainty. Furthermore, large positive foreign economic policy uncertainty shocks depress equity inflows more than smaller uncertainty shocks. This means that foreign economic policy uncertainty shocks affect the composition of capital flows. This has implications for domestic price and financial stability and requires mechanisms that mitigate the adverse effects.

Third, credit conditions tighten in response to heightened economic policy uncertainty shocks. They exhibit prolonged periods of tightening due to positive European, US and China economic policy uncertainty shocks. The composition of capital flows matters for credit conditions. Equity inflows amplify the tightening of credit conditions compared to debt inflows. Furthermore, the business confidence channel via the deterioration in business confidence exacerbates the decline in GDP due to foreign policy uncertainty shock.

Last, foreign economic policy uncertainty shocks depreciate the exchange rate of the rand to the US dollar, euro, Chinese Yuan and British pound, and risks to inflation are heightened. The repo rate tightens to curb positive inflationary pressures irrespective of whether foreign economic policy uncertainty shocks are endogenous or exogenous in the modelling. The decline in equity inflows and tightening credit conditions propagate the impact of monetary policy tightening on GDP growth.

The policy implication of the results is that there is presence of endogenous credit cycles or the financial accelerator mechanism in propagating the initial economic policy uncertainty shocks. The tightening in credit and financial conditions can result in higher agency costs and external premiums for raising capital in financial markets. Firms with poorer indicators of creditworthiness will be more constrained than those which are creditworthy, and this can negatively affect investment growth and output growth. Monetary policy enforces price stability irrespective of whether foreign economic policy is endogenous or exogenous in the model, albeit in small magnitudes, as indicated by the duration and the transitory nature of the responses. Tighter credit conditions due to foreign economic policy uncertainty shocks also induce the repo rate tightening, albeit at a slow pace due to positive inflation developments. The results imply that credit and domestic conditions matter for the magnitude and speed of the policy rate adjustment.

References

Baker, S., Bloom, N., and Davis, S. 2013. *Measuring Economic Policy Uncertainty*. Chicago Booth Research Paper.
Baker, S., Bloom, N., and Davis, S. 2015. *Measuring Economic Policy Uncertainty*. NBER Working Paper No. 21633.
Barsky, B.R., and Sims, E.R. 2008. *News Shocks*. NBER Working Paper No. 15312.
Bernanke, B.S., Gertler, M., and Girlchrist, S. 1996. The Financial Accelerator and the Flight to Quality. *The Review of Economics and Statistics*, 128(1), 1–15.
Bloom, N. 2014. Fluctuations in Uncertainty. *Journal of Economic Perspectives*, 28(2), 153–76.

Byrne, D., Fernald, J., and Reinsdorf, M. 2015. Does the United States Have a Productivity Slowdown or a Measurement Problem? Finance and Economics Discussion Series 2015–2016, Board of Governors of the Federal Reserve System (US).

Caldara, D., and Kamps, C. 2010. The Analytics of the Sign Restriction Approach to Shock Identification: A Framework for Understanding the Empirical Macro Puzzles. https://econpapers.repec.org/RePEc:red:sed010:335.

Caldara, D., Fuentes-Albero, C., Gilchrist, S., and Zakrajsek, E. 2014. *The Macroeconomic Impact of Financial and Uncertainty Shock*. Board of Governors of the Federal Reserve System International Finance Discussion Papers No. 1166.

Chudik, A., and Fratzscher, M. 2012. *Liquidity, Risk and the Global Transmission of the 2007–08 Financial Crisis and the 2010–11 Sovereign Debt Crisis*. ECB Working Paper Series No. 1416.

Dixit, A. 1989. Entry and Exit Decisions Under Uncertainty. *Journal of Political Economy*, 97, 620–38.

Farmer, R.E.A. 2011. *Confidence, Crashes and Animal Spirits*. NBER Working Paper No. 14846.

Fornari, F., and Straccay, L. 2011. *What Does a Financial Shock Do? First International Evidence*. ECB Working Paper Series No. 1522.

Glichrist, S., Sim, J.W., and Zakrajsek, E. 2013. *Uncertainty, Financial Frictions, and Investment Dynamics*. Finance and Economics Discussion Series (FEDS) Working Papers 2014-69.

Gumata, N., and Ndou, E. 2017. *Bank Credit Extension and Real Economic Activity in South Africa: The Impact of Capital Flow Dynamics, Bank Regulation and Selected Macro-prudential Tool*. Palgrave Macmillan. ISBN 978-3-319-43551-0.

Igan, D., and Tan, Z. 2015. *Capital Inflows, Credit Growth, and Financial Systems*. IMF Working Paper WP/15/193.

Kilian, L., and Vigfusson, R.J. 2011. Are the Responses of the U.S. Economy Asymmetric in Energy Price Increases and Decreases? *Quantitative Economics*, 2(3), 419–53.

Kiyotaki, N. 1999. Credit and Business Cycles. The Japanese Economic Review. *The Journal of the Japanese Economic Association*, 49(1), 18–39.

Kiyotaki, N., and Moore, J. 1995. *Credit Cycles*. NBER Working Paper No. 5083.

Part II

Global Policy Rates and The South African Economy

7

In Which Direction Is There a Momentum Effect in the Changes in the Spread Between the Repo Rate and Federal Funds Rate?

Learning Objectives

- Show the direction in which there is a momentum effect in the changes in the long-run spread between the repo rate and Federal Funds Rate (FFR).
- Establish the long-term relationship between the repo rate and the FFR.
- Estimate the deviations of the repo rate-FFR spread from the long-run relationship.
- Explore the nature of the association between the real interest rate spread and inflation.
- Establish whether there is an asymmetric adjustment in the repo rate-FFR spread.
- Determine whether the repo rate-FFR spread responds in a non-linear manner to own shocks.
- Determine whether key macroeconomic variables display asymmetric adjustments over the business cycle.

7.1 Introduction

This chapter explores the implications of the changes in the repo rate-Federal Funds Rate spread. This follows the lift-off of the Federal Funds Rate (FFR) by 25 basis points in December 2015. The US Fed has since continued on a gradual upward adjustment of the policy rate. What are the implications for a small open economy such as South Africa? According to the Mundell-Fleming open economy models, in a bilateral context, the small open economy should raise its interest rates following the large economy policy rate increase.[1] This rise will equilibrate the domestic interest rate to the global interest rate level. The transmission of interest rates changes from a large economy to the rest of the world occurs via changes in the bilateral exchange rate, changes in aggregate demand and shifts in the investment saving (IS) curve. Furthermore, the uncovered interest rate parity condition states that the bilateral interest rate differential or the spread should equal the expected exchange rate level.

The uncovered interest rate parity equation and the modified version are shown in Eqs. (7.1) and (7.2). Equation (7.2) suggests that the gap in changes in policy rates should be equal to changes in the expected exchange rate. This gives policymakers options to react in a bilateral way, taking into consideration the expected changes in the exchange rate.

$$Repo\ rate - FFR = spread = expected\ exchange\ rate \quad (7.1)$$

$$Change\ in\ repo\ rate - change\ in\ FFR = change\ in\ spread$$
$$= change\ in\ R/US\$ \quad (7.2)$$

With this bilateral relationship in mind, we assess the dynamics of the spread between the repo rate and FFR. We ask: In which direction is there a momentum effect in the changes to the long-run spread between the repo rate and FFR? Literature shows that key macroeconomic variables display asymmetric adjustments over the course of the business cycle. Is such asymmetric adjustment evident in the repo rate-FFR spread?

---

[1] This aspect is a simplified model and does not take into account the multilateral relationships and the potential effects of the divergence in global policy rates at a time when central banks also use un-conventional monetary policy tools.

First, we are motivated by the views of Laubach and Williams (2015),[2] which suggest that the real and natural rate of interest in the United States of America (US) is around zero. Taking the discussion further, Rachel and Smith (2015) estimate that the global neutral rate may remain low at around 1 per cent. Why should this matter from the South African policy perspective? It seems that US policymakers view the structurally low real and natural rate as a policy constraining factor on future policy decisions. This will be particularly binding when faced with adverse shocks. Brainard (2015) observes that the high probability of hitting the zero-lower bound implies pronounced asymmetry in policy flexibility. This requires risk management considerations, encompassing a cautious and gradual approach. As such, unconventional policy tools will probably continue playing an important role in the future (Laubach and Williams 2015; Rachel and Smith 2015).

Second, we are motivated by the trends in the evolution of the repo rate, the FFR and their spread over time in Fig. 7.1. The observed trends show that the policy rates do not move one-to-one. As a result, the spread has varied significantly over time. Furthermore, the period from late 2008 to the end of 2015 (shaded in grey), when the FFR was at the zero-lower bound, was characterised by the use of various unconventional monetary policy instruments. After the end of phase three of Quantitative Easing (QE3), the US Federal Reserve Bank asset holdings and reinvestments have been used to assist in maintaining accommodative financial conditions.

Third, we are motivated by literature which asserts the existence of the asymmetric adjustments of macroeconomic factors and policy responses over the course of the business cycle. It is for this reason that we do not assess the repo rate-FFR spread dynamics based on just a simple statistical difference. To be informative to policymakers, it is worthwhile to assess the spread as a deviation from the estimated long-run relationship or "equilibrium" rate.

---

[2] Partly responding to the scepticism in Hamilton et al. (2015), Laubach and Williams (2015) fail to establish evidence that the natural rate has adjusted and increased in line with the recovery of the US economy from the Great Recession. Similarly, Rachel and Smith (2015) establish that the global neutral real rate may have fallen. Lower expectations for trend growth, shifts in desired savings and investment preferences appear to be important in explaining the long-term decline. Fischer (2015) is of the view that the equilibrium real interest rate will probably remain low for the policy relevant horizon.

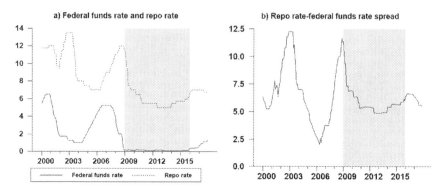

Fig. 7.1 The US Federal Funds Rate and repo rate. (Note: Grey-shaded area represents the period of the zero-lower bound for the US FFR. Source: South African Reserve Bank and Fred data. https://fred.stlouisfed.org/)

We fill research policy gaps by determining the long-run equilibrium repo rate. The analysis of the repo rate-FFR spread offers valuable policy lessons which can be learned from how historical adjustments based on relative deviations from the long-run equilibrium policy rate spread. Hence, we determine the nature and degree of the repo rate adjustments (corrections) from deviations below and above the estimated long-run rate. Implied in the assessment of the nature of the correction to deviations from the long-run rate is the assumption that the linearity about the spread adjustment is not ideal.

Furthermore, we fill policy gaps by adding on the Laubach and Williams (2015) argument that interest rates may change over time on account of highly persistent structural shifts in aggregate supply and demand. We do this by determining the extent of non-linearity, in the spread adjustment from the long-run level as well from the peak and trough of the spread. Therefore, the starting point matters as shown in Fig. 7.2. It is also evident that the repo rate-FFR spread hardly moved during the period of the FFR zero-lower bound. In fact, the level of the repo rate was the same as the spread. This means that the repo rate movements explain all the variation in the spread. However, the spread has adjusted as the US Federal Reserve (US Fed) started to increase the policy rate. Furthermore, the scatterplots in Fig. 7.2(b) indicate that the repo

7 In Which Direction Is There a Momentum Effect...

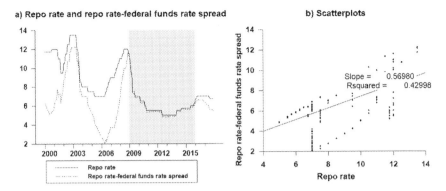

Fig. 7.2 The repo rate and the repo rate-FFR spread. (Note: Grey-shaded area represents the period of the zero-lower bound for the US FFR. Source: South African Reserve Bank and Fred data)

rate movements explain almost 42 per cent of the variation in the spread over the sample period.

The US Fed stated that policy adjustments will be done in a "very gradual" manner.[3] Is the adjustment in the repo rate-FFR spread the same from the trough and peak? Will the adjustments of the repo rate be different post the prolonged period of the zero-lower bound and quantitative easing? We believe that this evidence will anchor the debate on whether the current gradual and cautious pace of policy tightening by the South African Reserve Bank relative to historical episodes is still appropriate or not.

7.2 How Synchronised Are the Repo Rate and Federal Funds Rate Movements?

As the global financial crisis intensified in 2008, central banks in advanced economies co-ordinated interest rate cuts. What does the data tell us about the movements in the repo rate? We use the Geweke technique to

---

[3] In addition, the Fed Chair Yellen clarified that "gradual" does not mean mechanical, evenly timed and equally sized interest rate changes.

Table 7.1 Synchronisation of the repo rate and FFR during inflation targeting

Period	Geweke feedback measures
2000/2002	8.9[a]
2003/2004	14.9[a]
2005/2006	**37.0[a]**
2007/2008	16.3[a]

Source: Authors' calculations
[a]Imply significance at 1 per cent level

assess the strength of synchronised movements between the repo rate and FFR over two-year intervals. We use the Geweke technique to show synchronisation on the rate movements rather than changes in the level of the interest rates. In addition, we do not test whether the synchronisation is contemporaneous, lagged or leading. A higher value implies more synchronisation for that particular period. We use monthly data for the repo rate and the FFR for the sample period 2000M1 to 2017M12. The data is soured from the South African Reserve Bank and the Fred databases.

The results in Table 7.1 show that there was a higher degree of synchronisation during 2005/2006 when both policy rates were tightening. The estimates of the Geweke feedback measures are comparable for 2003/2004 and 2007/2008 when the policy stance was loosening, suggesting that there was some degree of synchronisation although weak.

7.3 What Approach Do We Adopt to Estimate the Persistence of Positive and Negative Interest Rate Spreads Deviations?

This section applies a momentum approach based on Enders and Siklos (2001) to establish whether positive interest rate spread deviations from the long-term equilibrium rate persist for substantially longer periods than negative interest rate spreads deviations. This approach uses Heaviside indicators which depend on the level of changes in the spread in the past period (lagged changes). This leads to a momentum threshold autoregressive model (M-TAR), as the changes in the spreads tend to display more momentum in one direction than to the other.

When is it ideal to use the momentum threshold approach? This approach is more informative when trying to identify the differences in the persistence of deviations and the rate at which the policy rate increases and decreases revert to the threshold. The Enders and Siklos (2001) M-TAR approach with asymmetric error-correction allows a variable to display differing degrees of autoregressive decay depending on whether it is increasing or decreasing.

Is it the best approach to use for the task at hand? Yes, it is an appropriate technique to answer the questions posed in this chapter. For instance, the Enders and Siklos (2001) M-TAR approach differs from the Engle-Granger and Johansen (1996) approach which assumes linear adjustments from the long-run equilibrium. Furthermore, the traditional cointegration techniques such as the Johansen (1988) approach assume that the adjustment to the long-run equilibrium is symmetric. Li and Lee (2013) show that such approaches are therefore unable to capture possible asymmetries resulting from positive and negative shocks. Ahmad and Hernandez (2013) indicate that the M-TAR approach is therefore appropriate as it can identify asymmetries compared to the Engel-ganger or Johansen linear cointegration models.

7.3.1 What Is the Long-term Relationship Between the Repo Rate and FFR During the Inflation Targeting Period?

The first step of the Enders and Siklos (2001) momentum threshold approach requires estimating the long-run relationship between the repo rate and FFR as shown in Eq. (7.3). Thereafter, we extract the residuals, namely the spread from the estimated long-run relationship, then use it to ascertain the long-term rate equilibrium via asymmetric error-correction tests.

$$Repo_t = 6.789 + 0.6677 \times FFR_t + Spread_t, \quad \bar{R}^2 = 29.12\% \quad (7.3)$$

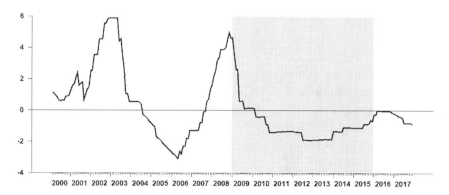

Fig. 7.3 The repo rate-FFR spread relative to the long-run estimated relationship. (Note: Grey-shaded area represents the period of the zero-lower bound for the US FFR. Source: Authors' calculations)

Why do we prefer this approach? It is because it is not only the long-run mean level repo rate that matters. The movements in the repo rate are not entirely explained by the FFR and the coefficient of the FFR. The value of the R^2 in Eq. (7.3) indeed suggests that domestic macroeconomic factors do play a much bigger role. The results from Eq. 7.3 show that the long-term mean repo rate is close to 7 per cent. We show the evolution of the estimated repo rate-FFR spread derived from Eq. (7.3) in Fig. 7.3.

It is evident that the repo rate-FFR spread does not adjust fully and does not remain in an equilibrium state. There are periods of prolonged deviation from the equilibrium in either direction. For instance, the spread was at an all-time high of around 6 per cent during the early 2000s and during the global financial crisis coinciding with high inflation episodes. However, during the period since 2010, the spread has been persistently negative, suggesting that the current repo rate is below the long-run equilibrium rate. This aspect is explored in further detail in later sections of this chapter exploring the relationship between the spread and inflation episodes.

7.3.2 The Second Stage: Is There a Momentum Effect in the Changes in Spread?

We proceed to the second stage which determines (i) the threshold, (ii) the cointegration relationship, and (iii) the speed of adjustment back to the long-run equilibrium. The analysis of these aspects of the repo rate and FFR spread are important in enabling us to understand the nature of the relationship and to derive appropriate policy implications. Hence, we estimate a momentum threshold autoregressive model (M-TAR) using the residuals derived from the cointegration Eq. (7.3) and shown in Fig. 7.3.

Is there a threshold in the change in the repo rate-FFR spread? If so, where does it occur? We determine the threshold endogenously using the consistent threshold estimator based on the Chan (1993) approach. This approach sorts the potential thresholds in an ascending order and excludes values within the lowest and highest 15th percentiles. Therefore, according to Chan's (1993) approach, the consistent estimate of the threshold is the one that yields the smallest residual sum of squares over the remaining 70 per cent. Based on this approach, we find a threshold value in the change of the spread of −0.163 per cent for the sample period January 2000 to November 2015.

$$\Delta Spread_t = -0.021 \times I_t \times Spread_{t-1} - 0.093 \times (1 - I_t)$$
$$\times Spread_{t-1} + \sum_{i=1}^{l} \beta_i \Delta Spread_{t-i} + \varepsilon_t \quad (7.4)$$

where

$$I_t = \begin{cases} 1 & \text{if } \Delta Spread_{t-1} \geq -0.163 \\ 0 & \text{if } \Delta Spread_{t-1} \leq -0.163 \end{cases} \quad (7.5)$$

Is there a cointegration relationship? In the second stage, we estimate and test two aspects of the bilateral relationship, namely, (i) the null hypothesis of no cointegration relationships and (ii) the convergence of the speed of adjustment. We then test whether the speed of adjustment above and below the estimated threshold is jointly equal to zero to determine the cointegration relationship based on the Enders and Siklos approach. We reject this null hypothesis in favour of cointegration relationship.[4]

---

[4] Since the T-max exceeds the statistics given by Enders and Granger (1998). In addition, based on Phi-value, we reject the null hypothesis of no cointegration.

Table 7.2 Cointegration and asymmetry tests

	Coefficient (t-values)	Implications
Sign of adjustment in change in spreads		
Impact when $\Delta Spread_{t-1} \geq$ threshold (ρ_1)	−0.021 (−1.82)[e]	Convergence
Impact when $\Delta Spread_{t-1} \leq$ threshold (ρ_2)	−0.093 (−2.56)[d]	Convergence
Threshold of $\Delta Spread_{t-1}$	−0.163	
Testing null hypothesis of no cointegration		
T-max[a]	−1.813	There is cointegration
Phi ... $\rho_1 = \rho_2 = 0$[b]	5.171	There is cointegration
Testing null hypothesis of no symmetry		
$\rho_1 = \rho_2$[c]	3.434	There is asymmetric adjustment

Source: Authors' calculations
[a]T-max exceeds EG statistics at 5 per cent
[b]Phi exceeds EG statistics at 10 per cent
[c]Testing equality which implies symmetric adjustment
[d]Implies significance at 5 per cent level
[e]Implies significance at 10 per cent level

The second aspect of the relationship involves determining the signs of the speed of adjustment coefficients and whether they are equal in Eq. 7.5 and Table 7.2. This means testing the null hypothesis of the symmetric speed of adjustments. The negative sign on the speed of adjustment indicates that there is convergence. This means that, having deviated, the spread does go back to the long-run equilibrium.

The small absolute value of (−0.021) indicates that the adjustments tend to persist more when the spread is widening (or increasing) as the change in the spread exceeds the threshold. In contrast, the adjustment value of (−0.093) implies that the pace of adjustment is relatively quick when the spread is narrowing from below the threshold. These findings of asymmetry suggest that the repo rate is adjusted differently to rising versus declining repo rate-FFR spread. Hence, we reject the null hypothesis of symmetry in the adjustment of the spread in favour of asymmetric adjustments. There is evidence of higher momentum in the adjustment of the repo rate when the spread is narrowing.

7.3.3 How Does the Repo Rate Adjust to the Spread Above and Below the Long-run Equilibrium?

Based on the preceding section and conclusion about the direction of momentum in the adjustment of the repo rate-FFR spread, this section estimates an asymmetric error-correction model. This entails determining whether previous repo rate and FFR changes matter for the current repo rate changes? The asymmetric error-correction model we estimate is shown in the equation below. The model allows us to examine the effects of short-term dynamics between changes in the repo rate and FFR. The model includes lags of changes in the repo rate and FFR.

Size of adjustment above threshold

Size of adjustment below threshold

$$\Delta Repo_t = -0.023 - \mathbf{0.0369} * I_t Spread_{t-1} - \mathbf{0.129} * (1 - I_t)\rho_2 Spread_{t-1} + A_i(L)\Delta Repo_{t-i} + B_i(L)\Delta FFR_{t-i} + \varepsilon_t$$

$\overline{R}^2 = 48.08\%$,   Durbin Watson test statistic $= 2.1$

Note: The bold indicates the values are high and significant at conventional statistically significance level. $A_i(L)\Delta Repo_{t-i}$ refers to lags 1, 2, 3, 5, 9 and 10. $B_i(L)\Delta FFR_{t-i}$ refers to lags 0, 2, 5, 6, 7 and 8.

Source: Authors' calculations

What do the coefficients of the adjustment mean? The results show that the repo rate adjusts faster when the spread is narrowing (-0.129) than when the spread is widening or increasing (-0.0369). In addition, the speed of adjustment differs below and above the threshold, indicating asymmetric adjustment. Since the repo rate cannot affect the policy rate of a large economy such as the US, we test whether changes in the FFR granger cause changes in the repo rate in Table 7.3.

The causality tests in Table 7.3 show that both lagged repo rates and FFR changes affect current movements in the repo rate.

Table 7.3 Granger causality test

Null hypothesis	F-test (p-value)	Decision
Impact of lagged FFR change is zero	5.753 (0.000)	Lagged FFR changes Granger cause repo changes
Impact of lagged repo rate changes is zero	10.725 (0.000)	Lagged repo rate changes are important

Source: Authors' calculations

7.3.4 Does the Spread Respond in a Non-linear Manner to Own Shocks?

If the repo rate-FFR spread matters for key policy relevant variables such as the exchange rate of the Rand per US dollar and the yield differentials, it is important to assess the non-linearities involved. In particular, movements at the peak and lowest points of spread series. Such an assessment is relevant since communication from the US Fed is by and large tilted towards a policy rate path characterised by a lower level of interest rates relative to the pre-crisis period. Furthermore, the US Fed has underperformed in achieving the inflation target and the inflation expectations have been declining. The US policymakers are constrained by policy objectives and have stated that adjustments to monetary policy are likely to be "gradual".

In fact, Brainard (2015) sums up these economic circumstances and states that, "With the nominal neutral interest rate lower than in the past and policy options highly limited in case economic conditions deteriorate than if inflationary pressures accelerate, the asymmetry in risk management considerations advices a cautious and gradual approach". This has implications for the design of the domestic monetary policy strategy if capital flows are highly responsive to the degree of changes in the FFR.

For this analysis, we calculate the repo rate-FFR spread for the period 2000M1 to 2017M12 as shown in Fig. 7.4. Thereafter, and we show policymakers that there exists a non-linear impulse response depending on the starting point. To show the differences in the adjustment process, we selected peak points such as points A and point C in Fig. 7.4 and lowest points such as point B in Fig. 7.4 in the spread. We also extend the analysis to show the adjustments during the period when the spread was relatively stable since 2011 such as point D in Fig. 7.4.

7 In Which Direction Is There a Momentum Effect... 133

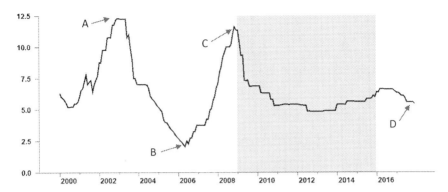

Fig. 7.4 Spread between repo rate and Federal Funds Rate. (Source: Authors' calculations)

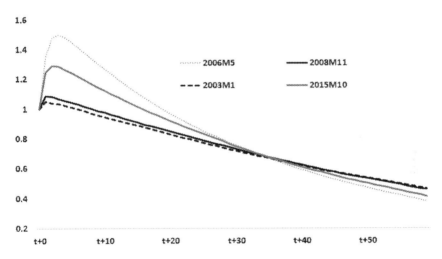

Fig. 7.5 Responses depending on the starting point of the spread between repo rate and Federal Funds Rate. (Source: Authors' calculations)

To assess whether the non-linearity matters from peak to lowest point, we use a positive 1 per cent shock to the repo rate-FFR spread. The responses showing the non-linearity of impulses depending on the starting point of the size of the spread are shown in Fig. 7.5. The results based on the momentum TAR approach show that the increases from points A, C and D are less aggressive compared to when the starting point was from a very low point such as in point B (2006M5). This shows that non-linearity plays a role in the adjustment of the repo rate-FFR spread. The move in the spread from point B also happens to be associated with one of the steepest increases in inflation during the inflation targeting regime. Hence, we address some aspects of the repo rate-FFR spread in relation to domestic factors in the next section.

7.4 How Did the Ex-post Real Repo Rate Evolve During the Period Under Review?

So far, we have estimated that the long-run nominal repo rate is nearly 7 per cent. Evidence shows that the actual and lagged FFR granger cause the repo rate. But the coefficient of the FFR suggests that domestic macroeconomic factors play a much bigger role. Furthermore, the repo rate-FFR spread does not fully revert to and remain in an equilibrium state. The repo rate-FFR spread has been persistently negative since 2010, suggesting that the current repo rate is below the long-run equilibrium rate. In addition, there are non-linearities in the adjustment process depending on the starting point.

We stated earlier that we are exploring the bilateral relationship between the repo rate and the FFR. But estimates of the global real and neutral rates are equally important. Why is the long-run global equilibrium rate relevant? According to Rachel and Smith (2015), real interest rates in emerging market economies closely co-move with those in advanced economies and the world. This indicates that the global neutral real rate affects country-specific equilibrium policy rates. As such, in the absence of distortions or shocks, the global real and neutral rate can be thought of as an "anchor" or "benchmark" to which country-specific equilibrium rates in small open economies will converge to in the long-term.[5]

If that is the case, as a point of departure, we show the Laubach and Williams (2015) estimates of the real and natural rate in the US in Fig. 7.6. Laubach and Williams (2015) show that real and the natural

---

[5] However, they show that the emerging market real interest rate has increased sharply and diverged from the advanced economies and world real interest rate since the beginning of 2015. This may largely reflect cyclical and structural country-specific factors that could result in temporary or persistent equilibrium rates higher than the global level.

7 In Which Direction Is There a Momentum Effect... 135

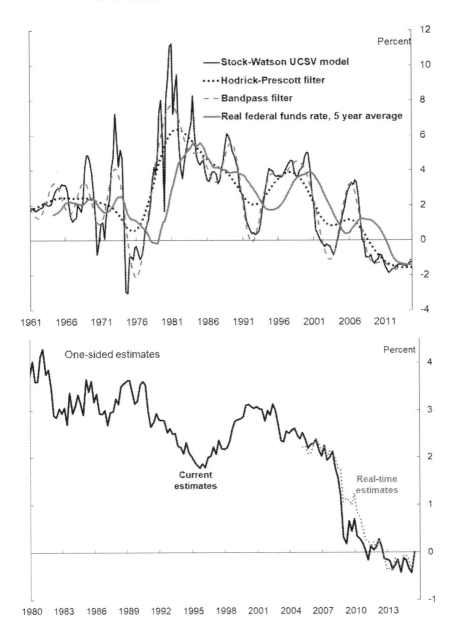

Fig. 7.6 US real interest rates and the natural rate as estimated in Laubach and Williams (2015). (Source: Laubach and Williams 2015)

rates in the US have declined structurally and this trend is likely to persist. If the expectation is that potential output and inflation will remain subdued in the US thus constraining policy decisions, this has implications for US nominal rates and the repo rate-FFR spread. Furthermore, most of the advanced economies are stuck at zero and negative rates. This means that domestic factors, in particular, the evolution of inflationary pressures in South Africa will drive the repo rate-FFR spread. Inflation differentials will play a larger role. Hence, we assess how the real repo rate has evolved relative to US real interest rates trends shown in Fig. 7.6 and make inferences based on selected historical episodes.

We look at two univariate series for the ex-post real repo rate calculated from averages and the Hodrick-Prescott filter. These are shown in Fig. 7.7. The trends show that the ex-post real repo rate has indeed declined post-2008 and averaged 0.63 per cent. The trend seems to be in line with developments in the US, in particular post-2008.

But what do the measures of the ex-post real interest rate, the nominal spread and inflation in relation to the peak and lows in the spread shown in Fig. 7.4 tell policymakers? The results based on mean values in Table 7.4 suggest that domestic factors such as inflation indeed play a meaningful role in the adjustment of the repo rate-FFR spread. For instance, the periods of policy tightening in May 2000 to November 2002; and May 2006 to January 2009 were characterised by different inflationary pressures.

Figure 7.8 shows the trends and the scatterplots depicting the relationship between the repo rate-FFR spread and inflation. The scatterplots in

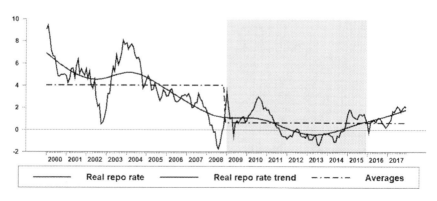

Fig. 7.7 Ex-post real repo rate. (Source: Authors' calculations)

7 In Which Direction Is There a Momentum Effect… 137

Table 7.4 Mean nominal repo rate-FFR spread, real repo rate and inflation

	Headline inflation	Repo rate	Repo rate-FFR spread	Real repo rate
May 2000 to November 2002	7.0	11.6	7.86	4.59
November 2002 May 2006	4.0	8.8	6.59	4.78
May 2006 to January 2009	8.3	10.0	6.29	1.78
January 2009 to December 2017	5.6	6.2	5.93	0.63

Source: Authors' calculations

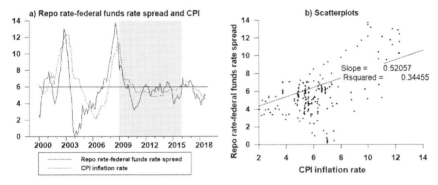

Fig. 7.8 Headline inflation and the repo rate-FFR spread. (Source: South African Reserve Bank, Fred data and authors' calculations)

Fig. 7.8(b) show that inflation is positively associated with repo rate-FFR spread. In addition, inflation explains about 34 per cent of the movements in the spreads. The slope of the relationship suggests that a one per cent rise in inflation raises the spread by about 0.52 per cent. The policy implication is that low and stable inflation has benefits for the level of the repo rate-FFR spread. Hence, the argument for the lowering of the inflation targeting band is further strengthened by these findings.

Has the tightening in the spread been similar during the two tightening periods based on the spread shown in Fig. 7.8? Evidence shows that the two spread tightening cycles differed in their speed, duration and prevailing economic conditions at the time. Hence, we ask, "Did the ability of inflation to explain spread vary over the two policy tightening cycles?" If so, what were the key differences in underlying factors? Alternatively, what other factors apart from inflation drove the differences in the tightening cycles?

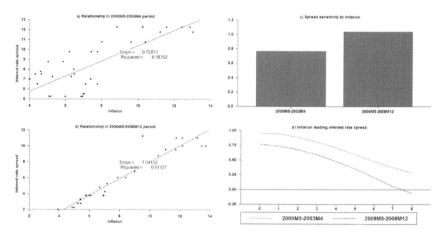

Fig. 7.9 Comparison of responses of repo rate-FFR spread and inflation over two policy tightening episodes. (Source: Authors' calculations)

We compare the effects of the tightening in spreads in the 2000M5 to 2003M2 and 2006M3 to 2008M12 in Fig. 7.9. We find that the spread was highly sensitivity to inflationary developments in 2006M3 to 2008M12 than in 2000M5 to 2003M2. Moreover, the R^2 shows that inflation explained about 91 per cent of the spread in 2006M3 to 2008M12 compared to 58 per cent in 2000M5 to 2003M2. This suggests that the repo rate response to inflation is a bigger driver of the spread than movements in the FFR. In addition, the cross correlations in Fig. 7.9(d) show that the spread is highly correlated with inflation in 2006M3 to 2008M12. This means that the spread is likely to increase when preceded by high inflation in 2006M3 to 2008M12 than in 2000M5 to 2003M2.

But it also happens that the key differences in macroeconomic conditions were glaring. For instance, the 2006 to 2008 policy tightening episode was characterised by high GDP growth, positive output-gap, low sovereign spreads and high credit growth relative to the period spanning 2000M5 to 2003M2. This suggests that it is more than inflation rate that drives spread. Hence, there are lessons from the comparison of previous tightening cycles. Ndou and Gumata (2017) showed that the exchange rate pass-through to inflation is influenced by prevailing macroeconomic conditions and these encompass the role of sovereign spreads, exchange rate volatility, output-gap, and GDP growth and credit growth.

7.5 Conclusion and Policy Implications

Against the background of the start of the Fed policy normalisation, this chapter explored the implications of the various aspects of the relationship between the repo rate and the FFR. We argue that the spread dynamics matter when viewed from deviations from the long-run equilibrium and the starting point (i.e the size of the current spread) of the adjustment. We establish that the long-run repo rate is at 7 per cent. The repo rate-FFR spread has been below the long-run repo rate since 2010.

There are asymmetries in the spread adjustment process. The adjustments tend to persist more when the spread is widening or increasing as the change in spread exceeds the threshold. In contrast, the pace of adjustments is relatively quick when the spread is narrowing from below the threshold. We conclude that this evidence points to higher momentum in the adjustment of the repo rate when the spread is narrowing. Furthermore, the spread adjusts non-linearly depending on the starting point.

Be that as it may, the FFR does not explain all the movements in the repo rate. Furthermore, evidence shows that the actual and lagged FFR changes granger-cause the repo rate. Domestic macroeconomic factors play a much bigger role. Inflationary pressures determine the pace and rate of adjustment in the repo rate, and ultimately the repo rate-FFR spread. For instance, the aggressive repo rate hike during 2006 was associated with a very low starting point of the repo rate-FFR spread. At the same time, inflation increased at a very steep rate for a prolonged period and peaked at the highest level during the inflation targeting regime. Furthermore, in line with the decline in the US real rate, we establish that the ex-post real repo rate has declined post-2008.

A key policy implication we derive from the evidence in this chapter is that, irrespective of whether the future Fed interest rate adjustments are constrained by the zero real and neutral FFR, South African domestic factors will dictate how policymakers adjust the repo rate. Central to the repo rate adjustments is the performance of inflation relative to the target. The policy implication is that low and stable inflation has benefits for the level of the repo rate-FFR spread. Hence, the argument for the lowering of the inflation targeting band is further strengthened by these findings.

References

Ahmad, H., and Hernandez, R.M. 2013. Asymmetric Adjustment between Oil Prices and Exchange Rates: Empirical Evidence from Major Oil Producers and Consumers. *Journal of International Finance Markets, Institutions and Money*, 27(C), 306–17.

Brainard, L. 2015. The US Economic Outlook and Implications for Monetary Policy. Speech at the Centre for Strategic and International Studies, Washington DC, 2 June 2015.

Chan, K.S. 1993. Consistency and Limiting Distribution of the Least Squares Estimator of a Threshold Autoregressive Model. *Annals of Statistics*, 21, 520–33.

Enders, W., and Granger, C.W.J. 1998. Unit-Root Tests and Asymmetric Adjustment with an Example Using the Term Structure of Interest Rates. *Journal of Business & Economic Statistics*, 16, 304–11.

Enders, W., and Siklos, P.L. 2001. Cointegration and Threshold Adjustment. *Journal of Business and Statistics*, 19, 166–76.

Engle, R.F., and Granger, C.W.J. 1987. Cointegration and Error Correction: Representation, Estimation and Testing. *Econometrica*, 55, 251-76.

Fischer, S. 2015. Central Bank Independence. Speech at the 2015 Herbert Stein Memorial Lecture National Economists Club, Washington, DC, 4 November 2015.

Hamilton, J.D., Harris, E.S., Hatzius, J., and West, K.D. 2015. The Equilibrium Real Funds Rate: Past, Present, and Future. Presented at the US Monetary Policy Forum, New York, 27 February 2015.

Johansen, S. 1988. Statistical Analysis of Cointegration Vectors. *Journal of Economic Dynamics and Control*, 12(2–3), 231–54.

Johansen, S. 1996. *Likelihood-Based Inference in Cointegrated Vector Autoregressive Models*. Oxford University Press: New York.

Laubach, T., and Williams, J.C. 2015. *Measuring the Natural Rate of Interest Redux*. Federal Reserve Bank of San Francisco Working Paper 2015–16.

Li, J., and Lee, J. 2013. ADL Tests for Threshold Cointegration. *Journal of Time Series Analysis*, 31, 241–54.

Ndou, E., and Gumata, N. 2017. *Inflation Dynamics in South Africa: The Role of Thresholds, Exchange Rate Pass-Through and Inflation Expectations on Policy Trade-offs*. Palgrave Macmillan. ISBN 978-3-319-46702-3.

Rachel, L., and Smith. T.D. 2015. *Secular Drivers of the Global Real Interest Rate*. Bank of England Staff Working Paper No. 571.

8

How Do Global Real Policy Rates Impact the South African GDP Growth and Labour Market Conditions?

Learning Objectives

- Determine the extent to which changes in the global real policy rate matter for policymakers regarding their effects on the South African economy and labour market conditions.
- Show what would have happened to the South African GDP growth and labour market conditions in the absence of elevated South African policy uncertainty.
- Establish what would have happened to the responses of GDP growth to positive exchange rate volatility shocks in the absence of elevated global real policy rate.
- Explore the extent to which monetary policy volatility shocks reinforce the effects of the exchange rate volatility shocks on economic growth.

8.1 Introduction

This chapter explores the impact of the global real policy rate on the South African economy. This is motivated by the degree to which the global real policy rate captures the global common interest rate and inflation shocks. In turn, these factors have a bearing on the interest rate differential, which is linked to the volatility of the domestic policy rate and the exchange rate.

We fill research gaps by showing the effects of the positive world real interest rate shocks on the South African GDP growth and labour market conditions. Second, we show what would have happened to the South African GDP growth and labour market conditions in the absence of elevated South African policy uncertainty changes. Third, we determine whether monetary policy volatility shocks reinforce the effects of the exchange rate volatility shocks on economic growth. These policy and academic research gaps need to be explored in literature and are covered in this chapter.

8.2 How Do the Effects of the Real Global Policy Rate Relate to Those of Positive Exchange Rate Volatility Shocks?

This section explores the impact of positive shocks to the real global policy rate and compares them to those arising from positive exchange rate volatility shocks on economic growth and labour market conditions. We separate the exchange volatility shocks into overall, permanent and transitory volatilities.[1] The labour market conditions index (LMCI) is sourced from Gumata and Ndou (2017) and the global real interest rate is sourced from King and Low (2014).[2] We estimate a VAR model which includes the exchange rate volatility indicator, repo rate, inflation, GDP growth, R/US$ exchange rate changes, SA-US policy rate differential and the labour market conditions index.[3] The volatility indicators are the R/US$ exchange rate volatility or the monetary policy volatility and they are included separately in the model. The world (global) real interest rate is

---

[1] See Chap. 21 for the graphical presentation of the exchange rate volatility components, and Ndou et al. (2017) for a detailed analysis of the exchange rate volatility components on other aspects of the South African economy.

[2] See King and Low (2014) for the details of how the global real interest rate is constructed.

[3] See Chap. 13 of Gumata and Ndou (2017) for the estimation of the labour market conditions index.

8 How Do Global Real Policy Rates Impact the South African... 143

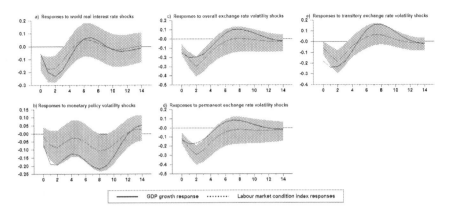

Fig. 8.1 GDP growth and labour market conditions responses. (Note: The grey-shaded bands denote the 16th and 84th percentile confidence bands. Source: Authors' calculations)

included as an exogenous variable in the model. The model is estimated with one lag using 10,000 Monte Carlo draws. The data is sourced from the South African Reserve Bank and the Fred databases. All growth rates are at an annual rate. The sample period spans 2000Q1 to 2011Q4 due to data availability for the global real rate.

Figure 8.1 shows that a positive global real rate shock leads to a contraction in the South African GDP growth. In addition, the labour market conditions index declines for nearly a year, implying tightening in labour market conditions. Positive monetary policy volatility shocks in Fig. 8.1(b) lead to GDP growth contraction and the tightening in the labour market conditions. Positive shocks to all the components of the exchange rate volatility lead to a significant contraction in GDP growth and tightening in labour market conditions in Fig. 8.1(c) to (e).

We extend the analysis to show the role of South African policy uncertainty[4] in transmitting positive global real interest rate shocks into the South African GDP growth by performing a counterfactual VAR analysis which shuts off the policy uncertainty to construct a counterfactual output response. Figure 8.2(a) shows that actual GDP growth declines more than the counterfactual suggests. Thus, elevated South African policy

---

[4] The policy uncertainty index is obtained from Hlatshwayo and Saxegaard (2016).

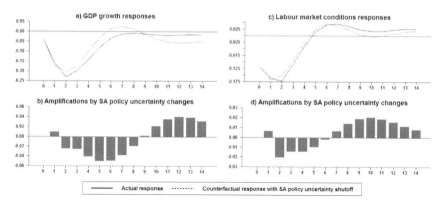

Fig. 8.2 GDP growth and LMCI responses to positive world real interest rate and role of South African policy uncertainty changes. (Source: Authors' calculations)

uncertainty leads to the worsening in GDP growth contraction. Figure 8.2(c) shows that labour market conditions tighten in the presence of heightened South African policy uncertainty than when it is shut off in the model.

8.3 Evidence from the Counterfactual VAR Analysis

This section performs the counterfactual analysis to show the role of the exchange rate and monetary policy volatilities. The VAR model estimated in this section includes the components of the R/US$ exchange rate volatility, annual changes in the R/US$ exchange rate, manufacturing production growth, repo rate, inflation and monetary policy volatility. The components of the exchange rate volatility are included separately in the model. The model is estimated using two lags and 10,000 Monte Carlo draws. Figure 8.3(a) shows that manufacturing output growth declines more in the presence of monetary policy volatility compared to when this variable is shut off in the model. The amplification shown in Fig. 8.3(b) is negative, meaning that elevated monetary policy volatility shocks accentuate the decline in manufacturing output growth following a positive exchange rate volatility shock. Thus, elevated monetary policy volatility

8 How Do Global Real Policy Rates Impact the South African... 145

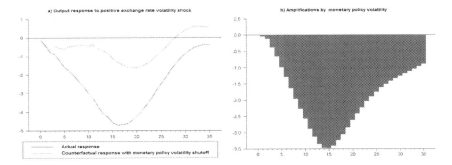

Fig. 8.3 Manufacturing output growth responses to positive exchange rate volatility shocks and the role of monetary policy volatility. (Source: Authors' calculations)

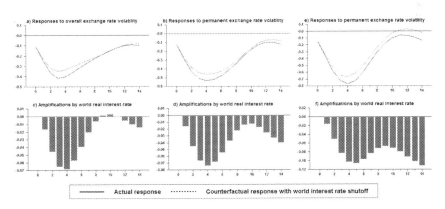

Fig. 8.4 GDP growth responses to positive exchange rate volatility shocks and the role of the world real interest rate. (Source: Authors' calculations)

shocks reinforce the effects of positive exchange rate volatility shocks on economic growth.

To conclude, the analysis examines the role of the world real interest rate in transmitting positive exchange rate shocks to GDP growth. Figure 8.4 shows that positive overall, permanent and transitory exchange rate volatility shocks lower GDP growth. However, the contraction in GDP growth is larger due to elevated world real interest rate than when this variable is shut off in the model. The size of the amplification by the world real interest rate is shown in the second row of Fig. 8.4, and these are negative. This evidence shows that GDP growth is likely to be sub-

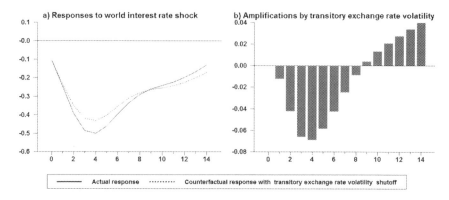

Fig. 8.5 Labour market conditions responses to positive world real interest rate shocks and the role of transitory exchange rate volatility. (Source: Authors' calculations)

dued for a prolonged period due to elevated exchange rate volatilities and rising global real rates.

Furthermore, Fig. 8.5 shows that positive world real interest rate shocks lower labour market conditions more during periods of elevated transitory exchange rate volatilities than when these are shut off in the model. The amplification effects are shown in Fig. 8.5(b).

8.4 Conclusion and Policy Implications

This chapter explored the effects of positive world real interest rate shocks on the South African GDP growth and labour market conditions. Evidence shows that a positive shock to the global real rate leads to contraction in the South African GDP growth. In addition, the labour market conditions decline for nearly a year, implying tightening in labour market conditions. Positive monetary policy volatility shocks also lead to GDP growth contraction and tightening in the labour market conditions. Similarly, positive shocks to all the components of the exchange rate volatility lead to a significant contraction in GDP growth and tightening in the labour market conditions.

What is the role of the South African policy uncertainty in transmitting positive global real interest rate shocks into the South African GDP growth? The results show that elevated South African policy uncertainty leads to the worsening in GDP growth contraction while labour market conditions tighten. Furthermore, we establish that elevated monetary policy volatility shocks reinforce the adverse effects of positive exchange rate volatility shocks on economic growth. Output growth declines more due to heightened monetary policy volatility. This implies that heightened monetary policy volatility shocks accentuate the decline in output growth following a positive exchange rate volatility shock. At the same time, evidence shows that GDP growth is likely to remain subdued and labour market conditions to remain tight for a prolonged period due to elevated exchange rate volatilities and rising global real rates.

References

Gumata, N., and Ndou, E. 2017. *Labour Market and Fiscal Policy Adjustments to Shocks: The Role and Implications for Price and Financial Stability in South Africa*. Palgrave Macmillan. ISBN 978-3-319-66520-7.

Hlatshwayo, S., and Saxegaard, M. 2016. *The Consequences of Policy Uncertainty: Disconnects and Dilutions in the South African Real Effective Exchange Rate-Export Relationship*. IMF Working Paper WP/16/113.

King, M., and Low, D. 2014. *Measuring the World Real Interest Rate*. NBER Working Paper 19887.

Ndou, E., et al. 2017. *Global Economic Uncertainties and Exchange Rate Shocks: Transmission Channels to the South African Economy*. Palgrave Macmillan. ISBN 978-3-319-62280-4.

Rachel, L., and Smith, T.D. 2015. *Secular Drivers of the Global Real Interest Rate*. Bank of England Staff Working Paper No. 571.

9

To What Extent Do Capital Inflows Impact the Response of the South African Economic Growth to Positive SA-US Interest Rate Differential Shocks?

Learning Objectives

- Show the extent to which capital inflows impact the response of the South African economic growth to positive SA-US interest rate differential shocks
- Determine if the role of capital inflow varies depending on whether it is equity versus debt flows

9.1 Introduction

The United States of America (US) the United States Federal Reserve Bank (US Fed) tightened monetary policy between December 2015 and January 2019. This was because economic fundamentals supported the Fed policy stance. These fundamentals include high US economic growth, very low unemployment rate and inflation moving towards the target level. The tightening of US monetary policy based on achieving the two policy objectives is expected to lead to elevated exchange rate volatility in emerging market economies' exchange rates due to the change in the direction of capital flows to the US.

The Mundell-Fleming model predicts, the exchange rate of the rand (E) would depreciate against the US dollar following an unexpected US monetary policy tightening. The currency depreciates from E0 to E1. The depreciation should shift the IS(E0) to IS(E1) in Fig. 9.1. All else being equal, the rand exchange rate depreciation should raise the South African net trade balance to point B relative to what it would be at point A. Three important aspects arise in this setting. First, the monetary policy tightening by the US Fed will lead to capital outflows from South Africa, thus leading to the rand exchange rate depreciation against the US dollar. Second, the US contractionary monetary policy is expected to be transmitted positively and not perversely to South African exports. Hence, the South African income is expected to rise when net exports increase following the rand exchange rate depreciation, *ceteris paribus*. Third, the rise in income should increase the transactions demand for money in South Africa (SA) thereby putting upward pressure on interest rates to rise. The Money demand rises as income rise. The increase in the SA policy rate to curb increased money demand should attract capital inflows, which in turn appreciates the exchange rate. The appreciation erodes the initial trade competitiveness due to the depreciated rand exchange rate. Depending on the magnitudes of the capital inflows and exchange rate appreciation, it is possible as shown in Fig. 9.1, for the IS curve to shift

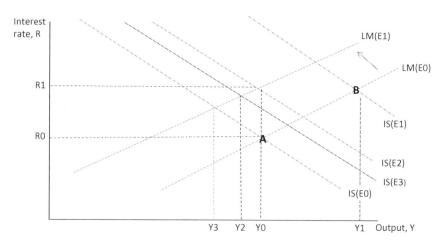

Fig. 9.1 Responses of the domestic economy following a tight US monetary policy shock under the Mundell-Fleming model. (Source: Authors' drawings)

all the way from IS(E1) to either IS(E2) or IS(E3) or IS(E0). The intersection of these curves with the LM(E1) indicates the possibility that output may be lower than original output (Y0) or return to the initial level as the exchange rate appreciation erodes trade competitiveness.

9.2 Why Is the Focus on Capital Flow Dynamics Important for This Study?

1. An increase in capital outflows from SA is expected to lead to the rand exchange rate depreciation following the US monetary policy tightening.
2. An increase in the SA policy rate is expected to attract capital inflows, which in turn appreciate the exchange rate of the rand and erodes the initial trade competitiveness due to the exchange rate depreciation.
3. Empirical evidence reveals that high capital inflows significantly raise economic growth (Ncube et al. 2016). But this study did not necessarily consider the role of the SA-US interest rate differential.

Due to the influence of increased capital inflows, two of the following outcomes can occur: First, output may decline below the initial level of output, when the exchange rate appreciates and erodes trade competitiveness. Second, output may return to its initial level. Given these possible influences of capital inflows on economic growth, it is important to ask the following questions: to what extent do capital inflows impact the response of the South African economic growth due to a positive SA-US interest rate differential (*hereafter referred to as the interest rate differential*) shocks? Does the role of capital inflows vary depending on whether it is equity inflows versus debt inflows?

This study is motivated by three reasons. First, the application of the interest rate parity condition may have been weakened post the recent global financial crisis. This is because the US and SA economic growth rates used to be highly synchronised or highly correlated before the onset of the global financial crisis in 2007. This has weakened recently as the US growth has been rising while the SA output growth has been very volatile and weak; and experienced a recession in between. This business cycle synchronisation pre-global financial crisis in 2007 made the implications of the economic growth repercussion theory pre-2007 global financial crisis to be easier in explaining the rise in the SA-US interest rate differential. According to the repercussion theory, an increase in the US GDP growth is expected to lead to increased demand for goods from other economies, including SA. This leads to synchronised economic growth. This raises the likelihood for actual GDP levels to exceed potential output in both economies, thus resulting in synchronised output-gaps. The synchronised output-gaps are expected to lead to synchronised inflationary pressures, that is, if the Philips curve holds. High inflation is expected to raise the demand for money. The rise in the money demanded would then lead to synchronised interest rate movements, instantaneously or with a lag, in turn curbing both actual and expected inflationary pressures.

The second motivation is based on the policy implications of asynchronised economic growth between high US GDP growth and weak SA GDP growth. Given the SA economic growth challenges, has international macroeconomics evolved with time to offer guidance on how the interest rate parity condition should be applied? This is because empirical studies have revealed that the size of exchange rate pass-through (ERPT) coefficients in South Africa has weakened over time and have become smaller (see for instance, Ndou et al. 2018; Kabundi and Mlachila 2018). The decline in the ERTP occurs during a period which the SA-US interest rate differential is narrowing. Third, there is a need to show and understand the optimal interest rate differential which should indicate what happens to capital inflows before reaching this threshold, at peak and after this threshold point. This is important especially if the US economic fundamentals keep on improving while the SA economic fundamentals weaken or take longer to improve. In addition, it is important for policy-makers to revisit the implications of the Laffer curve, which shows that increases in tax rates will lead to falling revenues after an optimal tax rate.

We therefore take this opportunity to apply the theory on international macroeconomics by linking the relationship between the size of capital inflows and the interest rate differential. As shown in Fig. 9.2, there should be an interest rate differential threshold such that, above this optimal limit, the size of capital inflows should start declining (or there is an increase in capital outflows). On the other extreme, there will be no capital inflows at zero the interest rate differential. As shown in Fig. 9.2, as the interest rate differential rises, capital inflows increase until the optimal interest rate

9 To What Extent Do Capital Inflows Impact The Response... 153

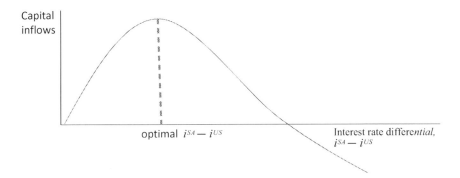

Fig. 9.2 Capital inflows and the interest rate differential. (Source: Authors' calculation)

differential is reached. Beyond the optimal interest rate differential, capital inflows may recede and capital outflows may be triggered. This is because investors may begin to weigh the adverse effects of the policy rate increases on the evolution of other pull factors such as business confidence, consumer confidence, economic growth, investment spending growth and household consumption changes. It is undisputable that high economic growth is an important pull factor in attracting capital inflows.

In addition, it is reasonable to assume that the optimal interest rate differential is much lower in a subdued economic growth environment compared to that during periods of high growth. Hence, the worsening in economic growth may lead to capital outflows despite the prevailing high interest rate differential. This happens if the economic growth has a higher weight in choices of inputs in the compilation of the investor portfolios.[1] Hence, it is important for policymakers to quantify the extent to which the interest rate differential attracts capital inflows compared to other pull factors. If other factors dominate the influence of the interest rate differential, this offers policymakers an opportunity to adopt alternative policy options, which may have less adverse effects on economic growth. Therefore, it is important to seriously consider the role of the interest rate differential in periods of asynchronised economic

---

[1] This is supported by literature which indicates the non-linear effect of policy rate on economic growth rate.

growth between the US and SA. This analysis fills policy research gaps by showing the extent to which capital inflows impact the transmission of positive interest rate differential shocks into SA economic growth. In addition, the analysis shows whether the role of capital inflows on GDP growth depends on whether it is equity inflows versus debt inflows.

9.3 Empirical Results

This analysis determines the role of the capital inflows channel in transmitting the positive interest rate differential shock into SA economic growth. Various counterfactual VAR models are estimated. In all instances, the counterfactual responses shut off the capital inflows channel in transmitting a positive one standard deviation interest rate differential shock into the South African GDP growth. The shock denotes nearly a 100-basis points increase in SA-US the interest rate differential. This analysis uses quarterly (Q) data spanning 1990Q1 to 2007Q2. All models are estimated using two lags and include a dummy for the adoption of the inflation targeting framework in 2000. The SA-US interest rate differential is measured as a difference between the repo rate and the US Federal Funds Rate.

9.3.1 Evidence from Three Variable VAR Model

This section estimates a baseline counterfactual VAR model with three variables. The model includes the SA-US interest rate differential, GDP growth and portfolio inflows as a percentage of GDP. In Fig. 9.3, the counterfactual GDP growth declines more than the actual GDP growth response. This evidence suggests that the portfolio inflow channel does not fully offset the decline in economic growth from an unexpected increase in the SA-US interest rate differential.

We further determine the robustness of the role of the portfolio inflows channel in the preceding model by replacing it with aggregated capital inflows variable. Figure 9.4(a) reveals that the counterfactual GDP growth declines more than the actual suggests. This indicates that increased capital inflows do not fully offset the decline in GDP growth following an unexpected increase in the SA-US interest rate differential.

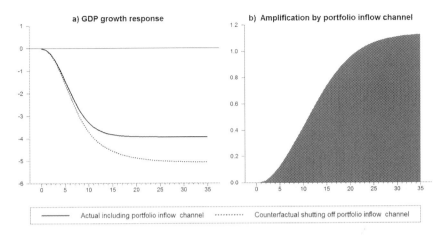

Fig. 9.3 Cumulative GDP growth responses to a positive interest rate differential shock and the role of portfolio inflows shock. (Source: Authors' calculations)

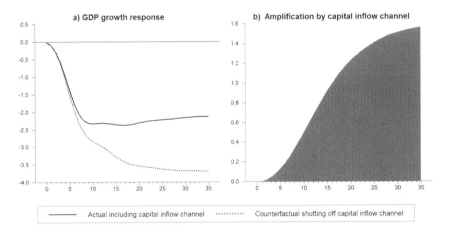

Fig. 9.4 Cumulative GDP growth responses to a positive interest rate differential shock and the role of the capital inflows shock. (Source: Authors' calculations)

9.3.2 Evidence from the Four-Variable Counterfactual VAR Model

The analysis further tests the robustness of the results in the preceding section by estimating an augmented baseline counterfactual VAR model. The augmented model includes the SA-US interest rate differential, GDP

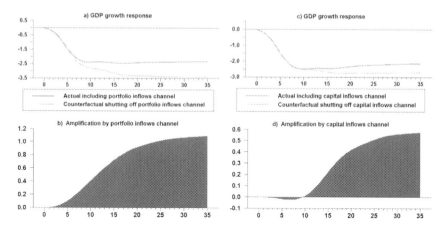

Fig. 9.5 Cumulative GDP growth responses to a positive interest rate differential shock and the role of the capital inflows shock. (Source: Authors' calculations)

growth, consumer price inflation and either portfolio inflows or capital inflows as a percentage of GDP. In Fig. 9.5, the counterfactual GDP growth declines more than the actual GDP growth response. This suggests that both portfolio and aggregated capital inflows channels do not fully offset decline in economic growth from an unexpected increase in the SA-US interest rate differential. The results are robust to using the aggregated capital inflow channel as shown in Fig. 9.5(c) and (d).

9.3.3 Evidence Based on Five Variables in the Model

The analysis further tests the robustness of the previous results by estimating an augmented baseline counterfactual VAR model. The model is augmented with the annual consumer price inflation and the annual growth in the nominal effective exchange rate (NEER). The new counterfactual VAR model includes the SA-US interest rate differential, GDP growth, consumer price inflation, the NEER growth rates and capital inflows as a percentage of GDP. The model is estimated using two lags and 10,000 Monte Carlo draws. The exogenous variables include the annual US GDP growth and annual US consumer price inflation and annual growth in the JSE All shares index. In Fig. 9.6, the counterfactual GDP growth declines more than the actual GDP growth response. This sug-

9 To What Extent Do Capital Inflows Impact The Response...

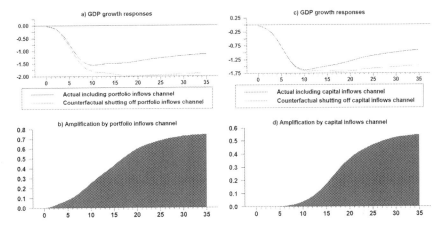

Fig. 9.6 Cumulative GDP growth responses to a positive interest rate differential shock and the role of the capital inflows shock in an expanded model. (Source: Authors' calculations)

gests that the portfolio inflows and aggregated capital inflows channel do not fully offset the decline in economic growth from positive interest rate differential shocks. The results are robust to the inclusion of the annual rand per US dollar exchange rate and the real effective exchange rate.

9.4 Does the Role of Capital Inflows Vary Depending on Whether It Is Equity Inflows Versus Debt Inflows?

We conclude the analysis by determining whether the different components of capital inflows differ in transmitting the positive interest differential shocks. The capital inflows channel is separated into debt inflows and equity inflows. These inflows are expressed as a percentage of GDP. The analysis estimates a baseline counterfactual VAR model with three variables. The model includes the interest rate differential, GDP growth and either debt inflows or equity inflows as a percentage of GDP. The model is estimated using two lags and 10,000 Monte Carlo draws. The capital inflows channel is shut off to calculate the counterfactual GDP growth response. In Fig. 9.7, the counterfactual GDP growth declines more than

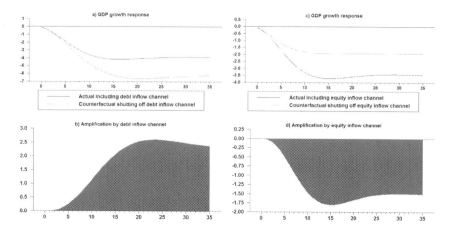

Fig. 9.7 Cumulative GDP growth responses to a positive interest rate differential shock and the amplification by the debt and equity inflows channels. (Source: Authors' calculations)

the actual GDP growth response when considering the debt inflow channel. This evidence suggests that the debt inflow channel mitigates the decline in economic growth from the increase in the interest rate differential. In contrast, the actual GDP growth responses decline more than the counterfactual when including the role of the equity inflows channel. This suggests that an equity inflows shock exacerbates the decline in GDP growth following positive SA-US interest rate differential shocks.

9.5 Conclusion and Policy Implications

To what extent do capital inflows impact the response of the South African economic growth to positive SA-US interest rate differential shocks? Evidence reveals that an unexpected increase in the interest rate differential lowers SA economic growth. The actual decline in economic growth is lower than what the counterfactual suggests. This implies that the increase in capital inflows following an unexpected increase in the SA-US interest rate differential does not fully prevent the decline in economic growth. This implies that capital inflows due to an unexpected increase in the interest rate differential are not large enough to raise economic growth to fully neutralise the adverse effects of a tight monetary policy stance. An effective outcome is achieved when the adverse effects of the interest rate differential shocks on GDP growth are fully offset by the beneficial effects of capital inflows on in stimulating economic growth. The policy implications of these findings is that, it is important to quantify the extent to which the interest rate differential compares to other pull factors in attracting capital inflows. If other factors dominate the influence of the interest rate differential, this offers policymakers the opportunity to adopt alternative policy options, which may have less adverse effects on economic growth. Second, there is a need to understand the optimal interest rate differential threshold which indicates what happens to capital inflows before reaching this limit, at peak and after this threshold point. This also requires the determination of whether the interest rate differential threshold differs between the high economic growth scenarios compared to very low growth or recessionary environment. The non-consideration of these threshold effects weakens the importance attached to the interest rate differential, especially during periods of asynchronous economic growth.

References

Kabundi, A., and Mlachila, M. 2018. *Monetary Policy Credibility and Exchange Rate Pass Through in South Africa*. Working Paper Number 4, WP/18/04.

Ncube, M., Ndou, E., and Gumata, N. 2016. *Global Growth and Financial Spill Overs and the South African Macro-economy*. Palgrave Macmillan. ISBN 978-1-137-51296-3

Ndou, E., Gumata, N., and Tshuma, M.M. 2018. *Exchange Rate Pass Through, Second Round Effects and Inflation Process, Evidence from South Africa*. Palgrave Macmillan. ISBN 978-3-030-13931-5.

Part III

Capital Flow Surges, Sudden Stops and Elevated Portfolio Inflows Volatility Effects

10

Economic Costs of Capital Flow Episodes in South Africa

Learning Objectives

- Determine whether the heightened global risk aversion shock matters more than the capital flow episodes shocks such as capital flow surges and capital flow sudden stops in driving economic activity in South Africa.
- Establish whether there are differential effects due to heightened global risk, capital flow sudden stop and capital flow surges episodes shocks on GDP growth.
- Show how the global risk aversion shock channel is linked to subdued GDP growth

10.1 Introduction

The VIX[1] index is currently at low levels by post-2008 standards as shown in Fig. 10.1. It is true that the unexpected increase in VIX is associated with the rand per US dollar (R/US$) exchange rate depreciation. At the

---

[1] VIX Index is the Chicago Board Options Exchange (CBOE) Volatility Index, see http://financial-dictionary.thefreedictionary.com/VIX for further details.

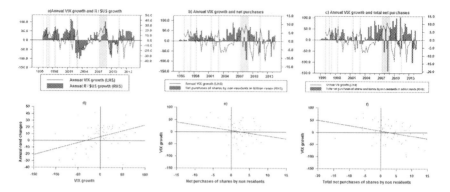

Fig. 10.1 VIX, net purchases by non-residents and the R/US$ changes. (Note: The shaded area denotes periods when VIX was equal to 31 per cent, which is equal to the size of VIX shock we use in the impulse response analysis)

same time, when VIX declines and is accompanied by an increase in net purchases by non-residents in the domestic market, the (R/US$) exchange rate appreciates in Fig. 10.1.

However, the nexus between global risk and capital flows goes beyond the effects on the R/US$ exchange rate. Forbes and Warnock (2011) show that capital flow volatility can amplify economic cycles as well as increase the financial system's vulnerability. Furthermore, Ndou et al. (2017) show that elevated policy uncertainty prevents GDP growth from rising more due to a capital flows surges shock and accentuates the decline due to the capital flow sudden stop shocks. Elevated domestic economic policy uncertainty shock raises the likelihood of capital flow sudden stop episodes and reduces the chances of capital flow surges episodes following an unexpected reduction in VIX.

So, does a global risk aversion shock matter more than the capital flow episode shocks in driving economic activity in South Africa? Is the global risk aversion shock channel linked to subdued GDP growth? The IMF WEO 2016 analysis on the drivers of capital flows to emerging market economies (EMEs) concludes that a protracted growth slowdown in EMEs and narrowed growth differentials relative to advanced economies implies that weaker gross capital inflows may not be reversed anytime soon. As a result, the diminished EME growth prospects relative to

10 Economic Costs of Capital Flow Episodes in South Africa

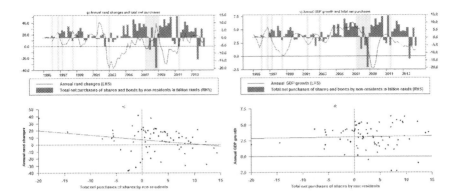

Fig. 10.2 Selected indicators of economic activity and net purchases by non-residents. (Note: The shaded area denotes the annual periods when VIX was equal to 31 per cent, which is equal to the size of VIX shock we use in the impulse response analysis. Source: South African Reserve Bank, Fred data and authors' calculations)

advanced economies counterbalance the effect of decreasing risk aversion, which would predict an increase in capital inflows to emerging market economies during this period. In addition, the real interest rate differential and other country characteristics do not outweigh the role of the growth differential in explaining capital flows.

Figure 10.2 shows that increased non-resident activity in the domestic markets is positively correlated with increased GDP growth indicative of the economic benefits of the capital flow surge episodes. If that is the case, how significant are the economic costs exerted by VIX shock relative to the capital flow surges and capital flow sudden stops shocks? We use the classification of capital flows episodes identified in Forbes and Warnock (2011).[2] In particular, we distinguish between the capital flow surges and capital flow sudden stops[3] on economic activity.

---

[2] These episodes differ to those identified in the IMF WEO April 2016 report. In addition, earlier evidence reported in other research notes indicates that US policy normalisation shock leads to a slowdown in activity in the stock and bond markets, including turnover activity, capital raised and other market activity.

[3] The analysis of sudden stops does not by any means suggest that the increased role of foreign currency reserves as a buffer is ignored.

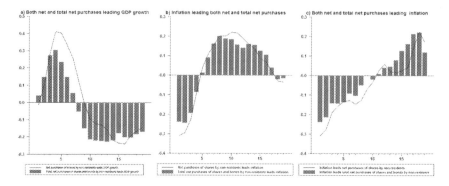

Fig. 10.3 Cross correlations. (Source: Authors' calculations)

Forbes and Warnock (2011) distinguish between capital flow waves according to (i) *sudden stops* that occur when foreign capital inflows suddenly slow or stop, (ii) *surges* which happen when foreign capital inflows increase rapidly, (iii) *retrenchment* which occurs when domestic investors liquidate their foreign investments and (iv) *capital flight* which occurs when domestic investors send large amounts of capital abroad. This classification also means that domestic investors are not cut off from global capital markets. Forbes and Warnock (2011) indicate that domestic investors have ample access to these markets and utilise them by moving their domestic funds abroad.[4]

What can possibly trigger a capital flight episode? This might happen if domestic investors with superior information foresee a negative shock to the local market or they see investment opportunities abroad. In anticipation of a negative shock to the local market, economic agents shift their money to global markets. According to Rothenberg and Warnock (2011), this leads to a net capital inflow decline. But the difference is that this decline is not prompted by foreign investors. We believe that these are relevant scenarios to assess in light of the recent and ongoing heightened domestic political and policy uncertainty.

As a precursor to the empirical analysis, Fig. 10.3 shows that non-resident activity matters for GDP growth and inflation dynamics. At the same time,

---

[4] Forbes and Warnock (2011) show that the reference definition of the data used in answering this question matters. There is a difference between using gross capital flows versus net capital flows in defining capital flow episodes.

price stability matters, as shown in Fig. 10.3 (c), as high inflation precedes a decline in net and total net purchases by non-residents.

So, if global risk appetite matters and drives capital flow dynamics, what are the effects of global risk aversion shocks on capital flows, the impact on episodes of capital flow surges, sudden stops and capital retrenchments?[5] Such capital flow episodes impose difficulties to policymakers because they render capital control policies redundant.

10.2 What Do Cross Correlations Suggest the Bilateral Relationships Between VIX and Capital Flow Episodes Is?

This section assesses the extent to which the capital flow episodes can be used to test some theoretical and econometric predictions. We estimate a VAR model with GDP growth, non-resident purchases of South African assets, VIX, trade balance components (imports and exports), inflation, JSE all-shares index, short-term interest rate and bond yields. We use the Choleski VAR decomposition and order each capital flows episode dummy before the South African macroeconomic variables. This suggests that the capital flow episode is independent of the South African variables. We use VIX as a proxy for global financial turmoil, economic risk and uncertainty. The VAR is estimated using two lags and 10,000 Monte Carlo draws.

To assess the extent to which these capital flow episodes can be used to test some theoretical and econometric predictions, we generate dummy variables that capture these episodes separately. This enables us to perform thorough econometric analysis of the potential effects of each event. We set the dummy variables equal to one for the period identified by Forbes and Warnock (2011) and zero otherwise. This is done for each capital flow wave episode namely (i) a capital flow sudden stop episode, (ii) capital flow surges episodes, (iii) capital flight episodes and (iv) capital retrenchment episodes. The capital flow dummies are used separately in the modelling.

---

[5] Capital retrenchments differentiate between changes in foreign and domestic investor behaviour. Domestic investor flows can become increasingly important as the change in net flows can no longer be driven by foreigner investors alone.

The sample for the estimations spans the period 1995Q1 to 2014Q3. We also construct two dummy variables for the (i) inflation targeting regime which is equal one for period beginning 2000Q1 up to the end of the sample, and zero otherwise and (ii) the recession which is equal to one for 2009Q1–2009Q3 and zero otherwise. The data is sourced from the South African Reserve Bank, IMF and Fred databases. All growth rates are at annual rate. The grey-shaded areas and the dotted lines around the impulse responses denote the confidence bands.

Figure 10.4 shows that capital flow sudden stops are negatively related to credit growth on impact, which suggests that credit growth slows down for prolonged periods when preceded by a capital flow sudden stop. On the other hand, VIX growth is negatively related to credit growth with a lag of four quarters. This suggests that elevated VIX and capital flow sudden stops episodes are adversely related to credit growth. In contrast credit growth is positively related to capital flow surges episodes.

Does this association occur on GDP growth? Yes, the cross correlations show that there is a positive (negative) association between capital flows surges episodes (capital flow sudden stops) and GDP growth, although with varying durations. Figure 10.5 shows the correlations between VIX, capital flow sudden stops, capital flow surges episodes and the trade balance components. We establish a negative (positive) association between imports and exports growth when they are preceded by VIX and capital flow sudden stops episodes (capital flow surges episodes) shock.

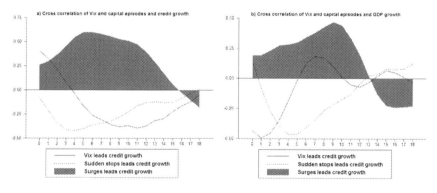

Fig. 10.4 Bilateral cross correlations. (Source: Authors' calculations)

10 Economic Costs of Capital Flow Episodes in South Africa

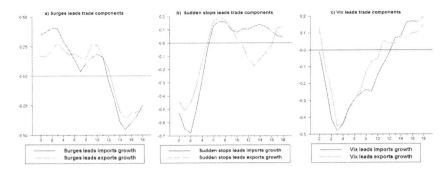

Fig. 10.5 Cross correlations between trade components and capital flow episodes. (Source: Authors' calculations)

10.3 Are There Any Economic Costs and Benefits of Capital Flow Wave Categories?

To answer this question, we estimate various VAR models to identify the various channels through which the capital flow channels are transmitted into the South African economy.

10.3.1 Do Global Risk Shocks Differ from Capital Flow Surges and Capital Flow Sudden Stops Shocks?

Are there real effects of capital flow sudden stops on the South African economy and how do these differ from those of capital flow surges episodes? Yes, evidence in Fig. 10.6 suggests that there are real effects. The impulse responses of GDP growth to heightened VIX and capital flow sudden stop shocks lower GDP growth significantly for nearly ten quarters while the capital flow surges shock leads to an increase in Fig. 10.6(a). Thus, capital flow surges shocks exert different effects on GDP growth compared to the VIX shocks. But Fig. 10.6(b) shows that although capital flow sudden stops and heightened VIX shocks depress output growth in the first three quarters, economic growth recovers quickly after a capital flow sudden stops shock compared to the VIX shock.

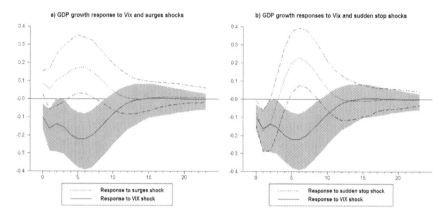

Fig. 10.6 Comparisons of GDP responses to VIX, capital flow sudden stops and capital flow surges shocks. (Source: Authors' calculations)

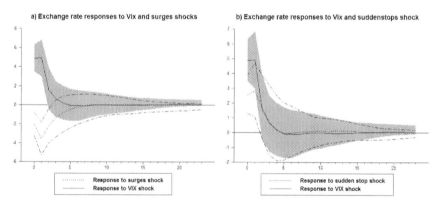

Fig. 10.7 Comparison of the exchange rate responses. (Source: Authors' calculations)

10.3.2 The Exchange Rate Channel

The capital flow surges shock leads to the R/US$ exchange rate appreciation with a peak of nearly 4 percentage points in the first quarter in Fig. 10.7. In contrast, heightened VIX and capital flow sudden stops shocks, respectively, lead to the R/US$ exchange rate depreciation on impact by about 5 percentage points within two quarters. It is evident that the capital flow surges episode shock effects differ from those of

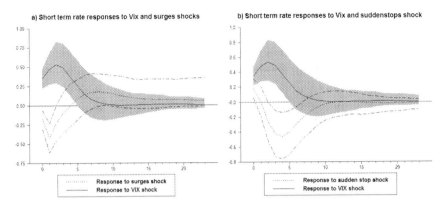

Fig. 10.8 Short-term interest rates responses. (Source: Authors' calculations)

capital flow sudden stops and heightened VIX despite the R/US$ exchange rate effects lasting only two quarters.

10.3.3 The Short-term Interest Rate Channel

This section assesses the responsiveness of the funding rates channel to capital flow surges episode shock. Evidence in Fig. 10.8 shows that a capital flow surges shock depresses money market rates for two quarters and the peak decline of 0.4 percentage points occurs in first quarter. Surprisingly, apart from the initial increase in short-term rates, a capital flow sudden stop shock lowers short-terms rates for long durations. In contrast, a heightened VIX shock increases short-term rates significantly for six quarters. We conclude that the heightened VIX shock leads to different effects compared to those of capital flow surges shock effects.

10.3.4 The Bond Yields Channel

The analysis is extended to bond yields in Fig. 10.9. Evidence shows that capital flow surges and capital flow sudden stops depress bond yields in contrast to heightened VIX shocks which lead to an increase in bond yields.[6]

---

[6] It is surprising why bond yields decline to a sudden stop shock.

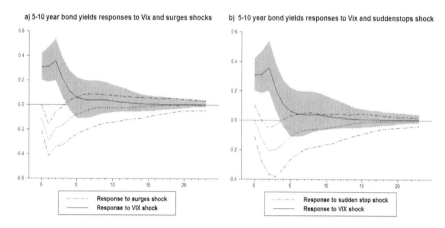

Fig. 10.9 Bond yield responses. (Source: Authors' calculations)

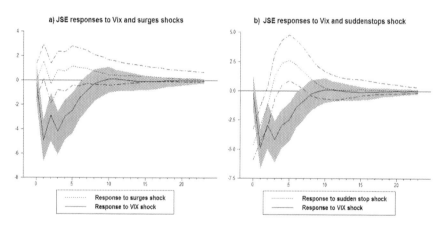

Fig. 10.10 Stock market responses. (Source: Authors' calculations)

10.3.5 The Equity Market Channel

How does the stock market (JSE all-shares index) respond to the capital flow surges, capital flow sudden stops and heightened VIX shocks? Figure 10.10 shows that a heightened VIX shock decreases the stock market growth by 4.5 percentage points in the second quarter and the decline lasts seven quarters.

10 Economic Costs of Capital Flow Episodes in South Africa

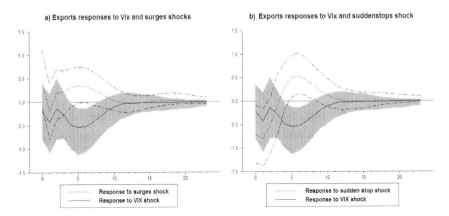

Fig. 10.11 Exports growth responses. (Source: Authors' calculations)

In addition, a capital flow sudden stop shock leads to a pronounced stock market growth contraction on impact. The stock market remains depressed for two quarters and recovers after three and seven quarters. In contrast, a capital inflow surges episode shock raises the stock market growth.

10.3.6 The Trade Balance Channel

Does the trade balance channel matter? Figure 10.11 shows that exports growth declines significantly for a long period due to a heightened VIX shock. In contrast, the capital flows surges episodes tend to increase exports growth. However, a capital flow sudden stop shock depresses exports growth for less than two quarters, which is later followed by a transitory improvement. This suggests that global risk aversion is a significant driver of domestic exports growth.

How does the imports growth channel react? The imports growth increases significantly for seven quarters due to the capital flow surges shock in Fig. 10.12. In contrast, imports growth declines due to heightened VIX and capital flow sudden stop shocks. This suggests that the South African trade, if it is mostly driven by imported intermediate goods, then risk aversion shocks may lead to a significant slowdown in economic activity.

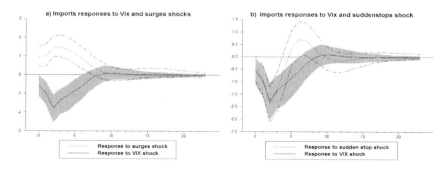

Fig. 10.12 Import growth responses. (Source: Authors' calculations)

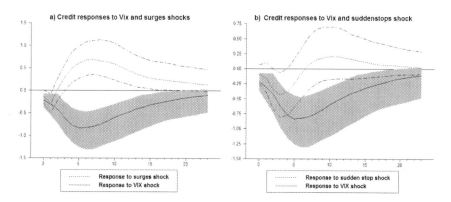

Fig. 10.13 Credit growth responses. (Source: Authors' calculations)

10.3.7 The Credit Channel

Does credit extension matter? Yes, it does. Figure 10.13 shows that a capital flow surges shock increases credit growth significantly between three and 16 quarters. On the other hand, a capital flow sudden stops shock depresses credit growth. Similarly, a heightened VIX shock leads to a significantly prolonged credit contraction for nearly 20 quarters. These results point to fact that credit growth contraction may lead to a slowdown in GDP growth.

10.4 Conclusion and Policy Implications

This chapter explored the significance of the economic costs exerted by VIX shock relative to capital flow surges and capital flow sudden stops shocks. We find that sudden stops as defined in Forbes and Warnock (2011) are associated with a significant slowdown in economic growth, stock market activity and the currency depreciation. In contrast, capital flow surges episode shocks raise economic growth, appreciate the exchange rate, lower inflation and raise the stock market activity. Global risk aversion (VIX) significantly raises the likelihood of capital flow sudden stops episodes and reduces the likelihood of capital flow surges episodes, and this has implications for how policymakers should deal with these capital flow episodes. In addition, VIX shocks lead to high GDP growth slowdown over a period longer than those due to capital flow sudden stops. This suggests that capital controls cannot completely insulate an economy against significantly large waves of capital flows. The implication is that policymakers should prioritise strengthening the country's ability to withstand their capital flow volatility, through policy intervention such as the accumulation of foreign currency reserves.

We conclude that the direction of all impulse responses is as expected and consistent with economic predictions. However, in most cases, we find that capital flow surges episode effects tend to last longer than those induced by capital flow sudden stops episodes. Capital flow sudden stops and capital flow volatility can have substantial economic costs, and this has implications for policymaking. The results presented in this chapter suggest that there is a need for a clear identification of capital flow episodes and their drivers. This is vital information in the design of policies to reduce the vulnerabilities and mitigating negative outcomes.

References

Forbes, K.J., and Warnock, F.E. 2011. *Capital Flow Waves: Surges, Stops, Flight, and Retrenchment*. NBER Working Paper No. 17351, August 2011.

Forbes, K.J., and Warnock, F.E. 2016. *Capital Flow Waves: Surges, Stops, Flight, and Retrenchment*. NBER Working Paper No. 17351.

IMF World Economic Outlook. 2016 October. Global Trade: What's Behind the Slowdown?

Ndou, E., Gumata, N., and Ncube, M. 2017. *Global Economic Uncertainties and Exchange Rate Shocks: Transmission Channels to the South African Economy*. Palgrave Macmillan. ISBN 978-3-319-62280-4.

Rothenberg, D.A., and Warnock, F.E. 2011. Sudden Flight and True Sudden Stops. *Review of International Economics*, 19, 509–24.

Rothenberg, D.A., and Francis, E., and Warnock, F.E. 2006. *Sudden Flight and True Sudden Stops*. NBER Working Paper No. 12726.

11

Capital Flow Surges, Sudden Stops and Elevated Portfolio Inflow Volatility Shocks: What is the Nature of Their Interaction with GDP Growth and Credit?

Learning Objectives

- Explore whether a net portfolio flow volatility shock can amplify economic cycles and increase the vulnerability of the financial system.
- Show the impact of elevated net portfolio flow volatility, capital flow surges and capital flow sudden stops shocks on credit growth.
- Show the effects of global risk on episodes of capital flow surges, capital flow sudden stops and capital flight and retrenchments
- Establish the spill-over effects into the R/US$ exchange rate, GDP growth and credit growth.

11.1 Introduction

The United States Federal Reserve Bank (US Fed) policy normalisation and its divergence with those of other advanced central banks is expected to alter the direction of capital flows to emerging market economies (EMEs).

This analysis is motivated by the potential adverse effects of a drastic change in the direction and composition of capital flows which should matter for the South African economy, given the current low growth environment, elevated sovereign risk and global risk aversion.

The analysis in this chapter examines the following question: do net portfolio flow volatility shocks impact credit growth dynamics? Forbes and Warnock (2011) distinguish between capital flow waves according to (i) sudden stops that occur when foreign capital inflows suddenly slow or stop, (ii) surges which happen when foreign capital inflows increase rapidly, (iii) retrenchment which occurs when domestic investors liquidate their foreign investments and (iv) capital flight which occurs when domestic investors send large amounts of capital abroad. This classification also means that domestic investors are not cut off from global capital markets. Using the classification of capital flows episodes identified in Forbes and Warnock (2011) we ask, "Do capital flow surges, sudden stops and elevated net portfolio flow volatility shocks impact credit dynamics?" In addition, if global risk appetite matters and drives capital flow dynamics, what are the effects of global risk on episodes of capital flow surges, sudden stops and capital flight and retrenchments? Do these spill-over to the R/US$ exchange rate, GDP growth and credit dynamics?

This chapter fills research policy gaps by assessing whether net portfolio flow volatility shocks can amplify economic cycles and increase the vulnerability of the financial system.[1] The chapter fills policy gaps by showing the impact of elevated net portfolio flow volatility, capital flow surges and capital flow sudden stops shocks on credit growth.

11.2 The Bilateral Relationships Between Net Portfolio Volatility, GDP Growth and Credit Growth

Much empirical evidence in literature has shown that GDP growth is a big driver of credit dynamics. This evidence is confirmed in Fig. 11.1 using scatterplots and cross correlations. The relationship is positive and bigger when GDP growth determines credit growth in Fig. 11.1(a) and

---

[1] Despite increasing financial vulnerability, economies benefit from capital inflows driven by domestic investors as they liquidate their foreign investments (Forbes and Warnock 2011).

11 Capital Flow Surges, Sudden Stops and Elevated Portfolio... 179

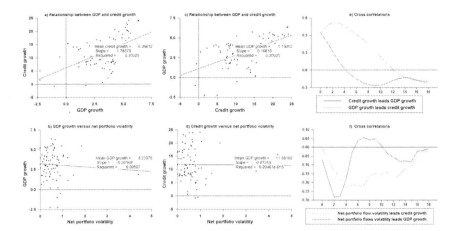

Fig. 11.1 Relationship between GDP growth, credit growth and net capital flows. (Source: Authors' calculations)

not the reverse in (b). In addition, the cross correlations in Fig. 11.1(c) show that the strength of the relationship is higher when GDP growth leads credit growth. Thus, robust and sustainable credit growth requires robust GDP growth.

Most studies establish a relationship between domestic credit growth and capital flows. For instance, Lane and McQuade (2013) find that domestic credit growth in European countries is strongly related to net debt inflows but not to net equity inflows.[2] They conclude that this connection between international debt flows and domestic credit growth suggests a direct role through the international funding activities of domestic banks. In addition, international debt flows can indirectly affect domestic macroeconomic and financial variables via the supply and demand for domestic credit growth. Similarly, Mendoza and Terrones (2012) also find that credit booms are classically associated with net capital inflows. On the other hand, Bruno and Shin (2013a, b) link global liquidity and the leverage cycle of global banks to credit growth via aggregate capital flows.

---

[2] Calderon and Kubota (2012) find that surges in gross debt inflows are a good predictor of subsequent credit booms.

What is the nature of the relationship between net portfolio volatility,[3] GDP growth and credit growth in South Africa? Figure 11.1(b) and (d) shows that net portfolio inflows volatility is negatively related to GDP growth and credit growth, but the effects differ. This shows that GDP growth as a key driver of credit growth is most impacted by net portfolio inflows volatility shock.

Furthermore, literature suggests that financial flows can result in excessive credit growth as they increase the ability of domestic banks to fund and extend loans (credit). The implication is that with an open financial system, a rise in cross-border financial flows can influence domestic credit growth through multiple channels. After all, the availability of international financial flows affects the funding and financial conditions faced by domestic banks. It also alters the menu of financial assets available to the banking sector.[4] What channels might be at play to facilitate this effect?

First, various studies establish a diverging trend between domestic deposits and credit growth in banking systems. This is because banks raise funds by borrowing short-term in the international interbank market and issue bonds. In addition, domestically owned banks linked to foreign affiliates use intra-bank funding. So, this is the cross-border bank-related financial flow channel that banks use to fund growth in domestic loans. Hence, most studies establish a systematic relationship between capital flows and domestic credit growth.[5]

Hoggarth et al. (2010) find that as banks increasingly resorted to wholesale cross-border funding, the tight correlation between bank deposits and credit growth began to break down. Was this the case at any point in South Africa? We show the breakdown of the South African bank liabilities and assets for the period 2000 to 2014 in Fig. 11.2.

It is evident that deposits continued to fund credit growth as both items constituted roughly 60 per cent of the liabilities and assets. Furthermore, rand deposits accounted for more than 80 per cent of total liabilities to the public. Further disaggregation of deposits in Fig. 11.3

---

[3] Net portfolio volatility is calculated as in Benigno et al. (2015).
[4] This applies to the non-banking sector as well.
[5] In relation to equity funding, foreign portfolio investors and foreign direct investors are important sources of shareholder capital for domestic banks.

11 Capital Flow Surges, Sudden Stops and Elevated Portfolio...

Fig. 11.2 South African bank assets and liabilities: 2000 to 2014. (Data for 2014 ends in December. Source: South African Reserve Bank and authors' calculations)

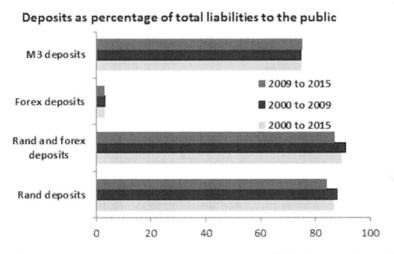

Fig. 11.3 South African bank deposits as per cent of liabilities to the public. (Source: South African Reserve Bank and authors' calculations)

shows that rand and foreign currency denominated deposits as a percentage of total liabilities to the public remained largely unchanged at around 90 per cent. Within the rand and foreign currency denominated deposits, foreign currency deposits were 3 per cent and rand deposits were 87 per cent of total liabilities to the public. M3 deposits which constitute M3 money supply have remained around 75 per cent of liabilities to the public.

What about interbank lending? Most studies document that an increase in domestic credit was facilitated by a large increase in cross-border interbank lending and the emergence of financial derivatives. These shifts in bank funding patterns associated with growth in cross-border bank-related financial flows suggest that a systematic relation might exist between international capital flows and domestic credit growth. Figure 11.2 shows that interbank deposits decreased from 10 per cent during 2000–2008 to 6 per cent 2009–2014 of banks' total liabilities. But further disaggregation of interbank deposits in Fig. 11.4 shows that interbank deposits as a percentage of foreign currency and rand-denominated deposits declined from 8 per cent to 3 per cent over the same period. Within interbank deposits, other interbank deposits (which include intra-bank deposits excluding negotiable certificates of deposits (NCD's) or promissory notes (PN's)) contribute 70 per cent of total interbank deposits and NCDs account for 30 per cent. Overall, the trends in the banks' balance sheets do not suggest much interaction or determination of their funding and credit growth by capital flows or foreign currency funding.

Nonetheless, Acharya and Schnabl (2009) also show that the overall current account balance is not necessarily a reliable indicator of the direc-

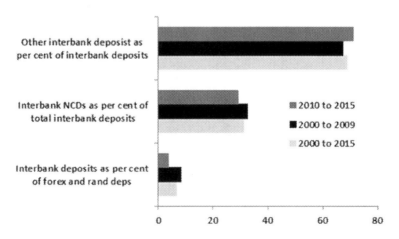

Fig. 11.4 South African bank interbank deposits as a percentage of total deposits. (Source: South African Reserve Bank and authors' calculations)

tion of bank-related capital flows in relation to the funding of banks. The sources of foreign funding for the banking system seem to give better information to policymakers. Lane and McQuade (2013) also confirm that the current account balance can be a misleading indicator in understanding the relationship between capital flows and domestic credit growth.

11.3 Evidence from a Bivariate VAR Model

This section estimates various VAR models which include a capital flow episode dummy based on the dates identified by Forbes and Warnock (2011), global investor risk perceptions based on the VIX index and the South African macroeconomic variables such as GDP growth and credit growth; and various categories of capital flows. The estimated VAR models have two lags including a constant and two dummy variables for the (i) inflation targeting which is equal one for period beginning 2000 up to the end of the sample and zero otherwise; and (ii) the recession which is equal to one for the period 2009Q1–Q3 and zero otherwise.[6] The sample size spans 1995Q1 to 2014Q1. The data is sourced from the South African Reserve Bank and Fred databases. All growth rates are at an annual rate. These impulse responses are accumulated responses to a one standard deviation shock in the capital flows episode shock. The model uses 10,000 Monte Carlo draws.

We examine three aspects which include (i) how the capital flow episode shocks impact credit growth and GDP growth, (ii) the historical contributions and (iii) the proportions of fluctuations in credit growth and GDP growth induced by these capital flow episode shocks. Capital flow dynamics are intertwined with changes in global investor perceptions. To assess for the impact of changes in global risk, we analyse the impact of positive VIX shocks on GDP growth and credit growth, capital flow sudden stops and capital flow surges episodes.

---

[6] We use the Choleski decomposition and order each capital flows episode dummy before the South African macroeconomic variables. This ordering of the variables indicates that the capital flow episode is independent of the South African variables.

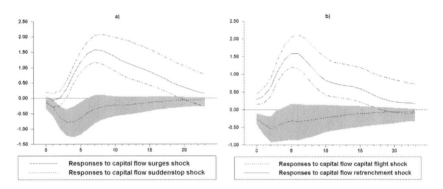

Fig. 11.5 Responses of credit growth. (Note: The grey-shaded areas denote the 16th and 84th percentile error bands. Source: Authors' calculations)

11.3.1 Evidence from the Bivariate VAR Impulse Responses

Figure 11.5(a) shows that credit growth responses due to capital flow surges and capital flow sudden stops episode shocks vary. We find that the capital flow surges shock increase credit growth with a peak effect of 1.5 per cent around 10 quarters. In contrast, a capital flow sudden stop shock leads to a contraction in credit growth which lasts nearly 6 quarters.

Figure 11.5(b) shows that credit growth responds differently to capital flow retrenchment shocks and capital flight shock. A capital flow retrenchment shock leads to a decline in credit growth, whilst a capital flight shock leads to an increase.

11.3.2 Evidence from the Historical Decompositions

This section applies a historical decomposition approach to determine which capital flow shock dominated the evolution of credit growth. Figure 11.6 shows that prior to 2004Q1 and after 2009Q3 the capital flow surges shocks were a drag on credit growth compared to all the other shocks. But between 2004Q2 and 2009Q1 the capital flow surges shock contributed positively to credit growth compared to other capital flow episodes shocks. Of particular interest is the different role played by

11 Capital Flow Surges, Sudden Stops and Elevated Portfolio...

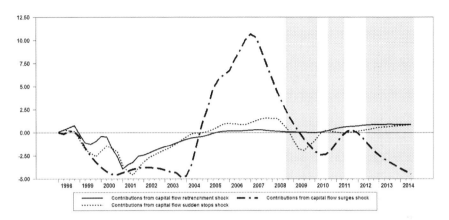

Fig. 11.6 Contributions of different capital flow categories' shocks to credit growth over time. (Source: Authors' calculations)

the capital flow surges episodes pre and post the global financial crisis. It is evident that the contribution of various capital flow episodes has been very muted and even negative in some instances post-2008. This is despite the surge in global liquidity associated with unconventional monetary policy interventions by various central banks.

This evidence concurs with earlier findings of an inverse transmission of global liquidity shocks on some domestic macroeconomic variables post-2008Q4.[7] It is evident that the sensitivity of credit growth to capital flow surges episodes changed post-2008, in line with GDP growth and exports growth.

11.3.3 Evidence from the Variance Decompositions of the Bivariate VAR Model

Do various capital flow shock episodes induce similar movements in credit growth? Figure 11.7 shows a comparison of the fluctuations in credit growth induced by various capital flow episode shocks. The capital flight shock episodes induce more movements in credit growth than other shocks.

---

[7] Gumata and Ndou (2017).

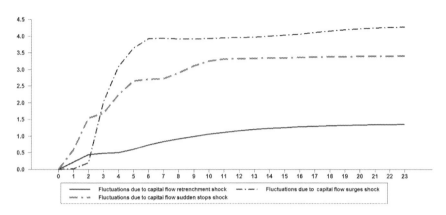

Fig. 11.7 Fluctuations in credit growth explained by different capital flow shocks. (Source: Authors' calculations)

But of great interest to policymaking are the effects of capital flow surges episodes and capital flow sudden stops. Evidence shows that the capital flow surges episodes shocks explain a relatively large proportion of fluctuations in credit growth more than capital flow sudden stops shocks. This could possibly be due to the fact that a large portion of domestic bank intermediated credit is domestically funded. The implication is that even in periods of severe capital outflow episodes, there might be disruptions in domestic bank lending activity, but they might not result in a complete freeze or dysfunction in banking activity.

11.4 Do Global Risk Aversion Shocks Impact Capital Flow Surges, Sudden Stops Episodes and Credit Growth?

One global element that features prominently in policy discussions is the presence or absence of risk appetite by foreign investors and its effects on domestic factors. To get the magnitude of the impact of changes in global investor risk, this section assesses the effects of positive VIX shocks on GDP growth and credit growth, capital flow sudden stops and capital flow surges episodes. We estimate various four-variable VAR models and

11 Capital Flow Surges, Sudden Stops and Elevated Portfolio... 187

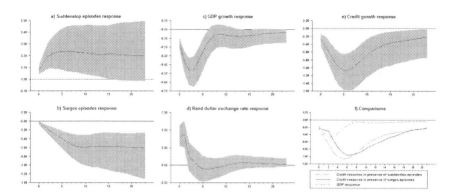

Fig. 11.8 The accumulated impulse responses to an unexpected positive one standard deviation VIX shock. (Note: The grey-shaded areas denote the 16th and 84th percentile error bands. Source: Authors' calculations)

show the response of credit growth in the presence of capital flow surges and capital flow sudden stops episodes to an unexpected one standard deviation (this is approximately 31 per cent) elevated level of global risk measured by the annual changes in VIX. The VAR models that are estimated in this section include VIX growth, a capital flow episode dummy, GDP growth, credit growth and the Rand/US$ exchange rate changes. Similar to the earlier sections, the VAR has two lags including a constant and two dummy variables for the inflation targeting and the recession. The sample size spans the period 1995Q1 to 2014Q1. All growth rates are at an annual rate. These impulse responses are accumulated responses to a one standard deviation shock in the capital flows episode shock. The model uses 10,000 Monte Carlo draws.

Figure 11.8(a) shows that a positive VIX shock increases significantly due to a capital flow sudden-stops episodes. This lowers the capital inflow surges episodes in Fig. 11.8(b) and leads to the R/US$ exchange rate depreciation for nearly a year in Fig. 11.8(d).

What happens to GDP growth and credit growth? In Fig. 11.8(c) and (d), GDP growth and credit growth decline for six and more quarters, respectively. However, in Fig. 11.8(f) credit growth declines much due to the global risk shock, and this holds irrespective of whether capital flow surges or capital flow sudden stops episodes are included in the model.

The implications of the VIX results reinforce the need for policy initiatives aimed at strengthening the ability of the financial system to withstand the episodes of large risk aversion and the change in the direction of capital flows.[8]

11.4.1 What Are the Implications for Credit Growth Dynamics: Evidence from a Large-scale VAR Model

The previous sections have shown that net portfolio flow volatility shocks have a negative association with economic activity and that capital flow surges shocks have opposite effects to those of a capital flow sudden stops episodes shock. However, we have not quantified the effects of net portfolio flows volatility shocks relative to those of capital flows surges and capital flows sudden stop episodes on credit growth and GDP growth.

This section estimates a VAR model which includes a capital flow surges or capital flow sudden stops episodes dummy, net portfolio flow volatility, GDP growth, inflation, repo rate, credit growth and the real effective exchange rate (REER). However, we only show the impulse responses for the variables of interest, namely, credit growth and GDP growth.

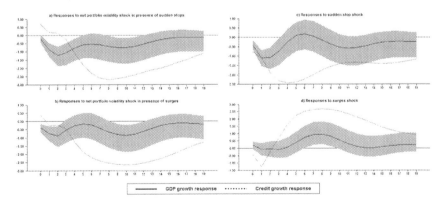

Fig. 11.9 Comparison of GDP growth and credit growth responses to capital flow episodes shocks. (Note: The grey-shaded areas denote the 16th and 84th percentile error bands. Source: Authors' calculations)

---

[8] Forbes and Warnock (2011).

Figure 11.9(a) and (b) shows that GDP growth and credit growth decline due to positive net portfolio flow volatility shocks, and this is irrespective of whether a capital flows surges and capital flows sudden stops are included.

The positive net portfolio flow volatility shock lowers credit growth more than GDP growth. Credit growth remains more depressed over long horizons. Figure 11.9(c) shows that a capital flow sudden stops shock lowers both GDP growth and credit growth but the credit growth is more responsive, whilst a capital flow surges shock raises credit growth more than GDP growth.

11.4.2 How Would GDP Growth and Credit Growth Have Evolved in the Absence of the Capital Flow Episode Shocks?

This section shows how the identified capital flow wave episodes contributed to the evolution of GDP growth and credit growth since 2003Q1. We use a historical decomposition approach and construct a counterfactual GDP growth and credit growth series by subtracting the contributions of the capital flow surges, sudden stops episodes and net portfolio flow volatility shocks individually from the actual growth. The results are estimated in separate models. We plot the actual and counterfactual GDP growth and credit growth series in Figs. 11.10 and 11.11, respectively.

The results show that actual GDP growth has been lower since 2011 suggesting that the presence of capital flow sudden stops and net portfo-

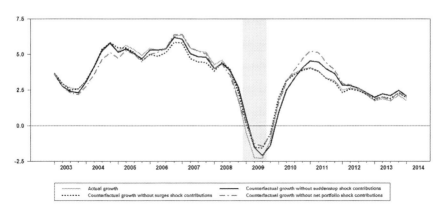

Fig. 11.10 Actual and counterfactual GDP growth. (Source: Authors' calculations)

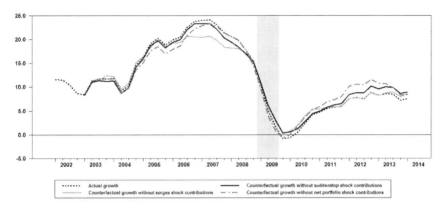

Fig. 11.11 Actual and counterfactual credit growth. (Source: Authors' calculations)

lio flow volatility shocks lead to lower GDP growth. A similar pattern is visible in the credit growth dynamics. Thus, we conclude that positive net portfolio flow volatility and capital flow sudden stops shocks have been a drag on GDP growth and credit growth. We find that capital flow shocks contributed to the uptick in GDP growth and credit growth between 2006 and around 2009Q4. This suggests that economic growth can remain positive even in periods characterised by capital flow surges or net portfolio flow volatility shocks or short-lived (abrupt) periods of capital flow reversals.

However, post 2011, we find that both actual GDP growth and credit growth are below their estimated counterfactual growth rates. This suggests that elevated net portfolio flow volatility, capital flow surges and capital flows sudden stops shocks were a drag on GDP growth and credit growth. Figure 11.12 shows that all capital flow episodes have been a drag on credit growth after 2009.

What can we learn about these shock effects during the recession? We conclude that there is evidence that these shocks can amplify the impact of negative shock on the economy. This was especially the case during the recession in 2009. Figure 11.13 shows that net portfolio flow volatility shocks tend to induce bigger fluctuations in credit growth and GDP growth in the first two years than capital flow surges shocks.

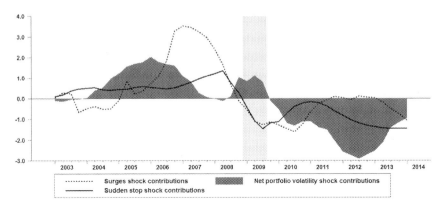

Fig. 11.12 Contributions of categories of various capital flow episodes on credit growth. (Source: Authors' calculations)

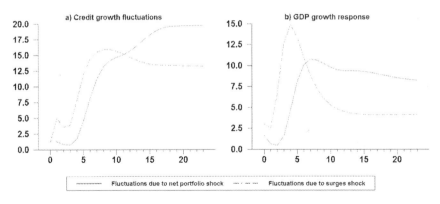

Fig. 11.13 Fluctuations in GDP growth and credit growth. (Source: Authors' calculations)

11.5 Conclusion and Policy Implications

Against the backdrop of the potential effects of the global policy divergence on the direction and composition of capital flows to EMEs, this chapter assessed whether net portfolio flow volatility, capital flow surges, capital flow sudden stops and elevated global risk shocks impact credit growth and GDP growth. First, we establish that GDP growth is a key driver of credit growth. This suggests that robust and sustainable GDP growth leads to higher credit growth. A positive net portfolio flow volatility shock has a larger negative effect on GDP growth and credit growth. In addition, positive net portfolio flow volatility, capital flow surges, capital flow sudden stops and global risk shocks can amplify the impact of shocks on the economy.

For instance, pre-2008 a capital flow surges shock contributed positively to credit growth compared to other capital flow categories. In contrast, a capital flow surges shock led to very little effect on credit growth post the global financial crisis. This concurs with findings of an inverse transmission of global liquidity shocks on some domestic macroeconomic variables post-2008Q4. All the categories of capital flows contributed little or negatively to credit growth post 2008, despite the surge in global liquidity associated with unconventional monetary policy interventions. Furthermore, evidence shows that they induce bigger fluctuations in credit growth and GDP growth, and this was particularly the case during the recession in 2009.

Evidence that global risk is a driver of capital flow volatility reinforces the need for policies aimed at strengthening the financial sector. The decline in the sensitivity of credit growth to capital flow surges changed meaningfully post-2008 amidst a surge in global liquidity shows the limited role of capital flows on bank credit growth. In policy terms, the results in this chapter reinforce the findings in Gumata and Ndou (2017) who failed to establish that excess global liquidity plays a significant role in domestic credit growth. Furthermore, the banking trends suggest limited intermediation of capital flows via the banking sector. As such, foreign funding plays a small role in driving banks' balance sheet items and credit growth. Therefore, we conclude that the positive contribution of capital flow surges to credit growth pre-2008 may be related to GDP growth pulling up credit growth in turn.[9] Hence there is no meaningful contribution during the post global financial crisis period characterised by excess global liquidity.

In addition, Gumata and Ndou (2017) showed that banks loosened lending criteria during the pre-2008 surge in the credit cycle and accommodated an unprecedented increase in house prices.[10] This therefore

---

[9] However, since this chapter only considered bank data, it does not preclude the role of capital flows to the extent that corporates funding directly in equity and debt markets. We note that some studies show that an exclusive reliance on banking-sector data may understate other linkages between capital flows and the supply and demand factors that determine credit growth.

[10] See Gumata and Ndou (2017) on the impact of low loan-to-value ratios on inflation expectations and how they reinforce the contractionary monetary policy stance.

means that, to the extent that credit extension growth is driven less by capital flows, the finding in Carstens (2015) that macroprudential policies are far less effective when they are not channelled through the banking system and, rather, are intermediated via market-based financing mechanisms still holds. Furthermore, these findings reinforce the case for the consideration of macro-prudential tools such as loan-to-value and repayment-to-income ratios as part of the macroprudential policies toolkit.

References

Acharya, V., and Schnabl, P. 2009. *Do Global Banks Spread Global Imbalances? The Case of Asset-Backed Commercial Paper during the Financial Crisis.* IMF Jaques Polak Annual Research Conference Paper.

Ahmed, S., Appendino, M., and Ruta, M. 2015. *Global Value Chains and the Exchange Rate Elasticity of Exports.* IMF Working Paper WP/15/252.

Ancharaz, V. 2011. *An Empirical Investigation of the Export-led Jobless Growth Hypothesis.* African Development Bank.

Benigno, G., Converse, N., and Fornaro, L. 2015. Large Capital Inflows, Sectoral Allocation, and Economic Performance. *Journal of International Money and Finance*, 55, 60–87.

Bruno, V., and Shin, H.S. 2013a. *Capital Flows, Cross-Border Banking and Global Liquidity.* NBER Working Paper No. 19038, May 2013.

Bruno, V., and Shin, H.S. 2013b. *Capital Flows, Cross-Border Banking and Global Liquidity.* NBER Working Paper No. 18942.

Calderon, C., and Kubota, M, 2012. *Gross Capital Inflows, Credit Booms and Crises.* World Bank Policy Research Working Paper No. WPS6270.

Carstens, A. 2015. Challenges for Emerging Economies in the Face of Unconventional Monetary Policies in Advanced Economies. Stavros Niarchos Foundation Lecture, Peterson Institute for International Economics, Washington, 20 April.

Eyraud, L. 2015. *End of the Super-cycle and Growth of Commodity Producers: The Case of Chile.* IMF Working Paper WP/15/242.

Forbes, K.J., and Warnock, F.E. 2011. *Capital Flow Waves: Surges, Stops, Flight, and Retrenchment.* NBER Working Paper No. 17351, August 2011.

Fornero, J., and Kirchner, M. 2014. *Learning About Commodity Cycles and Savings-Investment Dynamics in a Commodity Exporting Economy*. Working Papers Central Bank of Chile WP 727.

Gumata, N., and Ndou, E. 2017. *Bank Credit Extension and Real Economic Activity in South Africa: The Impact of Capital Flow Dynamics, Bank Regulation and Selected Macro-prudential Tools*. Palgrave Macmillan. ISBN 978-3-319-43551-0.

Hoggarth, G., Mahadeva, L., and Martin, J. 2010. *Understanding International Bank Capital Flows during the Recent Financial Crisis*. Bank of England Financial Stability Paper No. 08.

Lane, P.R., and McQuade, P. 2013. Domestic Credit Growth and International Capital Flows. *The Scandinavian Journal of Economics*, 116(1), 218–52.

Mendoza, E.G., and Terrones, M.E. 2012. *An Anatomy of Credit Booms and their Demise*. NBER Working Paper No. 18379, September 2012.

Michaely, M. 1977. Exports and Economic Growth: An Empirical Investigation. *Journal of Development Economics*, 4, 49–53.

Park, J.H., and Prime, P.B. 1997. Export Performance and Growth in China: A Cross Provincial Analysis. *Applied Economics*, 29, 1353–63.

Sachs, J.D., and Warner, A.M. 2001. The Curse of Natural Resources. *European Economic Review*, 45, 827–38.

12

Bank and Non-bank Capital Flows and The Sectorial Reallocation of Credit Away from the Household Sector

Learning Objectives

- Determine the extent to which capital inflows to bank or non-bank flows lead to sectorial shifts in credit.
- Establish the contributions of bank and non-bank flows to the share of credit to households.

12.1 Introduction

The wide policy implications of the relationship between capital flows, domestic credit growth and the real economy remain at the centre of the policy discussions. Excess global liquidity and funding conditions spill-over to emerging market economies via cross-border bank lending activity, and these are expected to lead to overheating credit markets. This chapter extends the analysis on the effects of global liquidity and capital flows on domestic credit markets by considering the role of bank and non-bank capital flows. Figure 12.1 shows the evolution of bank credit to households and companies as a percentage of total loans and advances.

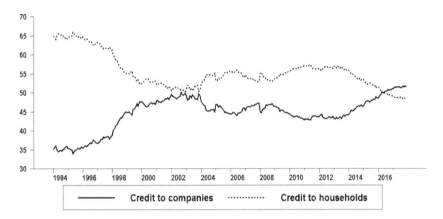

Fig. 12.1 Share of credit to households and companies. (Source: South African Reserve Bank)

Do foreign capital flows into non-banks and banks result in the sectorial reallocation of credit extension?

This is motivated by the argument in Samarina and Bezemer (2016) that since the 1990s foreign capital inflows resulted in the sectorial allocation of credit from non-financial businesses to households. They found evidence that foreign capital inflows into the non-bank sector are associated with lower shares of business lending in the domestic bank portfolios. Therefore, this chapter tests the hypothesis stated below.

Hypothesis 1 *Capital inflows into non-banks and banks are associated with a decrease in the share of domestic bank loans to households.*

Second, we are motivated by the empirical literature which indicates the presence of the substitution effect between domestic bank loans and foreign capital. This is attributed to limited profitable investment opportunities at a time when capital is abundant and highly mobile. This causes competition between domestic and foreign finances for investment opportunities and may result in a substitution effect. However, this substitution effect does not imply that total bank lending falls. Rather, that it induces sector reallocation of credit.

Third, we are motivated by theory which suggests that the abundance of (and in many cases) cheap capital allows domestic banks to fund domestic lending from international capital rather than from domestic bank deposits only. Hence, access to foreign sources of funding loosens banks' financing constraints. On the other hand, domestic non-financial businesses may demand less credit from banks as they can access funding from non-banks. So, banks can respond to the decline of demand by non-financial businesses by expanding lending to households and the share of non-financial business loans in the banks' portfolio declines.

In contrast to the above theory, we assess whether capital inflows lead to a reduction in lending to households as a share of the domestic banks' loan portfolio. To what extent do capital inflows to bank or non-bank flows lead to sectorial shifts in credit? The questions explored in this chapter have implications for the interaction of monetary policy and financial stability objectives. The monetary policy stance by triggering a favourable interest rate differential can attract capital flows. This may inadvertently facilitate for the sectorial credit shifts and lead to overheating in credit markets. These effects have a bearing on financial stability considerations and the design of macroprudential tools.

We fill research policy gaps by determining the extent to which bank and non-bank capital inflows lead to sectorial shifts in credit. We show the contributions of bank and non-bank flows to the share of credit to households.

12.2 What Is the Nature of the Relationship Between Credit to Households, Bank and Non-bank Capital Flows

To answer this question, this section uses quarterly (Q) data for the sample period 1994Q1 to 2015Q3. The data used in the study includes credit to households, capital flows, GDP growth, and the inflation rate. The capital flows include the foreign direct investment (FDI), portfolio

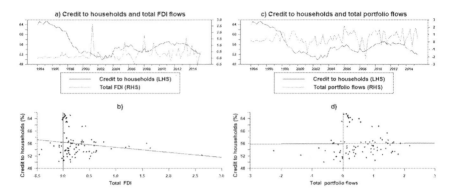

Fig. 12.2 Relationship between credit to households, total FDI flows and total portfolio capital flows. (Source: South African Reserve Bank and authors' calculations)

bank and non-bank capital flows, and total portfolio flows. All the capital flow categories are expressed as per cent of GDP. The capital flow categories are included individually in the model. Credit to households is expressed as a percentage of total loans and advances. The data is sourced from the South African Reserve Bank database. All growth rates are at an annual rate.

Figure 12.2(a) and (b) shows a negative relationship between credit to households and total FDI flows. On the other hand, the relationship between total portfolio flows and credit to households is flat in Fig. 12.2(c) and (d).

12.2.1 Does the Relationship Depend on the Definition of Capital Flows?

This section determines whether the earlier stylised relationships vary with the capital flow category. We apply more than one approach to determine the nature of the relationship between credit to households as a percentage of total credit and capital flows distinguished into bank and non-bank flows. This will reveal the robustness of the results to different capital flow categories.

12 Bank and Non-bank Capital Flows and The Sectorial... 199

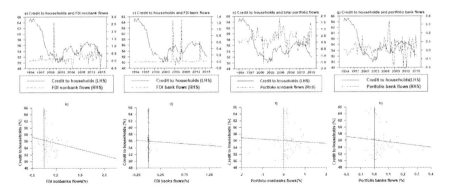

Fig. 12.3 Bilateral relationships between credit to households and capital flows. (Source: South African Reserve Bank and authors' calculations)

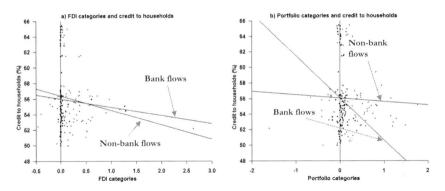

Fig. 12.4 The sensitivity of the credit to household relationship to disaggregated capital flows. (Source: Authors' calculations)

12.2.2 Evidence from Scatterplots

The analysis begins by looking at the bilateral relationship using scatterplots in Fig. 12.3, which establish a negative relationship. This implies that an increase in capital inflows leads to a reduction in the share of credit to household. This is the case for portfolio and foreign direct investment (FDI) bank and non-bank flows.

The robustness test of a negative relationship between the share of credit to the household sector, FDI and portfolio bank and non-banking flows is also visible in Fig. 12.4. Figure 12.4(a) and (b) compares the steepness of the slopes of the relationships and shows that this varies depending on capital flow categories assessed. The steepness of the negative relationship between the household sector credit share, FDI bank and non-bank flows and portfolio flows categories is different. The relationship is steeper between the share of credit to households and portfolio bank flows.

12.2.3 Evidence from Cross Correlations

This section applies the cross correlations approach to determine what happens to the share of credit to households when preceded by elevated banking and non-banking flows. Figure 12.5 shows a negative relationship for most periods in the early horizons. This suggests that the share of credit to households tends to decline for some time when preceded by elevated banking and non-banking flows. However, the correlations tend to be negative in the early first twelve quarters in Fig. 12.5(a) and (c) and become positive afterwards.

This means that elevated capital flows of all categories do not result in a strong increase in the share of credit to households on impact. The positive impact comes at a considerable lag. Even then it is very weak. The negative relationship between capital flows and the share of credit to households is indicative of credit reallocation dynamics, but it is very possible that they are very weak.

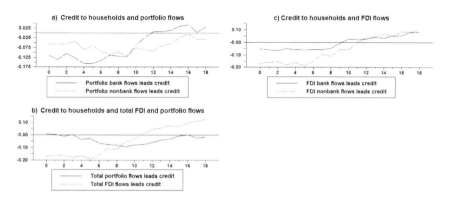

Fig. 12.5 Cross correlations between credit to households, banking and non-banking flows. (Source: Authors' calculations)

12.3 VAR Results

This section applies a VAR approach to determine the effects of capital flows and to establish whether they have any significant effects on the share of credit to households and the magnitudes of the peak effects. We estimate a VAR model with four variables, namely, the share of credit to households, capital inflows, GDP growth and the inflation rate. The capital inflows are foreign direct investment (FDI), portfolio bank and non-bank capital flows and total portfolio flows The capital flow categories as a percentage of GDP are included individually in the model. The VAR model is estimated using two lags as selected by the AIC and 10,000 bootstrap draws.

Similar to the findings in stylised sections, we find negative responses in Fig. 12.6. This indicates that banking and non-banking flows lead to sectorial credit reallocations from the household sector. However, the statistical significance of the responses differs. We find significant reallocation of credit to households due to FDI bank and non-bank flow shock in Fig. 12.6(a) and (b) as well as to portfolio bank flow shocks in Fig. 12.6(f). Amongst all the capital flows shocks, the decline in the share of credit to household does not exceed 0.25 per cent at peak response, which indicates that when the reallocations occur, they are very small.

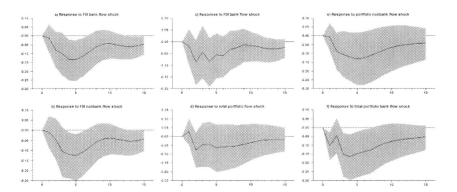

Fig. 12.6 Responses of credit to household to positive capital flow shock. (Note: The shaded area denotes the 16th and 84th percentiles. Source: Authors' calculations)

12.3.1 How Much of Fluctuations in the Share of Credit to Households Are Explained by Bank and Non-bank Flows?

This section determines the proportion of fluctuations in the share of credit to households induced by capital flows. Figure 12.7(a) shows that non-bank flows explain a larger proportion of movements in the share of credit to households than bank flows. Amongst the FDI flow categories in Fig. 12.7(c) the non-bank flows induce more fluctuations in the share of credit to households than bank flows.

In contrast, portfolio bank flows explain more of the fluctuations in the share of credit to households than portfolio non-bank flows in Fig. 12.7(d).

12.3.2 Counterfactual Contributions

This section applies a historical decomposition approach to determine periods in which bank and non-bank flows increased and were a drag on the share of credit to households. The historical contributions decompose the share of credit to households into its own contributions and those from other variables in the model. To calculate the counterfactual share of credit to households, we purge the contributions of bank and non-

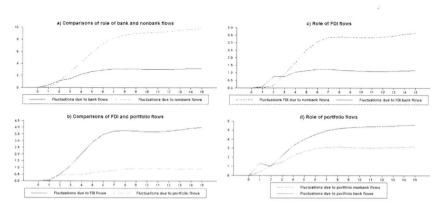

Fig. 12.7 Fluctuations in credit to households due to FDI, portfolio flows, bank and non-bank flows. (Source: Authors' calculations)

bank flows, respectively. The purged series is the counterfactual share of credit to households.

Figures 12.8(a) and 12.9(a) show the actual and counterfactual shares of credit to households, while the contributions from bank and non-bank flows are shown in Figs. 12.8(b) and 12.9(b). In Fig. 12.8(a) the difference between actual and counterfactual share of credit to households is very small suggesting that bank flows contributions play a small role in the share of credit to households. This is further corroborated by the magnitude of less than one per cent at the peak contributions in

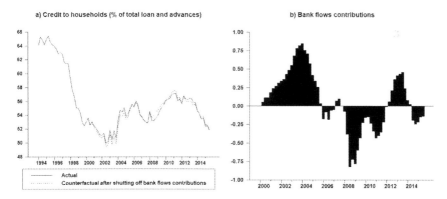

Fig. 12.8 The contributions of aggregated bank flows. (Source: Authors' calculations)

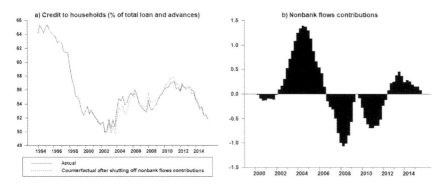

Fig. 12.9 The contributions of aggregated non-bank flows. (Source: Authors' calculations)

Fig. 12.8(b) during the recent credit and house price boom. During the period of the financial crisis and recession, bank flows only contributed a maximum of one per cent in dragging credit to households.

On the other hand, the non-bank flows made positive contributions to credit to households in Fig. 12.9(a) during 2002–2005 and after 2014. The contributions were negative between 2006 and 2013. In terms of magnitudes, the peak increase contribution is nearly 1.5 per cent and the peak decline is below 1 per cent. These magnitudes indicate that non-bank flow contributions play a small role in driving in the share of credit to households.

12.4 Conclusion and Policy Implications

This chapter searched for evidence of the sector reallocation of the share of household credit due to bank and non-bank capital flows. We find a negative relationship between the share of credit to the households and all categories of capital flows. The magnitudes of the negative effects though statistically significant are small suggesting this is not a big problem in South Africa. Although the magnitudes are small, these results suggest that capital mobility has detrimental effects on the domestic allocation of bank credit. The negative effects are particularly evident when capital is flowing into the non-bank sector. Despite small magnitudes, if the negative effects occur over a prolonged period, this means that they can crowd out domestic credit to households. This can create a significant change in the banks' loan portfolios and concentration of risks.

However, from a financial stability and macroprudential regulation perspective, the small magnitude probably offers no sense of comfort. Regulators know that small and localised financial practices can mask severe threats to financial stability. Although small, the impact of bank and non-bank capital flows on the reallocation of credit suggests close monitoring and regulation of these sectorial patterns so that policymakers are not caught off guard. In addition, these findings suggest that prudential targeted regulations, as opposed to broad regulations, may be more effective.

References

Ancharaz, V. 2011. *An Empirical Investigation of the Export-Led Jobless Growth Hypothesis*. African Development Bank.

Eyraud, L. 2015. *End of the Super-Cycle and Growth of Commodity Producers: The Case of Chile*. IMF Working Paper WP/15/242.

Michaely, M. 1977. Exports and Economic Growth: An Empirical Investigation. *Journal of Development Economics*, 4, 49–53.

Park, J.H., and Prime, P.B. 1997. Export Performance and Growth in China: A Cross Provincial Analysis. *Applied Economics*, 29, 1353–63.

Samarina, A., and Bezemer, D. 2016. Do Capital Flows Change Domestic Credit Allocation? *Journal of International Money and Finance*, 62(C), 98–121. Elsevier.

13

Banking and Non-banking Capital Flows and The Sectorial Reallocation of Credit Away from Companies

Learning Objectives

- Show the extent to which foreign capital flows result in domestic bank lending to be dominated by credit to companies.
- Determine the proportion of variation in the share of credit to companies explained by various categories of capital flows.
- Show the amplifying role of capital flows in the response of the repo rate to positive inflation shocks.
- Establish the contribution of various capital flows in the evolution of the share of credit to companies over time.

13.1 Introduction

Ndou and Gumata (2018) showed that credit conditions, bank lending criteria, house prices and the monetary policy stance have a disproportionate impact on the sectoral credit extension. In addition, evidence in Chap. 12 showed that bank and non-bank capital flows are negatively related to the households share of credit. The negative effects are

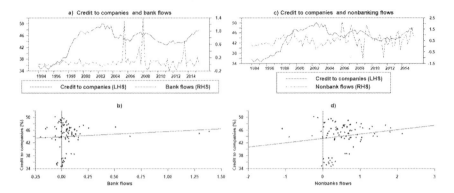

Fig. 13.1 Relationship between credit to companies and bank and non-bank capital flows. (Source: South African Reserve Bank and authors' calculations)

small, suggesting that capital flows do not induce large sectoral reallocations in bank credit. However, trends shown in Chap. 12 indicate that the share of bank lending to companies is increasing relative to that to households. Hence, this chapter extends the analysis by looking at the dynamics of the credit share to companies. To what extent do foreign capital flows result in domestic bank lending to be dominated by credit to companies? Samrina and Bezemer (2016) found evidence that foreign capital inflows into the non-banking sector are associated with lower shares of business lending in the domestic bank portfolios. We test the relevance of this hypothesis in South Africa as stated below:

Hypothesis 1 *Are capital inflows into non-banks and banks associated with a decrease in the share of domestic bank loans to companies?*

Empirical literature shows that the link from larger capital inflows to more fragile bank loan portfolios runs via foreign capital into the non-bank sector. This link is particularly strong when investment opportunities are fewer. This has implications for macroprudential policy and the regulation of capital flows. Before we infer policy implications, Fig. 13.1 shows the relationship between the share of credit to companies,[1] foreign

---

[1] The share of credit to companies as per cent of credit.

direct investment (FDI) and portfolio flows into banks and non-banks. The relationship between the share of credit to companies and aggregated bank and non-bank flows is positive. This is different to the findings in relation to the share of credit to the household sector in Chap. 12, in which we established robust evidence of a negative relationship between the share of credit to the household sector and FDI and portfolio bank and non-banking flows.

Does the sectoral credit substitution matter? Yes, it matters. Empirical literature indicates the presence of a substitution effect between domestic bank loans and foreign capital. This is attributed and mostly relevant in the economies with limited investment opportunities because domestic and foreign finances are more likely to compete for investment opportunities. However, the substitution effect does not imply that total bank lending falls, but that financial openness tends to cause domestic sector specific lending credit booms. It allows domestic banks to fund domestic lending from international capital rather than from domestic bank deposits only.

Hence, we argue that access to foreign sources of funding loosens the banks' financing constraint. In addition, banks can experience a decline in the demand for their loans by domestic non-financial businesses as other sources of funding become more competitive. It can then happen that banks respond to this by reducing lending to households and increase the companies' loan share in the domestic bank portfolios. Hence, we assess whether capital inflows lead to an increase in credit to companies at the expense of the households' credit share in the domestic bank loan portfolios.

This chapter fills existing academic and policy research gaps by extending work that assessed the impact of capital flows on the household sector credit share. As in the case of the household sector, we argue that the findings in this chapter have implications for the design of macroprudential and regulatory tools. This is also of policy relevance given the relationship between the monetary policy tightening cycles and capital inflows which can in turn inadvertently lead to an increasing share of credit to companies. This can be an additional channel that can result in the increase in credit to companies.

13.2 Does the Relationship Depend on the Definition of Capital Flow Category?

This section determines whether there are any stylised relationships and whether they vary with the definition of the capital flows category used. We divide capital flows into bank and non-bank flows. This will reveal the robustness of the results to different capital flow categories. We examine the bilateral relationship by using scatterplots. We find a positive relationship in Fig. 13.2 which suggests that increased capital inflows, whether in the form of bank and non-bank flow, lead to an increase in the share of credit to companies.

This positive relationship between the share of credit to companies and bank and non-banking flows is robust evidence as it holds for FDI and portfolio flows in Fig. 13.3(a) and (b). Does the relationship vary between aggregated bank and non-bank flows? Yes, it does. Figure 13.3(a) and (b) shows that the steepness of the correlations varies between the bank and non-bank flows in the FDI and portfolio flows categories. The share of credit to companies is more sensitive to bank portfolio inflows compared to the non-bank category.

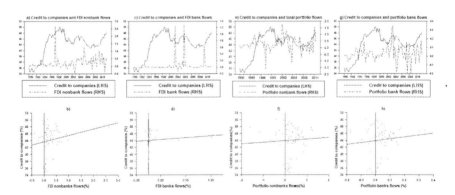

Fig. 13.2 Bilateral relationships between credit to companies and capital flows. (Source: South African Reserve Bank and authors' calculations)

13 Banking and Non-banking Capital Flows and The Sectorial…

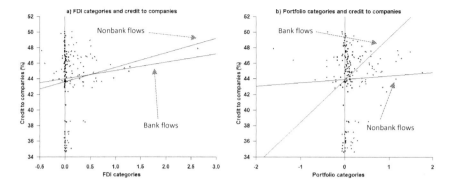

Fig. 13.3 Sensitivity of credit to companies to disaggregated capital flows. (Source: Authors' calculations. Note: Capital flows are expressed as a percentage of GDP)

These results indicate that there is a positive relationship between capital flows and the share of credit to companies. This evidence supports the theory of the prevalence of the credit reallocation from the households sector towards companies.

13.3 VAR Results

This section estimates a VAR model with four variables from 1994Q1 to 2015Q3. The four variables include GDP growth, the inflation rate, the share of credit to companies and capital flow categories. The capital flow categories refer to (i) total FDI or FDI bank flow or non-bank flows; (ii) total portfolio or portfolio bank or non-bank flows. The capital flow categories are expressed as per cent of GDP and the share of credit to companies is expressed as per cent of total credit. The capital flow categories are included separately in the model. The VAR model is estimated using two lags selected by AIC and 10,000 Monte Carlo draws. The results are robust to different orderings. All growth rates are at an annual rate. The data is sourced from the South African Reserve Bank database.

We find positive impulse responses in Fig. 13.4 for the share of credit to companies due to various capital flow shocks. This indicates that banking and non-banking flows lead to sectorial credit reallocations towards companies. We find a significant increase in the reallocation of credit to companies due to positive portfolio flows, portfolio bank flows and

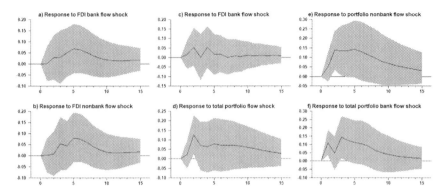

Fig. 13.4 Responses of credit to companies to positive capital inflow shocks. (Note: The shaded area denotes the 16th and 84th percentiles. Source: Authors' calculations)

non-bank flow shock in Fig. 13.4(d), (e) and (f), respectively. However, amongst all the capital flow shocks, the increase in the share of credit to companies does not exceed 0.3 per cent of GDP. This indicates that although the reallocation of credit towards companies occurs, it is in very small magnitudes. However, we note that in absolute terms, this positive impact is much higher compared to the negative impact of 0.25 per cent at peak response of these capital flow categories on the household sector credit share established in Chap. 12.

Does the disaggregation of FDI and portfolio flows into banking and non-banking flows impact the relationship between credit to companies and capital flows? To answer this question, we estimate a VAR model similar to earlier sections. Figure 13.5(a) and (b) shows that the share of credit to companies rises due to a positive bank and non-bank flow shock. However, the increase is significant towards non-bank flows shocks in Fig. 13.5(c). The share of credit to companies rises for nearly ten quarters.

13.3.1 How Much Fluctuations in Credit to Companies Is Explained by the Bank and Non-bank Flows Shocks?

We determine the proportion of fluctuations in credit to companies induced by capital flows shocks. Figure 13.6(a) shows that non-bank

13 Banking and Non-banking Capital Flows and The Sectorial... 213

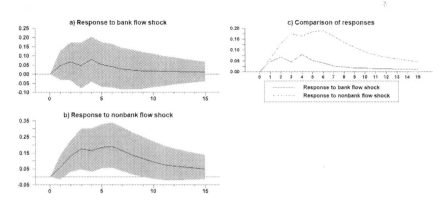

Fig. 13.5 Credit to companies' responses to bank and non-bank flows shocks. (Note: The shaded area denotes the 16th and 84th percentiles. Source: Authors' calculations)

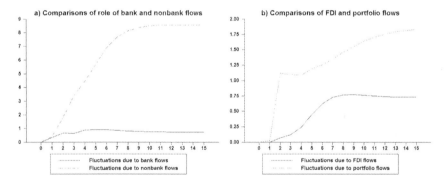

Fig. 13.6 Fluctuations in credit to companies due to FDI, portfolio, bank and non-bank flows. (Source: Authors' calculations)

flows explain more movements in the share of credit to companies than bank flows. Figure 13.6(b) shows that portfolio inflow shocks induce more fluctuations in credit to companies than FDI flows shock.

On a comparative basis, we found that non-bank flows explain more movements in the share of credit to households than bank flows, in particular FDI non-bank than bank flows. On the other hand, portfolio bank flows explain more fluctuations in the share of household credit than portfolio non-bank flows.

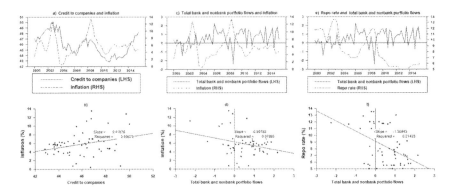

Fig. 13.7 Relationships between credit to companies and selected macroeconomic indicators. (Source: South African Reserve Bank and authors' calculations)

13.3.2 Counterfactual Contributions

This section determines the amplifying role of capital flows in the response of the repo rate to positive inflation shocks. That is, is the repo rate response different in the presence of capital flows than when it is shut off in the model? Figure 13.7 shows that the increased share of credit to companies is positively related to inflation.[2] At the same time, portfolio flows reduce inflation and the rate at which the repo rate responds to inflation shocks. In comparative terms, the magnitude in the inflation decline due to portfolio flows is larger than the size of the inflation increases due to the increased share of credit to companies. This means that increased capital flows neutralise inflationary pressures and this has implications for the repo rate adjustments. The repo rate declines due to increased portfolio flows. The results underscore the role of portfolio flows on the exchange rate channel in the repo rate response to inflationary pressures.

---

[2] See Fig. 13.12 in the Appendix for the comparison of the household credit share relationship with inflation. The negative relationship holds even for the level of credit growth in Fig. 13.13. We show the relationship between credit growth to companies and households with headline CPI in Fig. 13.13 in the Appendix. This shows that the positive relationship between credit to companies and headline inflation is robust to measurement, that is, as a share to total credit and the growth rate in the level of credit to companies.

13 Banking and Non-banking Capital Flows and The Sectorial...

We estimate a four-variable VAR model as done in the previous section to determine the actual and counterfactual repo rate responses to positive inflation shocks. We shut off each capital flow category, respectively, to determine the counterfactual repo rate response to positive inflation shocks. The gap between the actual repo rate in the presence of capital flows and counterfactual response when the capital flow channel is shut off gives the estimate of the amplification or dampening magnitudes. We show the cumulative repo rate responses following a 1 per cent positive inflation shock.

Figure 13.8 shows the response of the repo rate to positive inflation shocks in the presence of portfolio flows and when the portfolio flows are shut off. The counterfactual repo rate responses exceed the actual repo rate response. This shows that increased portfolio flows induce a lower increase in the repo rate than when capital flows are shut off in the model. In cumulative terms, the repo rate may be lower by 0.4 percentage points over long horizons.

We extend the analysis to other capital flow categories shown in Fig. 13.9. The results concur with those in the earlier sections. The counterfactual repo rate exceeds the actual repo rate. This means that increased capital flow activity lowers the rate at which the repo rate increases in response to positive inflation shocks. This is possibly linked to the appreciation in the exchange rate that is usually associated with an increase in capital flows. Overall, the results reveal that the repo rate will respond to positive inflation shocks, irrespective of capital flow activity.

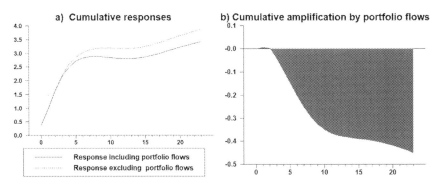

Fig. 13.8 Cumulative repo rate responses to positive inflation shocks and amplification by portfolio flows channel. (Source: Authors' calculations)

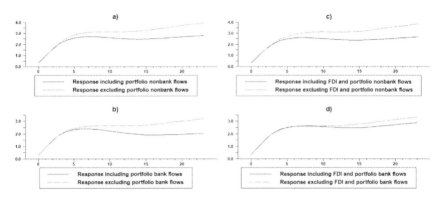

Fig. 13.9 Cumulative repo rate responses to positive inflation shocks and amplification by various capital flow categories. (Source: Authors' calculations)

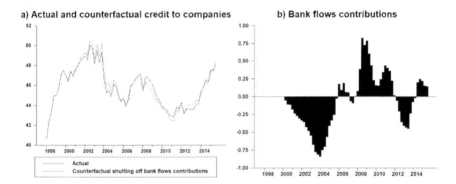

Fig. 13.10 Actual and counterfactual credit to companies and the contributions of bank flows. (Source: Authors' calculations)

13.3.3 Historical Decomposition

This section applies a historical decomposition approach to determine periods during which bank flows as well as combined bank and non-bank flows increased and were a drag on the share of credit to companies. The counterfactual credit to companies refers to credit that would prevail when bank flows and combined banks and non-bank flows contributions are shut off in the model. Figure 13.10 shows that bank flows increased credit to companies between 2005 and 2012 and mid-2014 and thereafter.

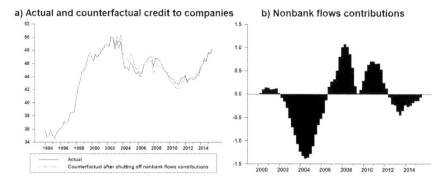

Fig. 13.11 Actual and counterfactual credit to companies and the contributions of bank and non-bank flows. (Source: Authors' calculations)

This contrasts with the trends observed in their contributions to household's credit.

On the other hand, the contributions of both non-bank and bank flows in Fig. 13.11 were largely negative between 2000 and 2007 due to the contribution of non-bank flows. It also seems to be the case that non-bank flows were neutralising the positive impact of bank flows towards the end of the sample period shown in Fig. 13.10.

13.4 Conclusion and Policy Implications

The results in this chapter suggest that capital mobility may lead to an increase in the domestic allocation of bank credit towards companies. In addition, portfolio flow shocks induce more fluctuations in credit to companies than FDI flow shock. This contrasts with the findings that non-bank flows explain more movements in credit to households than bank flows in Chap. 12. This evidence supports the theory of the prevalence of credit reallocation from the households sector towards companies.

Furthermore, the counterfactual scenarios which determine the responses of repo rate to positive inflation pressures show that the repo rate rises to curb inflationary pressures. However, the policy tightening is larger in the absence of increased capital flow activity. This means that increased capital flow activity makes the repo rate to increase by smaller magnitudes to curb inflationary pressures. This is linked to the exchange rate appreciation response to capital flows that tends to dampen inflationary pressures. In a nutshell, the inflation target is binding, and policymakers respond to positive inflationary pressures irrespective of the sources. For prudential policy, the evidence of the prevalence of credit reallocation from the households sector towards companies means that capital flows can result in excesses in some market segments. To mitigate the build-up of such imbalances and the potential negative spillover effects requires targeted regulatory tools instead of broad regulation.

Appendix

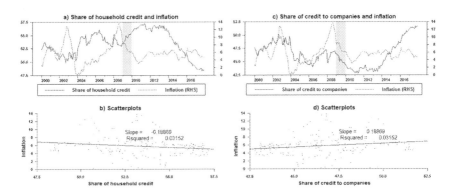

Fig. 13.12 Household and corporate credit share relationship with inflation. (Source: South African Reserve Bank and authors' calculations)

13 Banking and Non-banking Capital Flows and The Sectorial... 219

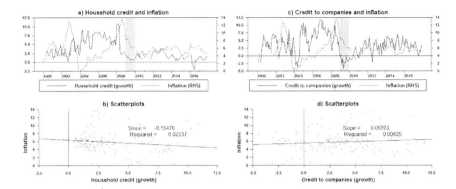

Fig. 13.13 Household and corporate credit growth relationship with inflation. (Source: South African Reserve Bank and authors' calculations)

References

Ancharaz, V. 2011. *An Empirical Investigation of the Export-Led Jobless Growth Hypothesis*. African Development Bank.

Eyraud, L. 2015. *End of the Super-Cycle and Growth of Commodity Producers: The Case of Chile*. IMF Working Paper WP/15/242.

Michaely, M. 1977. Exports and Economic Growth: An Empirical Investigation. *Journal of Development Economics*, 4, 49–53.

Park, J.H., and Prime, P.B. 1997. Export Performance and Growth in China: A Cross Provincial Analysis. *Applied Economics*, 29, 1353–63.

14

Equity, Debt Inflows and the Price Stability Mandate

Learning Objectives

- Establish whether equity and debt inflows matter in the attainment of the price stability mandate.
- Determine whether debt and equity capital inflows propagate the effects of inflation shocks on GDP growth and the repo rate.
- Explore whether the propagation effects of debt and equity capital inflows affect the repo rate responses to positive inflationary shocks.
- Determine whether positive debt and equity inflow shocks lead to sectoral credit reallocation.

14.1 Introduction

Earlier chapters showed that capital flows play a dampening role in the response of the repo rate due to positive inflation shocks. Increased portfolio flows induce a lower rate of increase in the repo rate due to the propagation role of the exchange rate channel on inflationary pressures. Furthermore, the disaggregation of equity and debt inflows into banking and non-banking capital inflows leads to sectoral reallocation of credit between households and companies.

This analysis is motivated by the findings in Davis (2015), which indicate that debt capital inflows have different effects on various macroeconomic indicators compared to equity capital inflows. This is because debt capital inflows directly involve the balance sheet of financial intermediaries and lead to the domestic financial accelerator effects compared to equity capital inflows.

This analysis fills policy research gaps by exploring whether debt and equity capital inflows propagate the effects of positive inflation shocks on the repo rate. Is the repo rate adjusted differently to positive inflationary shocks in the presence of capital inflows compared to the counterfactual scenario when the capital inflows are shut off? Do equity and debt inflows matter in the attainment of the price stability mandate?

14.2 Stylised Analysis

First, this section examines the differences between equity and debt inflows based on descriptive statistics using quarterly (Q) data for the period 1997Q1 to 2015Q3. For this analysis, equity and debt inflows are expressed as per cent of GDP. The equity inflows mean value is larger than the debt inflows in Fig. 14.1(a). In addition, equity inflows exhibit

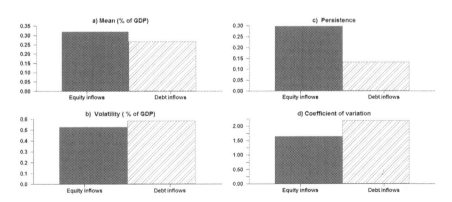

Fig. 14.1 Comparison of descriptive statistics. (Source: Authors' calculations)

14 Equity, Debt Inflows and the Price Stability Mandate

more persistence than debt inflows in Fig. 14.1(c). The persistence based on the coefficient of the AR (1) process suggests a slight influence of the past equity inflows. The coefficient of variation (CV) defined as the ratio of the standard deviation to the mean in Fig. 14.1(d) shows that debt inflows are more variable relative to their mean. On the other hand, debt inflows are more volatile than equity-based capital inflows in Fig. 14.1(b).

What is the relationship between inflation, equity and debt inflows? The trends and scatterplots are shown in Fig. 14.2 and depict a negative relationship indicating that rising inflation deters equity and debt inflows.

In addition, the steepness of the slopes, the magnitudes of the slope coefficients and R-square values in Fig. 14.3(a) reveal a steeper negative relationship which indicates that rising inflation leads to a bigger decline in equity inflows than debt inflows.

The comparison of the magnitudes of the impact of inflation shows that the impact on equity inflows is three times larger than that on debt inflows. In addition, in Fig. 14.3(c) inflation explains 10 per cent of variations in equity inflows. This variation is four times more than the variation explained in debt inflows.

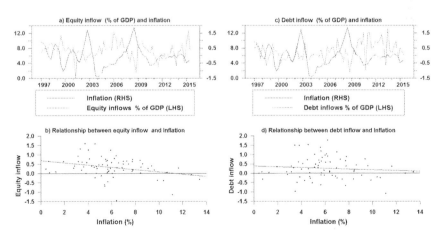

Fig. 14.2 Relationship between inflation, equity inflows and debt inflows. (Source: South African Reserve Bank and authors' calculations)

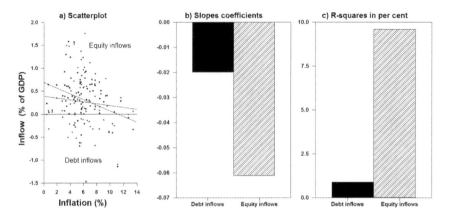

Fig. 14.3 Comparison of bilateral relationships. (Source: Authors' calculations)

14.3 Empirical Analysis: Responses to a Positive Inflation Shock

This section estimates various VAR models to examine the effects of positive inflation shocks. We use quarterly (Q) data from 1997Q1 to 2015Q3 sourced from the South African Reserve Bank database. The various VAR models serve as further tests of the robustness of the effects. The baseline model includes inflation, GDP growth, repo rate, credit growth and other variables which are added depending on the assumptions stated. The various VAR models differ depending on whether, (i) equity and debt inflows are included together in the model, (ii) equity inflows only are included in the model and (iii) debt inflows only rae included in the model. In later sections, we add the rand per US dollar (R/US$) exchange rate. Because the main intention is to assess the impact of inflation shocks, we place all measures of capital inflows last in the model. This is consistent with the role of inflation as a pull-and-push factor on capital flows. The models are estimated using two lags selected by AIC and 10,000 Monte Carlo draws. All growth rates are at an annual rate.

Figure 14.4 shows that a positive inflation shock raises the repo rate significantly for five quarters followed by a significant decline between 6 and 12 quarters. Inflation has adverse effects on GDP growth and credit growth.

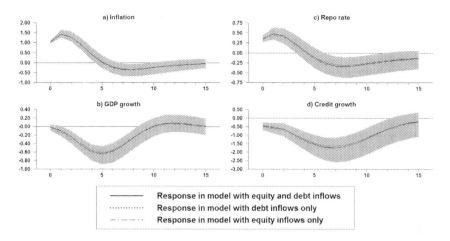

Fig. 14.4 Repo rate, GDP growth and credit growth responses to a positive inflation shock. (Note: The grey-shaded areas denote the 16th and 84th percentile error bands. Source: Authors' calculations)

GDP growth declines significantly for 9 quarters, which is a shorter duration compared to 13 quarters of the decline in credit growth.

Despite the different assumptions incorporated into the model, the lack of a statistically significant difference indicates that the results are robust to different specifications and the ordering of the variables in the models. The results are robust to whether equity and debt inflows are included together or separately in the model.

14.3.1 Are the Effects of the Rand Depreciation Shock Influenced by Debt and Equity Inflows?

Indeed, the results in Fig. 14.5 show that the R/US$ exchange rate depreciation shock leads to significant inflationary pressures for nearly two years and exert upward pressure on the policy rate. This is because the R/US$ exchange rate depreciates on impact by nearly 10 per cent and returns to the pre-shock level after five quarters. The combined effects of rising inflation and upward pressure on the repo rate leads to a significant GDP growth contraction for three years in Fig. 14.5.

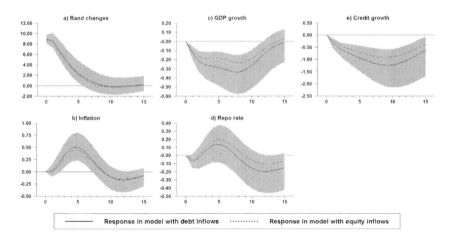

Fig. 14.5 Responses to the R/US$ exchange depreciation shocks. (Note: The grey-shaded areas denote the 16th and 84th percentile error bands. Source: Authors' calculations)

GDP growth slows by less than 0.4 percentage points at the peak period, credit growth declines significantly and remains depressed for over 15 quarters.

14.3.2 Do the Responses of Debt Flows and Equity Flows Differ Due to Positive Inflation and R/US$ Exchange Rate Depreciation Shocks?

Figure 14.6 shows that a positive inflation shock leads to a significant decline in equity inflows which lasts for five quarters, while debt securities do not. Similarly, we find that positive inflation shocks lead to a significant reduction in (i) portfolio banking and non-banking flows and (ii) FDI banking and non-banking inflows. However, the portfolio and FDI banking flows remain depressed for a prolonged period. Thus, high inflation deters equity, banking and non-banking inflows.

Do the responses of equity and debt inflows due to a positive inflation shock vary from those due to the R/US$ exchange rate depreciation shock? In Fig. 14.7, we find that the R/US$ exchange rate depreciation shock exerts a negative effect on equity and debt inflows, but the responses are insignificant.

14 Equity, Debt Inflows and the Price Stability Mandate

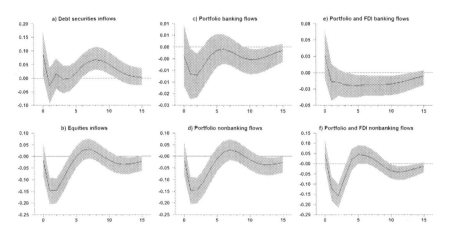

Fig. 14.6 Capital inflow responses to positive inflation shocks. (Note: The grey-shaded areas denote the 16th and 84th percentile error bands. Source: Authors' calculations)

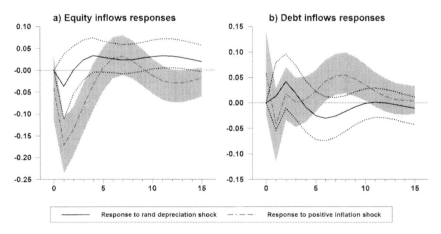

Fig. 14.7 Responses to rand depreciation and positive inflation shocks. (Note: The grey-shaded areas denote the 16th and 84th percentile error bands. Source: Authors' calculations)

In contrast, inflation leads to a significant contraction in equity inflows for a year. Debt securities do not react significantly but tend to rise transitorily after six quarters. Yes, we conclude that equity and debt inflows respond differently to positive inflation and R/US$ exchange rate depreciation shocks.

14.3.3 Do Positive Debt and Equity Flow Shocks Lead to the Reallocation of Credit Between Household and Companies?

This section determines whether positive debt and equity inflow shocks lead to the reallocation of credit between the companies and households. In the preceding two chapters, we established that total portfolio, foreign direct investment (FDI) and banking and non-banking inflows lead to sectorial credit reallocation.

Evidence in Fig. 14.8 confirms that positive debt and equity inflow shocks lead to credit reallocation as the credit share to household contracts and that to companies increases. Other capital inflow shocks also induce a sectoral credit reallocation.

14.4 Counterfactual Repo Rate Responses to Positive Inflation Shocks

This section performs a counterfactual analysis to determine what the response of the repo rate to unexpected inflation rate shocks is in the absence and presence (active role) of (i) debt and equity inflows, (ii) debt and equity outflows, and (iii) banking and non-banking inflows.

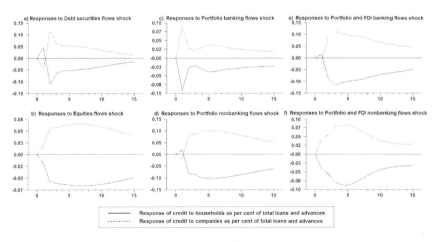

Fig. 14.8 Households and companies credit share responses to positive capital inflow shocks. (Source: Authors' calculations)

14.4.1 The Role of Debt and Equity Inflows

Figure 14.9(a) shows that the repo rate increases more due to positive inflation shocks when the equity or debt inflows are not shut off in the model than when they are shut off. The peak increase suggests that the repo rate tends to respond more aggressively to positive inflation shock in a model with equity inflows compared to that with debt inflows. In cumulative terms, the repo rate would be 0.5 percentage points lower at the peak in the presence of equity inflows. This is five times larger than the size of the repo rate increase that would prevail when considering debt inflows.

What could explain the differential effects? Evidence shows that the difference could be linked to the ability of equity inflows and debt inflow shocks to influence inflation and the R/US$ exchange rate. In Fig. 14.10(a), inflation declines significantly for five quarters, while it does not decline in Fig. 14.10(b) due to debt inflow shocks. In addition, equity inflow shocks appreciate the R/US$ exchange rate for three quarters. Furthermore, at peak magnitudes, the equity inflows appreciate the R/US$ exchange rate by 3 percentage points which is larger than the 2 percentage points due to debt inflows.

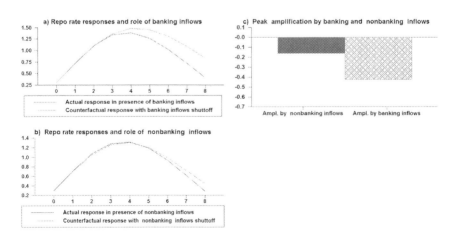

Fig. 14.9 Repo rate responses to positive inflation shocks and the role of equity and debt inflows. (Source: Authors' calculations)

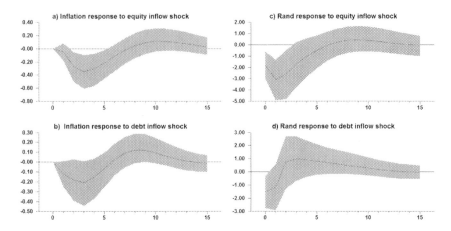

Fig. 14.10 Responses to equity and debt inflow shocks. (Note: The grey-shaded areas denote the 16th and 84th percentile error bands. Source: Authors' calculations)

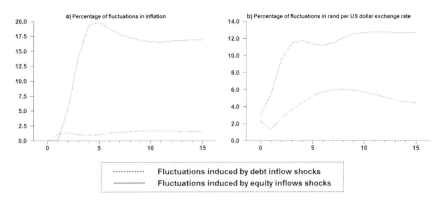

Fig. 14.11 Comparison of fluctuations induced by positive equity and debt inflow shocks. (Source: Authors' calculations)

Furthermore, the proportion of fluctuations in inflation and the R/US$ exchange rate induced by positive equity and debt flow shocks in Fig. 14.11 indicate that equity inflows explain a higher proportion of fluctuations in inflation and the R/US$ exchange rate compared to debt inflow shocks. This is further evidence on why the repo rate may respond less aggressively to inflation pressures in the presence of equity inflows than debt inflow shocks.

Overall, the results indicate that positive equity and debt inflow shocks have different effects on the repo rate response to inflation shocks. Positive equity inflow shocks lower inflation and appreciate the R/US$ exchange rate. However, the repo rate response indicates that monetary policymakers enforce price stability irrespective of equity and debt inflow shocks.

14.4.2 The Role of Debt and Equity Outflow

This section examines the response of the repo rate to positive inflation shocks when considering equity and debt outflows. We find that the repo rate rises slightly higher due to positive inflation shocks when equity and debt outflows are included in the model than when they are shut off in the model. In comparison to the results in Fig. 14.12, equity and debt outflows lead to much larger interest rate increases than would prevail when the capital outflows are shut off in the model.

In contrast to earlier findings, debt outflows induce about 0.1 percentage points increase in the repo rate than when they are not shut off in the model. This peak effect exceeds that from equity outflows.

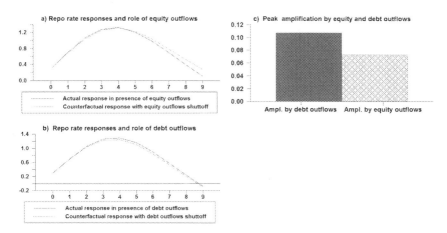

Fig. 14.12 Repo rate responses to positive inflation shocks and the role of equity and debt outflows. (Source: Authors' calculations)

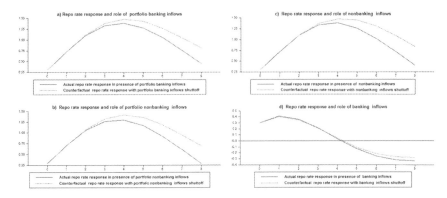

Fig. 14.13 Repo rate responses to positive inflation shocks and the role of banking and non-banking flows. (Source: Authors' calculations)

14.4.3 The Role of Banking and Non-banking Inflows

This section concludes the analysis by examining the role of portfolio and FDI banking and non-banking inflows. Figure 14.13(a), (b) and (c) shows that the repo rate would be higher in the absence of banking inflows compared to when banking inflows are not shut off in the model. The actual repo rate would be much lower than the counterfactual repo rate. This suggests that the increase in portfolio banking and non-banking inflows via the exchange rate appreciation lowers inflation which leads to less aggressive policy adjustment than that would prevail when these are shut off in the model.

14.5 Conclusion and Policy Implications

This chapter explored whether equity and debt inflows matter in the attainment of the price stability mandate. First, we establish that the mean value of equity inflows is larger than that of debt inflows. In addition, equity inflows exhibit more persistence than debt inflows. Debt inflows are more volatile than equity capital inflows. Furthermore, rising inflation deters equity and debt inflows, in particular equity inflows decline more compared to debt inflows. The impact of inflation on equity inflows is three times larger than that on debt inflows.

Second, evidence shows that positive inflation shocks lead to a significant decline in equity inflows while debt securities do not decline. Similarly, positive inflation shocks lead to a significant reduction in (i) portfolio banking and non-banking flows and (ii) FDI banking and non-banking inflows. However, the portfolio and FDI banking flows remain depressed for a prolonged period. Thus, high inflation deters equity, banking and non-banking inflows. Furthermore, the results corroborate earlier evidence that capital flows induce sectoral credit reallocation. Evidence shows that positive debt and equity inflow shocks lead to sectoral credit reallocation as the credit share to households contracts and that to companies increases.

Third, evidence shows that the repo rate tends to respond more aggressively to positive inflation shock in a model with equity inflows compared to that with debt inflows. In cumulative terms, the repo rate would be 0.5 percentage points lower at the peak in the presence of equity inflows. This is five times larger than the size of the repo rate increase that would prevail when considering debt inflows. Evidence shows that the differential effects could be linked to the ability of equity inflow and debt inflow shocks to influence inflation and the R/US$ exchange rate. The equity inflow shocks appreciate the R/US$ exchange rate by a larger magnitude and for a prolonged period compared to positive debt inflow shocks. Thus, positive equity inflow shocks lower inflation, appreciate the R/US$ exchange rate and affect the rate at which the repo rate responds to inflationary shocks. Hence, equity inflows matter more in the attainment of the price stability mandate.

References

Cesa-Bianchi, A., Cespedes, L.F., and Rebucci, A. 2015. *Global Liquidity, House Prices, and the Macroeconomy: Evidence from Advanced and Emerging Economies*. IMF Working Paper WP/15/23.

Davis, S.J. 2015. The Macroeconomic Effects of Debt-and Equity-Based Capital Inflows. *Journal of Macroeconomics*, 46, 81–95.

Samarina, A., and Bezemer, D. 2016. Do Capital Flows Change Domestic Credit Allocation? *Journal of International Money and Finance*, 62(C), 98–121. Elsevier.

15

Do Local Investors Play a Stabilising Role Relative to Foreign Investors After Economic Shocks?

Learning Objectives

- Show the extent to which local investors play a stabilising role relative to foreign investors after economic shocks to US and SA GDP growth and policy rates.
- Show how foreign and domestic investors react to GDP growth and policy rates shocks in the US and SA.
- Find whether domestic investors repatriate their assets due to US GDP growth and the Federal Funds Rate (FFR) shocks.
- Establish how domestic investors respond to the repo rate-FFR spread and VIX shocks.

15.1 Introduction

This chapter explores whether local investors play a stabilising role relative to foreign investors after economic shocks. We explore this question against the background of diverging macroeconomic factors between the United States of America (US) and South Africa (SA). This is motivated by the US Fed, which has continued the gradual policy normalisation path since December 2015, because of the high US employment growth and GDP growth resulting in the decline to pre-crisis levels in the unemployment rate. At the same time, GDP growth outcomes in SA are very weak and the unemployment rate has averaged 25 per cent post-2009. However, the policy rate was slightly loosened as inflation has remained within the 3–6 per cent inflation target range. To what extent do local investors play a stabilising role relative to foreign investors after economic shocks to US and SA GDP growth and policy rates?

This analysis is further motivated by the divergence between the policy rates and GDP growth rates in the US and SA. The divergence does not support repercussions theory of the influence of the big economy on a small economy and synchronised economic growth and policy rate adjustments. Literature shows that although the interest rate differentials are an important factor in attracting capital flows, it seems that growth differentials and investor risk appetite matter more.[1] Hence the key question posed in this chapter: When faced with shocks to GDP growth and policy rates in the US and SA, how do foreign and domestic investors react? Do domestic investors repatriate their assets due to shocks to US GDP growth and the Federal Funds Rate? How do domestic investors respond to shocks to the repo rate-FFR spread and positive VIX shocks?

In addition, we are motivated by evidence of a cointegration relationship between the repo rate and the FFR established in Chap. 7. We estimated that the long-term repo rate is close to 7 per cent. Furthermore, evidence indicated that the adjustments in the repo rate-FFR spread tend to persist more when the spread is widening or increasing. There exists a non-linear response from peak to the lowest point of the repo rate-FFR spread. Figure 15.1 shows that the repo rate is positively related to FFR, but the relationship has changed during the sample period 2000Q1 to 2017Q4.

The slope of the positive relationship is much steeper for the entire sample period relative to the period 2000M1 to 2017M12. In addition, the mean repo rate was 15.62 per cent during the sample periods 1990M1 to 1999M12 compared to 8.12 per cent during 2000M1 to 2017M12.

---

[1] See for instance, Bernanke (2007) and IMF WEO (2016).

15 Do Local Investors Play a Stabilising Role Relative to Foreign…

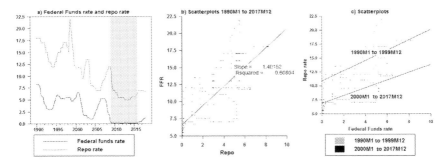

Fig. 15.1 Relationship between repo rate and FFR. (Source: South African Reserve Bank, Fred and authors' calculations)

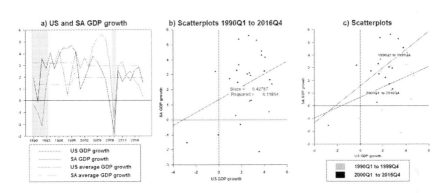

Fig. 15.2 Relationship between the US and SA GDP growth. (Source: South African Reserve Bank, IMF and authors' calculations)

We have shown that GDP growth differentials matter for capital flows. Furthermore, Fig. 15.2 shows how the relationship between US and SA GDP growth has evolved since the 1990s. The period 2000Q1 to 2016Q4 was characterised by the divergence of the GDP growth rates and the weakening in the strength of the positive association between the countries' output growth rates.

Figure 15.2(c) shows that the slope of the association between US and SA GDP growth, although still positive, has become much gentler (flatter). This means that for the period 2000Q1 to 2016Q4 positive US GDP growth did not necessarily translate to much higher SA GDP growth. There are other countries and factors that play a more meaningful role in SA GDP growth than US GDP growth alone. For instance, Chap. 2 showed that robust Chinese growth is important for sustaining high SA GDP growth in response to positive US, euro area, G7 and Chinese GDP growth shocks. Robust Chinese growth amplifies the response of euro area GDP growth response to positive US GDP growth shocks. This suggests that these economies will grow more when US GDP growth occurs concurrently with robust Chinese growth. In addition, China growth shocks and those of advanced economies including the US are transmitted via other countries (third countries) before impacting South Africa.[2]

With this background on US and SA GDP growth and policy rates, we determine the extent to which local investors play a stabilising role in capital flows. Do domestic investors play an offsetting role by repatriating foreign assets following a positive disturbance to the US policy rate and GDP growth shocks? How do gross capital inflows react to positive disturbances to SA GDP growth and repo rate shocks? Do persistent and non-persistent SA GDP growth and repo rate shocks exert different effects on gross capital inflows and outflows? These are pertinent and relevant questions to policymakers.

15.2 Do Domestic Monetary Policy Conditions Matter for Capital Flow Activity?

This section begins the analysis by showing the scatterplots between the repo rate and gross capital inflows and outflows. In line with recent literature, we define gross capital inflows (outflow) as capital movement in

---

[2] Furthermore, evidence in earlier chapters showed that there was a persistent divergence and decline in SA GDP growth post-2013 when global and US growth recovered and continued to increase. Had SA GDP growth data remained at 2010 and 2011 growth rates and maintained the growth momentum, SA GDP growth would have compared favourably with average global GDP growth.

15 Do Local Investors Play a Stabilising Role Relative to Foreign...

international liabilities (assets) of a country. We use the inflow and outflow categories as some researchers argue that net capital flows are less informative. According to Adler et al. (2016), a decline in gross capital outflows due to an increase in the policy rate means asset repatriation by local investors. In contrast, a decline in gross capital inflows implies foreign investors' retrenchment. Therefore, a decline in capital outflows means that local investors will repatriate their foreign assets. On the other hand, a positive relationship between the repo rate and gross capital inflows suggests that foreign investors do retrench their capital investments following a repo rate increase. Is there evidence of repatriation and retrenchment activities following a repo rate increase?

Yes, the relationship between the repo rate and gross capital outflows is negative in Fig. 15.3. This suggests that an increase in the repo rate will lead to a decline in gross capital outflows. On the other hand, gross capital inflows are positively correlated to the repo rate. The relationships depicted by the scatterplots support that from the cross correlations in Fig. 15.3(e) and (f). The negative cross correlation suggests that gross capital inflows decline when preceded by an increase in the repo rate. The positive cross correlation suggests that gross capital inflows increase when preceded by elevated repo rate.

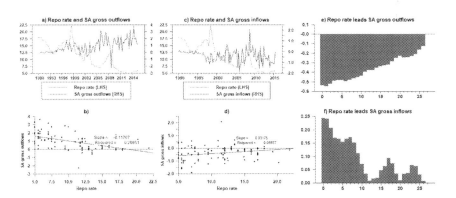

Fig. 15.3 Relationship between the repo rate and gross capital inflows and outflows. (Source: South African Reserve Bank and authors' calculations)

15.3 Empirical Evidence

The empirical analysis section applies a VAR approach, which includes US GDP growth, US FFR, SA GDP growth, SA gross capital outflows and inflows. The data is on a quarterly (Q) frequency for the sample period 1990Q1 to 2015Q3. The VAR model is estimated using the ordering that suggests that US variables are exogenous to the model and capital inflows and outflows depend on GDP growth and the policy rate. The capital inflows and outflows are expressed as per cent of trend GDP. The trend GDP is based on the Hodrick-Prescott filter. The model is estimated using two lags as selected by AIC and 10,000 Monte Carlo draws. The growth rates are at annual rate. The data is sourced from the South African Reserve Bank, Fred and IMF databases.

15.3.1 How Do Foreign and Domestic Investors React to Positive GDP Growth and Policy Rate Shocks?

This section looks at the effects of positive US GDP growth and monetary policy tightening shocks on capital flows. News of positive economic growth from the US are expected to induce US monetary tightening which pushes capital flows away from emerging market economies (EMEs). In contrast, better economic prospects and a positive interest rate differential in favour of EMEs is expected to attract capital flows to these markets. Thus, to what extent does SA GDP growth respond to a positive US GDP shock? Does the response deter foreign investor capital retrenchment from South Africa?

Figure 15.4 shows that a positive US GDP growth shock despite having a positive effect on SA GDP growth is followed by an increase in the US FFR.[3] Gross capital outflows increase while gross inflows decline on impact but with differing durations in Fig. 15.4(e) and (g), respectively. Figure 15.4(h) shows that gross capital inflows decline transitorily due to

---

[3] We tested for the robustness of the results to ordering by changing the ordering and placing inflows before outflows.

15 Do Local Investors Play a Stabilising Role Relative to Foreign…

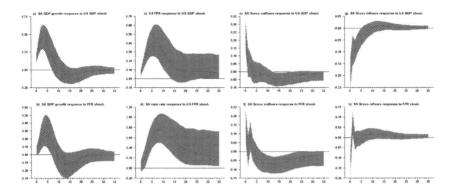

Fig. 15.4 Responses to positive US GDP growth and FFR shocks. (Note: The grey-shaded areas denote the 16th and 84th percentile error bands. Source: Authors' calculations)

FFR tightening. The response to the FFR tightening shock is highly transitory relative to that of a positive GDP growth shock. This difference is because the US policy rate increases significantly following positive US GDP growth shocks leading to a prolonged period of foreign investor retrenchment. This is different to the responses due to the tightening of the US policy rate only. The results suggest that the effects via GDP growth linkages far outweigh the impact via the interest rate differential channels in driving foreign investor retrenchment in South Africa.

Do local investors repatriate their assets due to positive US GDP growth and FFR tightening shocks? Evidence shows that a statistically significant asset repatriation by local investors occurs with a long delay following tightening in the US policy rate relative to the US GDP growth shock. The decline in gross capital inflows indicates that foreign investors retrench capital from South Africa. In addition, the surge in gross capital outflows indicates that local investors accumulate external assets. We conclude that local investors do not play a stabilising role following a positive US GDP growth shock. They do play a stabilising role with a long delay due to positive US policy rate shocks. These results suggest that a tightening in the US monetary policy that occurs following an improving GDP growth and outlook will have significant effects on South Africa through foreign investor retrenchments in Fig. 15.4(g).

Fact 1 *Local investors do not play a stabilising role following a positive US GDP growth shock. An increase in the US monetary policy rate that occurs following an improving GDP growth outlook has significant effects on South Africa through foreign investor retrenchments.*

15.3.2 Can Interest Rate Arbitrage Due to Positive GDP Growth and Interest Rate Shocks Be a Driver of Gross Flows Dynamics?

This section starts by showing the relationship between the repo rate-FFR spread and gross capital flows (inflow and outflows). The repo rate-FFR spread refers to the repo rate minus the US FFR. We use scatterplots, cross correlations and impulse responses to determine the effects of the repo rate-FFR spread. The VAR model estimated in this section includes US GDP growth, SA GDP growth, repo rate-FFR spread, SA gross capital outflows and inflows. The scatterplots in Fig. 15.5(a) reveal a much steeper relationship between the repo rate-FFR spread and gross capital outflows than with gross capital inflows.

In addition, the cross correlations in Fig. 15.5(b) indicate that gross capital outflows decline for a prolonged period compared to an increase in gross capital inflows when preceded by a higher repo rate-FFR spread.

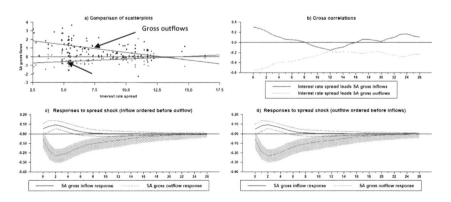

Fig. 15.5 Relationship between the repo rate-FFR spread and gross capital flows. (Note: The grey-shaded areas denote the 16th and 84th percentile error bands. Source: Authors' calculations)

Moreover, the impulse responses in Fig. 15.5(c) and (d) indicate that gross capital outflows respond significantly compared to gross capital inflows due to a positive repo rate-FFR spread shock. This evidence indicates that gross capital outflows are more responsive to the repo rate-FFR spread in favour of the repo rate. A positive repo rate-FFR spread shock (in favour of SA) leads to a significant repatriation of assets by domestic investors more than it induces reluctance in foreigners to retrench their assets in South Africa.

Fact 2 *Gross capital outflows are more responsive to the repo rate-FFR spread in favour of the repo rate. A shock to the repo rate-FFR spread in favour of SA leads to a significant repatriation of assets by domestic investors.*

15.3.3 Interest Rate Arbitrage from Positive Disturbances to the US Policy Rate

The preceding results did not show the interest rate arbitrage conditions that may arise following positive US GDP growth and FFR shocks. The results only showed that a positive repo rate-FFR spread shock does matter for gross capital outflows. Figure 15.6(a) shows that the FFR rises following a positive US FFR shock, leading to a negative differential relative

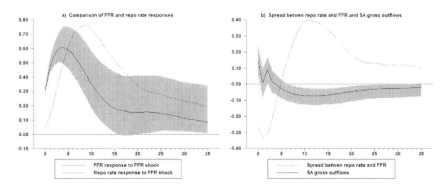

Fig. 15.6 The repo rate-FFR differential and South African gross capital outflows. (Note: The grey-shaded areas denote the 16th and 84th percentile error bands. Source: Authors' calculations)

to the repo rate. It is only after five quarters that the repo rate increases more than the FFR. Hence, the interest rate differential peaks around ten quarters.

Figure 15.6(b) shows that a positive and rising interest rate differential induces local investors to start a stabilising role as shown by a significant decline in gross capital outflows. Thus, a positive repo rate-FFR spread due to the US FFR policy tightening accompanied by a delayed repo rate tightening leads to a delay in the repatriation of assets by local investors. The increased gross capital outflow within a year means that domestic investors do not play a stabilising role on impact in responses to the US monetary policy tightening. This reflects that foreign and domestic investors tend to move in the same direction but with different sensitivities and magnitudes. Furthermore, Adler and Tovar (2015) suggest that the movement of foreign and domestic investors in the same direction may indicate that investors seek existing arbitrage opportunities in the short-term interest rate differential.

Fact 3 *A positive and rising interest rate differential induces local investors to play a stabilising role as shown by a significant decline in gross capital outflows.*

15.3.4 The Interest Rate Arbitrage from A Positive US GDP Growth Shock

Would the conclusions in the preceding sections differ if the US interest rate increase is due to improved GDP growth? To test for this, we estimated the VAR model in the previous sections but included US GDP growth in the model so that we can interpret the tight US interest rate shock to reflect improved economic conditions. This approach differs from a purely monetary shock analysed earlier and can have different implications in terms of the impact on capital flows into the South African economy. So, does an improvement in US GDP growth impact the stabilisation role of domestic investors? To answer this question, we compare the responses of US GDP growth and the FFR in Fig. 15.7(a) and (b). Consistent with GDP growth spill-overs and lower multiplier effects, SA GDP growth increases due to a positive US growth shock. The increase,

15 Do Local Investors Play a Stabilising Role Relative to Foreign... 245

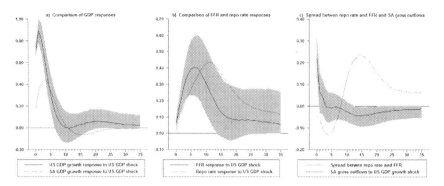

Fig. 15.7 Responses of repo rate-FFR spread and domestic gross capital outflows due to positive US GDP growth shock. (Note: The grey-shaded areas denote the 16th and 84th percentile error bands. Source: Authors' calculations)

although significant, reaches a peak that is far below that of the US GDP growth. In addition, after five quarters the GDP growth responses tend not to be significantly different from each other.

Despite the repo rate and FFR rising, the repo rate increases with a delay but reaches a higher peak than the FFR. The developments in gross capital outflows reflect those in the interest rate spread dynamics. Gross capital outflows rise in the beginning and then decline significantly between 15 and 20 quarters when the interest rate differential reaches its peak effects. This suggests that assets repatriation by local investors happens with big lag following a US GDP growth shock. Thus, improved economic prospects and news from the South African economy can improve prospects of the repatriation of assets by local investors.

Fact 4 *Improved economic prospects and news from the South African economy can improve the repatriation of assets by local investors.*

15.3.5 Comparison of the Effects of the Interest Rate Arbitrage

Figure 15.8 shows that the interest rate differential induced by the US policy rate shock seems to be more potent in inducing asset repatriation as it results in a bigger repo rate-FFR spread than that emanating from a positive US growth shock.

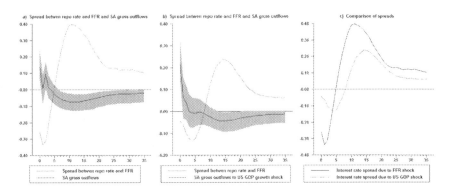

Fig. 15.8 The impact of pure and growth-driven US interest rate shock. (Note: The grey-shaded areas denote the 16th and 84th percentile error bands. Source: Authors' calculations)

Fact 5 *The interest rate differential induced by the US policy rate shock is more potent in inducing asset repatriation.*

15.4 The Role of Positive VIX Shocks

We stated earlier that changes in global investor risk perceptions impact the direction of capital flows. Large changes in global risk aversion shocks during the global financial crises and the taper tantrum in May 2013 were experienced. Literature suggests that episodes of changes in global investor risk appetite and net capital flow reversals were driven by declines in gross capital inflows (foreign investors retrenching from EMEs) and surges in gross capital outflows (local investors accumulating external assets). Other studies find that episodes of reversals of gross capital inflows did not entail a reversal of net capital inflows (residents have a fully offsetting effect on the behaviour of non-resident investors). The results in Fig. 15.9(c) show that a positive VIX shock leads to an insignificant decline in gross capital outflows on impact but this is followed by a transitory and significant increase in the second quarter. This suggests that local investors do not significantly repatriate their assets.

US GDP growth declines for nearly five quarters in response to elevated risk in Fig. 15.9(a). In addition, gross capital inflows do not react

15 Do Local Investors Play a Stabilising Role Relative to Foreign...

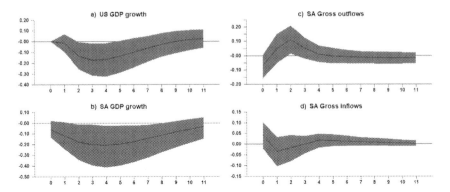

Fig. 15.9 Responses of US and SA GDP growth to positive VIX shocks. (Note: The grey-shaded areas denote the 16th and 84th percentile error bands. Source: Authors' calculations)

significantly. Based on Fig. 15.9(a) and (b), this means that elevated risk aversion shocks are detrimental to GDP growth in the US and SA economies.

Fact 6 *Elevated risk aversion shocks are detrimental to GDP growth in the US and SA economies.*

15.4.1 Do Domestic Conditions Matter for Repatriation of Domestic Assets by Local Investors?

This section compares the effects of a positive 1 per cent SA GDP growth shock to those due to a positive 1 per cent repo rate shock. Figure 15.10(a) shows that SA GDP growth rises significantly for nearly a year due to a positive GDP growth shock. In contrast, GDP growth declines for nearly ten quarters due to 1 per cent tightening in the repo rate. The GDP growth and repo rate shocks impact gross outflows in the same direction in this first year in Fig. 15.10(b). But a positive repo rate shock leads to a bigger and prolonged decline in gross capital outflows than a positive GDP growth shock. Thus, asset repatriation by local investors rises significantly following a policy tightening shock.

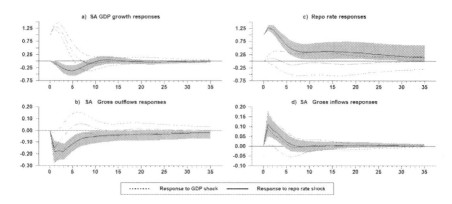

Fig. 15.10 Comparison of responses to positive domestic GDP growth and repo rate shocks. (Note: The grey-shaded areas denote the 16th and 84th percentile error bands. Source: Authors' calculations)

So, is there retrenchment of capital by foreign investors? No, based on the results in Fig. 15.10(d), the gross capital inflows rise significantly for nearly six quarters following a 100-basis points repo rate increase. In contrast, the positive GDP growth shock increases gross capital inflows significantly for two quarters. Based on the peak effects, the 100-basis points repo rate increase leads to a slightly higher per cent of gross capital inflows relative to that of a positive GDP shock. Hence, the evidence indicates that episodes of reversals in gross inflows do not entail a reversal in outflows. This means that domestic residents do not fully offset the behaviour of non-resident investors.

Fact 7 *Episodes of reversals in gross capital inflows do not entail a reversal in capital outflows. Hence, domestic residents do not fully offset the behaviour of non-resident investors.*

15.4.2 Does the Persistence of A Positive Repo Rate Shock Matter?

The results in Fig. 15.11 indicate that a persistently increasing repo rate shock leads to an increase in gross capital inflows compared to a non-persistent repo rate shock in Fig. 15.11(b). This suggests that a high repo

15 Do Local Investors Play a Stabilising Role Relative to Foreign... 249

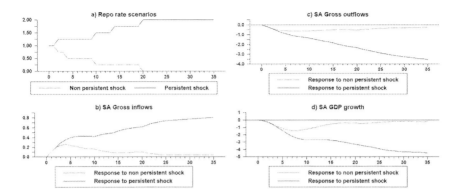

Fig. 15.11 The impact of persistent and non-persistent repo rate shocks on gross capital flows. (Source: Authors' calculations)

rate does not induce foreign investor to retrench their assets from South Africa.

The decline in South African gross capital outflows in Fig. 15.11(c) is large when the repo rate shock is persistently increasing leading local investors to repatriate their assets for a prolonged period. But SA GDP growth declines persistently by a bigger magnitude due to a persistently increasing repo rate.

Fact 8 *A persistently increasing repo rate induces local investors to repatriate their assets for a prolonged period. But, domestic GDP growth declines persistently by a bigger magnitude due to a persistently increasing repo rate.*

15.4.3 Does the Persistence of A Positive GDP Growth Shock Matter for Capital Flows?

In this section, we distinguish between a persistently rising GDP growth shock and non-persistent shock in Fig. 15.12(a). A persistently rising GDP growth shock in Fig. 15.12(b) leads to more gross capital inflows compared to a non-persistent GDP growth shock. In addition, the results in Fig. 15.12(c) indicate that a persistently rising GDP growth shock leads to a decline in South African gross capital outflows suggesting that local investors repatriate their assets.

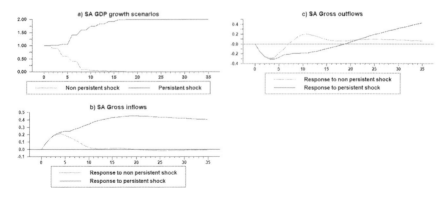

Fig. 15.12 The impact of persistent and non-persistent positive GDP growth shocks on gross capital flows. (Source: Authors' calculations)

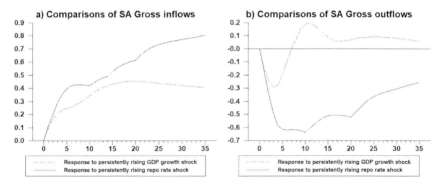

Fig. 15.13 Comparison of domestic gross capital flow responses. (Source: Authors' calculations)

The repatriation of assets lasts for a longer period when GDP growth is persistently rising relative to when it is a non-persistent shock. We conclude that the persistence of positive GDP growth shocks matters for the repatriation of assets by local investors and the deterrence of retrenchment by foreign investors. Furthermore, in Fig. 15.13 a persistently rising repo rate shock increases gross capital inflows more than positive GDP growth shocks do.

In addition, a persistently rising repo rate shock leads to a bigger decline in gross capital outflows, suggesting that local investors repatriate assets more due to a repo rate shock compared to the GDP growth shock. We showed in the earlier sections that GDP growth declines more and persistently in response to a persistently rising repo rate shock.

Fact 9 *A persistently rising repo rate shock leads to a larger repatriation of assets by local investors compared to a positive GDP growth shock. But, a persistently rising repo rate shock leads to a decline in GDP growth.*

15.5 How Important Are the Foreign Shocks in Driving Movements in Gross Capital Outflows and Inflows?

Which US shock matters for gross capital outflows and inflows? To answer this question, this section estimates the forecast error variance decompositions to determine the fluctuations in gross capital outflows and inflows induced by US GDP growth and FFR shocks. Figure 15.14(a) shows that a positive US GDP growth shock induces more fluctuations in gross capital inflows compared to gross capital outflows over all forecast horizons.

In contrast, the results in Fig. 15.14(b) indicate that the US FFR shock induces more fluctuations in SA gross capital inflows in the first ten quarters. This suggests that in the short-term US GDP growth and FFR shocks matter much for foreign investor activities in South Africa.

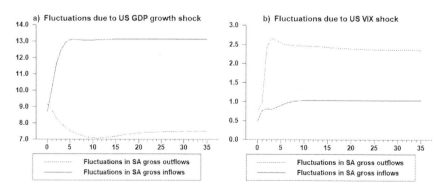

Fig. 15.14 Proportion of fluctuations in gross capital outflows and inflows due to US positive GDP growth and FFR shocks. (Source: Authors' calculations)

Fact 10 *The US FFR shock induces more fluctuations in SA gross capital inflows because in the short-term, US GDP growth and FFR dynamics matter much for foreign investor activities in South Africa.*

15.5.1 Which South African Shock Matters for Gross Capital Outflows and Inflows?

This section concludes the analysis by investigating the influence of positive SA GDP growth and repo rate shocks on gross capital outflows and inflows. Figure 15.15(a) and (b) shows that positive SA GDP growth and repo rate shocks induce more fluctuations on gross capital outflows than in gross capital inflows.

However, the SA GDP growth shock does not explain more than 5 per cent over all forecast horizons of gross capital flows in Fig. 15.15(a). A positive repo rate shock in Fig. 15.15(b) explains nearly 15 per cent of fluctuations in gross capital outflows, which is nearly three time more than gross capital inflows

Fact 11 *A positive repo rate shock explains nearly 15 per cent of fluctuations in gross capital outflows, which is nearly three time more than gross*

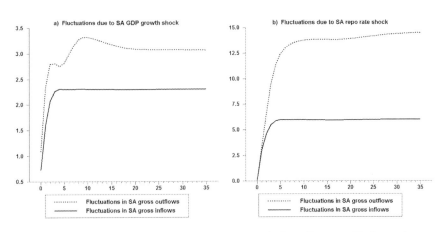

Fig. 15.15 Proportion of fluctuation in gross capital outflows and inflows due to positive SA GDP growth and repo rate shocks. (Source: Authors' calculations)

capital inflows compared to less than 5 per cent variation due to domestic a positive GDP growth shock.

15.6 Conclusion and Policy Implications

The chapter explored the extent to which local investors play a stabilising role relative to foreign investors after economic shocks to US and SA GDP growth and policy rates. Evidence indicates that there is repatriation and retrenchment activity following repo rate changes. The repo rate is negatively (positively) associated with gross capital outflows (inflows). This suggests that an increase (decline) in the repo rate will lead to a decline (increase) in gross capital outflows (inflows).

Do domestic investors play an offsetting role by repatriating foreign assets following a positive US policy rate and GDP growth shocks? We establish different responses to positive US GDP growth and FFR shocks. The results suggest that the effects via GDP growth linkages far outweigh the impact via the interest rate differential channels in driving foreign investor retrenchment in South Africa. Furthermore, local investors do not play a stabilising role following a positive US GDP growth shock. But they do play a stabilising role with a long delay due to positive US policy rate shocks. The results suggest that a tightening in the US monetary policy that occurs following an improving GDP growth and outlook will have significant effects on South Africa through foreign investor retrenchments.

How do gross capital inflows react to positive SA GDP growth and repo rate shocks? The results show that gross capital outflows decline for a prolonged period compared to an increase in gross capital inflows due to a positive repo rate-FFR spread shock. This evidence indicates that gross capital outflows are more responsive to the repo rate-FFR spread in favour of the repo rate. A shock to the repo rate-FFR spread in favour of SA leads to significant repatriation of assets by domestic investors than it induces reluctance in foreigners to retrench their assets in South Africa. Furthermore, assets repatriation by local investors occurs following a positive US GDP growth shock. This implies that improved economic prospects and news from the South African economy can improve the repatriation of assets by local investors.

On the other hand, a positive repo rate-FFR spread due to the US FFR policy tightening is accompanied by a delayed repo rate tightening which leads to a delay in the repatriation of assets by local investors. The increased gross capital outflow means that domestic investors do not play a stabilising role on impact in response to US monetary policy tightening. This reflects that foreign and domestic investors tend to move in the same direction but with different sensitivities and magnitudes. The movement of foreign and domestic investors in the same direction may indicate that investors seek existing arbitrage opportunities in the short-term interest rate differential. Thus, a positive repo rate-FFR spread shock does matter for gross capital outflows.

References

Adler, G., Djigbenou, M.L., and Sosa, S. 2016. *Global Financial Shocks and Foreign Asset Repatriation: Do Local Investors Play a Stabilizing Role?* IMF Working Paper WP/16/60.

Adler, G., and Tovar, C.E. 2015. Global Financial Shocks and their Economic Impact on Emerging Market Economies. *Journal of International Commerce, Economics and Policy*, 4(2), 1–27.

Bernanke, Ben S. 2007. Global Imbalances: Recent Developments and Prospects. Speech delivered at Bundesbank, Berlin, 11 September.

Bernanke, Ben S. 2008. Remarks on the Economic Outlook. International Monetary Conference, Barcelona, Spain, 3 June.

IMF World Economic Outlook. 2016. Too Slow for Too Long. https://www.elibrary.imf.org/view/IMF081.

16

Do Investors' Net Purchases and Capital Retrenchment Activities Impact the Monetary Policy Response to Positive Inflation Shocks?

Learning Objectives

- Test whether net purchases or total purchases or capital flow surges or retrenchments amplify or dampen the GDP growth responses to monetary policy tightening shocks.
- Explore the effects of net purchases or total purchases or capital flow surges or retrenchments on the inflation response to rand depreciation shocks.
- Establish whether the repo rate response to positive inflation shocks is amplified or dampened by net purchases or total purchases or capital flow surges or retrenchment shocks.
- Establish whether the R/US$ exchange rate depreciation shocks deter net purchase by non-residents and increase risk aversion.
- Explore whether the R/US$ exchange rate depreciation and inflationary shocks have adverse effects on (i) investors' net purchases of stocks and bonds and (ii) capital flow surges and sudden stops episodes.

16.1 Introduction

The earlier chapters exploring the role of capital flow episodes did not address the amplification effects of capital flow episodes on economic activity and the policy implications thereof. We are motivated by lack of empirical evidence which distinguishes between the amplification effects of sudden stops episodes, capital flow surges episodes and net purchases of shares and bonds by non-residents on the responses of selected macroeconomic indicators to various economic shocks. The amplification effects explored in this chapter are not only restricted to their role on price stability via their impact on inflation responses to the rand per US dollar (R/US$) exchange rate depreciation shocks. We also assess their impact on the GDP growth responses to monetary policy tightening shocks. This will enable us to derive appropriate policy prescriptions based on the role of capital flow episodes in the evolution of GDP growth, inflation and the policy rate.

This chapter differs from Dahlhaus and Vasishtha (2014), who found reduced capital inflow activity into South Africa due to the expected US policy normalisation shock. In contrast to these authors, we determine the amplification effects of selected capital flow episodes. Furthermore, we classify capital flows as either sudden stops or surges. Thereafter, we estimate the economic costs of capital flow episodes. To classify the capital flow episodes, we apply the Forbes and Warnock classification of episodes. Forbes and Warnock (2011) assert that capital flow volatility can amplify economic cycles as well as increase the financial system vulnerability. We show policymakers that the rand exchange rate depreciation and inflationary shocks have adverse effects on investors' net purchases of stocks and bonds, and capital flow surges and sudden stops episodes. The findings in this chapter suggest that price stability and the exchange rate stability matter.

Similar to earlier chapters, we apply the Forbes and Warnock (2011) classification of capital flow episodes for the analysis. First, we fill research gaps by showing that the R/US$ exchange rate depreciation and inflationary shocks have adverse effects on investors' net purchases of stocks and bonds, capital flow surges and sudden stops episodes. Second, we determine whether price stability and the exchange rate stability matter. We apply counterfactual analysis to test whether net purchases or total purchases or capital flow surges or retrenchments amplify or dampen the responses of (i) GDP growth to monetary policy tightening shocks, (ii) inflation responses to the R/US$ exchange rate depreciation shock and (iii) repo rate responses to positive inflation shocks. Furthermore, we determine whether the R/US$ exchange rate depreciation shocks (i) deter net purchase by non-residents, increase risk aversion and sudden stops episodes and (iii) reduce capital flow surges episodes. Despite increasing financial vulnerabilities, Forbes and Warnock (2011) noticed that during the time of global liquidity contraction, economies benefitted from capital inflows driven by domestic investors as they liquidated their foreign investments (or retrenchment activities). Hence, we examine the amplification effects of these retrenchment episode effects. Furthermore, the analysis shows policymakers the extent to which these capital flow episodes can amplify GDP growth, inflation and policy rate responses to various shocks.

16.2 How Does Literature Classify Capital Flow Episodes, and Does It Separate Between Foreign and Domestic Investor Activities?

We bring the least-discussed differentiation in the classification of capital flow episodes and the potential policy dilemmas they present. Forbes and Warnock (2011) show that the reference definition of the data used in answering this question matters. There is a difference between using gross versus net capital flows in defining capital flow episodes. It is noted in literature that the following are the shortcomings of using net capital flows to define episodes: (i) the failure to differentiate between changes in foreign and domestic investor behaviour; (ii) the size and volatility of gross flows can increase while net capital flows have become more stable; (iii) domestic investor flows can become increasingly important. Therefore, the change in net flows can no longer be driven by foreigner investors alone. This is particularly important when considering the relaxation of exchange controls on residents in recent years and (iv) the increased incidence of capital flow sudden stops and retrenchment resulting from investors liquidating their foreign investment positions.

We argue that the South African discussions on capital flows should discern capital flow waves according to (i) the sudden stops that occur when foreign capital inflows suddenly slow or stop and (ii) surges which happen when foreign capital inflows increase rapidly.[1]

16.3 Do Macroeconomic Fundamentals Matter?

As stated in earlier paragraphs, we use episodes identified by Forbes and Warnock (2011) for four capital flow wave categories to investigate the effects associated with capital flow dynamics on South African macroeconomic variables. We generate dummy variables that capture the capital flow episodes separately. We set the dummy variables equal to one for the capital flow episodes identified by Forbes and Warnock and zero otherwise. This is done for each capital flow wave episode, namely: (i) a capital flow sudden stops episode; (ii) capital inflow surges episodes. Thereafter, we estimate various VAR models with five variables, namely a capital flow dummy, GDP growth, VIX changes, inflation and the repo rate. The capital flow dummy is for (i) the capital flow surges episodes, (ii) the capital flow sudden stops episodes and (iii) the capital flow retrenchment episodes. These capital flow dummy variables enter the VAR models separately. The other two dummy vari-

---

[1] Retrenchments occur when domestic investors liquidate their foreign investments and capital flight which occurs when domestic investors send large amounts of capital abroad. This also means that domestic investors are not cut off from global capital markets. Domestic investors have ample access to these markets and utilise them by moving their domestic funds abroad (Forbes and Warnock 2011). What could possibly trigger the latter episode of capital flows? This might happen if domestic investors with superior information foresee a negative shock to the local market. In anticipation of this shock, they shift their money to global markets. This leads to net capital inflows decline, but the difference is that this decline is not prompted by foreign investors (Rothenberg and Warnock 2011).

ables are for the (i) adoption of the inflation targeting framework which is equal one for period beginning 2000 up to the end of the sample and zero otherwise; and (ii) the recession which is equal to one for 2009Q1–Q3 and zero otherwise.

The VAR models are estimated using two lags including a constant and two dummies. The data is on quarterly (Q) basis spanning the period 1995Q1 to 2014Q3. The data is sourced from the South African Reserve Bank data base. We use the Choleski decomposition and place each capital flows episode dummy as the first variable suggesting that it is the most exogenous variable. This suggests that the capital flow episode is independent of the South African variables. All growth rates are at annual rate. The confidence bands are based on 10,000 Monte Carlo draws. Shocks are a one standard deviation the variable of interest.

16.3.1 The R/US$ Exchange Rate Depreciation Shocks

We begin the analysis in this section by looking at the effects of the R/US$ exchange rate depreciation shocks. Figure 16.1(a) shows that the R/US$ exchange rate depreciation shock leads to a transitory increase in a sudden stops episode which lasts two quarters. In contrast, the

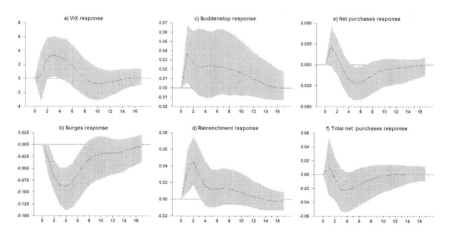

Fig. 16.1 Responses to the rand per US dollar exchange rate depreciation shocks. (Note: The grey-shaded areas denote the 16th and 84th percentile error bands. Source: Authors' calculations)

capital flow surges episodes decline significantly for eight quarters. The net purchases of South African assets by non-residents decline significantly between four and eight quarters whereas total net purchases on South African assets by non-residents do not respond significantly. We find that the R/US$ exchange rate depreciation leads to domestic investors' retrenchment over a year. These responses suggest that a stable exchange rate matters.

16.3.2 Evidence from Positive Inflation Shocks

The determinants of capital flows are classified into pull-and-push factors and high inflation is a deterrent factor to capital inflows. We determine the extent to which positive inflation shocks impact the capital flow sudden stops, surges episodes, risk aversion, net purchases of domestic shares by non-residents, total net purchases of shares and bond by non-residents, and domestic investors' retrenchment of capital flows. The impulses responses are shown in Fig. 16.2. Evidence suggests that positive inflationary shocks transitorily raise risk aversion and sudden stops episodes and lead to significant declines in net purchases of domestic shares by non-residents. Total net purchases of domestic shares and bonds by non-residents declines much more compared to net purchases of domestic shares by non-residents. In addition, domestic investors' retrenchments declines but not significantly.

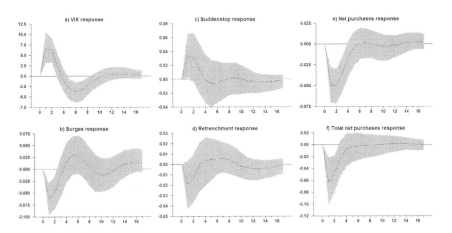

Fig. 16.2 Responses to positive inflation shocks. (Note: The grey-shaded areas denote the 16th and 84th percentile error bands. Source: Authors' calculations)

This evidence concludes that high inflation significantly deters capital flow surges episodes and net purchases of domestic shares by non-residents. Therefore, stable inflation is important for domestic and non-resident investors' activities. These results suggest that price stability should be enforced.

16.3.3 Monetary Policy and Economic Growth

To derive policy implications regarding the response of inflation to the R/US$ exchange rate depreciation shocks, this section applies a counterfactual approach which shuts off the effects of capital flow retrenchments, risk aversion and net purchases of domestic shares by non-residents, respectively. The VAR model estimated in this section includes the repo rate, inflation, GDP growth, capital flow retrenchment, VIX, net purchases of domestic shares by non-residents and a capital flow sudden stops episode dummy variable. The analysis focuses on the activities of domestic investors. We then compare the counterfactual GDP growth with the actual responses when these variables are not shut off in the model. The model is estimated using two lags and 10,000 Monte Carlo draws.

Figure 16.3 shows that actual GDP growth would be much lower in the presence of a capital flow sudden stops episode and elevated VIX

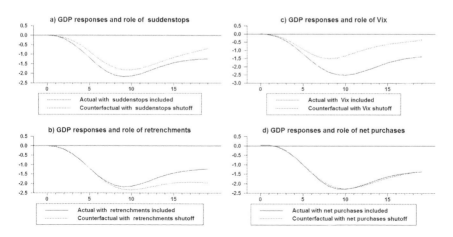

Fig. 16.3 Counterfactual and actual cumulative GDP growth responses to positive repo rate shocks. (Source: Authors' calculations)

compared to the counterfactual. In contrast, the GDP growth response would not decline much in the presence of domestic investors' retrenchment compared to when it is shut off in the model.

16.3.4 Inflation Adjustment to the R/US$ Exchange Rate Depreciation Shocks

This section derives the policy implications regarding the response of inflation to the R/US$ exchange rate depreciation shocks. To derive the policy implications, a counterfactual approach VAR model which shuts off the effects of capital flow retrenchment, risk aversion and net purchases of domestic shares by non-residents is estimated. The focus of the analysis is on the activities of investors and their effects are compared to the counterfactual and actual inflation responses when these variables are not shut off in the model. Figure 16.4 shows that actual inflation would be lower in the presence of net purchases and domestic capital retrenchment compared to the counterfactual inflation rate.

In contrast, the inflation response would be higher in the presence of elevated VIX than when it is shut off in the model. The domestic investors' capital flow retrenchment has a bigger impact in dampening infla-

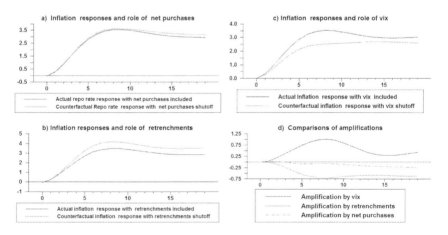

Fig. 16.4 Counterfactual and actual cumulative inflation responses to the rand per US dollar exchange rate depreciation shocks. (Source: Authors' calculations)

tionary pressures due to the R/US$ exchange rate depreciation shocks than due to net purchases of domestic shares by non-residents.

16.3.5 Is the Monetary Policy Response to Positive Inflation Shocks Impacted?

To derive policy implications regarding the response of the repo rate to positive inflation shocks, this section applies a counterfactual VAR approach similar to the previous section. The repo rate responses are then compared with the responses when these channels are not shut off in the model. The results in Fig. 16.5 show that the counterfactual repo rate would be higher when the capital flow surges episodes, retrenchments and net purchases of domestic shares by non-residents are shut off in the model than when these are included. This suggests that increased capital flow surges episodes, capital flow retrenchment episodes and increased net purchases of domestic shares by non-residents lead to the appreciation in the R/US$ which lowers the inflation rate, thus leading to a lower level of the repo rate.

In contrast, the actual repo rate would be higher in the presence of elevated VIX than when it is shut off in the model. This suggests that higher risk aversion as shown in Fig. 16.5 leads to the R/US$ exchange rate depreciations which has inflationary pressures, leading to aggressive

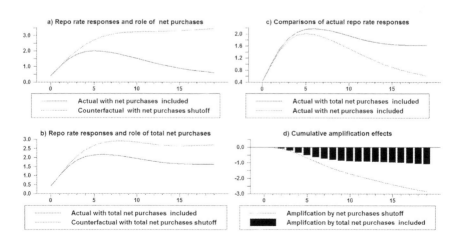

Fig. 16.5 Counterfactual and actual cumulative repo rate responses to positive inflation shocks. (Source: Authors' calculations)

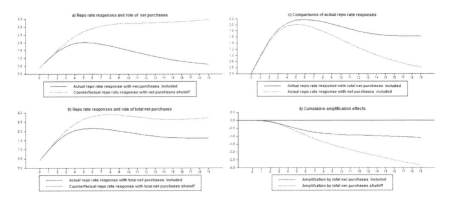

Fig. 16.6 Comparison of the cumulative effects of total and net purchases of domestic shares by non-residents. (Source: Authors' calculations)

policy tightening. It is evident in Fig. 16.6 that the impact of increased net purchases of domestic shares by non-residents matters for the responses of the repo rate to positive inflation shocks. The results show that the actual repo rate is lower than the counterfactual rate, which suggests that increased net purchases of domestic shares by non-residents through the appreciation of the R/US$ exchange rate leads to lower inflation and repo rate responses to inflation shocks. This suggests that increased net purchases of domestic shares by non-residents dampen the repo rate responses to positive inflation shocks.

Overall, the results indicate that the repo rate is tightened to positive inflation shocks consistent with enforcing the price stability mandate irrespective of capital flow surges, capital flow retrenchments, net purchases of domestic shares by non-residents and risk aversion shocks.

16.4 Conclusion and Policy Implications

This chapter distinguished between the amplification effects of capital flow sudden stops episodes, capital flow surges episodes and net purchases of domestic shares and bonds by non-residents on the responses of selected macroeconomic indicators to various economic shocks. First, the results indicate that the R/US$ exchange rate depreciation shocks leads to a transitory increase in a sudden stops episodes, whereas the capital flow surges episodes decline. The R/US$ exchange rate depreciation also leads to domestic investors' retrenchment. Hence, a stable exchange rate matters. Second, high inflation is a deterrent factor to capital inflows. Evidence suggests that inflationary shocks transitorily increase risk aversion, a sudden stops episodes and lead to a significant decline in net purchases of domestic shares by non-residents. Therefore, stable inflation environment is important for domestic and non-resident investors' activities.

What are the amplification effects of capital flow sudden stops episodes, capital flow surges episodes and net purchases of domestic shares and bonds by non-residents on the responses of selected macroeconomic indicators to various economic shocks? Evidence shows that capital flow sudden stops and elevated VIX propagate the negative effects of high inflation on GDP growth responses. Furthermore, VIX and domestic investors' capital flow retrenchment have a bigger impact in propagating inflationary pressures due to the R/US$ exchange rate depreciation shock. Higher risk aversion leads to the R/US$ exchange rate depreciation which has inflationary pressures leading to aggressive policy tightening. On the other hand, increased capital flow surges, retrenchment episodes and net purchases of domestic shares by non-residents due to the appreciation in the R/US$ lower the inflation rate, thus leading to a lower level of the repo rate. Similarly, increased net purchases of domestic shares by non-residents through the appreciation of the R/US$ exchange rate dampen the repo rate responses to positive inflation shocks.

References

Dahlhaus, T., and Vasishtha, G. 2014. *The Impact of U.S. Monetary Policy Normalization on Capital Flows to Emerging-Market Economies*. Bank of Canada Working Paper 2014-53.

Forbes, K.J., and Warnock, F.E. 2011. *Capital Flow Waves: Surges, Stops, Flight, and Retrenchment*. NBER Working Paper No. 17351, August 2011.

Rothenberg, A.D., and Warnock, F.E. 2011. Sudden Flight and True Sudden Stops. *Review of International Economics*, 19, 509–24.

Part IV

The Transmission of Sovereign Debt Credit Ratings Downgrades and Upgrades into the Credit Markets and the Real Economy

17

What Role Does Business Confidence Play in Transmitting Sovereign Debt Credit Ratings Upgrades and Downgrades Shocks into the Real Economy?

Learning Objectives

- Show the effects of the simultaneous occurrence of low business confidence and heightened risk of a sovereign debt credit ratings upgrades and downgrades on the domestic real economy
- Determine the role of the business confidence channel in transmitting sovereign debt credit ratings upgrade and downgrades shocks to GDP growth
- Show the indirect role of the business confidence channel in explaining the transmission of sovereign rating downgrades and upgrades on GDP growth.

17.1 Introduction

The risk of a further sovereign debt credit ratings downgrade remains elevated in 2019. At the same time, consumer and business confidence levels have continued to deteriorate and remain at historic low levels. Almeida et al. (2014) find that via the *sovereign ceiling channel*, sovereign debt credit ratings downgrades lead to an increase in the cost of debt, decline in investment and leverage of firms. In addition, Adelino and Fereira (2014) establish that banks increase loan spreads during sovereign debt credit ratings downgrades. Thus, the real effects of sovereign debt credit ratings downgrades are not only transmitted via fundamentals such as interest rates and crowding-out effects. Furthermore, the negative externalities are regardless of private firms' financial soundness. This implies that public debt management generates negative externalities for the private sector and real economic activity. So, what does the simultaneous occurrence of low business confidence and the heightened risk of a sovereign debt credit ratings upgrade and downgrade do to the domestic real economy? Does business confidence play a role in transmitting a sovereign debt credit ratings upgrades and downgrades shocks to GDP growth?

A large body of literature shows that confidence plays a role in transmitting stimulatory policy decision. Barsky and Sims (2009) categorise the role of confidence in macroeconomics into two views. First, is the animal spirits view, which suggests autonomous fluctuations in beliefs that in turn have causal effects on economic activity. Second, is the news view (the impact of positive news about the performance of the economy) regarding the causal relationship between confidence and the subsequent macroeconomic activity. This is underpinned by the fact that confidence measures contain fundamental information about the current and future states of the economy. In most studies, the channel linking confidence and subsequent macroeconomic activity is changes is future productivity. Without taking any view, we illustrate the role of confidence and the responses of expectations to expansionary monetary policy in Fig. 17.1. We use changes in interest rates to demonstrate the impact of accommodative monetary policy on output when consumer and business confidence are high and low. A decline in interest rates results in a much higher response in output (Y_0 to Y_2) when confidence is high, and agents have better expectations about the economic outlook, compared to Y_0 to Y_1, when confidence and expectations are low.

In addition, the stylised facts in Fig. 17.2 show that business confidence is positively related to GDP growth. Furthermore, consumer confidence has a bigger effect on GDP growth than business confidence in Fig. 17.2(c). This is consistent with findings in Farmer (2011) that consumer sentiment leads to private activity and does not passively reflect the

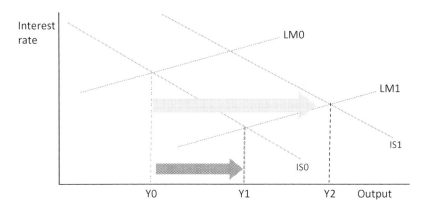

Fig. 17.1 The role of confidence and expectations in responding to stimulatory policy shocks. (Source: Authors' drawings)

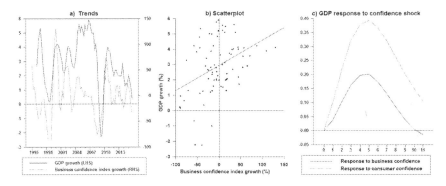

Fig. 17.2 GDP growth, consumer and business confidence. (Source: South African Reserve Bank and Authors' calculations)

current state of the economy. In addition, Barsky and Sims (2012) find that consumer confidence results in an increase in GDP growth largely via changes in future productivity compared to the contribution of pure animal spirits. Nonetheless, Barsky and Sims (2012) conclude that the contribution of animal spirts is non-negligible.

Evidence shows that confidence directly influences GDP growth. In addition, it is possible that confidence plays a role as an indirect channel in transmitting other economic shocks to GDP growth such as sovereign debt credit ratings downgrades and upgrades. The debate about the effects of an increase in government debt (and budget deficits) on economic growth remains unsettled. For instance, on the one hand, studies find that because debt (tax)-financed deficits trigger high interest costs (tax rates), these then decrease productivity growth and deter private investment. On the other, deficit spending is found to complement business investment and stimulate economic productivity.

Similarly, studies report mixed findings on the role of consumer and business confidence in the propagation of expansionary fiscal policy shocks to promote economic activity. For instance, Bachman and Sims (2012) find high fiscal multipliers during periods of economic slack compared to normal times. The authors attribute this to the systematic response of confidence following an increase in government spending. The key channel of transmission of confidence is the information it contains about future productivity improvements. On the other hand, Jia and Kim (2015) fail to establish a positive role for consumer confidence as a propagation mechanism for positive government spending shocks. They find that increases in the government spending generate consumer pessimism, which may weaken the fiscal policy effect on GDP growth.

17.2 Stylised Relationships

What do the stylised facts suggest is the nature of the relationship between government debt, GDP growth and confidence indicators? Figure 17.3 shows that consumer and business confidence and GDP growth are negatively related to changes in government debt. The slope of the negative relationship is much steeper between changes in government debt and business confidence. The negative relationship is robust to using confidence indicators in levels and the government debt-to-GDP ratio.

What might explain this negative association of changes in government debt and business confidence? Ratings agencies look at several variables when assessing the creditworthiness of a sovereign state. The level of government debt and its ratio to GDP are amongst the key factors that are flagged as risk indicators which have an important bearing on sovereign debt credit risk and the ratings. In turn, Adelino and Fereira (2014) show that sovereign debt credit ratings represent a strong upper bound

17 What Role Does Business Confidence Play in Transmitting... 273

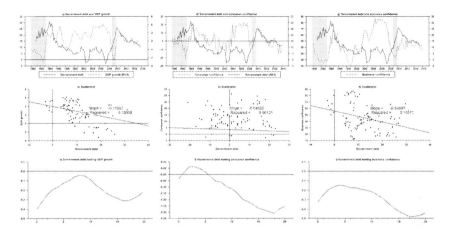

Fig. 17.3 Government debt growth, GDP growth, and consumer and business confidence. (Source: South African Reserve Bank and authors' calculations)

and have an important effect on the firms' cost of debt, investment decisions and leverage through the sovereign ceiling channel.

Furthermore, the evidence of the lead-lag relationships based on cross correlations shown in Fig. 17.3(c), (f) and (i) is consistent with findings in literature that show that exogenous shocks to government spending support consumption but tend to be negative for both residential and non-residential investment.[1] In addition, Fig. 17.4 shows that government debt is negatively associated with productivity. At the same time, business confidence is positively related to productivity growth.

The negative association of government debt growth with productivity is a possible channel through which changes in government debt result in lower business confidence. Hence, this chapter investigates the effects of sovereign debt credit ratings downgrades shocks and the role of business confidence in the transmission of these effects to economic growth. That is, to what extent does business confidence react to sovereign debt credit ratings downgrades and upgrades shocks and does it amplify the transmission of these shocks to output? What are the implications for monetary policy? What is the counterfactual repo rate under different scenarios of sovereign debt credit ratings downgrades and upgrades?

---

[1] See for example, Blanchard and Perotti (2002), Fatás and Mihov (2001) and Mountford and Uhlig (2000).

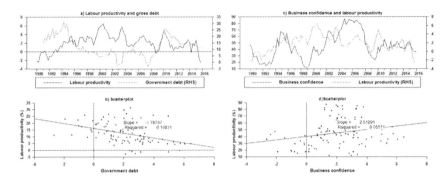

Fig. 17.4 Government debt growth, labour productivity and business confidence. (Source: South African Reserve Bank and authors' calculations)

17.3 Do Positive GDP Growth Shocks Impact Sovereign Debt Credit Ratings Upgrade and Downgrades?

GDP growth performance matters in sovereign debt credit ratings. As such, the empirical analysis begins by examining the extent to which positive GDP growth shocks affect sovereign debt credit ratings upgrades and downgrades decisions. Are there differential responses between sovereign debt credit ratings downgrades and upgrades following a positive GDP growth shock? To do this, we estimate a VAR model with GDP growth, inflation, repo rate, sovereign debt credit ratings dummy and business confidence changes. We construct dummy variables for the three rating agencies, namely Standard & Poor's (S&P), Fitch and Moody's based on the changes in the sovereign debt credit ratings shown in Table 17.1 in the Appendix. The sample period for the estimations spans the period 1995Q1 to 2015Q4. The VAR model is estimated with two lags as chosen by AIC and 10,000 Monte Carlo draws. All growth rates are at an annual rate.

Figure 17.5 shows that a positive GDP growth shock increases the likelihood of sovereign debt credit ratings upgrades, while the downgrades tend to decline. The decline is more significant for S&P and Fitch but insignificant due to Moody's. This evidence shows that GDP growth matters in reducing the likelihood of sovereign debt credit ratings downgrades and improves the possibilities of sovereign debt credit ratings upgrades. The results are robust to different ordering of the variables in the model.

17 What Role Does Business Confidence Play in Transmitting... 275

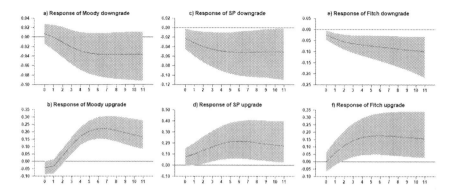

Fig. 17.5 Responses of sovereign debt credit ratings to positive GDP growth shocks. (Note: The grey-shaded area bands denote the 16th and 84th percentile confidence bands. SP denotes Standard & Poor's. Source: Authors' calculations)

17.3.1 What Are the Effects of Different Ratings Agencies' Upgrades and Downgrades Shocks on Output Growth?

To model the effects of sovereign debt credit ratings outcomes on GDP growth, we estimate the VAR model in the previous section. Figure 17.6 shows that shocks to the sovereign debt credit ratings downgrades dummy lead to lower output growth. In contrast, the sovereign debt credit ratings upgrades dummy variables lead to increases in output growth.

The difference is that the Moody's sovereign debt credit ratings upgrades shock leads to a significant decline in output growth followed by an insignificant recovery. The Fitch sovereign debt credit downgrades shock lowers output growth by 0.4 percentage points, which is worse than 0.2 percentage points due to Moody's and S&P shocks, respectively. These results show the heterogenous effects of the sovereign debt credit ratings downgrades shocks. In addition, the analysis so far shows that there is strong feedback between GDP growth and the sovereign debt credit ratings upgrades and downgrades. A positive GDP growth shock tends to raise the likelihood of sovereign debt credit ratings upgrades. At the same time, the sovereign debt credit ratings downgrades (upgrades) lower (increase) output growth.

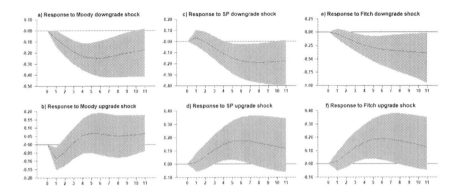

Fig. 17.6 GDP growth responses to sovereign debt credit ratings upgrades and downgrades shocks. (Note: The grey-shaded area bands denote the 16th and 84th percentile confidence bands. SP denote Standard & Poor's. Source: Authors' calculations)

17.4 Why Does Confidence Matter?

The analysis in this section shows the importance of the confidence channel in the propagation of the sovereign debt credit ratings changes on GDP growth. We estimate the responses of selected variables to positive confidence shocks. In the estimations of the VAR model, we include two-year credit default spreads (CDS), the Emerging Market Bond Index (EMBI SA), the sovereign spread and the rand per US dollar (R/US$) exchange rate. The sovereign spread is measured by the gap between the three-month London Interbank-Offered rate (Libor) and the three-month South African Treasury bill rate. In Fig. 17.7, the CDS, sovereign spreads and R/US$ exchange rate decline in response to a positive business confidence shock, suggesting that the risk of a potential sovereign debt credit ratings downgrade or default declines, sovereign risk subsides and the currency appreciates.[2]

On the contrary, we show that a negative (unexpected rise) in CDS and EMBI SA spread shock results in a decline in GDP growth in Fig. 17.8. GDP growth declines significantly due to positive CDS and sovereign spread shocks.

---

[2] See Kganyago (2016) on the potential impact of a sovereign credit downgrade on the government debt-servicing costs, bank interest rate spreads and poor households.

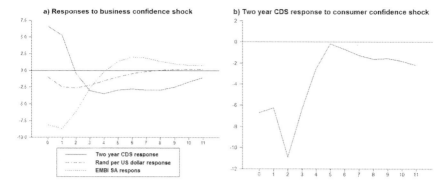

Fig. 17.7 The responses to positive business confidence shocks. (Source: Authors' calculations)

17.4.1 Are There Any Asymmetric Effects of Positive Business Confidence Shocks on GDP Growth?

We apply the Kilian and Vigfussion (2011) approach to determine the asymmetric effects of negative business confidence shocks. The size of the shocks is measured by the standard deviation (SD). The results in Fig. 17.9 indicate that GDP growth declines more due to bigger declines in business confidence than small-sized shocks. This suggests that negative business confidence changes are likely to depress economic growth by big magnitude for long periods.

In addition, it is possible to test the effect characterised by periods of economic uncertainty, such as unstable growth and global growth and economic policy uncertainty as was the case for the period 2009Q1 to 2015Q4. Table 17.1 in the Appendix shows that the sovereign debt ratings downgrades occurred during this period. We set a dummy equal to one for the period 2009Q1 to 2015Q4 and zero otherwise. We estimate a counterfactual VAR model with the variables as in the previous section and an additional dummy for the period 2009Q1 to 2015Q4, alternatively, an economic uncertainty dummy variable. The model is estimated using two lags and 10,000 Monte Carlo draws. The counterfactual response refers to the response estimated in the model where the dummy for the period 2009Q1 to 2015Q4 (economic uncertainty dummy) is

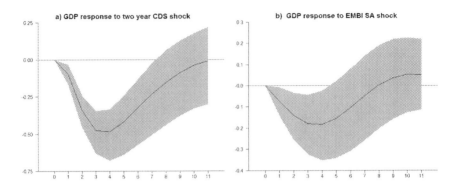

Fig. 17.8 GDP growth responses to positive CDS and EMBI shocks. (Note: The grey-shaded area bands denote the 16th and 84th percentile confidence bands. Source: Authors' calculations)

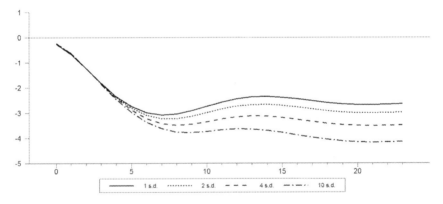

Fig. 17.9 GDP growth responses to negative business confidence shocks. (Source: Authors' calculations)

shut off to explore the role of the economic uncertainty channel characterised by unstable growth and global growth and economic policy uncertainty.

Figure 17.10 shows that a sovereign debt credit ratings downgrades shock during the period 2009Q1 to 2015Q4 worsened the deterioration in business confidence than when the economic uncertainty dummy was shut off in the model.

17 What Role Does Business Confidence Play in Transmitting... 279

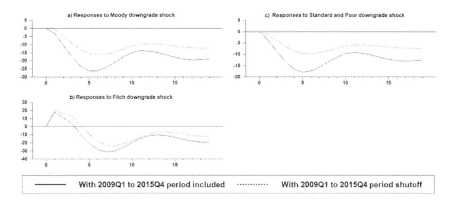

Fig. 17.10 Business confidence responses to downgrades shocks and the role of post-2008 periods. (Source: Authors' calculations)

17.4.2 The Amplification of the Business Confidence Channel on GDP Growth Based on the Endogenous–Exogenous VAR Approach

We perform further counterfactual analysis to determine how the confidence channel influences GDP growth responses to sovereign debt credit ratings downgrades shocks using the endogenous–exogenous VAR approach. In the estimation of the model, business confidence is assumed to be endogenous in one model and exogenous in another model. The gap between the GDP growth impulse responses under the two models will reveal whether the business confidence channel worsened or amplified the responses of GDP growth due to the sovereign debt credit ratings downgrades shocks. Figure 17.11 shows that GDP growth declines much more due to a Fitch downgrade shock when the business confidence channel is exogenous than when it is endogenous in the model. This shows that the business confidence channel plays an important role in the transmission of sovereign debt credit ratings downgrades shocks to GDP growth.

On the other hand, in the endogenous–exogenous VAR approach the responses to sovereign debt credit ratings upgrades shocks shown in Fig. 17.12 indicate that the business confidence channel amplifies the

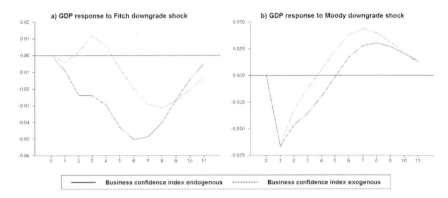

Fig. 17.11 Selected GDP growth responses to downgrades shocks. (Source: Authors' calculations)

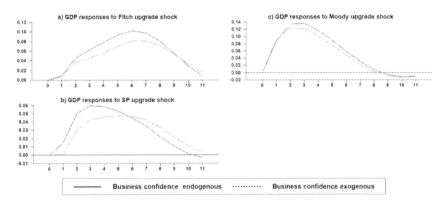

Fig. 17.12 GDP growth responses to sovereign debt credit ratings upgrades shocks. (Note: SP denotes Standard & Poor's. Source: Authors' calculations)

GDP growth responses to the sovereign debt credit ratings upgrades shocks. The amplification is much bigger due to Fitch compared to the S&P sovereign debt credit ratings upgrades shocks. This result is robust evidence indicating that the business confidence channel plays a role in the transmission of sovereign debt credit ratings shocks to GDP growth.

17.4.3 What About the Consumer Confidence Channel? Does It Amplify the Effects of the Sovereign Debt Credit Rating Revisions Shocks on GDP Growth?

To answer the question posed in this section, we modify the Pentecôte and Rondeau (2015) approach based on Cerra and Saxena (2008) to determine the amplifications effects due to consumer confidence. We apply the approach to Eq. (17.1).

$$GDP_t = constant + \sum_{i=1}^{4} \beta_i GDP_{t-i} + \sum_{i=0}^{4} w_i CCI_{t-i} + \sum_{i=0}^{4} q_i Repo_{t-i}$$
$$+ \sum_{i=0}^{4} h_i Inflation_{t-i} \sum_{i=0}^{4} q_i Rating\_Dummy_{t-i} + \varepsilon_t, \quad (17.1)$$

where ε_t denotes an error term and CCI denotes the consumer confidence index. $Rating\_Dummy_{t-i}$ denotes a sovereign debt credit ratings downgrades revisions dummy. We determine the actual and counterfactual GDP growth responses to sovereign debt credit ratings revisions dummy. The actual (counterfactual) responses refer to GDP growth responses when the consumer confidence channel is included (shut off) in the model. The propagating (magnifying) or restraining (stifling) ability of the consumer confidence channel is determined by the gap between the actual and counterfactual GDP growth responses.

Based on the gaps between the actual and counterfactual GDP growth responses in Fig. 17.13, it is evident that the consumer confidence channel plays a role in the transmission of sovereign debt credit ratings revisions shocks to GDP growth.

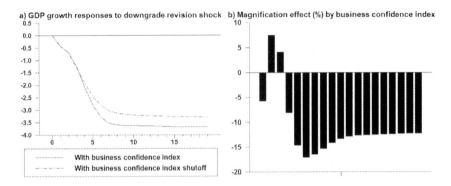

Fig. 17.13 Cumulative responses of GDP growth to S&P sovereign debt credit ratings revisions shocks and the role of consumer confidence. (Source: Authors' calculations)

17.5 What Is the Counterfactual Repo Rate Under the Different Scenarios?

The analysis in this section concludes by applying a historical decomposition approach to isolate the contributions of certain variables in the evolution of inflation. These contributions are shut off in the inflation equation to construct the counterfactual inflation rate. The contributions are shut off in separate models that include the sovereign debt credit ratings downgrades dummy, business confidence channel and GDP growth.

Figures 17.14 and 17.15 show that GDP growth is influenced by the trajectory of the repo rate post 2009. The counterfactual repo rate which shuts off the effects of GDP growth remains higher than the actual repo rate. In addition, Fig. 17.14(b) shows that the policy rate adjustment would have not been aggressive towards inflation developments such as those observed in the peaks around 2003 and 2008. This shows that GDP growth influenced the pace of change in the policy rate responses towards inflation developments.

Figure 17.15(a) shows the effects of combined sovereign debt credit ratings downgrades contributions to the evolution of the repo rate. The counterfactual repo rate exceeds the actual repo rate suggesting that the sovereign debt credit ratings downgrades shocks lead to a slightly less aggressive policy rate adjustment. Figure 17.15(b) shows that lower business confidence leads to lower actual repo rate than the counterfactual

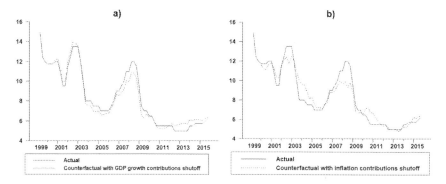

Fig. 17.14 Actual and counterfactual repo rate responses to GDP growth shocks. (Source: Authors' calculations)

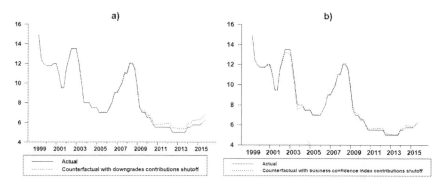

Fig. 17.15 Actual and counterfactual repo rate responses and the role of sovereign debt credit ratings downgrades confidence shocks. (Source: Authors' calculations)

suggests. All these results suggest that the policy rate adjustments do consider the influence of business confidence, GDP growth and inflation shocks in the adjustment of the policy rate.

17.6 Conclusion and Policy Implications

The risk of a further sovereign debt credit ratings downgrade remains elevated in 2019. At the same time, consumer and business confidence have deteriorated and have remained weak. Against this backdrop, this chapter asked: What does the simultaneous occurrence of low business confidence and the heightened risk of a sovereign debt credit ratings upgrades and downgrades do to the domestic real economy? We establish that GDP growth and confidence indicators are negatively related to changes in government debt growth. The negative relationship is pronounced in relation to government debt and business confidence. Furthermore, government debt growth is negatively associated with productivity. At the same time, business confidence is positively related to productivity growth. This means that the productivity channel partly explains why high government debt growth leads to low business confidence.

A positive GDP growth shock tends to raise the likelihood of sovereign debt credit ratings upgrades. However, a sovereign debt credit ratings downgrades shock lowers GDP growth. In, addition we find that there are heterogeneous effects of sovereign debt credit ratings downgrades shocks. GDP growth declines more due to S&P and Fitch sovereign credit sovereign debt credit ratings downgrades. The Fitch sovereign debt credit ratings downgrades shocks lower output by 0.4 percentage points, whilst Moody's and S&P shocks lower GDP growth by 0.2 percentage points, respectively. The confidence channel plays an important role in the propagation of the sovereign debt credit ratings changes on GDP growth. In the endogenous–exogenous VAR approach, the confidence channel amplifies the GDP growth responses to a sovereign debt credit ratings upgrades shocks. In turn, sovereign debt credit ratings downgrades and GDP growth influence the trajectory of the repo rate towards inflation shocks such as those observed in the peak around 2003 and 2008. This shows that GDP growth influenced the pace of changes in the policy rate responses towards positive inflation shocks. Overall, lower business confidence and subdued GDP growth play a role in the adjustment of the repo rate to inflationary pressures.

Appendix

Table 17.1 Sovereign debt credit ratings of South Africa's government long-term debt

Moody's		Standard & Poor's		Fitch's	
downgrade	Upgrade	downgrade	Upgrade	downgrade	Upgrade
27-Sep-2012	30-May-1995	12-Oct-2012	03-Oct-1994	10-Jan-2013	22-Sep-1994
06-Nov-2014	29-Nov-2001	13-Jun-2014	20-Nov-1995	04-Dec-2015	19-May-2000
	11-Jan-2005		25-Feb-2000		27-Jun-2000
	16-July-2009		07-May-2003		02-May-2003
			01-Aug-2005		25-Aug-2005

Source: South African Reserve Bank.

References

Adelino, M., and Miguel, A.F. 2014. *Does Sovereign Credit Risk Affect Bank Lending? Evidence from Sovereign Rating Downgrades*. Working Paper, Duke University.

Almeida, H., Igor, C., Miguel, A.F., and Felipe, R. 2014. *The Real Effects of Credit Ratings: Using Sovereign Downgrades as a Natural Experiment*. Working Paper, University of Illinois at Urbana Champaign.

Barsky, R.B., and Sims, E.R. 2009. *News Shocks*. NBER Working Paper No. 15312.

Barsky, R.B., and Sims, E.R. 2012. Information, Animal Spirits, and the Meaning of Innovations in Consumer Confidence. *American Economic Review*, 102, 1343–77.

Blanchard, O., and Perotti, R. 2002. *An Empirical Characterization of the Dynamic Effects of Changes in Government Spending and Taxes on Output*. NBER Working Paper No. 7269.

Cerra, V., and Saxena, S.W. 2008. Growth Dynamics: The Myth of Economic Recovery. *American Economic Review*, 98(1), 439–57.

Cespedes, L., Chang, R., Velasco, A. 2004. Balance-sheet and Exchange Rate Policy. *American Economic Review*, 94(4), 1183–93.

Farmer, R.E.A. 2011. *Confidence, Crashes and Animal Spirits*. NBER Working Paper No. 14846.

Fatás, A., and Mihov, I. 2001. *The Effects of Fiscal Policy on Consumption and Employment: Theory and Evidence*. CEPR Discussion Paper No. 2760.

Jia, B., and Kim, H. 2015. *Government Spending Shocks and Private Activity: The Role of Sentiments*. MPRA Paper No. 66263.

Kganyago, L. 2016. Keynote Address at SAICA's Courageous Conversation Session Nelson Mandela Centre of Memory, Johannesburg, 26 September 2017.

Kilian, L., and Vigfusson, R.J. 2011. Are the Responses of the U.S. Economy Asymmetric in Energy Price Increases and Decreases?. *Quantitative Economics*, 2(3), 419–53.

Mountford, A., and Uhlig, U. 2000. *What Are the Effects of Fiscal Policy Shocks?* CEPR Discussion Papers No. 3338, C.E.P.R. Discussion Papers.

Ndou, E., and Gumata, N. 2017. *Inflation Dynamics in South Africa: The Role of Thresholds, Exchange Rate Pass-through and Inflation Expectations on Policy Trade-offs*. Palgrave Macmillan. ISBN 978-3-319-46702-3.

Ndou, E., Gumata, N., Ncube, M., and Olson, E. 2013. *An Empirical Investigation of the Taylor Curve in South Africa*. African Development Bank Working Paper No. 189

Pentecôte, J.S., and Rondeau, F. 2015. Trade Spill Overs on Output Growth during the 2008 Financial Crisis. *Journal of International Economics*, 143, 36–47.

18

Are Sovereign Debt Credit Ratings Shocks Transmitted Via Economic Growth to Impact Credit Growth?

Learning Objectives

- Determine the extent to which weak credit growth post-recession in 2009 could be linked to the sovereign debt credit ratings downgrades shock effects.
- Establish whether GDP growth shocks exacerbate the transmission of sovereign debt credit ratings downgrades shocks to credit growth.

18.1 Introduction

This chapter extends the analysis in the previous chapters by examining the extent to which weak credit growth post-recession in 2009 could be linked to the sovereign debt credit ratings downgrades shock effects. The chapter examines the role of GDP growth in transmitting sovereign debt credit ratings shocks to credit growth. In addition, this chapter examines whether the GDP growth channel can exacerbate the transmission of sovereign debt credit ratings downgrades shocks to credit growth. This is motivated by fact that such a channel of transmission, including its relative importance due to sovereign debt credit ratings downgrades

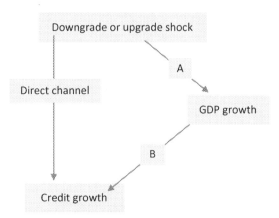

Fig. 18.1 Schematic representation of the transmission of the sovereign debt credit ratings downgrades and upgrades shock to credit growth. (Source: Authors' drawings)

and upgrades shocks, has not been explored as a potential driver of the slowdown in credit growth. Hence, this chapter shows the direct effects of sovereign debt credit ratings downgrades and upgrades shock effects indicated by the *direct channel* in Fig. 18.1. In addition, Fig. 18.1 depicts the *indirect channel* via economic growth shown by arrows A and B.[1]

How does the chapter determine the relative importance of the indirect channel of the transmission of sovereign debt credit ratings shocks? The evidence about the relative importance of the sovereign debt credit ratings indirect channel of transmission is determined using several approaches to ascertain that the evidence is not just specific to one technique. First, we apply a counterfactual VAR approach in which the role of GDP growth is shut off. Second, we use the endogenous–exogenous VAR approach in which GDP growth is assumed exogenous in one model and endogenous in another. Third, we use a single-equation approach that performs a counterfactual analysis by shutting off the role of GDP growth to determine its effects in transmitting the sovereign debt credit ratings shocks to credit growth.

Why is it important to look at the sovereign debt credit ratings channel? First, we are motivated by the argument in Chen et al. (2016) that one

---

[1] The gap between the direct and indirect channels shows the effects of remaining channels. See Kganyago (2016) on other possible channels of transmission.

country's sovereign debt credit ratings revision may affect other countries' economic growth via the financial channels. However, the transmission of the sovereign debt ratings revisions depends on the interactions with other factors. In addition, Allen and Gale (2000) indicate that creditors assessing the downgraded country may tighten credit lines of other countries exposed to the risk of potential losses. Second, we are motivated by the suggestion in Gande and Parsely (2014) that a negative sovereign debt credit ratings revision leads to significant net capital outflows from the downgraded countries. Chen et al. (2016) argue that sovereign debt credit ratings-downgraded countries suffer from damages in terms of trade and trade-credit enabling other economies to benefit from economic growth. This is because the downgraded economy becomes less able to compete in the international product markets. Thus, when a country experiences a sovereign debt credit ratings downgrade, its trade counterparties may also suffer income effects with a downturn in economic activity, reduced imports by the downgraded countries and, possibly, investment growth. Third, we are motivated by the assessment in Bekaert and Harvey (1998, 2000) that economies with better sovereign debt credit ratings will benefit from net capital inflows and the interest rate differential spill-over, which increases the severity of the cumulative downgrade effects abroad and enables better credit countries to improve economic growth.

We fill research policy gaps, as none of the literature discussed so far has shown the role of GDP growth as a conduit in the transmission of sovereign debt credit ratings downgrades and upgrades shocks to credit growth. Second, this chapter fills research policy gaps in South Africa by showing that sovereign debt credit ratings changes do impact credit growth directly and indirectly via the economic growth channel.

18.2 Does Economic Growth Matter for the Transmission of Sovereign Debt Credit Ratings Revisions Shocks to Credit Growth Dynamics?

The examination of the role of GDP growth in transmitting sovereign debt credit ratings shocks to credit growth is examined using Eq. (18.1).

$$Credit\ growth_t = constant + \sum_{i=1}^{4} \beta_i Credit\ growth_{t-i}$$
$$+ \sum_{i=0}^{4} q_i GDP\ growth_{t-i} + \sum_{i=0}^{4} w_i Rating\ dummy_{t-i} + \varepsilon_t, \quad (18.1)$$

where ε_t denotes an error term and *Rating dummy* denotes the sovereign debt credit ratings revisions dummy. This equation is estimated using quarterly (Q) data from 1995Q1 to 2015Q4. For each sovereign debt credit ratings agency, Standard and Poor's (S&P), Fitch and Moody's, we create a dummy variable separated into sovereign debt credit ratings downgrades and upgrades. Each sovereign debt credit ratings downgrade dummy for the three ratings agencies is equal to one, two and three for each grade change in the sovereign debt credit downgrade rating and zero otherwise. Similarly, the sovereign debt credit ratings upgrade dummy is equal to one, two and three for each grade Change in the sovereign debt credit upgrade rating and zero otherwise. The counterfactual credit growth impulse response is determined by setting the coefficients of GDP growth to zero in Eq. (18.1). The equation is estimated using 10,000 bootstrap draws.

The results in Fig. 18.2 show that the effect of a sovereign debt credit ratings downgrades (upgrades) shocks lower (raise) credit growth. This evidence indicates that sovereign debt credit ratings revisions shocks impact credit growth. How would credit growth have responded in the presence (absence) of GDP growth? Does economic growth play a meaningful

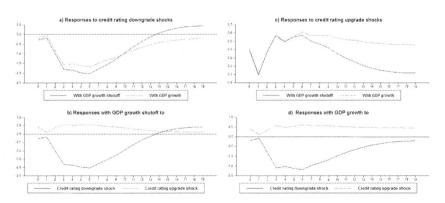

Fig. 18.2 Responses of credit growth to sovereign debt credit ratings downgrades and upgrades shocks and the role of economic growth. (Source: Authors' calculations)

role in the transmission of the sovereign debt credit ratings revisions? We find that the sovereign debt credit ratings downgrades shocks lead to a large peak decline when economic growth is allowed to operate in the model than when it is shut off. In contrast, a sovereign debt credit ratings upgrades shock raises credit growth much more in the presence of economic growth than when this channel is shut off in the model. This evidence confirms that economic growth matters for the transmission of sovereign debt credit ratings downgrades and upgrades shocks to credit growth.

Is there asymmetry in the reaction of credit growth to sovereign debt credit ratings downgrades and upgrades shocks? Evidence shows that credit growth declines by big magnitudes du to sovereign debt credit ratings downgrades shocks than it rises due to upgrades shocks. In addition, the asymmetry holds irrespective of whether economic growth is shut off or is allowed to operate in the model. These findings imply that it is important to avoid a sovereign debt credit ratings downgrade as it leads to a pronounced contraction in credit growth. This means that the financing required to stimulate economic growth may remain weak for prolonged periods.

Would the results differ when using the Fitch, Moody's and Standard and Poor's sovereign debt credit ratings agencies downgrades and upgrades shocks? Figure 18.3 shows the responses of credit growth to sovereign debt credit ratings downgrades and upgrades shocks according to the three sovereign debt credit ratings agencies to determine the robustness of the role of economic growth in transmitting shocks to credit growth

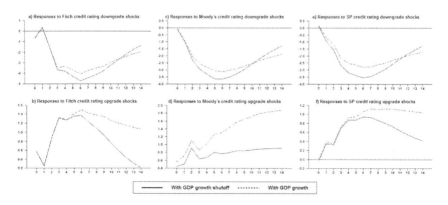

Fig. 18.3 Responses of credit growth to the ratings agency sovereign debt credit ratings downgrades and upgrades shocks and the role of economic growth. (Note: SP denotes Standard and Poor's. Source: Authors' calculations)

responses. We find that credit growth declines much more due to the sovereign debt credit ratings downgrades shocks when economic growth is allowed to operate in the model than when it is shut off. Similarly, a sovereign debt credit ratings downgrade shock has a bigger impact on credit growth than an upgrade shock confirming the asymmetric effects.

18.3 A VAR Approach

We apply a VAR approach to determine the responses of credit growth and GDP growth to sovereign debt credit ratings downgrades and upgrades shocks and the role of economic policy uncertainty. The model is estimated using quarterly data spanning 1995Q1 to 2015Q4 and includes the sovereign debt credit ratings upgrades or downgrades dummy, GDP growth, credit growth and changes in the South African economic policy uncertainty index. The economic policy uncertainty index is sourced from Hlatshwayo and Saxegaard (2016) and the data for all the other variables is sourced from the South African Reserve Bank database. The model is estimated using two lags and 10,000 Monte Carlo draws. All growth rates are at an annual rate. The impulse responses refer to one standard deviation shock.

The results show that a sovereign debt credit ratings downgrades shock lowers credit growth significantly between three and six quarters in Fig. 18.4. But credit growth remains lower than the pre-shock levels over

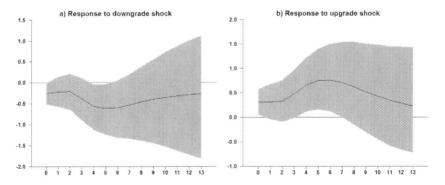

Fig. 18.4 Credit growth responses to sovereign debt credit ratings downgrades and upgrades shocks. (Note: The grey-shaded areas denote the 16th and 84th percentile confidence bands. Source: Authors' calculations)

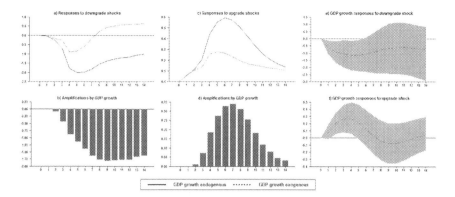

Fig. 18.5 Credit growth responses to sovereign debt credit ratings downgrades and upgrades shocks in the endogenous–exogenous model. (Note: The grey-shaded areas denote the 16th and 84th percentile confidence bands. Source: Authors' calculations)

all horizons. On the other hand, the sovereign debt credit ratings upgrades shock raises credit growth significantly between three and eight quarters.[2]

We apply the endogenous–exogenous VAR approach for robustness analysis. The approach uses GDP growth as an endogenous variable in one model and exogenous in the other model. The gap between credit growth responses based on whether GDP growth is endogenous or exogenous in the model indicates the role of GDP growth in the transmission of sovereign debt credit ratings revisions shocks.

Figure 18.5(a) and (c) shows that sovereign debt credit ratings downgrades (upgrades) shocks lower (increase) credit growth more when GDP growth is endogenous in the model than when it is exogenous. The gap in Fig. 18.5(b) and (e) shows the size of the amplification by GDP growth contraction due to a sovereign debt credit ratings downgrades shock. The additional increase in credit growth is due to the increase in GDP growth following a sovereign debt credit ratings upgrades shock in Fig. 18.5(d) and (f). In addition, in absolute terms, the sovereign debt credit ratings downgrades shocks lead to bigger credit growth responses than those from the upgrades shock, indicating asymmetric effects.

Figure 18.6 shows the percentage of fluctuations induced by the sovereign debt credit ratings downgrades and upgrades shocks on credit growth.

---

[2] The results are robust to different orderings of the variables.

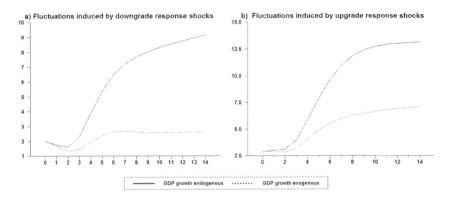

Fig. 18.6 Percentage of fluctuations in credit growth explained by the sovereign debt credit ratings downgrades and upgrades shocks. (Source: Authors' calculations)

The fluctuations depend on whether GDP growth is endogenous or exogenous in the model. We find that sovereign debt credit ratings upgrades and downgrades shocks explain more fluctuations in credit growth when GDP growth is endogenous in the model than when it is exogenous.

18.3.1 Do Revisions in the Sovereign Debt Credit Ratings Shocks Matter?

We extend the analysis of the effects of the sovereign debt credit ratings by assessing the effects of shocks to revisions in the upgrades and downgrades on credit growth and the role of GDP growth. Evidence in Fig. 18.7 shows that sovereign debt credit ratings downgrades (upgrades) revisions shocks lower (increase) credit growth more in the presence of GDP growth in the model than when it is shut off. However, the sovereign debt credit ratings revisions shocks do not lead to a permanent decline in credit growth and GDP growth.

Furthermore, in Fig. 18.8, shocks to sovereign debt credit ratings revisions lead to big fluctuation in credit growth when GDP growth is endogenous in the model than when it is exogenous. This shows that allowing for the feedback effects leads to a bigger amplification role for GDP growth.

18 Are Sovereign Debt Credit Ratings Shocks Transmitted...

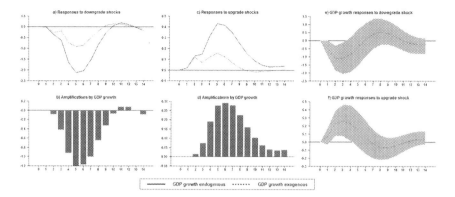

Fig. 18.7 Credit growth responses to sovereign debt credit ratings downgrades and upgrades revisions shocks in the endogenous–exogenous model. (Note: The grey-shaded areas denote the 16th and 84th percentile confidence bands. Source: Authors' calculations)

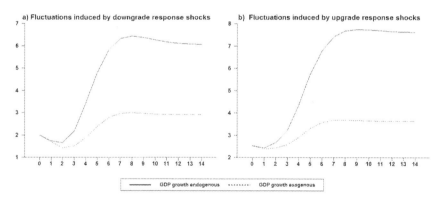

Fig. 18.8 Percentage of fluctuations in credit growth explained by shocks to sovereign debt credit ratings revisions to downgrades and upgrades. (Source: Authors' calculations)

18.3.2 Evidence from a Counterfactual VAR

The preceding section applied the endogenous–exogenous VAR approach to determine the role of GDP growth in transmitting the sovereign debt credit ratings downgrades and upgrades shocks to credit growth. The section complements the previous results by applying a counterfactual VAR

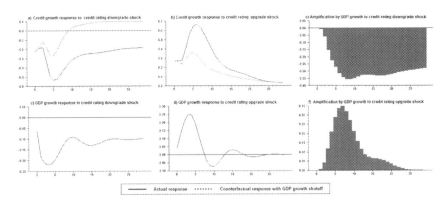

Fig. 18.9 Credit growth responses to sovereign debt credit ratings downgrades and upgrades shocks in a counterfactual VAR model. (Source: Authors' calculations)

approach using the same variables in the previous model. All variables are endogenous in the counterfactual VAR model. The counterfactual VAR approach shuts off the GDP growth variable to determine the counterfactual impulse responses. The differences between the actual and counterfactual determines the magnitudes of the amplifying role of GDP growth. Figure 18.9 shows the responses to sovereign debt credit ratings downgrades and upgrades shocks and the size of amplification due to the GDP growth shock. Indeed, in Fig. 18.9 the sovereign debt credit ratings downgrades (upgrades) shock lower (increase) credit growth. The decline (increase) is much more pronounced when GDP growth is included in the model than when it is shut off. This evidence shows that GDP growth is an important transmitter of sovereign debt credit ratings downgrades and upgrades shock to credit growth.

We further examine the role of GDP growth in transmitting the individual sovereign debt credit ratings agencies' shocks to credit growth. We apply the counterfactual VAR approach as described above but use the sovereign debt credit ratings upgrades and downgrades shocks for Moody's, Fitch and Standard and Poor's individually. Similarly, Fig. 18.10 shows that actual credit growth responses decline more due to sovereign debt credit ratings downgrades (upgrades) shocks when GDP growth is included in the model than when it is shut off. The counterfactual results confirm that GDP growth amplifies credit growth responses to sovereign debt credit ratings shocks.

18 Are Sovereign Debt Credit Ratings Shocks Transmitted...

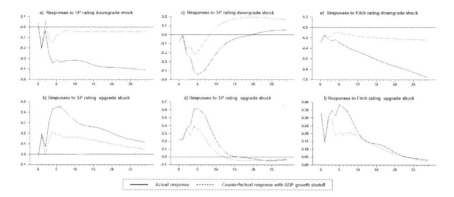

Fig. 18.10 Credit growth responses to sovereign debt credit ratings downgrades and upgrades shocks in a counterfactual VAR model. (Note: SP denotes Standard and Poor's sovereign debt credit ratings. Source: Authors' calculations)

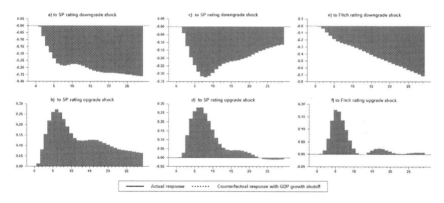

Fig. 18.11 Credit growth amplifications by GDP growth response to sovereign debt credit ratings agency downgrades and upgrades shocks. (Note: SP denotes Standard and Poor's sovereign debt credit ratings. Source: Authors' calculations)

Figure 18.11 shows the sizes of the amplification by GDP growth due to sovereign debt credit ratings revisions by individual rating agencies. The decline (increase) in GDP growth due to the sovereign debt credit ratings downgrades (upgrades) shocks worsen (improve) credit growth contraction (acceleration).

18.4 Conclusion and Policy Implications

This chapter examined the extent to which weaker credit growth post-recession in 2009 could be linked to successive sovereign debt credit ratings downgrades and whether GDP growth dynamics exacerbate the transmission of these shocks to credit growth. We establish that indeed the sovereign debt credit ratings downgrades (upgrades) shock lower (increase) credit growth. The decline (increase) is more pronounced when GDP is endogenous to the model than when it is shut off. We established whether there is asymmetry in the reaction of credit growth to sovereign debt credit ratings downgrades and upgrades shocks. Evidence shows that credit growth declines by big magnitudes due to sovereign debt credit ratings downgrades shocks compared to the increase due to upgrades shocks. In addition, the asymmetry holds irrespective of whether economic growth is shut off or is allowed to operate in the model. These findings imply that it is important to avoid a sovereign debt credit ratings credit downgrade as it leads to a pronounced contraction in credit growth. This means that the financing required to stimulate economic growth may remain weak for prolonged periods. Evidence shows that that sovereign debt credit ratings upgrades and downgrades shocks explain more fluctuation in credit growth when GDP growth is endogenous in the model than when it is exogenous.

Furthermore, shocks to sovereign debt credit ratings revisions lead to big fluctuations in credit growth when GDP growth is endogenous in the model than when it is exogenous. This shows that allowing for feedback effects leads to a bigger amplification role for GDP growth. This evidence shows that GDP growth is transmitter of sovereign debt credit ratings downgrades and upgrades shock to credit growth.

References

Allen, F., and Gale, D. 2000. Financial Contagion. *Journal of Political Economy*, 108, 1–33.

Bekaert, G., and Harvey, C.R. 1998. Time-Varying World Market Integration. *Journal of Finance*, 50, 403–44.

Bekaert, G., Harvey, C.R., and Lundblad, C.T. 2000. Liquidity and Expected Returns: Lessons from Emerging Markets. *Review of Financial Studies*, 20, 1783–831.

Chen, S.-S., Chen, H.-Y., Yang, S.-L., and Chang, C.-C. 2016. Output Spillovers from Changes in Sovereign Credit Ratings. *Journal of International Money and Finance*, 63, 48–63.

Gande, A., and Parsley, D.C. 2014. News Spillovers in the Sovereign Debt Market. *Journal of Financial Economics*, 75, 691–734.

Hlatshwayo, S., and Saxegaard, M. 2016. *The Consequences of Policy Uncertainty: Disconnects and Dilutions in the South African Real Effective Exchange Rate-Export Relationship*. IMF Working Paper WP/16/113.

Kganyago, L. 2016. Keynote Address at SAICA's Courageous Conversation Session Nelson Mandela Centre of Memory, Johannesburg, 26 September 2017.

19

Does the Cost of Government Borrowing Transmit Sovereign Debt Credit Ratings Downgrades Shocks to Credit Growth?

Learning Objectives

- Assesses whether the indirect effects of the sovereign debt credit ratings downgrades shocks are transmitted via the cost of government debt.
- Determine the prevalence of the spill-over effects of the sovereign debt credit ratings downgrades shocks via the cost of government debt.
- Examine the role of the cost of government debt channel in the amplification of the sovereign debt credit ratings downgrades shock effects on credit growth.

19.1 Introduction

The previous chapters examined the effects of the sovereign debt credit ratings downgrades shocks but did not empirically explore the cost of government borrowing channel as a transmission channel.[1] This chapter

---

[1] See Kganyago (2016) on the discussion of the potential impact of a sovereign debt credit ratings downgrade on the government debt-servicing costs, bank interest rate spreads and poor households.

assesses the indirect effects of the sovereign debt credit ratings downgrades shocks transmitted via the costs of government debt and borrowing. This is motivated by the rising government debt-to-GDP ratio and the increased share of debt servicing costs. Hence, it is likely that it will spill-over into other real economic indicators. Is there a spillover channel of the sovereign debt credit ratings downgrades shocks via the cost of government debt? We determine the role of the cost of government debt and borrowing in the amplification of the sovereign debt credit ratings downgrades shock effects on credit growth.

We apply different techniques to determine the robustness of the evidence. The analysis starts by using the endogenous–exogenous VAR approach in which the cost of government debt and borrowing is used as an endogenous variable in one model and an exogenous variable in another model. Second, we apply a counterfactual VAR approach, where the gap between the two impulse responses indicates the size of amplifications induced by the cost of government debt and borrowing. Third, we use disaggregated data on the sovereign debt credit ratings by each of the three ratings agencies individually, to assess the robustness of the results to changes in the model specification.

19.2 Evidence from the Endogenous–Exogenous VAR Model

The models estimated in this chapter use quarterly (Q) data from 1995Q1 to 2015Q4, two lags and 10,000 Monte Carlo draws. The endogenous VAR model includes a sovereign debt ratings credit downgrade dummy, credit growth, gross government loan debt as a ratio of GDP and the weighted cost of government debt. The exogenous variables in the VAR models include changes in the South African economic policy uncertainty changes, the recession dummy and the inflation targeting dummy. The inflation targeting dummy equals one for the period 2000Q1 till the end of the sample period and zero otherwise. The recession dummy equals one for the period 2009Q1 to 2009Q3 and zero

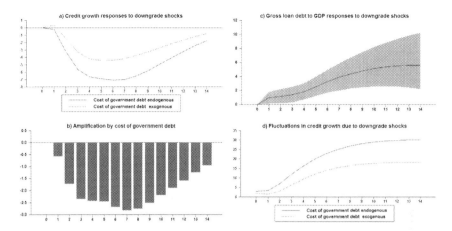

Fig. 19.1 Credit growth responses to sovereign debt credit ratings downgrades shocks. (Note: The grey-shaded area denotes the 16th and 84th percentile confidence bands. Source: Authors' calculations)

otherwise. The data is sourced from the South African Reserve Bank database, and the South African policy uncertainty variable is sourced from Hlatshwayo and Saxegaard (2016). All growth rates are at an annual rate.

Figure 19.1(a) shows that a sovereign debt credit rating downgrade shock lowers credit growth and the decline is bigger when the cost of government debt and borrowing is endogenous in the model than when it is exogenous. This means that allowing for the feedback of the cost of government debt and borrowing propagates the adverse shock effects of the sovereign debt credit ratings downgrade on credit growth. Figure 19.1(b) shows the size of the amplification effects of the cost of government debt and borrowing on credit growth following a sovereign debt credit ratings downgrades shock.

19.2.1 Evidence from the Counterfactual VAR Model

This section applies a counterfactual VAR approach which shuts off the cost of the government borrowing channel in the model to determine the counterfactual credit growth impulse response. The counterfactual

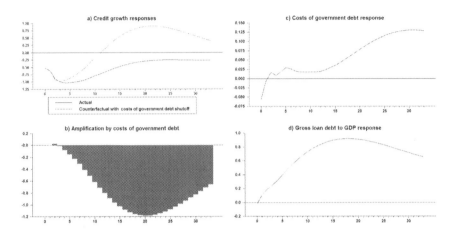

Fig. 19.2 Credit growth, cost of government debt and gross government loan-to-GDP ratio responses to a sovereign debt credit ratings downgrades shock. (Source: Authors' calculations)

impulse response is then compared to actual response which arises when this cost of government debt and borrowing channel is not allowed to operate in the model. In Fig 19.2(a), credit growth declines more when the cost of government debt is allowed to operate in the model than when it is shut off. The sizes of the amplifications in Fig 19.2(b) show the extent to which the sovereign debt credit ratings downgrades shocks are negative and their amplification of the decline in credit growth via the cost of government debt and borrowing channel. In addition, Fig 19.2(c) and (d) shows that the sovereign debt credit rating downgrades shock increases the cost of government debt and the gross loan to GDP ratio.

19.2.2 Evidence-based Specific Agency Credit Downgrade Shock

The preceding sections focused on the role of aggregated sovereign debt credit ratings downgrades shock effects. This section conducts the robustness analysis by using the individual ratings agency sovereign debt credit ratings downgrades shocks, namely the Moody's, Fitch and Standard and Poor's. Figure 19.3 shows that credit growth declines follow-

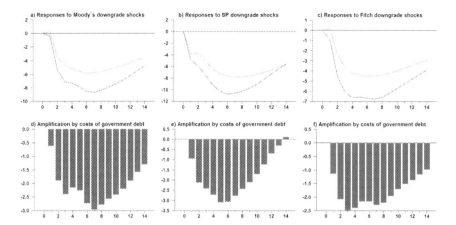

Fig. 19.3 Credit growth responses to rating agency-specific sovereign debt credit downgrades shocks. (Note: SP denotes Standard and Poor's. Source: Authors' calculations)

ing a sovereign debt credit ratings downgrades shock by each ratings agency. In addition, similar to earlier sections, the decline in credit growth decline is pronounced when the cost of government debt and borrowing is endogenous in the model than when it is exogenous. This evidence shows that the cost of government debt and borrowing is a potent transmitter of the sovereign debt credit rating downgrades shocks.

19.3 Conclusion and Policy Implications

This chapter assessed whether the indirect effects of the sovereign debt credit ratings downgrades shocks are transmitted via the cost of government debt and borrowing. Evidence shows that the sovereign debt credit ratings downgrades shocks are transmitted via the cost of government debt and borrowing to impact credit growth. This is because the sovereign debt credit ratings downgrades shocks increase the cost of government debt and borrowing as well as the ratio of gross government loan debt-to-GDP. This implies that policymakers should implement policies that avert sovereign debt credit ratings downgrades. The ratings downgrades shocks spill-over into credit growth via the cost of government debt and borrowing channel.

References

Hlatshwayo, S., and Saxegaard, M. 2016. *The Consequences of Policy Uncertainty: Disconnects and Dilutions in the South African Real Effective Exchange Rate-Export Relationship*. IMF Working Paper WP/16/113.

Kganyago, L. 2016. Keynote Address at SAICA's Courageous Conversation Session Nelson Mandela Centre of Memory, Johannesburg, 26 September 2017.

Part V

The Output–Inflation Trade-off, External Shocks, Labour Market Conditions and Inflation Expectations

20

The Output-gap, Nominal Wage and Consumer Price Inflation Volatility Trade-off

Learning Objectives

- Show the responses of the output growth volatility to an unexpected positive inflation volatility shock.
- Determine whether the correlation between inflation and the output-gap is a time-varying or constant process.
- Establish the extent to which positive demand and supply shocks impact the inflation and output-gap volatilities.

20.1 Introduction

The heightened uncertainty and anaemic growth following the global financial crisis and the euro area sovereign debt crisis lead to a persistent debate on what role monetary policy should be playing in trying to stimulate growth. At the same time, the domestic economy has been subjected to several severe supply-side shocks, such that the output-gap has remained persistently negative and inflation expectations remain very close to the upper part of the target band. As such, the Monetary Policy

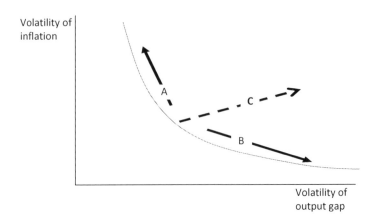

Fig. 20.1 Efficient policy frontier. (Source: Authors' drawings)

Committee (MPC) has been facing tough policy choices as it tries to support the hesitant recovery and bring inflation to well within the target range.[1] Figure 20.1 depicts the policy choices facing the MPC along the efficient policy frontier. At any given point in time, the MPC is confronted with four policy choices in Fig. 20.1.

This chapter assesses whether the policy-efficient frontier shifted over time. Which periods were associated minimum inflation and output volatilities?

First, in a *strict inflation targeting* monetary policy framework, which minimises inflation volatility at the expense of higher output volatility, the policy trade-off leans more towards the direction shown by arrow B. Second, in a *flexible inflation targeting*, which allocates more or less equal weight in minimising the inflation and output volatilities, the policy choices tend to converge around the centre of the efficient policy frontier. Third, in *output targeting* the main objective is the minimisation of the output volatility and less on inflation volatility, and the policy choices move towards arrow A. Last, policymakers can choose to allow

---

[1] The objectives of monetary policy as given through the inflation target by the minister of finance state that primary objective is to ensure that CPI inflation remains within the 3–6 per cent inflation band but it also makes clear that, in so doing, the MPC should be mindful of the implications of its policy actions on growth.

the policy frontier to shift outwards. This leads to high output and inflation volatility as shown by arrow C.

20.2 The Taylor Curve in South Africa

To empirically assess the efficient policy frontier in Fig. 20.1, there is a need to understand the correlation between the output and inflation volatilities as stated in the central bank loss function.[2] This trade-off between the inflation and output volatilities along the efficient policy frontier in Fig. 20.1 is known as the Taylor curve. Taylor (1979) also refers to the Taylor curve as a second-order Phillips curve in which there is a permanent trade-off between the variance of inflation and the variance of the output-gap. The trade-off arises because monetary policy cannot simultaneously offset both types of variabilities. Hence, the trade-off allows for the construction of an efficiency frontier for monetary policy that traces the points of minimum inflation and output-gap variability.[3]

As stated earlier, the trade-off in the Taylor curve implies policy choices which involves the selection of a loss function that represents the social costs of deviations of inflation from the target and of deviations of growth from its long run or potential. The trade-off between the inflation and output-gap volatilities generates a negatively sloped policy curve in Fig. 20.1. Hence, the positioning on the Taylor curve best describes policy choices available to policymakers (Taylor 1999a, b).

Furthermore, theory asserts that the optimal point on the output–inflation efficiency frontier can only be achieved when a central bank has the independence to set policy without political interference. This brings to the fore the role of *constrained discretionary policymaking* as the central bank can choose the appropriate inflation variability aversion parameter

---

[2] The specification of a loss function that represents the social costs of the deviations of inflation from the inflation target and the deviations of output growth from its long-run rate or potential output.
[3] See Cecchetti and Ehrmann (2001) for the analysis of the identification of aggregate demand and supply shocks and the different effects they exert on the inflation and output.

to solve the minimisation problem.[4] Economic growth regimes do constrain policy decisions especially during periods of heightened inflation and growth uncertainty. In addition, Ndou and Gumata (2017) show that the lowest average inflation and output-gap volatilities occurred in 2000Q1 to 2007Q2. This period also achieved the highest average growth rate of 4.2 per cent. On the other hand, the lowest average growth of 1.98 per cent was during 1975Q1 to 1999Q4, which had the highest inflation and output-gap volatilities. They conclude that the highest macroeconomic performance in terms of higher average growth tends to be associated with periods of more negative trade-off in volatilities.[5]

20.3 Evidence of Negative Trade-off

This section uses a bivariate VAR analysis with three lags as selected by Schwarz-Bayesian Criterion (SBC) to determine the trade-off between inflation and output volatilities. The analysis uses monthly data from 1990M1 to 2012M3. All the variables used in the estimation have been multiplied by 100 prior to transformation. We calculate the consumer price inflation and nominal wage inflation volatilities by using the Garch (1,1) model. We approximate GDP growth by using month-on-month manufacturing production growth and derive the growth volatility from the conditional variance using the Garch(1,1) model. We examine the effects of a one standard deviation positive shock to the inflation volatility on output growth volatility. The data is sourced from the South African Reserve Bank database.

---

[4] See Evans and Wachtel (1993) on the role the characteristics of regime shifts play in the estimation of the effects of inflation uncertainty. Similarly, Friedman (1977) postulates that higher inflation levels lead to increased inflation uncertainty. Chang and He (2010) show that inflation volatility raises social costs and further impairs the economic system. Miles and Schreyer (2009) argue that inflation and the distortions induced by misaligned in nominal and real exchange rates have a negative impact on welfare. On the other hand, Bloom (2009) shows that both macro- and micro volatility vary over the business cycle.

[5] King (2013) attributed the period of the lowest inflation and output volatilities, alternatively the inward shift in the Taylor curve, to well-anchored inflation expectations which led to a huge reduction in inflation volatility. Carney (2013) asserts that this distinguished the inflation targeting from other policy regimes and propelled the consensus regarding its superiority.

20 The Output-gap, Nominal Wage and Consumer... 313

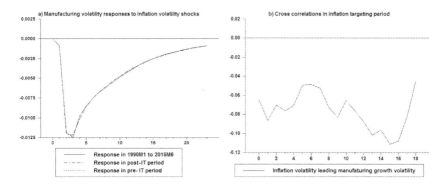

Fig. 20.2 Trade-off between output growth volatility and inflation volatility. (Note: IT means inflation targeting period. Source: Authors' calculations)

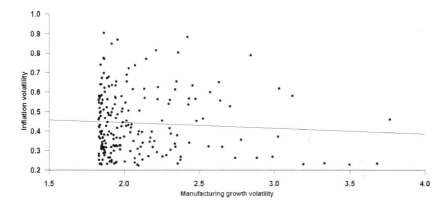

Fig. 20.3 Scatterplot between output growth volatility and inflation volatility. (Source: Authors' calculations)

Figure 20.2(a) shows that output growth volatility tends to decline with varying magnitudes due to an unexpected positive inflation volatility shock. The trade-off is more pronounced in the first ten months and the decline retracts towards the pre-shock level, suggesting that the inflation–output growth volatility trade-off weakens over time. This trade-off is evident in the samples for pre- and post-inflation targeting framework.

Is the trade-off between inflation volatility and output-growth volatility dependent on the technique used? No, Fig. 20.2(b) further corroborates the negative responses of output growth volatility to elevated inflation volatility during the inflation targeting period. In addition, the bilateral

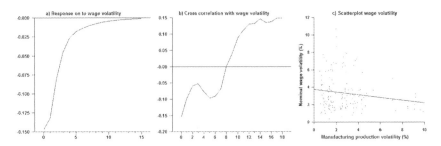

Fig. 20.4 Impulse responses, cross correlation and scatterplot between output volatility and nominal wage inflation volatility. (Source: Authors' calculations)

scatterplots in Fig. 20.3 also confirm a negative relationship between inflation volatility and output growth volatility.

Similarly, Fig. 20.4(a) shows that manufacturing production growth volatility declines and remains depressed in response to a positive nominal wage inflation volatility shock. At the same time, the cross correlation in Fig. 20.4(b) shows that manufacturing production growth volatility declines for the first ten months quarters. The scatterplot in Fig. 20.4(c) corroborates the robustness of the negative association between manufacturing production growth volatility and nominal wage inflation volatility.

20.4 Inflation and Output-gap Volatility Responses to Positive Demand and Supply Shocks

Figure 20.5 shows the demand and supply shocks' own effects and the impulse responses of output and inflation volatilities to these shocks as done in Ndou and Gumata (2017). First, we find evidence that demand and supply shocks are not persistent. The shocks do not have long-lasting effects on their own movements.

Second, the effects of the shocks on the conditional volatilities of output and inflation are short-lived. Since the responses of conditional volatilities to demand and supply shocks are not persistent. The results imply that departures or deviations from the Taylor curve should be short-lived

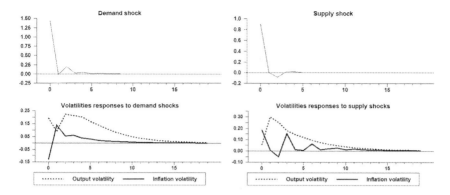

Fig. 20.5 Effects of positive demand and supply shocks on conditional volatilities. (Source: Authors' calculations)

if the central bank operates efficiently. For robustness tests, we estimated the model using different samples, and the results indicate that demand and supply shocks have transitory effects on the inflation and output growth volatilities. This suggests that the results are robust to the consideration of the recession in 2009 and period of global uncertainty since 2010.

20.5 Conclusion and Policy Implications

This chapter empirically investigated the relationship between output growth volatility and inflation volatility. The results show that output growth volatility tends to decline with varying magnitudes due to an unexpected positive consumer inflation and nominal wage volatility shock. This trade-off is evident in the samples for pre- and post-inflation targeting framework. The negative relationship between consumer price inflation and nominal wage volatility and output growth volatility is strong pre- and post-inflation targeting. In addition, the results show that the effects of demand and supply shock on the consumer price inflation, nominal wage and output-gap volatilities are not persistent. The policy implication is that departures or deviations from the Taylor curve should be short-lived if the central bank operates efficiently.

References

Bloom, N. 2009. The Impact of Uncertainty Shocks. *Econometrica*, 77(3), 623–85. May.

Carney, M. 2013. Monetary Policy after the Fall. Remarks at the Eric J. Hanson Memorial Lecture University of Alberta, Edmonton, AB.

Cecchetti, S.G., and Ehrmann, M. 2001. *Does Inflation Targeting Increase Output Volatility? An International Comparison of Policymakers' Preferences and Outcomes.* NBER Working Paper No. 7426. National Bureau of Economic Research: Cambridge, MA.

Chang, K.L., and He, C.W. 2010. Does the Magnitude of the Effect of Inflation Uncertainty on Output Growth Depend on the Level of Inflation? *The Manchester School*, 78(2), 126–48.

Chatterjee, S. 2002. The Taylor Curve and the Unemployment-Inflation Trade-off. *Business Review*. Federal Reserve Bank of Philadelphia. www.phil.frb.org/research review/2002/q3/brq302sc.pdf.

Evans, M., and Wachtel, P. 1993. Inflation Regimes and the Sources of Inflation Uncertainty. *Journal of Money, Credit and Banking*, 25(3, Part 2), 475–511.

Friedman, M. 1977. Nobel Lecture: Inflation and Unemployment. *Journal of Political Economy*, 85, 451–72.

IMF. 2017. *World Economic Outlook, Seeking Sustainable Growth*. Washington, DC.

King, M. 2013. Monetary Policy: Many Targets, Many Instruments. Where Do We Stand? Remarks at the IMF Conference on 'Rethinking Macro Policy II: First Steps and Early Lessons', Washington, DC.

Kganyago, L. 2017. Monetary Policy: Why We Target Inflation. Address at the University of KwaZulu-Natal, Durban, 25 April 2017.

Miles, W., and Schreyer, S. 2009. Inflation Costs, Uncertainty Costs and Emerging Markets. *Journal of Economic Development, Chung-Ang University, Department of Economics*, 34(2), 169–83. December.

Miles, D., Panizza, U., Reis, R., and Ubide, A. 2017. And Yet It Moves: Inflation and the Great Recession, 19th Geneva Report on the World Economy, ICMB and CEPR.

Ndou, E., and Gumata, N. 2017. *Inflation Dynamics in South Africa: The Role of Thresholds, Exchange Rate Pass-through and Inflation Expectations on Policy Trade-offs*. Palgrave Macmillan. ISBN 978-3-319-46702-3.

Ndou, E., Gumata, N., Ncube, M., and Olson, E. 2013. *An Empirical Investigation of the Taylor Curve in South Africa*. African Development Bank Working Paper No. 189.

Olson, E., Enders, W., and Wohar, M.E. 2012. An Empirical Investigation of the Taylor Curve. *Journal of Macroeconomics*, 34(2), 380–90.
Taylor, J.B. 1979. Estimation and Control of a Macroeconomic Model with Rational Expectations. *Econometrica*, 47(5), 1267–86.
Taylor, J.B. 1980. Aggregate Dynamics and Staggered Contracts. *Journal of Political Economy*, 88, 1–23.
Taylor, J.B. 1999a. A Historical Analysis of Monetary Policy Rules. In *Monetary Policy Rules*. University of Chicago Press, pp. 319–48.
Taylor, J.B. 1999b. Staggered Price and Wage Setting in Macroeconomics. In J.B. Taylor and M. Woodford (eds.) *Handbook of Macroeconomics*. Elsevier.
Taylor, J.B. 2000. Low Inflation, Pass-through, and the Pricing Power of Firms. *European Economic Review*, 44, 1389–408.
Taylor, J.B. 2006. Comments on "Trade-offs in Monetary Policy" by Milton Friedman. Unpublished manuscript, Stanford University. www.stanford.edu/~johntayl/CommensOnMiltonFriedman's.doc.
Taylor, J.B. 2007. Housing and Monetary Policy. Remarks presented at the Federal Reserve Bank of Kansas City Symposium "Housing, Housing Finance, and Monetary Policy" Jackson Hole, Wyoming. www.nber.org/papers/w13682.
Yellen, J. 2017. The U.S. Economy and Monetary Policy. Speech delivered at the Group of 30 International Banking Seminar, 15 October, Washington, DC.

21

The Output-Gap and Inflation Volatility Trade-off: Do External Shocks and Inflation Expectations Shift the Taylor Curve

Learning Objectives

- Determine the impact of positive external shocks such as the US Federal Funds Rate, heightened US and UK economic policy uncertainty on the domestic Taylor curve.
- Show the extent to which the exchange rate, commodity prices, terms of trade and inflation expectations shocks impact the inflation and output-gap volatility trade-off.
- Show the impact of the propagation effects of heightened global economic policy uncertainties via the gross capital outflows channel on the output-gap and inflation volatility trade-off.
- Show the impact of positive inflation expectations shocks above the 6 per cent inflation threshold on the output-gap and inflation volatilities.

21.1 Introduction

The previous chapter established that output growth volatility tends to decline with varying magnitudes due to an unexpected positive consumer price inflation and nominal wage volatility shock. In addition, the achievement of low and stable inflation and the solid anchoring of inflation expectations is the primary objective of the monetary policy. In certain situations there may be tough choices regarding the output-gap and inflation trade-off, hereafter referred to as Taylor curve. The analysis of the drivers of the output-gap and inflation trade-off in this chapter is extended by asking: Do inflation expectations shocks, external shocks and economic policy uncertainty shocks shift the Taylor curve?

This analysis is motivated by the persistently negative output-gap post-2009, various persistent supply-side shocks, and economic policy uncertainty shocks that have hit the domestic economy. The analysis is motivated by the political and economic policy uncertainties which have been heightened and are an important macroeconomic policy issue. Global political and economic policy uncertainty encompasses factors such as the following: (i) when and how will the US Fed normalise the policy rate and unwind the balance sheet activity, (ii) how will the Brexit process unfold and what will be the effects on the Bank of England decisions, and (iii) how will the open-ended European Central Bank asset purchase programme and the achievement of the price stability mandate spill-over to the global economy? It is these developments in the global economy that motivate the investigation of the extent to which the domestic Taylor curve responds to positive external shocks such as the US Fed policy rate increases, heightened US and UK economic policy uncertainty shocks.

In addition, these global developments have a bearing on commodity prices and terms of trade and, in turn, have an impact on the inflation and output growth volatility trade-off. This is because heightened uncertainty induces capital flow volatility, the exchange rate depreciation and inflation expectations.

This chapter fills research policy gaps by showing that gross capital outflows do exert an influence on the output-gap and inflation trade-off. Second, we show that positive inflation expectations shocks shift the output-gap and inflation volatilities. Third, we contribute to literature by showing that there are asymmetric effects depending on whether inflation is above and below 6 per cent inflation threshold.

21.2 How Does a Positive US Federal Funds Rate and Policy Uncertainty Shock Affect the Output and Inflation Volatilities?

This section estimates a counterfactual VAR model that includes the US Federal Funds Rate (FFR), the domestic Taylor curve, repo rate and current account as a ratio of GDP. The Taylor curve is captured by the output-gap and inflation volatilities. The sample spans the period 2000Q1 to 2016Q1. The data is sourced from the South African Reserve Bank and the St Louis Federal Reserve databases. However, the equations that include current, one-year and two-year ahead inflation expectations shocks are estimated using quarterly (Q) data from 2002Q3 to 2015Q3 due to data availability. The various inflation expectations maturities are included separately in the model. The model is estimated using one lag and 10,000 Monte Carlo draws. Shocks refer to a one positive standard deviation shock. The model includes the repo rate-FFR spread and the current account because theory suggests that the current account is partly determined by the interest rate spreads. This means that there is a link between interest rate spreads and the current dynamics following the FFR shock.

Figure 21.1 shows the responses of the Taylor curve, the policy rates, the repo rate-FFR spread to a positive FFR shock. As expected, a positive FFR shock leads to an immediate increase in Federal Funds Rate but results

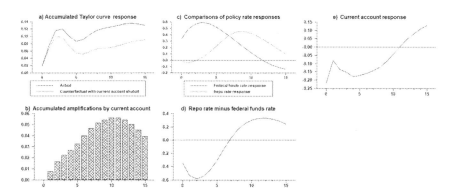

Fig. 21.1 Responses to a positive Federal Funds Rate shock. (Source: Authors' calculations)

in an increase in the repo rate with a delay. The repo rate-FFR spread decline is followed by an increase after six quarters. At the same time, Fig. 21.1(e) and (d) shows that the current account and the repo rate-FFR spread deteriorate. In Fig. 21.1(a), the Taylor curve increases more when the current account is not shut off in the model compared to when it is shut off. The increase in the Taylor curve may be because of the amplification effects of the exchange rate depreciation shocks on inflation.

Thus, evidence shows that the FFR shocks do impact the domestic Taylor curve. But since positive foreign economic policy uncertainty shocks also impact domestic inflation and output: What are the effects of foreign economic policy uncertainty shocks on the domestic Taylor curve? In the estimated VAR model, the FFR is replaced with the foreign economic policy uncertainty variable. The foreign economic policy uncertainty variable enters the model as annual growth rates. Figure 21.2 shows that the Taylor curve rises due to positive US and UK policy uncertainty shocks.

Figure 21.2(e) and (f) show that the gross capital outflows increase following a positive policy uncertainty shock. Second, the actual Taylor curve in Fig. 21.2(a) and (c) is higher than the counterfactual response in the first three quarters following the uncertainty shock. Figure 21.2(b) and (d) show that increased gross capital outflows magnify the Taylor curve responses following elevated economic policy uncertainty shocks.

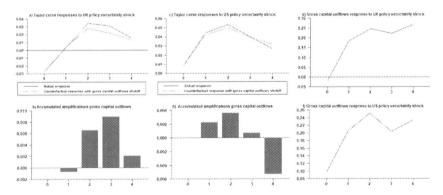

Fig. 21.2 Cumulative responses to positive UK and US economic policy uncertainty shocks. (Source: Authors' calculations)

21.2.1 The Effects of Positive Commodity Price, Exchange Rate and Terms-of-trade Shocks

We stated earlier that economic policy uncertainty has an impact on the exchange rates, commodity prices and terms of trade. Hence this section focuses on the effects of the exchange rate depreciation, commodity prices and terms-of-trade shocks on the inflation and output-gap volatilities trade-off. The exchange rate, commodity prices and terms-of-trade shocks represent outcomes of global and domestic supply and demand shocks. Their impact on the Taylor curve may vary depending on whether these shocks are persistent, non-persistent and their magnitudes. Intuition, suggests that non-persistent (persistent) demand and supply shocks should lead to transitory (highly persistent) increases in the inflation and output-gap volatilities.

So, what does a positive commodity price shock do to the Taylor curve? Figure 21.3 shows that positive commodity price shock increases the Taylor curve and results in the tightening of the repo rate.

We also show the responses to a negative terms-of-trade shock. The Taylor curve increases in Fig. 21.4(a), and the repo rate is tightened in Fig. 21.4(b) due to a negative terms-of-trade shock. How is this possible? This happens when a negative terms-of-trade shock leads to the exchange rate depreciation, induces inflation and leads to contraction in GDP growth. These dynamics increase inflation and output growth volatility trade-off.

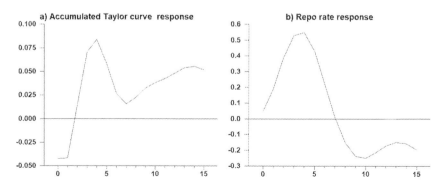

Fig. 21.3 Responses to positive commodity price shocks. (Source: Authors' calculations)

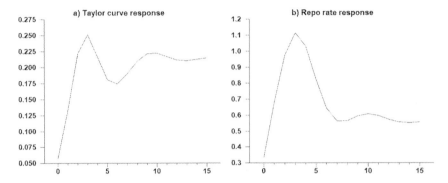

Fig. 21.4 Responses to a negative terms-of-trade shock. (Source: Authors' calculations)

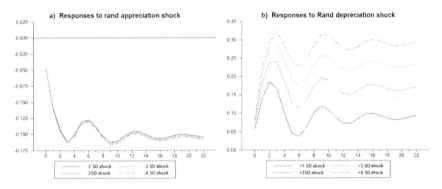

Fig. 21.5 The Taylor curve responses to the Rand per US dollar exchange rate shock. (Note: S.D. denotes the standard deviation shocks. Source: Authors' calculations)

We use the modified Kilian and Vigfusson (2011) bivariate VAR model to assess the asymmetries of exchange rate shocks of different magnitudes on the inflation and output growth volatility trade-off. Figure 21.5 shows that the exchange rate appreciation (depreciation) shock has a negative (positive) effect on the Taylor curve. Large and small rand exchange rate depreciation shocks result in different changes in the Taylor curve. On the other hand, different magnitudes of the exchange rate appreciation seem to have no noticeable differential effects on Taylor curve in Fig. 21.5(a).

21.2.2 The Role of Inflation Expectations on the Policy Trade-off

We conclude the analysis by looking at the role of inflation expectations. A notable feature of the South African inflation expectations is that they have been persistently above the upper part of the inflation target band. So, what is the impact of positive inflation expectations shocks on the Taylor curve? The inflation expectations shocks are measured by a one positive standard deviation in the current, one-year and two-year ahead inflation expectations shocks. The different maturities of inflation expectations shocks enter the equation individually. The role of the inflation expectations shock on the policy trade-off is examined using Eq. (21.1).

$$Taylor\ curve_t = constant + \sum_{i=1}^{4} \beta_i Taylor\ curve_{t-i}$$
$$+ \sum_{i=0}^{4} q_i Inflation\ expectations_{t-i} + \varepsilon_t, \quad (21.1)$$

where ε_t denotes an error term and *Inflation expectations* denotes inflation expectations over different time horizons. We determine the responses of the Taylor curve to the positive inflation expectations shocks. Figure 21.6

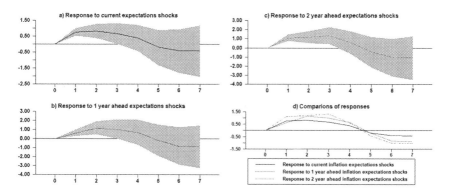

Fig. 21.6 The responses of the Taylor curve to positive expectations shocks. (Note: The grey-shaded bands denote the 16th and 84th percentile confidence bands. Source: Authors' calculations)

shows that the Taylor curve shifts outwards indicating that inflation and output growth volatilities increase following a positive inflation expectations shock.

So, does it matter where inflation expectations are in relation to the upper band of the inflation target? We answer this question by distinguishing between the effects when current inflation expectations exceed or are below the 6 per cent threshold. Such a distinction enables us to assess the role of (i) unanchored; (ii) poorly anchored; and (iii) well-anchored inflation expectations. We use three dummy variables in the estimations, and they are included separately in the model. The first dummy is equal to one when current inflation expectations exceed 6 per cent and zero otherwise. The second dummy is equal to one when current inflation expectations are below 6 per cent and zero otherwise. The third dummy variable is equal to one for inflation expectations below 4.5 per cent and zero otherwise. The model is estimated using one lag and 10,000 bootstraps draws.

Figure 21.7(a) shows that positive inflation expectations shocks increase the Taylor curve when inflation expectations exceed 6 per cent. Inflation expectations shocks have absolutely no effect in Fig. 21.7(b) when inflation expectations are below 6 per cent. This suggests that elevated and unanchored

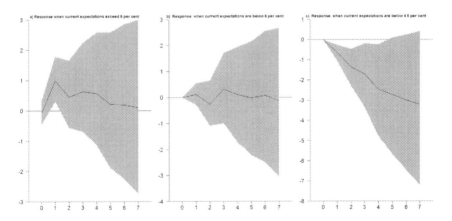

Fig. 21.7 The responses of the Taylor curve to positive inflation expectations shocks. (Note: The grey-shaded bands denote the 16th and 84th percentile confidence bands. Source: Authors' calculations)

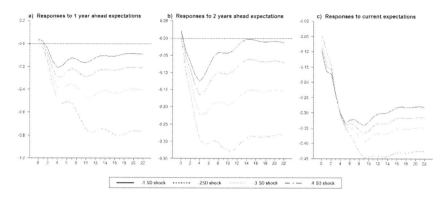

Fig. 21.8 The responses of the Taylor curve to negative inflation expectations shocks relative to the 6 per cent inflation threshold. (Source: Authors' calculations)

inflation expectation induce a shift in the Taylor curve. The negative effects due to inflation expectations below 4.5 per cent indicate that the Taylor curve is minimised via the reduced output growth and inflation volatilities.

Furthermore, we apply the modified Kilian and Vigfusson (2011) bivariate VAR model to assess the asymmetries of different magnitudes of negative deviations in inflation expectations from 6 per cent. Figure 21.8 shows the asymmetric responses based on the size of negative shocks to inflation expectations at various horizons. Large negative shocks exert more negative effects on the Taylor curve due to current inflation expectations.

21.3 Conclusion and Policy Implications

This chapter assessed whether inflation expectations shocks, external shocks and economic policy uncertainty shocks, shift the Taylor curve. Evidence in this chapter shows that a positive FFR shock leads to a delayed effect of an increase in the repo rate, a decline in the repo rate-FFR spread and deterioration in the current account. In addition, the Taylor curve increases more when the current account is not shut off in the model. This may be because of the amplification effects of the exchange rate depreciation on inflation. At the same time, foreign economic policy uncertainty shocks also result in the increase in the domestic Taylor curve. Furthermore, elevated economic policy uncertainty shocks due to increased gross capital outflows magnify the Taylor curve responses.

Economic policy uncertainty shocks have an impact on exchange rates, commodity prices and terms of trade. This chapter also explored the effects of positive shocks to the exchange rate, commodity prices and terms of trade on the inflation and output growth volatilities trade-offs. We find that a positive commodity price shock increases the Taylor curve and results in the tightening of the repo rate. On the other hand, a negative terms-of-trade shock increases the Taylor curve and the repo rate is tightened. This is because a negative terms-of-trade shock leads to the exchange rate depreciation and induces inflation but leads to a contraction in GDP growth. The combined effects of these shocks lead to increases in the inflation and output growth volatilities trade-off.

What is the impact of positive inflation expectations shocks on the Taylor curve? Evidence shows that positive inflation expectations shocks shift the Taylor curve outwards indicating that the inflation and output growth volatilities increase following positive inflation expectations shocks. The results show that a positive inflation expectations shock when inflation expectations are above 6 per cent increases the Taylor curve. On the other, inflation expectations have absolutely no effect on the Taylor curve when inflation expectations are below 6 per cent. Hence, elevated and unanchored inflation expectations induce a shift in the Taylor curve. However, inflation expectations below 4.5 per cent indicate that the Taylor curve is minimised via reduced output growth and inflation volatilities.

In addition, we establish that there are asymmetric shock effects. First, large and small rand exchange rate depreciation shocks result in different changes in the Taylor curve. At the same time, different magnitudes of the exchange rate appreciation have no noticeable differential effects on Taylor curve. Second, large negative current inflation expectations shocks exert more negative effects on the Taylor curve compared to other maturities.

References

Cerra, V., and Saxena, S.W. 2008. Growth Dynamics: The Myth of Economic Recovery. *American Economic Review*, 98(1), 439–57.

Kilian, L., and Vigfusson, R.J. 2011. Are the Responses of the U.S. Economy Asymmetric in Energy Price Increases and Decreases? *Quantitative Economics*, 2(3), 419–53.

Pentecôte, J.S., and Rondeau, F. 2015. Trade Spill Overs on Output Growth During the 2008 Financial Crisis. *Journal of International Economics*, 143, 36–47.

Poirson, H., and Weber, S. 2011. *Growth Spill-over Dynamics from Crisis to Recovery*. International Monetary Fund WP/11/218.

22

Do Adverse Global Trade Shocks Impact the Trade-off Between the Inflation and Output-Gap Volatilities

Learning Objectives

- Determine the impact of negative global trade shocks on labour market conditions, the inflation and output growth volatility trade-off.
- Show the role of the labour market conditions in the propagation of negative global trade shocks on the output growth and inflation volatilities.
- Examine the role of the exchange rate in the response of the repo rate to a negative global trade shock.

22.1 Introduction

This chapter extends the analysis of the impact of global developments of the domestic Taylor curve. However, the analysis in this chapter focuses on the impact of negative global trade shocks on the inflation and output growth volatility trade-off. This is motivated by the fact that global trade shocks are demand shocks and these constitute part of the secular stagnation hypothesis, which is defined as a persistent period of below-potential output growth put forward by Summers (2013). The authors argue that secular deficiency in aggregate demand, investment and insufficient fiscal stimulus explain a large part of subdued global growth. We are also motivated to determine the extent to which the role of labour market conditions transmit the effects of negative global trade shocks into the output growth and inflation volatility trade-off. The thrust of the argument contained in this chapter is that adverse global trade developments matter for monetary policy decisions aimed at minimising the trade-off between inflation and output growth volatilities. At the same time, these decisions have a bearing on labour market conditions which are impacted by negative global trade shocks. Figure 22.1 shows the labour market condition index. The labour market conditions index is tight when negative values are recorded and loose when positive values are recorded.

Methodologically, this chapter fills policy and academic research gaps by using the endogenous–exogenous VAR approach to determine the role of labour market conditions in the transmission of negative global trade shocks into inflation and output growth volatilities. To derive monetary policy implications, the chapter shows the responses of the exchange rate and the repo rate to negative global trade shocks. The intention is to show that the exchange rate depreciation shocks are sources of risks to the inflation outlook and volatility. In addition, we fill policy gaps by establishing whether labour markets adjust via changes in wages (prices) and employment growth (quantities). This adjustment mechanism has implications for the fiscus as it impacts tax revenue sources and the tax base.

The analysis of the labour markets adjustment via either prices or quantities has not been explored in policy and academic research in South

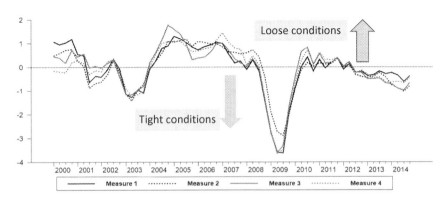

Fig. 22.1 Labour market conditions index. (Source: Authors' calculations)

Africa. The dominant channels of adjustment in the labour market matter for policy decision-makers tasked with the mandates of price and financial stability as well as their impact on maximum employment.

22.2 What Is the Impact of a Negative Global Trade Shock on the Taylor Curve?

This section examines the role of a negative global trade shock on the Taylor curve and its components. We estimate a model using quarterly (Q) data spanning 1995Q1 to 2014Q1. The variables used in the model include global trade growth, tax revenue growth, the Taylor curve and the labour market conditions index. However, in later sections we replace the Taylor curve with its components, namely the inflation and output growth volatilities. We also use selected components of the labour market conditions index, namely remuneration per worker (wages) and employment growth. The data is sourced from the International Monetary Fund and South African Reserve Bank databases. The labour market conditions index is sourced from Gumata and Ndou (2017). The model is estimated using two lags and 10,000 Monte Carlo draws. All variables enter the model as annual growth rates. The shock is a one standard deviation.

Figure 22.2 shows the responses of the Taylor curve and the labour market conditions index to a negative global trade shock. A negative

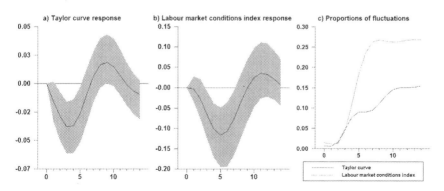

Fig. 22.2 Responses to a negative global trade shock and in a longer sample. (Note: The grey-shaded bands denote the 16th and 84th percentile confidence bands. Source: Authors' calculations)

global trade shock has a significant negative effect on the Taylor curve, suggesting that the Taylor curve shifts inwards.

In addition, a negative global trade shock lowers the labour market conditions index implying that labour market conditions tighten. Furthermore, a negative global trade shock induces more fluctuations in labour market conditions than on the Taylor curve. The implication is that labour markets adjust more to negative global trade shocks compared to the output and inflation volatility trade-offs. Negative global demand shocks via the trade channel exert pronounced adverse effects on labour market conditions than on the Taylor curve. This implies that negative trade shocks which are demand shocks exert a disproportionately negative effect on labour market conditions than the output growth and inflation volatilities. The results are consistent with the findings in Gumata and Ndou (2017), who show evidence of the inverse transmission of excess global liquidity associated with central bank asset purchases.

Figure 22.3 shows selected responses of the variables included in the labour market conditions index. Figure 22.3(a) shows that total tax revenue declines more than remuneration per worker and non-agricultural employment growth. However, employment growth (quantity) adjusts more than remuneration per worker (price). This shows that the responses of labour conditions to negative global trade shocks are adjusted more via

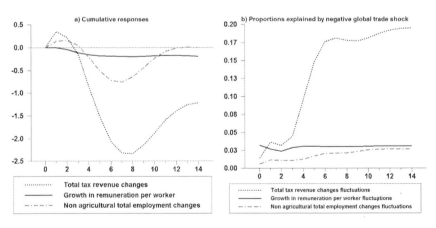

Fig. 22.3 Tax revenue growth and selected labour market indicators responses to negative global trade shocks. (Source: Authors' calculations)

a decline in employment growth (quantity or numbers) than through lower remuneration per worker (price).

22.2.1 The Transmission of Negative Global Trade Shock Effects Via the Output and Inflation Volatilities

The Taylor curve consists of the inflation and output growth volatilities. To determine which component of the Taylor curve is the biggest driver of the trade-off, we examine the responses of the inflation and output growth volatilities to negative global trade shocks. We assess what happens to the inflation and output growth volatilities following a negative global trade growth shock. Figure 22.4 shows that inflation and output growth volatilities decline significantly for nearly six and eight quarters following a negative global trade shock. But the output growth volatility declines more than the inflation volatility, especially for the sample period 1995Q1 to 2014Q1.

The labour market conditions tightening is comparable to that of the decline in the output volatility. The negative reaction of the inflation and output growth volatilities and the labour market tightening occurs in sample periods 1995Q1 to 2014Q1 and 2000Q1 to 2014Q1, suggesting that the responses are robust to sample size adjustments.

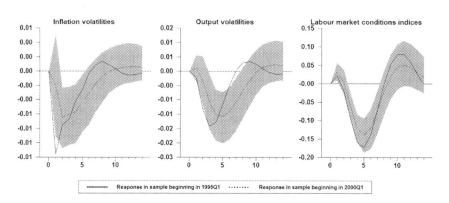

Fig. 22.4 The Taylor curve responses based on the endogenous–exogenous VAR approach. (Note: The grey-shaded bands denote the 16th and 84th percentile confidence bands. Source: Authors' calculations)

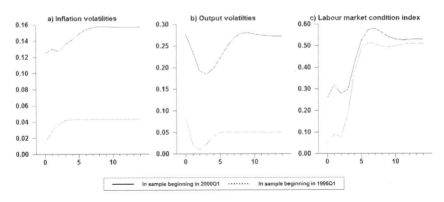

Fig. 22.5 Proportion of fluctuations induced by global trade shocks. (Source: Authors' calculations)

Furthermore, evidence in Fig. 22.5 shows that a negative global trade shock induces a bigger proportion of fluctuations in the labour market conditions and inflation and output growth volatilities during the sample period 2000Q1 to 2012Q1 compared to 1995Q1 to 2014Q1.

On a comparative basis, negative global trade shocks induce a large proportion of movements in output growth volatility and labour market conditions than in the inflation volatilities in the sample beginning in 2000Q1. This suggests that negative global trade shocks are transmitted more via the output growth and employment growth channels than the inflation channel. The negative global trade shocks explain more than 20 per cent and 50 per cent of fluctuations in the output growth volatility and labour market conditions index after five quarters.

22.2.2 To What Extent Are Negative Global Trade Shocks Amplified Via the Labour Market Conditions Channel

This section examines the role of labour market conditions in transmitting negative global trade shocks into the inflation and output growth volatilities. This is examined via estimating an endogenous–exogenous VAR model. The labour market conditions index is assumed to be endogenous in one model and exogenous in the other model. We assess the robustness

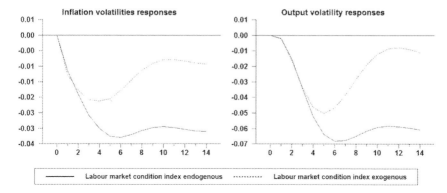

Fig. 22.6 Cumulative responses to a negative global trade shock and the role of the labour market conditions index (1995Q1 to 2014Q1). (Source: Authors' calculations)

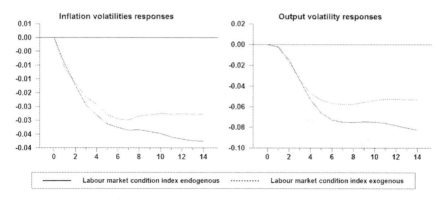

Fig. 22.7 Cumulative responses to a negative global trade shock and the role of labour market conditions index (2000Q1 to 2014Q1). (Source: Authors' calculations)

of the results to changes to the sample sizes of 1995Q1 to 2014Q1 and 2000Q1 to 2014Q1.

Figures 22.6 and 22.7 show the cumulative inflation and output volatilities responses to a negative global trade shock and distinguish results based on whether the labour market conditions index is endogenous or exogenous in the model. The results show that inflation and output volatilities decline more when the labour market conditions index is endogenous in the model than when it is exogenous. The gap between the impulse responses shows the amplification by tight labour market conditions. The results are robust to changes in the sample size.

22.2.3 How Should Monetary Policy Respond Following a Negative Global Trade Shock?

This section concludes the analysis by examining how monetary policy should respond following a negative global trade shock. The variables enter the model as changes on an annual basis. We estimate a VAR model using two lags and 10,000 Monte Carlo draws. The model includes global trade growth, inflation and output growth volatilities and either the repo rate or the exchange rate changes. We use the sample starting in 2000Q1. Figure 22.8(a) shows that repo rate declines but the inflationary risks posed by the R/US$ exchange rate and nominal effective exchange rate (NEER) depreciation against basket of currencies neutralise the repo rate decline following a negative global trade shock.

In addition, Fig 22.8(b) shows that the exchange rates fluctuate more than the repo rate due to a negative global trade shock. This means that the exchange rate remains a risk to the minimisation of the inflation and output growth volatilities following a negative global trade shock.

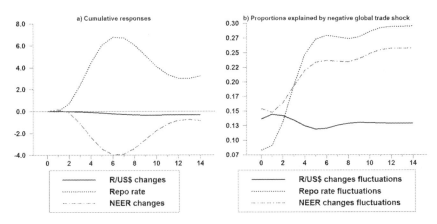

Fig. 22.8 Cumulative responses and fluctuation due to a negative global trade shock. (Source: Authors' calculations)

22.3 Conclusion and Policy Implications

This chapter assessed the impact of negative global trade shocks on labour market conditions, inflation and output growth volatility trade-off. Evidence establishes that a negative global trade shock has a negative effect on the Taylor curve and labour market conditions. This suggests that the Taylor curve shifts inwards, and the labour market conditions tighten. Furthermore, we establish that a negative global trade shock induces more fluctuations in labour market conditions than to the Taylor curve. The implication is that labour markets adjust more to negative global trade shocks compared to the output growth and inflation volatilities. Negative global demand shocks via the trade channel exert pronounced adverse effects on labour market conditions than the Taylor curve. In addition, a disaggregated analysis of the labour market conditions index shows that employment growth (quantity) adjusts more than remuneration per worker (price) to negative global trade shocks. The negative global trade shocks explain more than 20 per cent and 50 per cent of fluctuations in the output growth volatility and labour market conditions index after five quarters.

Furthermore, evidence shows that a negative global trade shock induces a bigger proportion of fluctuations in the labour market conditions, inflation and output growth volatilities. However, on a comparative basis, negative global trade shocks induce a large proportion of movements in output growth volatility and labour market conditions than in inflation volatilities. This suggests that negative global trade shocks are transmitted more via the output growth and employment growth channels than the inflation channel. At the same time, the exchange rate depreciation following a negative global trade shock poses risks to the inflation and output growth volatilities and neutralises the policy rate responses to inflation shocks.

References

Gumata, N., and Ndou, E. 2017. *Labour Market and Fiscal Policy Adjustments to Shocks: The Role and Implications for Price and Financial Stability in South Africa*. Palgrave Macmillan. ISBN 978-3-319-66520-7.

Ndou, E., and Gumata, N. 2017. *Inflation Dynamics in South Africa: The Role of Thresholds, Exchange Rate Pass-through and Inflation Expectations on Policy Trade-offs*. Palgrave Macmillan. ISBN 978-3-319-46702-3.

Summers, L. 2013. U.S. Economic Prospects: Secular Stagnation, Hysteresis, and the Zero Lower Bound. *Business Economics*, 49(2), 65–73. National Association for Business Economics.

Summers, H., Wessel, D., and Murray, J.D. 2018. Rethinking the Fed's 2 Per cent Inflation Target: A Report from the Hutchins Centre on Fiscal and Monetary Policy at Brookings. https://www.brookings.edu/wp-content/uploads/2018/06/ES_20180607_Hutchins-FedInflationTarget.pdf.

23

Do the Labour Market Conditions Shocks Impact the Trade-off Between the Inflation and Output-Gap Volatilities?

Learning Objectives

- Examine the extent to which loose and tight labour market conditions shocks impact the Taylor curve and whether the effects depend on the 6 per cent inflation threshold.
- Show extent to which loose and tight labour market conditions shocks impact the policy rate responses via the output-gap and inflation volatilities channels.

23.1 Introduction

The previous chapter showed that labour markets adjust more to adverse global demand shocks via the global trade channel compared to the output-gap and inflation volatilities. We are motivated by the finding that employment growth (quantity) adjusts more than remuneration per worker (price) to negative global trade shocks. In addition, we showed in earlier chapters that monetary policy decisions are aimed at minimising the inflation and output-gap volatilities along the efficient policy frontier. We are also motivated by the finding in previous chapters that the wage inflation process

© The Author(s) 2019
N. Gumata, E. Ndou, *Capital Flows, Credit Markets and Growth in South Africa*, https://doi.org/10.1007/978-3-030-30888-9_23

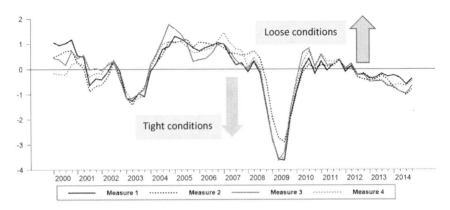

Fig. 23.1 Labour market conditions index. (Source: Authors' calculations)

and the effects it exerts on consumer price inflation matter for the monetary policy decision-making process. This chapter extends the analysis of the interaction of the labour market conditions and the inflation and output-gap volatility trade-off known as the *Taylor curve*. Do labour market conditions shocks impact the Taylor curve? Do their effects differ depending on whether inflation is above or below the 6 per cent threshold? The evolution of labour market conditions index is shown in Fig. 23.1. The labour market conditions index is estimated in Ndou and Gumata (2017). Positive (negative) values denote loose(tight) labour market conditions.

We fill policy research gaps by examining the extent to which loose and tight labour market conditions shocks impact the Taylor curve and whether the effects depend on the 6 per cent inflation threshold. In addition, we show the extent to which loose and tight labour market conditions shocks impact the policy rate responses via the output-gap and inflation volatilities channels.

23.2 Evidence from Linear Regressions

This chapter uses several econometric approaches ranging from single equations, endogenous–exogenous VAR models and counterfactual VAR models to assess the robustness of the results. This section starts by using a modified Pentecôte and Rondeau (2015) approach in Eq. (23.1).[1] The aim

---

[1] Taylor curve data is based on data estimated using techniques in Ndou et al. (2013).

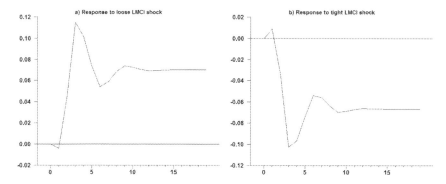

Fig. 23.2 Taylor curve responses to loose and tight labour market conditions shocks. (Note: LMCI denotes labour market conditions index. Source: Authors' calculations)

is to test for the labour market conditions shock effects on the Taylor curve. The analysis distinguishes between loose and tight labour market conditions index. The tight (loose) labour market conditions index dummy is equal to negative (positive) values of the labour market conditions index and zero otherwise. The role of the labour market conditions index is captured by the (*Labour market condition dummy*$_{t-i}$) in Eq. (23.1).

$$Taylor\ curve_t = constant + \sum_{i=1}^{4} d_i Taylor\ curve_{t-i}$$
$$+ \sum_{i=0}^{4} \beta_i\ Labour\ market\ condition\ dummy_{t-i} + \varepsilon_t, \quad (23.1)$$

where ε_t denotes an error term.[2] The sample uses quarterly (Q) data for the period 2000Q1 to 2014Q4. The data is sourced for the South African Reserve Bank database. All growth rates are at annual rate and shocks are a one positive standard deviation. The model is estimated using two lags and 10,000 bootstrap draws.

Figure 23.2 shows the cumulative responses of the Taylor curve to loose and tight labour market conditions shocks. A positive loose labour mar-

---

[2] We also use the output and inflation volatilities, rand per US dollar exchange rate and the repo rate in the estimations.

ket conditions shock exerts a positive effect on the Taylor curve. In contrast, a positive tight labour market conditions shock has a negative effect on the Taylor curve. Thus, evidence shows that loose and tight labour market conditions shocks exert opposing effects on the Taylor curve.

23.3 Does the Level of Inflation Play a Role?

This section assesses the robustness of the Taylor curve responses to labour market conditions shocks and the role of inflation relative to the 6 per cent threshold. We use the counterfactual VAR models and the endogenous–exogenous VAR models to answer this question. The endogenous–exogenous VAR model approach uses inflation as an endogenous variable in one model while it is exogenous in the other model. The VAR model includes the labour market conditions index dummy and the Taylor curve as endogenous variables. Two inflation dummy variables are created. The first (second) inflation dummy equals values of inflation above (below) the 6 per cent threshold and zero otherwise. The inflation dummy is an exogenous variable in the model. The model is estimated with two lags and 10,000 Monte Carlo draws.

Evidence in Fig. 23.3 shows that the Taylor curve increases due to a positive shock to loose labour market conditions index. The Taylor curve increases more when inflation exceeds the 6 per cent threshold. In contrast, tight labour market conditions shocks have a negative effect on the

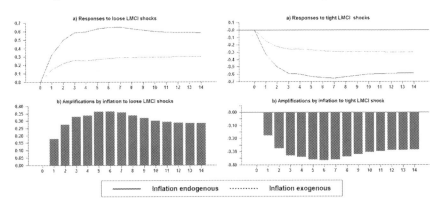

Fig. 23.3 Taylor curve responses based on the endogenous–exogenous VAR approach. (Note: LMCI denotes labour market conditions index. Source: Authors' calculations)

Taylor curve and result in a pronounced decline in inflation when inflation is above the 6 per cent inflation threshold.

Are the results sensitive to changes in the sample size? For the robustness test of the results to changes in the sample size, we change the sample from 1995Q1 to 2014Q4 and use 2000Q1 to 2014Q4. The impulse responses in Fig. 23.4 show that loose labour market conditions shocks have a positive effect on the Taylor curve.

In contrast, the tight labour market conditions have a negative impact on Taylor curve. The responses are much bigger when inflation is endogenous rather than when it is exogenous in the model. We conclude that the findings are robust to different sample sizes.

We change the estimation approach and use the counterfactual VAR approach to show the responses of the repo rate. The VAR model includes the repo rate, the labour market conditions index dummy, the Taylor curve and inflation. The model is estimated using two lags and 10,000 Monte Carlo draws. Like earlier results, loose (tight) labour market conditions shocks exert a positive (negative) effect on the Taylor curve in Fig. 23.5. The repo rate is tightened due to positive labour market conditions shocks as inflation rises and the Taylor curve increases. On the other hand, the repo rate is loosened due to tight labour market conditions shocks as inflationary pressures subside and the Taylor curve declines.

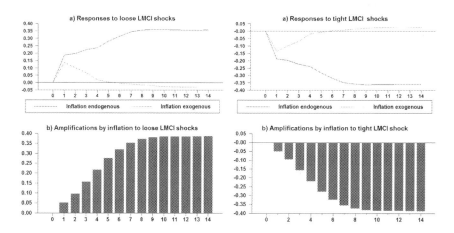

Fig. 23.4 Taylor curve responses based on the endogenous–exogenous VAR approach (1995Q1 to 2014Q4). (Note: LMCI denotes labour market conditions index. Source: Authors' calculations)

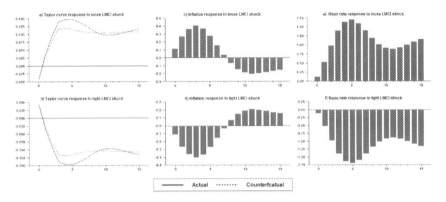

Fig. 23.5 Responses from a counterfactual VAR approach. (Note: LMCI denotes labour market conditions index. Source: Authors' calculations)

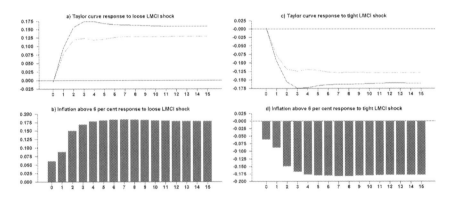

Fig. 23.6 Taylor curve responses to labour market conditions shocks and role of the 6 per cent inflation threshold. (Note: LMCI denotes labour market conditions index. Source: Authors' calculations)

23.3.1 Evidence Using One-year Rolling Taylor Curve

Are the results established earlier of the responses of the Taylor curve to loose and tight labour market conditions shocks when inflation is above the 6 per cent threshold sensitive to the measurement of the Taylor curve? This section uses the one-year rolling Taylor curve to test for the robustness of the results to changes in the model specification. Figure 23.6 shows that the Taylor curve increases (declines) due to loose (tight) labour market conditions shocks. Tight labour market conditions shocks exacerbate the decline in inflation when inflation is above the 6 per cent threshold. Thus, like earlier results, loose labour market conditions shocks raise inflation while tight labour conditions lower inflation. In addition, when inflation exceeds the 6 per cent threshold, tight labour market conditions shocks assist in lowering inflation and shifting the Taylor curve inwards.

23.3.2 How Do Inflation and Output-Gap Volatility Components React to Loose and Tight Labour Market Conditions Shocks?

To answer this question, we use the components of the Taylor curve, namely the output-gap and inflation volatilities. Evidence in Fig. 23.7 shows that a loose (tight) labour market conditions shock exerts a positive (negative) effect on the output-gap and inflation volatilities but the effects

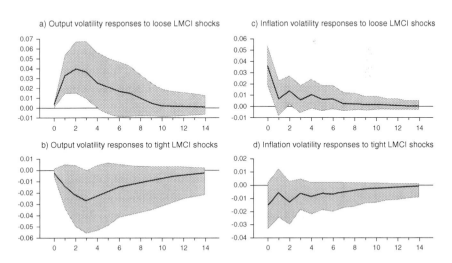

Fig. 23.7 Output-gap and inflation volatility responses to loose and tight labour market conditions shocks. (Note: The grey-shaded bands denote 16th and 84th percentile confidence bands. LMCI denotes labour market conditions index. Source: Authors' calculations)

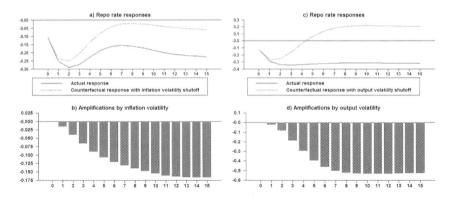

Fig. 23.8 Cumulative responses to tight labour market shocks and the role of the output-gap and inflation volatility shocks. (Source: Authors' calculations)

differ. Tight labour market conditions shocks exert a severe negative impact on the output-gap volatility compared to inflation volatility.

What are the implications for the repo rate adjustments following a tight labour market conditions shock and the role of the inflation and output-gap volatilities? To answer this question, we estimate a four-variable counterfactual VAR model which includes tight labour conditions, output-gap or inflation volatility, rand per US dollar exchange rate changes and the repo rate. The inflation and output-gap volatilities are shut off in the model to determine the counterfactual repo rate. The counterfactual refers to the policy rate that would prevail after shutting off the output-gap and inflation volatilities.

Figure 23.8 shows the actual and counterfactual repo rate responses to tight labour market conditions and size of amplification induced by the inflation and output-gap volatilities, respectively. The results show that the actual repo rate is lowered more when the inflation and output-gap volatilities are included in the model than when these are shut off. This means that the decline in the output-gap and inflation volatilities following tight labour market conditions shocks induces a highly accommodative monetary policy. In addition, the decline in the output-gap volatility accentuates the decline in the repo rate than the inflation volatility. This suggests that tight labour markets shocks are transmitted much through the output channel than the inflation channel.

23.4 Conclusion and Policy Implications

This chapter explored whether labour market conditions shocks impact the Taylor curve. If so, do the effects differ depending on whether inflation is above or below the 6 per cent threshold? First, evidence shows that loose and tight labour market conditions shocks exert opposing effects on the Taylor curve. Loose (tight) labour market conditions shocks result in an increase (decline) in the output-gap and inflation volatilities. Furthermore, tight labour market conditions shocks result in a pronounced decline in inflation when inflation is above the 6 per cent inflation threshold. Consequently, the repo rate is tightened due to positive labour market conditions shocks as inflation rises and the Taylor curve increases. On the other hand, the repo rate is loosened due to tight labour market conditions shocks as inflationary pressures subside and the Taylor curve declines.

Nonetheless, tight labour market conditions shocks exert a severe negative impact on the output-gap volatility compared to inflation volatility. In addition, when inflation exceeds the 6 per cent threshold, tight labour market conditions shocks assist in lowering inflation and shifting the Taylor curve inwards. As a result, the decline in the output-gap volatility accentuates the decline in the repo rate than the inflation volatility. The decline in the output-gap volatility following tight labour market conditions shocks induces highly accommodative monetary policy. This suggests that tight labour markets shocks are transmitted much through the output channel than the inflation channel. Thus, there are price stability benefits that accrue from changes in the labour market conditions and these spill-over into the monetary policy settings.

References

Cerra, V., and Saxena, S.W. 2008. Growth Dynamics: The Myth of Economic Recovery. *American Economic Review*, 98(1), 439–57.

Kilian, L., and Vigfusson, R.J. 2011. Are the Responses of the U.S. Economy Asymmetric in Energy Price Increases and Decreases? *Quantitative Economics*, 2(3), 419–53.

Ndou, E., and Gumata, N. 2017. *Inflation Dynamics in South Africa: The Role of Thresholds, Exchange Rate Pass-through and Inflation Expectations on Policy Trade-offs*. Palgrave Macmillan. ISBN 978-3-319-46702-3.

Ndou, E., Gumata, N., Ncube, M., and Olson, E. 2013. *An Empirical Investigation of the Taylor Curve in South Africa*. African Development Bank Working Paper No. 189.

Pentecôte, J.S., and Rondeau, F. 2015. Trade Spill Overs on Output Growth During the 2008 Financial Crisis. *Journal of International Economics*, 143, 36–47.

Part VI

The Policy Ineffectiveness Issues

24

The *Output Gap–Inflation* Trade-off and the Policy Ineffectiveness

Learning Objectives

- Establish the size of *output gap–inflation* trade-off and reveal the extent of the applicability of the policy ineffectiveness proposition.
- Show the extent to which the *output gap–inflation* trade-off is impacted by the role of the 6 per cent inflation threshold.
- Determine whether inflation regimes impact the transmission of nominal demand shocks to the *output gap–inflation* trade-off parameter.
- Explore whether trend consumer price and nominal wage inflation have an impact on the magnitudes of the demand management policies on real GDP growth.

24.1 Introduction

This chapter looks at the policy ineffectiveness propositions posited by the new Keynesian and new classical theories regarding the effects of positive nominal demand shocks shown in Fig. 24.1.

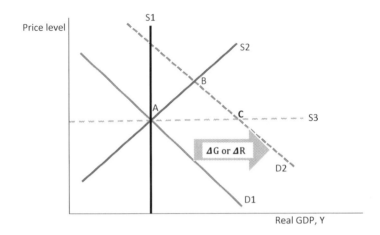

Fig. 24.1 Theoretical effects of expansionary policy shock on output and inflation. (Source: Authors' drawings)

Depending on the slope of the aggregate supply curve (S), a nominal demand shock such as expansionary policy, for example, increased government spending ΔG or monetary stimulus ΔR, will shift the aggregate demand (D) curve from D1 to D2 resulting in three outcomes for output inducing a trade-off between output and inflation outcomes.

The outcomes are dependent on the slope of supply curve. Given a *vertical supply curve* S1, output does not change, and prices react fully, suggesting that expansionary policy is fully passed through to prices. On the other hand, based on a *flat or horizontal supply curve* S3, the expansionary policy is fully passed through to output changes without any effect on prices. For the *upward sloping supply curve* S2, both output and prices respond to an expansionary policy shock. These different slopes of the aggregate supply curve induce an *output gap–inflation* trade-off due to an expansionary policy shock.

The size of *output gap–inflation* trade-off can reveal the extent of the applicability of the policy ineffectiveness proposition. Does the *output gap–inflation* trade-off exist in South Africa? To what extent is it impacted by the role of the 6 per cent inflation threshold? In addition, does inflation impact the transmission of nominal demand shocks to the *output gap–inflation* trade-off parameter? This chapter determines the policy ineffectiveness hypotheses based on the new Keynesian theory on nominal rigidities. Does trend consumer price and nominal wage inflation have an impact on the magnitudes of the demand management policies on real GDP growth?

Ball et al. (1988) show the importance of menu costs in the new Keynesian theory and that the real effects of nominal demand shocks depend on how often price adjustments are made.[1] The faster (slower) the speed of price adjustments, the smaller (larger) are the real effects of nominal demand shocks and therefore the steeper (flatter) the Philips curve. In addition, Ball et al. (1988) postulated that demand policies would be less effective in countries with high trend inflation because prices are less rigid, which leads agents to alter prices frequently as opposed to quantities.

24.2 How Is the Short-run *Output Gap–Inflation* Trade-off Measured?

This section shows how the short-run *output gap–inflation* trade-off is measured in literature and how this can be linked to the theoretical predictions in Fig. 24.1. To capture the theoretical predictions in Fig. 24.1, Ball et al. (1988) show that the short-run *output gap–inflation* trade-off (τ) can be derived by estimating Eq. (24.1).

$$\text{Real GDP}_t = constant + \tau \times \Delta \text{Nominal GDP growth}_t + \beta \times trend + \varepsilon_t, \quad (24.1)$$

where Δ*Nominal GDP growth*$_t$ captures the nominal demand shock, β captures the coefficient associated with *trend* consumer price and nominal wage inflation and ε_t is the error term. Equation (24.1) implies that output movements due to aggregate demand disturbances can be decomposed into the long-run time trend and short-run fluctuations. It is the intuition

---

[1] The new classical economics suggest that policy interventions should not occur because inflation is costly than unemployment. The short-run Philips curve is very steep and the economy is *self-correcting*, and this works smoothly and quickly. In contrast, the new Keynesian theory suggests policy interventions because unemployment is costlier than inflation. The Philips curve is flat or horizontal, and the self-correcting mechanism is rather slow and unreliable.

behind Eq. (24.1) that matters for the analysis in this chapter as τ captures the short-run effects of nominal disturbances in real output. The parameter τ measures the *output gap–inflation* trade-off, which is the slope of the Philips curve. The change in aggregate demand can be transmitted to (i) real output or (ii) prices or (iii) or both prices and output. If the coefficient of parameter $\tau = 1$, this implies that nominal demand shocks are passed through to real output for one to one. On the other hand, if the coefficient on parameter $\tau = 0$, this implies a full pass-through of nominal demand shocks to prices. Last, if the coefficient on the parameter lies between $0 < \tau < 1$, this implies that changes in nominal demand shocks are partially passed through to real output and prices.[2]

24.3 Is There a Short-run *Output Gap– Inflation* Trade-off?

This section examines the effectiveness of nominal demand policy by estimating the size and significance of the *output gap–inflation* trade-off. The size and significance of the *output gap–inflation* trade-off is measured by the response of output to a change in nominal demand as in Lucas (1973) and Ball et al. (1988).

Does a positive nominal demand shock exert any real effects on GDP growth or induce the *output gap–inflation* trade-off? In addition, given the prevalence of inflation regimes in South Africa, we determine whether the *output gap–inflation* trade-off is impacted by whether inflation exceeds or is below the 6 per cent inflation threshold. We use the 6 per cent inflation threshold to demarcate the inflation regimes. Periods of inflation above (below) the 6 per cent inflation threshold signify high- (low-) inflation regimes.

As a result, two regime-dependent VAR models are estimated under three model assumptions to deal with the econometric issues raised in

---

[2] The parameter τ refers to the proportion of demand changes that are passed into prices. The larger (smaller) the coefficient for parameter τ, the larger (smaller) is the effect of changes in demand on the real economy. Thus, a small τ implies that nominal disturbances have more effects on prices.

24 The Output Gap–Inflation Trade-off and the Policy...

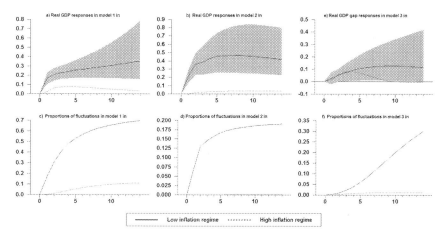

Fig. 24.2 Responses to a positive nominal demand shock. (Note: The grey-shaded bands denote the 16th and 84th confidence bands. Source: Authors' calculations)

literature regarding the validity and robustness of estimations derived from Eq. (24.1). *Model 1* uses real and nominal GDP growth rates to deal with the criticism of spurious regression. *Model 2* uses the Ball et al. (1988) specification of real GDP in log level and nominal GDP growth. Literature permits systems which explicitly model stationary and non-stationary variables.[3] *Model 3* follows Odedokun (1991) and uses the real GDP gap and nominal GDP growth. The real GDP gap is derived from the difference between actual real GDP and the Hodrick-Prescott filter real GDP trend. Thus, the analysis in this chapter uses GDP data in growth rates, log level and deviations from trend (gap) to assess for the robustness of the results. To conduct further robustness analysis, the same models are estimated but consumer price inflation is replaced with nominal wage inflation. The data is sourced from the South African Reserve Bank database. The sample spans the period 1990Q1 to 2017Q1. The models are estimated using two lags and 10,000 Monte Carlo draws. The shocks refer to a positive one standard deviation shock.

Figure 24.2 shows the response of real output due to a nominal demand shock or the *output gap–inflation* trade-off parameter. Evidence in Fig. 24.2

---

[3] See Blanchard and Quah (1989) and Dungey and Fry (2008).

shows the existence of the *output gap–inflation* trade-off.[4] Real GDP growth rises due to a positive nominal demand shock irrespective of the model specifications and inflation regimes. But the results show that real output rises more in a low inflation regime than in a high inflation regime. This means that the *output gap–inflation* trade-off is much higher in a low inflation regime relative to a high inflation regime. This suggests that a nominal demand policy shock that affects nominal demand will have a bigger effect on real output in a low inflation regime than in a high inflation regime.

As in Fig. 24.2, the low *output gap–inflation* trade-off in a high inflation regime implies that the nominal demand shock is passed through to consumer and nominal wage inflation pressures than to real output. The slope of the Philips curve is steeper in the high inflation regime than in the low inflation regime. Hence, a nominal demand shock raises consumer and nominal wage inflation rather than stimulate real output growth.

In addition, Fig. 24.2(c) and (d) shows the proportion of fluctuations in real output induced by a nominal demand shock in different inflation regimes. Evidence shows that irrespective of the inflation regime, a nominal demand policy shock induces more fluctuations in real output in the low inflation regime than in the high regime. This evidence further shows that a higher degree of the *output gap–inflation* trade-off movements happens in the low inflation regime. A positive nominal demand policy initiative will have a bigger effect in the low inflation regime. Thus, evidence from the impulse responses and variance decompositions reinforces the conclusion that inflation regimes play a role in explaining the *output gap–inflation* trade-off dynamics.

24.3.1 Evidence from Three Variable VAR Models

Would the results change if consumer price inflation is included as an endogenous variable in the models? To test for the robustness of the evi-

---

[4] The results that use nominal wage inflation to test for the robustness of the results to the changes in the model specification are shown in Fig 24.7. In the estimation of these models, consumer price inflation is replaced with nominal wage inflation.

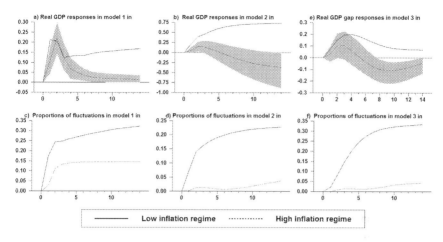

Fig. 24.3 Responses to a positive nominal demand shock in different VAR models. (Note: The grey-shaded bands denote the 16th and 84th confidence bands. Source: Authors' calculations)

dence in the preceding section, consumer price inflation is included in the analysis to determine whether inflation regimes play an important role in impacting the *output gap–inflation* trade-off. Several studies use real and nominal GDP without consumer price inflation in the modelling. This analysis includes consumer price inflation in the two models specified above for further robustness analysis. Evidence in Fig. 24.3 shows that irrespective of the model specifications, inflation regimes play an important role in the *output gap–inflation* trade-off. The *output gap–inflation* trade-off is significantly higher in the low inflation regime than in the high inflation regime. Thus, evidence is robust to changes in the model specification.

In addition, Fig. 24.4 compares the responses of real GDP and inflation to positive a nominal demand shock. The responses in Fig. 24.4(a) and (b) are based on the model which includes real GDP growth, while the results in Fig. 24.4(c) and (d) are based on the model which includes the real GDP gap. Evidence shows that a positive nominal demand shock affects the inflation rate more than real output. However, the inflation reaction is low or muted in the low inflation regime than in the high inflation regime. The peak inflation increases are smaller in the low inflation regime than in the high regime. In addition, real output rises persistently higher in the low inflation regime than in the high infla-

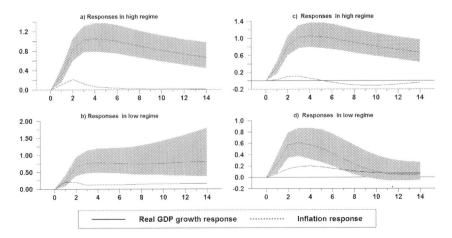

Fig. 24.4 Responses to a positive nominal demand shock in high and low inflation regimes. (Note: The grey-shaded bands denote the 16th and 84th confidence bands. Source: Authors' calculations)

tion regime. This suggests that a nominal demand shock is likely to provide more stimulus on real output in the low inflation regime. The low inflation regime also has benefits of low consumer and wage inflationary pressures compared to the high inflation regime. The responses of nominal wage inflation are shown in Fig. 24.8 in the Appendix.

24.3.2 Price Changes

Ball et al. (1988) argue that menu costs cause prices to adjust infrequently. For a given frequency of individual price adjustments, the staggering contracts slows the adjustment of the price level. In addition, evidence in Sun (2012) and some other studies shows that price inflation is state dependent. Implying that in a high inflation environment, consumer prices tend to change more often. Hence, this section explores whether price adjustments differ above and below the 6 per cent threshold. We use a three variable VAR model in the preceding section which includes real GDP growth.

Evidence in Fig. 24.5 shows that inflation increases more in the high inflation regime than in the low inflation regime following a nomi-

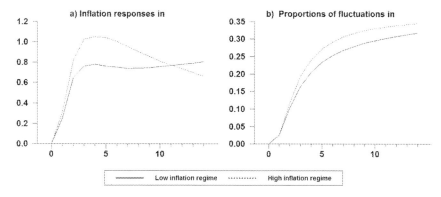

Fig. 24.5 Inflation responses and fluctuations to positive a nominal demand shock. (Source: Authors' calculations)

nal demand shock. Furthermore, inflation fluctuates much more due to nominal demand shocks in the high inflation regime than in the low inflation regime. The results are robust to using the specification in Model 2.

24.3.3 What Are the Implications of the Inflation Channel on the *Output Gap–Inflation* Trade-off?

This section explores the implications of the inflation channel for the *output gap–inflation* trade-off by estimating a regime-dependent counterfactual VAR model based on inflation regimes. The inflation regimes are delineated based on the 6 per cent inflation threshold. Where a high (low) inflation regime refers to inflation above (below) 6 per cent. The model estimated includes real and nominal GDP growth and consumer price inflation. The inflation rate is shut off in the model to determine the counterfactual GDP growth responses due to a nominal demand shock. The gap between the actual and counterfactual GDP growth measures the size of the amplification induced by the inflation channel. The models are estimated using two lags and 10,000 Monte Carlo draws.

Evidence in Fig. 24.6 shows that the amplification role of inflation differs between the low and high inflation regimes. In the high inflation regime in Fig. 24.5(a), inflation plays a dampening role in transmitting the impact of a positive nominal demand shock on real GDP growth. In

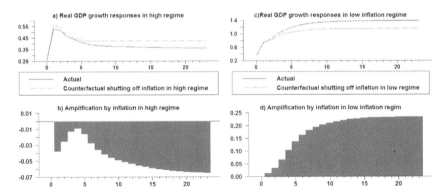

Fig. 24.6 Cumulative responses to positive a nominal demand shock and the role of inflation. (Source: Authors' calculations)

contrast, in Fig. 24.5(c) inflation amplifies real GDP growth responses to a positive nominal demand shock. Thus, evidence shows that a positive nominal demand shock has a bigger effect on GDP growth in the low inflation regime than in the high inflation regime. Hence, a low inflation regime matters for the pass-through effects of a positive nominal demand policy shock in Fig. 24.6.

This evidence confirms the new Keynesian hypothesis, which implies that demand policy interventions are less effective in countries with high trend inflation and where prices are less rigid. In addition, Sun (2012) shows that in case of nominal rigidity arising from the adjustment costs or staggered contracts, prices do not adjust fully to compensate for shifts in nominal demand. This is why changes in nominal demand have real effects.

24.4 Conclusion and Policy Implications

This chapter explored whether the *output gap–inflation* trade-off exists in South Africa? If so, to what extent is it impacted by the role of the 6 per cent inflation threshold? In addition, does inflation impact the transmission of positive nominal demand shocks to the *output gap–inflation* trade-off parameter? Evidence in this chapter shows the existence of the *output gap–inflation* trade-off. Real GDP growth rises due to a positive nominal demand shock. But the results show that real output rises more in a low inflation regime than in a high inflation regime. In addition, evidence shows that a higher degree of the *output gap–inflation* trade-off movement occurs in the low inflation regime. This means that the *output gap–inflation* trade-off is much higher in a low inflation regime relative to a high inflation regime. The policy implication is that a positive nominal demand policy shock that affects nominal demand will have a bigger effect on real output in a low inflation regime than in a high inflation regime.

The findings of the impact of inflation regimes on the *output gap–inflation* trade-off are particularly important given the prevalence of high inflation regimes in South Africa. Evidence showing that the *output gap–inflation* trade-off is low in the high inflation regime implies that a positive nominal demand shock is passed through to consumer and nominal wage inflation pressures than to real output. The slope of the Philips curve is steeper in the high inflation regime than in the low inflation regime. Hence, a positive nominal demand shock raises consumer and nominal wage inflation rather than stimulate real output growth. Thus, evidence reinforces the conclusion that inflation regimes play a role in explaining the *output gap–inflation* trade-off dynamics. The data supports the new Keynesian hypothesis, which implies that demand policy interventions are less effective in countries with high trend inflation and where prices are less rigid.

Appendix

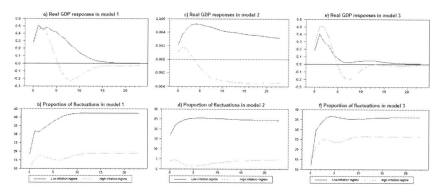

Fig. 24.7 GDP responses to positive a nominal demand shock in models with nominal wage inflation. (Source: Authors' calculations)

Fig. 24.8 Nominal wage responses to a positive nominal demand shock in high- and low inflation regimes. (Source: Authors' calculations)

References

Ball, L., and Mankiw, N.G. 1994. Asymmetric Price Adjustment and Economic Fluctuations. *Economic Journal, Royal Economic Society*, 104(423), 247–61.

Ball, L., Mankiw, N.G., and Romer, D. 1988. The New Keynesian Economics and the Output Inflation Trade-off. *Brookings Paper on Economic Activity*, 19, 1–65.

Ball, L., and Romer, D. 1989. Are Prices Too Sticky? *Quarterly Journal of Economics*, 104(3), 507–24.

Ball, L., and Romer, D. 1990. Real Rigidities and the Non-neutrality of Money. *Review of Economic Studies*, 57(2), 183–203.

Blanchard, O., and Quah, D. 1989. The Dynamic Effects of Aggregate Demand and Supply Disturbances. *The American Economic Review*, 79, 655–73.

Dungey, M., and Fry, R. 2008. The Identification of Fiscal and Monetary Policy in a Structural VAR. https://www.rbnz.govt.nz/media/ReserveBank/Files/Publications/Seminars%20and%20workshops/October2008/3410301.pdf?la=en.

Lucas, R.E., Jr. 1973. Some International Evidence on Output-Inflation Trade-Offs. *American Economic Review, American Association*, 63(3), 326–34, June.

Odedokun, M.O. 1991. Alternative Econometric Approaches for Analysing the Role of the Financial Sector in Economic Growth: Time-Series Evidence from LDCs. *Journal of Development Economics*, 50(1), 119–46.

Sun, R. 2012. *Nominal Rigidity and Some New Evidence on the New Keynesian Theory of the Output-Inflation Trade-off*. MPRA Paper No. 45021.

25

Inflation Regimes and the Transmission of Positive Nominal Demand Shocks to the Price Level

Learning Objectives

- Show the inflation rate at which a positive nominal demand shock pass through to the consumer price level minimised.
- Explore whether inflation regimes affect the transmission of nominal demand shocks to the consumer price level.
- Establish the policy implications of the pass-through of a nominal demand shock to inflation when inflation is below the midpoint (4.5 per cent) of the inflation target range.

25.1 Introduction

The previous chapter showed that the South African data supports the new Keynesian hypothesis, which implies that nominal demand policy interventions are less effective in countries with high trend inflation and where prices are less rigid. This chapter extends the analysis of the pass-through of a positive nominal demand shock. Figure 25.1 shows that a nominal demand shock pass-through to the price level depends on the slope of the

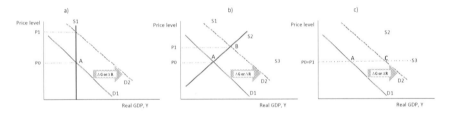

Fig. 25.1 Theoretical depiction of the price level response to a positive nominal demand shock. (Source: Authors' drawings)

aggregate supply curve. A positive nominal demand shock impacts prices (P) only if the supply curve is perfectly inelastic as in Fig. 25.1(a).

In contrast, there can be no pass-through to the price level if the supply curve is perfectly inelastic as in Fig. 25.1(c). The pass-through of a nominal demand shock can be distributed to the price level and real GDP growth with varying degrees when the supply curve is upward sloping. Hence, this chapter asks: Under which inflation rate is a positive nominal demand shock such as increased government spending ΔG or expansionary monetary policy ΔR, pass-through to the consumer price level minimised?

For instance, Fig. 25.1(c) shows that when the consumer price level reacts very little or not all, real output reacts more to a positive nominal demand shock. On the other hand, when the consumer price level rises more as in Fig 25.1(a), real output does not react. These theoretical dispositions seem to concur with the predictions of the role of menu costs as argued by Ball et al. (1988). The new Keynesian theory asserts that the real effects of a positive nominal demand shock depend on the frequency of price adjustments and the speed of adjustment. Ball et al. (1988) show that the faster the speed of adjustment of prices, the smaller are the real effects of a nominal demand shock. Alternatively, the slower the speed of adjustment of prices, the larger are the real effects of a nominal demand shock. However, Fig. 25.1 does not show the role of inflation regimes. This chapter extends the analysis by exploring whether inflation regimes affect the transmission of positive nominal demand shocks to the consumer price level.

This chapter shows that there exists a certain inflation level within the current inflation target band of 3–6 per cent that is consistent with the minimisation of the pass-through of nominal demand shocks to the consumer price level. The previous chapter did not examine the long-run pass-through of a nominal demand shock to the consumer price level and the speed of correction towards the long-run equilibrium, when inflation is above and below the 6 per cent threshold. This chapter is also specific in assessing the implications of the pass-through of a nominal demand shock to inflation when inflation is below 4.5 per cent, which is the midpoint of the 3–6 per cent inflation target range. Furthermore, we show that the implications of nominal demand shocks are different for real GDP growth when inflation is anywhere below 6 per cent relative to specifically below 4.5 per cent.

Holmes (2000) argues that price flexibility allows for the adjustment of prices rather than quantities, which leads to no real effects due to a nominal demand shock. Thus, if demand management policy effectiveness depends on price rigidities, the analysis in this chapter examines the extent to which price rigidities affect the effectiveness of these policies and whether it depends on inflation regimes. Sun (2012) shows that due to nominal rigidity arising from the adjustment costs or staggered contracts, prices do not adjust fully to compensate for shifts in nominal demand. As a result, changes in nominal demand have real effects. Hence, a nominal demand shock will have real effects if prices are rigid or less flexible. This follows the new Keynesian hypothesis predictions that demand policies are less effective in periods of high trend consumer price inflation and where prices are less rigid.

25.2 Empirical Methodology

This section follows Holmes (2000) to estimate the long-run relationship between the consumer price level P_t and nominal GDP using Eq. (25.1) and ε_t represents the deviation from the long-run equilibrium.

$$P_t = \text{constant} + \beta \times \text{Nominal GDP}_t + \varepsilon_t, \quad (25.1)$$

when $\beta = 0$, this implies that there is zero price flexibility, meaning that the movements in nominal demand shocks are not associated with move-

Table 25.1 Unrestricted cointegration rank test (trace)

Hypothesised No. of CE(s)	Eigenvalue	Trace Statistic	Critical value	Prob.a
None	0.371039	58.80378	20.26184	0.0000**
At most 1	0.072997	8.262043	9.164546	0.0740

Source: Authors' calculations
Note: Trace test indicates 1 cointegrating eqn(s) at the 0.05 level; * denotes rejection of the hypothesis at the 0.05 level; ** denotes rejection of the hypothesis at the 0.01 level; a denotes MacKinnon-Haug-Michelis (1999) p-values

ments in consumer prices. When $\beta < 1$, this implies long-run price rigidities and theory suggests that in this case nominal income changes will have real effects. When $\beta = 1$, this implies that movements in nominal demand are matched one-to-one by changes in the price level. However, when $\beta > 1$, this suggests that a nominal demand shock is matched by much larger increase in the price level changes. Holmes (2000) suggests that this is consistent with increases in nominal income which causes a wage–price spiral, and this puts downward pressure on real output growth.

The analysis in this chapter is based on variables shown in Fig 25.1. To properly estimate Eq. (25.1), we begin by testing the stationarity properties for consumer prices, nominal wages and nominal GDP in levels. The sample uses quarterly (Q) data from 1990Q1 to 2017Q1. Evidence shows that consumer prices, nominal wages and nominal GDP are non-stationary in levels (are not I(0)) and become stationary after first differencing (are I(1)). This enables the estimation of the cointegration relationships. The cointegration tests are done using the Johannsen cointegration test. The trace and maximum eigenvalue test results are reported in Tables 25.1 and 25.2.[1] The trace test indicates one cointegration relationship.

The Maximum Eigenvalue test in Table 25.2 also concludes that there is one cointegration relationship.

What are the pass-through magnitudes of nominal GDP shocks to the consumer price level and nominal wages in the long run? The impact of nominal demand shocks on the consumer price level are shown in Table 25.3.[2]

Evidence in Table 25.3 shows that the pass-through is less than one and this is robust to changes in the sample size. The magnitudes of the

---
[1] The results for nominal wages are shown in Tables 25.5 and 25.6 in the Appendix.
[2] The results for nominal wages are shown in Table 25.7 in the Appendix.

Table 25.2 Unrestricted cointegration rank test (maximum eigenvalue)

Hypothesised No. of CE(s)	Eigenvalue	Max-Eigen Statistic	Critical value	Prob.a
None	0.371039	50.54174	12.89210	0.0000**
At most 1	0.072997	8.262043	9.164546	0.0740

Source: Authors' calculations

Note: Max-eigenvalue test indicates 1 cointegrating eqn(s) at the 0.05 level; * denotes rejection of the hypothesis at the 0.05 level; ** denotes rejection of the hypothesis at the 0.01 level; a denotes MacKinnon-Haug-Michelis (1999) *p*-values

Table 25.3 Estimates of the long-run coefficients based on the inflation regimes

	1960Q1–2017Q1	1970Q1–2017Q1	1980Q1–2017Q1	1990Q1–2017Q1
No regime	0.702 (0.004)	0.727 (0.005)	0.693 (0.008)	0.566 (0.007)
High regime	0.748 (0.007)	0.748 (0.007)	0.708 (0.010)	0.566 (0.008)
Low regime	0.684 (0.004)	0.695 (0.010)	0.524 (0.011)	0.524 (0.011)
Below 4.5% regime	0.683 (0.004)	0.521 (0.018)	0.521 (0.018)	0.521 (0.018)

Source: Authors' calculations

Note: *p*-values are in parentheses

pass-through decline depending on inflation regimes. The results show that high inflation regimes are associated with a high pass-through compared to when inflation is low and particularly below the 4.5 per cent inflation threshold. This shows that the pass-through of nominal demand shocks to consumer price and nominal wage inflation is bigger in the high inflation regime.

Given evidence of price rigidities in the low inflation regime, it is therefore possible that the pass-through to real GDP is much higher in the low inflation regime than in the high inflation regime. Any evidence in support of such an outcome will suggest that policymakers have considerable scope to engage in short-run demand management policies in the low inflation regime than in the high inflation regime. This is because there is a substantial degree of policy effectiveness in the low inflation regime and prices become more rigid as consumer price and nominal wage inflation move below the 4.5 per cent inflation threshold, alternatively, a low inflation regime.

Table 25.4 The speed of price adjustment or the error-correction coefficients

	1960–2017		1980–2017		1990–2017	
No regime	−0.022	(0.006)	−0.018	(0.008)	−0.064	(0.017)
High regime	−0.012	(0.006)	−0.016	(0.007)	−0.065	(0.019)
Low regime	−0.010	(0.006)	−0.015	(0.011)	−0.024	(0.025)

Source: Authors' calculations
Note: *p*-values are in parentheses

The speed of adjustments or the error-correction coefficients provide information about the short-run responsiveness of inflation to nominal demand shocks. The speed of adjustment or the error-correction provides information about how consumer prices and nominal wage inflation adjust back to the long-run equilibrium after the disturbance due to a nominal demand shock. Holmes (2000) suggests that the closer to zero the speed of adjustment is, the less flexible consumer price and nominal wage inflation are in the short-run. Evidence in Table 25.4[3] shows that the speed of adjustments is relatively large in the high inflation regime than in the low inflation regime.

This suggests that there is more prices flexibility in the high inflation regime compared to the low inflation regime. Therefore, nominal demand shocks are unlikely to generate much inflation in the low inflation regime relative to the high inflation regime.

25.2.1 Evidence from a Regime-Dependent VAR Approach

This section shows the effects of a nominal demand shock on inflation depending on inflation regimes. Several inflation regime-dependent bivariate VAR models are estimated using two lags and 10,000 Monte Carlo draws. The first model (Model 1) includes consumer price inflation and nominal GDP growth. The second model (Model 2) to test for the robustness of the results uses the reverse ordering of the variables in Model 1. All the growth rates are at an annual rate. In the models, nominal GDP growth captures the nominal demand shock that emanates from either expansionary fiscal or monetary policies. The three inflation regimes are (i) the high inflation regime when inflation exceeds the 6 per cent threshold (ii) the low inflation regime when inflation is below the 6

---

[3] The results for nominal wages are shown in Table 25.8 in the Appendix.

25 Inflation Regimes and the Transmission of Positive Nominal… 371

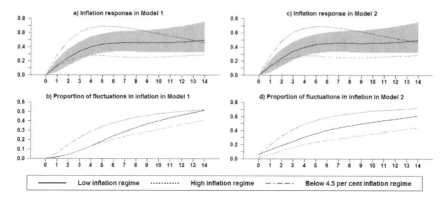

Fig. 25.2 Inflation responses and fluctuations due to a positive nominal demand shock in 1990Q1 to 2017Q1 period. (Note: The grey-shaded bands denote the 16th and 84th percentile error bands. Source: Authors' calculations)

per cent threshold and (iii) the inflation regime below the 4.5 per cent inflation threshold. Figure 25.2(a) and (b) shows that there is a high degree of the nominal demand shock pass-through to consumer price inflation in the high regime than in the low inflation regime. Inflation rises less when inflation is below or equal to 4.5 per cent. This means inflation regimes matter for the impact of nominal demand shocks on inflation.

In addition, Fig. 25.2(b) and (d) show the proportions of inflation fluctuations explained by the nominal demand shock in different inflation regimes. Evidence shows that inflation fluctuates more in the high inflation regime than when it is below the 4.5 per cent inflation threshold. This shows that inflation tends to be rigid in the low inflation regime than in the high inflation regime. This evidence is robust to changes in the sample size in Fig. 25.3 for the inflation targeting period and the period 1980Q1–2017Q1 in Fig. 25.8 in the Appendix.

25.2.2 What Are the Implications for Real GDP Growth?

To answer this question, this section applies the preceding regime-dependent bivariate VAR models but replaces consumer price inflation with real GDP growth. The objective is to determine the nature of the relationship between real GDP growth responses to positive nominal demand shocks in different

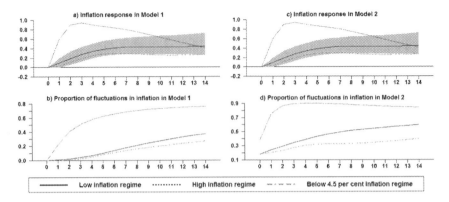

Fig. 25.3 Inflation responses and fluctuations due to a positive nominal demand shock during the inflation targeting period. (Note: The grey-shaded bands denote the 16th and 84th percentile error bands. Source: Authors' calculations)

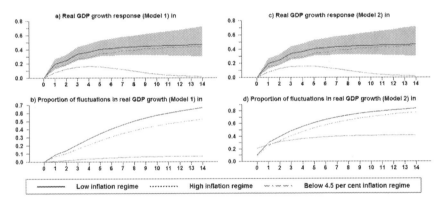

Fig. 25.4 Real GDP growth responses due to a positive nominal demand shock and the role of inflation regimes during the inflation targeting period. (Note: The grey-shaded bands denote the 16th and 84th percentile error bands. Source: Authors' calculations)

inflation regimes. Figure 25.4 shows that a positive nominal demand shock leads to an increase in real GDP growth, but the rate of increase is less in the high inflation regime compared to the low inflation regime and when inflation is below the 4.5 per cent inflation threshold.

In addition, real GDP growth fluctuates more in the low inflation regime compared to the high inflation regime. Positive nominal demand shocks induce more fluctuations in the real effects in the low inflation

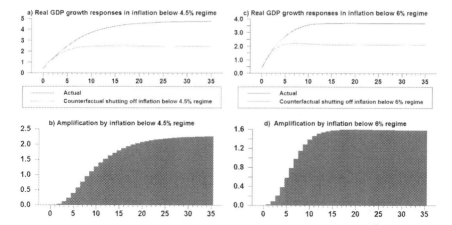

Fig. 25.5 Accumulated actual and counterfactual real GDP growth responses due to a positive nominal demand shock and the role of inflation regimes (2000Q1–2017Q1). (Source: Authors' calculations)

regime compared to the high inflation regime. These findings support the view that weak inflationary pressures in the low inflation regime tend to be accompanied by high levels of real GDP growth following a positive nominal demand shock. This further corroborates earlier findings that a positive nominal demand shock has real effects when prices are rigid in the low inflation environment and that the adjustment occurs via quantities.

Does it matter whether inflation is just below the 6 per cent or 4.5 per cent inflation threshold? The differential effects induced by inflation thresholds are assessed by using a counterfactual VAR analysis. We estimate a number of counterfactual VAR models to determine the role of different inflation regimes relative to the 4.5 per cent inflation threshold in transmitting the nominal demand shocks to real GDP growth. The estimated regime-dependent counterfactual VAR models include consumer price inflation, nominal and real GDP growth. The model is estimated using one or two lags depending on the inflation regime and 10,000 Monte Carlo draws. The counterfactual responses are calculated by shutting off the role of inflation in transmitting positive nominal demand shocks to real GDP growth. The size of amplification due to the inflation regime is determined by the gap between the counterfactual and actual responses. Figure 25.5 shows that real GDP growth increases more in the low inflation regime compared to what the counterfactual responses suggest.

This indicates that the low inflation regime amplifies the reaction of real GDP growth to positive nominal demand shocks. In addition, the amplification effects are pronounced when inflation is below the 4.5 per cent inflation threshold than when it is just anywhere below the 6 per cent inflation threshold. This shows that low inflation matters for the transmission of nominal demand shocks to stimulate real GDP growth. Thus, deviations from the 4.5 per cent midpoint of the inflation target range play a meaningful role in the transmission and amplification effects of positive nominal demand shock to real economic activity.

25.2.3 Robustness Analysis

Are the preceding results robust to changes in the sample size? This section tests the robustness of the previous results by using a counterfactual analysis for the sample 1990Q1 to 2017Q1. Figure 25.6 shows that the high (low) inflation regime dampens (magnify) the real GDP growth response to a positive nominal demand shock. The findings are robust to changes in the sample size.

In addition, a comparison of the amplifications by inflation regimes in Fig. 25.7 shows that inflation below the 4.5 per cent inflation

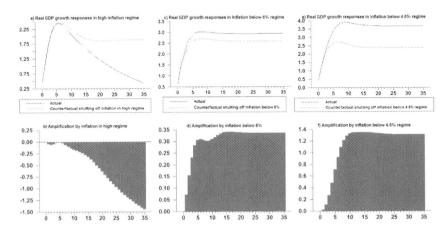

Fig. 25.6 Accumulated actual and counterfactual real GDP growth responses due to a positive nominal demand shock and the role of inflation regimes (1990Q1–2017Q1). (Source: Authors' calculations)

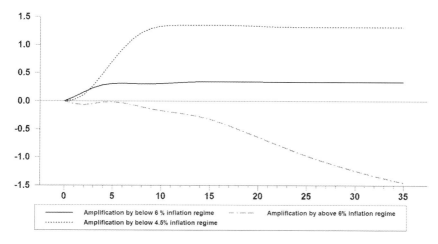

Fig. 25.7 Comparison of amplification of nominal demand shocks by inflation regimes. (Source: Authors' calculations)

threshold leads to a pronounced amplification of real GDP growth responses to positive nominal demand shocks.

25.3 Conclusion and Policy Implications

This chapter assessed the inflation threshold under which a positive nominal demand shock such as increased government spending or expansionary monetary policy pass-through to the consumer price level and nominal wages is minimised. Furthermore, the policy implications of the pass-through of a positive nominal demand shock to consumer price and nominal wage inflation when inflation is below the midpoint (4.5 per cent) of the 3–6 per cent inflation target range were examined. Evidence in this chapter shows that the pass-through is less than one and the magnitudes of the pass-through decline depending on inflation regimes. High inflation regimes are associated with a high pass-through compared to when inflation is low and particularly below the 4.5 per cent inflation threshold. This shows that the pass-through of positive nominal demand shocks to consumer price and nominal wage inflation is bigger in the high inflation regime.

The speed of adjustment or the error-correction coefficient is relatively large in the high inflation regime than in the low inflation regime.

Furthermore, evidence shows that inflation fluctuates more in the high inflation regime than when it is below the 4.5 per cent threshold. This shows that inflation tends to be rigid in the low inflation regime than in the high inflation regime. This indicates that policymakers have considerable scope to engage in short-run demand management policies in the low inflation regime than in the high inflation regime. This is because there is a substantial degree of policy effectiveness in the low inflation regime and prices become more rigid as consumer price inflation moves below the 4.5 per cent inflation regime. Therefore, nominal demand shocks are unlikely to generate much inflation in the low inflation regime relative to the high inflation regime. In addition, the amplification effects are pronounced when inflation is below the 4.5 per cent inflation threshold than when it is just anywhere below the 6 per cent inflation threshold. Thus, deviations from the 4.5 per cent midpoint of the inflation target range play a meaningful role in the transmission and amplification effects of nominal demand shock to real economic activity.

Appendix

Table 25.5 Unrestricted cointegration rank test (trace)

Hypothesised No. of CE(s)	Eigenvalue	Trace Statistic	Critical value	Prob.a
None*	0.11352	20.69188	15.49471	0.0075**
At most 1	0.02490	3.58096	3.84146	0.05844

Source: Authors' calculations
Note: Trace test indicates 1 cointegrating eqn(s) at the 0.05 level; * denotes rejection of the hypothesis at the 0.05 level; ** denotes rejection of the hypothesis at the 0.01 level; a denotes MacKinnon-Haug-Michelis (1999) p-values

Table 25.6 Unrestricted cointegration rank test (maximum eigenvalue)

Hypothesised No. of CE(s)	Eigenvalue	Max-Eigen Statistic	Critical value	Prob.a
None *	0.113522	17.11093	14.26460	0.0173**
At most 1	0.024903	3.580962	3.841466	0.0584

Source: Authors' calculations
Note: Max-eigenvalue test indicates 1 cointegrating eqn(s) at the 0.05 level; * denotes rejection of the hypothesis at the 0.05 level; ** denotes rejection of the hypothesis at the 0.01 level; a denotes MacKinnon-Haug-Michelis (1999) p-values

Table 25.7 Estimates of the long-run coefficients based on the inflation regimes

	1980Q1–2017Q1		1990Q1–2017Q1	
No regime	0.811	(0.000)	0.630	(0.007)
High regime	0.809	(0.000)	0.757	(0.000)
Low regime	0.657	(0.000)	0.627	(0.008)
Below 4.5% regime	0.602	(0.009)	0.482	(0.030)

Source: Authors' calculations
Note: p-values are in parentheses

Table 25.8 The speed of adjustment or error-correction

	1980–2017		1990–2017	
No regime	−0.019	(0.004)	−0.076	(0.039)
High regime	−0.018	(0.005)	−0.063	(0.006)
Low regime	−0.016	(0.009)	−0.053	(0.005)

Source: Authors' calculations
Note: p-values are in parentheses

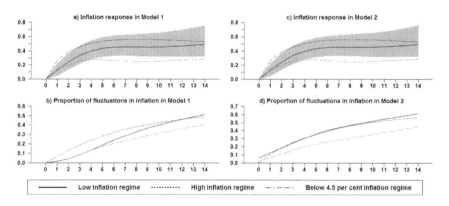

Fig. 25.8 Robustness based on 1980Q1–2017Q1 sample. (Note: The grey-shaded bands denote the 16th and 84th percentile error bands. Source: Authors' calculations)

References

Ball, L., and Mankiw, N.G. 1994. Asymmetric Price Adjustment and Economic Fluctuations. *Economic Journal, Royal Economic Society,* 104(423), 247–61.

Ball, L., Mankiw, N.G., and Romer, D. 1988. The New Keynesian Economics and the Output-Inflation Trade-off. *Brookings Paper on Economic Activity,* 19, 1–65.

Ball, L., and Romer, D. 1989. Are Prices Too Sticky? *Quarterly Journal of Economics*, 104(3), 507–24.

Ball, L., and Romer, D. 1990. Real Rigidities and the Non-neutrality of Money. *Review of Economic Studies*, 57(2), 183–203.

Blanchard, O., and Quah, D. 1989. The Dynamic Effects of Aggregate Demand and Supply Disturbances. *The American Economic Review*, 79, 655–73.

Holmes, M.J. 2000. The Output-Inflation Trade-off in African Less Developed Countries. *Journal of Economic Development*, 25(1), 41–55, June 2000.

MacKinnon, J.G., Haug, A.A., and Michelis, L. 1999. Numerical Distribution Functions of Likelihood Ratio Tests for Cointegration. *Journal of Applied Econometrics*, 14, 563–77.

Sun, R. 2012. *Nominal Rigidity and Some New Evidence on the New Keynesian Theory of the Output-Inflation Trade-off*. MPRA Paper No. 45021.

Index

A

Absorption channel, 29
Actual and counterfactual responses, 60
Adjustment costs/staggered contracts, 367
Aggregate supply curve, 366
Aggregated capital inflow channel, 156
Amplification effects, 146
Animal spirits view, 270
AR (1) process, 223
Asset purchase programme, 320
Asymmetric effects, 292, 293
Asymmetric shock effects, 328

B

Bank and non-bank flows, 101, 103–104, 195, 197–200, 202, 203
Barsky, R.B., 271
Bloom, N., 101
Bond yields channel, 171–172
Bootstrap draws, 343
Brainard, L., 123
Brexit process, 320
BRICS (excluding China), 33, 35, 39
and BIITS, 35
BRICS GDP growth, 25–53
BRICS GDP growth shocks, 25–27, 38, 40, 52

---

[1] Note: Page numbers followed by 'n' refer to notes.

Business confidence index, 109, 110
Business confidence shocks, 55

C

Capital flight, 166
Capital flow
 in driving economic activity, 163
 surges, viii, 12, 20
Capital flow channels, South African economy and, 169
Capital inflows, 149–159
 economic growth and, 151
 exchange rate and, 150
Chinese exchange rate, 42
Chinese GDP growth, 25–27, 33, 35, 41, 43–53
Chinese policy uncertainty, 25, 28, 41–45, 49
Choleski decomposition, 259
Choleski VAR decomposition, 167
Cointegration relationship, 236
Collateral constraints and financial frictions, 99
Commodity prices and terms-of-trade shocks, 323
Commodity price shock before the financial crisis, 36–37
Competition
 prices and, 72
Complementarity in price setting, 73
Conditional volatilities of output and inflation, 314
Confidence and expectations, 11, 270, 271
Constrained discretionary policymaking, 311
Consumer price inflation channel, 62
Counterfactual, 40

Credit and financial conditions, 98, 107, 116
Credit channel, 174–175
Credit conditions channel, 100, 106–114
Credit conditions index (CCI), 99
Credit default spreads (CDS), 276
Creditworthiness, 108, 116
Cross border bank-related financial flows, 182
Cross-border bank-related financial flow channel, 180
Currency appreciates by large magnitude, 57
Current account balance, 182

D

Debt and equity outflow, 231
Debt (tax) financed deficits, 272
Debt inflow channel, 158
Debt inflows are more volatile than equity, 223
Direct channel, 288
Domestic and foreign finances are more likely to compete for investment, 209
Domestic firms
 pricing strategies, 72
Dominant firms
 pricing power of, 71
Dummy for the recession, 58

E

Economic costs of capital flow episodes, 163–175
Economic growth
 capital inflows and, 153

Efficient policy frontier, 310, 311
Emerging Market Bond Index (EMBI SA), 276
Emerging market economies (EMEs)
  drivers of capital flows to, 164
  excluding China, 33, 35
Employment growth, 334, 339
Enders, W., 126, 127
Endogenous–exogenous VAR approach, 109, 113, 114
Engle-Granger and Johansen (1996) approach, 127
Equity vs. debt flows, 149
Equity and debt inflows, 100, 115
Equity market channel, 172–173
ERPT dynamics, trade tensions and, 70
Excessive credit growth, 180
Exchange rate
  changes, 75
  channel, 170–171
  depreciation shocks, 69–83
  effective real interest rate and, 71
  monetary policy volatilities, 144
  volatility shocks, vii, 17, 141–145, 147
Exchange rate pass-through (ERPT)
  high trade-openness reduces size of, 74
  size of, 69
Export and import channels, 61
  business confidence shocks and, 61

Farmer, R., 270
Federal Funds Rate (FFR), 122
First differencing, 368

Fiscal multipliers, 272
Fiscal stimulus, 332
Fitch sovereign credit, x, 284
Fitch sovereign debt credit, 19
Flexible inflation targeting, 310
Forbes, K.J., 164
Foreign direct investment (FDI), 197, 199, 201
Foreign sources of funding loosens the banks' financing constraint, 209
Forex reserves, 42
Funding and financial conditions, 180

Garch (1, 1) model, 312
GDP growth
  differentials matter for capital flows, 237
  elevated policy uncertainty, 164
(G7) GDP growth shock, 26
GDP, portfolio or capital inflow as per cent of, 156
Geweke technique, 125
Global and domestic supply and demand shocks, 323
Global demand via the absorption channel, 29
Global growth, 25–53
Global interest rate, 122
Globalisation of economic activity, 71
Global liquidity and capital flows, 195
Global policy uncertainty, 87
Global real interest rate, 142, 142n2, 143, 146

Global risk aversion shock channel, 163
Government debt and borrowing channel, 19, 304, 305
Government debt and business confidence, viii, 12, 272, 284
Government debt channel, 301
Government spending, 272, 273
Gross fixed capital formation, 55
Gross loan to GDP ratio, 304
Growth differentials and investor risk appetite, 236
G7 growth, 27, 31, 32, 35, 36, 40, 52
    dynamics, 31

H

Heightened global risk aversion shock, 163
High interest costs (tax rates), 272
Highly accommodative monetary policy, 348, 349
Historical decompositions, 184–185
Hlatshwayo, S., 143n4
Hodrick-Prescott filter, 240

I

Imports and exports growth, 168
Import-substituting goods, substitutability and, 56
Indirect channel, 288
Inflation
    channel, 348, 349
    expectations and targets, 71
Inflation forecast errors, small pass-through and, 71
Inflation path
    transparency of, 71
Inflation targeting dummy, 302
Interbank lending, 182
Interest rates
    trade balance and, 57
Intermediate imports, 57
International financial flows, 180
International Monetary Fund, 88
Investment saving (IS) schedule, 57
Investment spending
    exports and, 57

J

Johannsen cointegration test, 368
JSE All shares index, 156

K

Kilian, L., 28, 37, 37n13
King, M., 142, 142n2

L

Labor market condition index (LMCI), 89
Laffer curve, tax rates and, 152
Laubach, T., 123, 123n2, 124, 134, 135
Long-run equilibrium, 124, 127–131, 134, 139
Long-run relationship/"equilibrium" rate, 123
Loose (tight) labour market conditions shock, 347
Low, D., 142, 142n2
Low-inflation regime, 57

Index

M

Macroeconomic fundamentals matter, 258–264
Maximum eigenvalue, 368, 369, 376
Maximum employment, 333
Minimum inflation and output volatilities, 310
Monetary policy, 71
    changes, 66
    expansionary *vs.* contractionary, 66
    settings, 349
Money demand, 150
Monte Carlo draws, 344, 345
Moody's sovereign debt credit ratings, 275
M-TAR approach, 127
Mundell-Fleming model, 150
Mundell-Fleming open economy models, 122

N

Negative global trade shocks, xii, 18, 331, 334–339
Net capital inflow decline, 166
Net capital outflows, 289
Net portfolio flow volatility, 177, 178, 188–191
Net purchase by non-residents, 255, 257
Net purchases of shares and bond by non-residents, 260
New Keynesian and new Classical theories, 353
Nominal demand shock, xii, 354–364
Nominal effective exchange rate (NEER), 43
Nominal rigidity, 367
Non-residents activity in domestic market, 165
Non-stationary, 368

O

One positive standard deviation, 343
Optimal interest rate differential, 153
Organization for Economic Co-operation and Development, 88
Output channel, 348, 349
Output targeting, 310
Overall, permanent and transitory volatilities, 142

P

Pass-through, 365–369, 371, 375
Pentecôte, J.S., 27, 33, 33n11
Persistently rising shock, 249–251
Philips curve, 152, 355, 355n1, 356, 358, 363
Poirson, H., 28, 46, 48
Policy ineffectiveness, 353–363
Poorly anchored, 326
Portfolio bank and non-bank capital flows, 197–198, 201
Positive inflationary pressures, 113, 116
Price and financial stability, 333
Price flexibility, 367
Price setting, 114, 116
    high trade integration and, 73
    inflation thresholds and, 57
    mandate, 221–233

Price variation
  minor volatilities in, 71
Pricing power
  reduction in, 72
Pricing to market practices, 73
Productivity channel, viii, 12, 284
Productivity growth, viii, 12, 272, 273, 284
Profit margins, outsourcing productions and, 73
Propagating (magnifying)/restraining (stifling) abilities of specific channels, 33
Prudential policy, ix, 208, 218

R

Rachel, L., 123, 123n2, 134
Real effective exchange (REER), 43
Recession dummy, 302
Regime dependent VAR approach, 370–371
Relationship between capital flows and domestic credit growth, 183
Relationship between ERPT and trade openness, 69
Remuneration per worker, 334, 339
Repo rate-FFR spread, 16, 242, 245
Repo rate, 87, 88, 94–95, 101, 110, 113–116
Repo rate changes
  negative, 65
Repo rate-FFR rate spread, 236
Repo rate-FFR spread, 242–245, 253, 254
Repo rate-FRR spread, 128–130, 132, 133, 136, 139
Retrenchment, 166
Rondeau, F., 27, 33, 33n11

S

SA GDP growth, 31, 41, 46, 48
S&P, x, 19, 274, 275, 280, 282, 284
SA-US interest rate differential shocks, 149–159
SA-US policy rate differential, 142
Saxegaard, M., 143n4
Sectorial reallocation of credit extension, 196
Secular stagnation hypothesis, 331
Share of credit to companies, 207–214, 208n1, 216
Share of domestic bank loans to households, 196
Short-term interest rate channel, 171
Siklos, P., 126, 127
Sims, E., 271
Slope coefficients, 223
Smith, T.D., 123, 123n2, 134
South African Reserve Bank, 88
Sovereign ceiling channel, 269, 273
Sovereign debt credit ratings upgrade and downgrade, 269, 270
Speed of adjustment, 366, 370, 375, 377
Speed of correction towards the long-run equilibrium, 367
Spill-over, 349
  effects, 98
Strict inflation targeting monetary policy framework, 310
Substitution effect, 209
Sudden stops, 166
Summers, L.H., 331
Surges, 166
Synchronised inflationary pressures, output-gaps and, 152
Systematic relationship between capital flows and domestic credit growth, 180

T

Tariffs imposition
  on goods imported, 55
Taylor curve, 311–312
Terms of trade and trade-credit, 289
Third-country transmissions, 48, 56
  costs of US tariffs linked to, 66
Three-month London Interbank-Offered rate (Libor), 276
Three-month South African Treasury bill rate, 276
Tight and loose monetary policy regimes, 65
Total portfolio flows, 198, 201
Trace test, 368, 376
Trade balance channel, 173–174
Trade-off between the inflation and output volatilities, 311
Trade-openness
  degree of competition, 72
  lower ERPT, 72
  measuring, 58
  monetary policy transmission and, 57
Trade openness channel, 56
  inflation reaction and, 69
Trade policy, 71
Transmitting a credit rating shocks to credit growth, 288

U

Unanchored, 326, 328
Uncertainty shock, 35
Unconventional monetary policy instruments, 123
Uncovered interest rate parity condition, 122
Unrestricted cointegration rank test, 368, 369, 376
US growth *vs*. SA growth, policy implications, 152
US monetary policy, tightening of, 149

V

Vigfusson, R.J., 28, 37, 37n13
VIX Index, Chicago Board Options Exchange (CBOE) Volatility Index, 163n1

W

Wage-price spiral, 368
Warnock, F.E., 164
Weber, Sebastian, 28, 46, 48
Weighted cost of government debt, 302
Well anchored inflation expectations, 326
Williams, J.C., 123, 123n2, 124, 134, 135
World (global) real interest rate, 142

Z

Zero lower bound, vi, 7, 123–125

Printed in the United States
By Bookmasters